The Persecution and Genocide of Christians in the Middle East

Prevention, Prohibition, & Prosecution

Qaraqosh, Iraq. Prayer book found on
the floor of destroyed Syriac Catholic church.

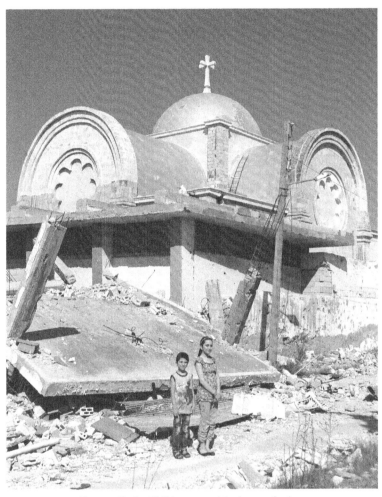

Qusayr, Syria. Children stand in front of what was their parish church of St. Elijah (September, 2016).

The Persecution and Genocide of Christians in the Middle East

Prevention, Prohibition, & Prosecution

Edited by
Ronald J. Rychlak
Jane F. Adolphe

Angelico Press

First published
by Angelico Press 2017
© Ronald J. Rychlak
& Jane F. Adolphe 2017

All rights reserved

No part of this book may be reproduced or transmitted,
in any form or by any means, without permission.

For information, address:
Angelico Press
4709 Briar Knoll Dr.
Kettering, OH 45429
www.angelicopress.com

pbk: 978-1-62138-280-5
cloth: 978-1-62138-281-2
ebook: 978-1-62138-279-9

Cover photo: St. Joseph Cultural Center in the
Christian village of Karamless, Iraq, January 10, 2017
(the Arabic written next to the cross reads "Let the Cross fall and break")
Cover design: Michael Schrauzer

CONTENTS

Foreword *by Jane F. Adolphe* 1

Preface *by Ronald J. Rychlak* 13

1 ISIS Genocide of Christian Communities in Iraq and Syria 17
   Nina Shea

2 Genocide, Statecraft, and Domestic Geopolitics 59
   Robert A. Destro

3 Historical and Theological Reflections on the Persecution of Christians 93
   Robert Fastiggi

4 International Humanitarian Law (IHL): Five Key Dynamics Shaping the Global Landscape, Security, and Freedom of Religion and the Way Ahead 119
   Kevin H. Govern

5 Sexual Violence as a Tactic of Terror: The Plight of Christian Women and Girls 141
   Jane F. Adolphe

6 Sharia Law, the "Islamic" State, and the Persecution of Christians: Moving Past Phobia and Neologisms 183
   Geoffrey Strickland

7 The Theory of Religious Freedom 207
   Fr. Piotr Mazurkiewicz

8 The Holy See's Diplomatic Response to the Crisis in Syria 245
   John M. Czarnetzky

9 Using the Torture Act Against the Persecution of Christians 265
   Mark Healy Bonner

10 International Criminal Law 283
    Kevin Cieply

11 Persecution of Christians in the Middle East: The Failed Promise of the International Criminal Court 323
    Ronald J. Rychlak

12 The Zhejiang Cross Problem: An Argument for an International Convention Prohibiting (Religious) Cultural Genocide 343
    Richard V. Meyer

13 Under Caesar's Sword: A Report on the Conference 363
    Al Kresta

    Glossary 383

    Contributor Biographies 388

Photograph Credits

iii	Photo courtesy of Aid to the Church in Need
iv	Photo courtesy of Aid to the Church in Need (Sept. 2016)
title page	Photo courtesy of Aid to the Church in Need (2017)
x	Photo courtesy of Martha Hudson (Jan. 2017)
xii	Photo courtesy of Aid to the Church in Need (Dec. 2016)
11	Photo courtesy of Stephen Rasche (Apr. 2017)
12	Photo courtesy of Aid to the Church in Need (Jan. 2016)
15	Photo courtesy of Aid to the Church in Need (Jan. 2016)
16	Photo courtesy of Aid to the Church in Need
57	Photo courtesy of Martha Hudson (Oct. 2016)
58	Still from video released by ISIS (Feb. 2015)
91	Photo courtesy of Stephen Rasche (Aug. 2016)
92	Photo courtesy of Stephen Rasche (2016)
117	Photo courtesy of Stephen Rasche (2016)
118	Photo courtesy of Stephen Rasche (Apr. 2017)
139	Photo courtesy of Stephen Rasche (2017)
140	Photo courtesy of Martha Hudson (Jan. 2017)
182	Still from Boko Haram video (Oct. 2016)
206	Photo courtesy of Stephen Rasche (2016)
243	Photo courtesy of Martha Hudson (Mar. 2017)
244	Photo courtesy of Martha Hudson (2015)
263	Photo courtesy of Stephen Rasche (2016)
264	Photo courtesy of Stephen Rasche (2016)
282	Photo courtesy of Aid to the Church in Need (Apr. 2016)
322	Photo courtesy of Aid to the Church in Need (Jan. 2016)
342	Photo courtesy of Peter Bityou (Nov. 2016)
362	Photo courtesy of Aid to the Church in Need (Dec. 2016)
382	Photo courtesy of Aid to the Church in Need (Apr. 2016)

Bartella, Iraq. Burned bible (January, 2017).

For Mary Helen Rychlak
*With gratitude for this young woman who was born
in the United States and grew up safe and free*

Karamles, Iraq. A young Syriac Catholic priest in the Mar Addai church with statue of the Sacred Heart decapitated by ISIS (December, 2016).

Foreword

Jane F. Adolphe

IN HIS ADDRESS to the European Parliament on November 25, 2014, Pope Francis graphically described the persecution of Christians. During the hours and days following the Address, little was said about these particular comments in the mainstream media. Something particularly surprising, given the media's penchant for violence:

> Here I cannot fail to recall the many instances of injustice and persecution which daily afflict religious minorities and Christians in particular, in various parts of our world. Communities and individuals today find themselves subjected to barbaric acts of violence: they are evicted from their homes and native lands, sold as slaves, killed, beheaded, crucified or burned alive, under the shameful and complicit silence of so many.[1]

Silence, the recent film from Martin Scorsese about a Jesuit missionary priest ministering in a seventeenth-century Japan hostile to Christians, has been described as the "search for God in circumstances defined by His absence."[2] In the face of drownings, beheadings, and other blood lettings of the Christians hiding from shogun's forces, the perennial question is posed: Where was God? Several underlying assumptions are implicit: there is a God to intervene; God cares about the human person and his or her dignity; God has the capacity and power to intervene; and God should intervene.[3]

---

1. Pope Francis, *Address to the European Parliament*, Strasbourg, France, November 25, 2014.
2. Robbie Collin, "Scorsese's Search for God is Scalding Work of Art," *The Sunday Telegraph*, December 11, 2016.
3. Ataloa Snell Woodin, "Speak, O Lord: The Silence of God in Human Suffering," *Direction*, spring 1996, vol. 25 No. 1, 29–54.

Persecution & Genocide of Christians in the Middle East

Within the biblical context, Job, in the Old Testament, poses the question about why God is seemingly silent during his human suffering, which testifies to the cosmic dimension of all human suffering: the battle between good and evil and the mystery of God's apparent absence. For his part, Pope Francis has fiercely proclaimed, "God is not indifferent! God cares about mankind! God does not abandon us!"[4] In support, he has underlined important points in salvation history, where God has reminded man of his responsibility toward his brothers and sisters, from the origin of human history culminating in the coming of Jesus, the Son of God, who took on flesh and identified with us in all things but sin, including suffering, sorrow, misery, and death.[5] Rather, it is man who has shown indifference to a loving God, which in turn has provoked an unresponsiveness to one's neighbor, something that has occurred in every period of history.[6]

In specific regard to Christians in the Middle East and North Africa, they continue to be tortured, beheaded, crucified, burnt alive, and brutally driven from their native lands, where Christianity was born and from where they have been present from apostolic times.[7] Indifference to their needs and fundamental human rights reached global dimensions when silence virtually became a matter of international consensus. Only recently have the sufferings, persecution, and even genocide of Christians been admitted in some quarters, and only after the relentless and courageous efforts of a few. In this regard, most notable are the labors of Christians, especially members of the Catholic Church, commencing with Pope Francis, certain members of the hierarchy, individual priests, sisters, and members of the laity, including academics, politicians, and relief workers, individually and in collaboration with entities such as the Hudson Institute, the Knights of Columbus, Alliance Defending Freedom, Aid to the Church in Need, Open Doors, and the European Center for Law and Justice.

In July 2015, Pope Francis was one of the first global leaders to use the term "genocide" in the context of persecuted Christians in the

---

4. Pope Francis, *World Day of Peace Message, Overcome Indifference and Win Peace*, 1 January 2016, No. 1.
5. Ibid., No. 5.
6. Ibid., No. 3.
7. Pope Francis, *Letter to the Christians in the Middle East*, 21 December 2014.

Foreword

Middle East, which propelled the subsequent recognition of the genocide of Christians by the European Parliament[8] and the United States government,[9] something certain bodies and officials of the United Nations System continue to resist.[10] The Pope stated:

> Today, we are dismayed to see how in the Middle East and elsewhere in the world many of our brothers and sisters are persecuted, tortured, and killed for their faith in Jesus. This too needs to be denounced: in this third world war, waged piecemeal, which we are now experiencing, a form of genocide—I insist on the word—is taking place, and it must end.[11]

Genocide is, above all, a legal concept, a crime in international law for which individuals may be indicted.[12] For example, State Parties to the 1948 Convention on the Prevention and Punishment of Genocide (Genocide Convention) are obliged to prevent and punish this crime; the competent authorities to define a particular event as genocide include competent domestic tribunals, where the atrocities occurred, or an international penal tribunal with jurisdiction accepted by States.

How the political designation relates to the Genocide Convention and a State Party's legal obligation remains an open question. In this regard, many issues are raised, which include the following: when does the legal obligation of a State party to prevent genocide begin?

---

8. *European Parliament resolution of 4 February 2016 on the systematic mass murder of religious minorities by the so-called 'ISIS/Daesh'* (2016/2529(RSP)).

9. See the U.S. Department of State, *Remarks of John Kerry, Secretary of State*, Press Briefing Room, Washington, DC, 17 March 2017.

10. See, e.g., Donna Rachel Edmunds, "U.N., West, Accused of Ignoring Plight of Syria's Christians," *Breibart.Com*, 7 October 2016 ("The United Nations and Western nations including Britain have been accused of abandoning Syria's Christians in the face of widespread persecution by Islamic State and their Muslim countrymen—even within refugee camps); see also Nina Shea, "The U.S. and U.N. Have Abandoned Christian Refugees," *Wall Street Journal*, 7 October 2016.

11. Pope Francis, Apostolic Journey to Ecuador, Bolivia and Paraguay (July 5–13, 2015), *Address for the Second World Meeting of Popular Movements*, Bolivia, July 9, 2015.

12. The term genocide is also the subject of research by social scientists and scholars on matters pertaining to the history of genocide as well as its dynamics, conditions, and causes. This particular research is arguably useful in relation to the legal obligation to prevent genocide after its onset in so far as it forms the backdrop to the development of appropriate political, social, legal, and economic initiatives.

Does the term "prevention" refer to stopping something from occurring and/or to halting something from ongoing? Does the duty to prevent include the use of force, or in such a case, would one be confusing prevention with intervention?[13] Unfortunately, the text of the Genocide Convention offers little clarity.

Certainly, when the United States declared the events against Christians and other ethnic and religious minorities as genocide, it followed with the promotion of an independent investigation and to this end the collection, documentation, preservation, and analysis of evidence of atrocities with a view to holding the perpetrators accountable. Theoretically, it should have the positive effect of raising international awareness and compelling other States to act as well as the international community as a whole. It should also lead to special concern for the plight of Christians and respect for their fundamental human rights in specific regard to protection, rehabilitation, reparation, resettlement, return, and reintegration into their ancestral homelands, including the ability to reclaim their property.

Similarly, the French Minister of Foreign Affairs and International Development chaired a meeting of the U.N. Security Council on the victims of ethnic and religious violence.[14] During an interview, he argued that "Christians are being eradicated from the Middle East."[15] An International Conference on the Victims of Ethnic and Religious Violence in the Middle East was convened in Paris co-chaired by France and Jordon. It gathered together fifty-six countries and eleven international and regional organizations to discuss the communities (e.g., Muslims, Eastern Christians, Yazidis, Turkmens, Kurds, Shabak, and all those, be they Shia or Sunni) targeted by Daesh and other terrorist groups.[16]

---

13. See e.g., Eyal Mayroz, "The Legal Duty to 'Prevent': after the Onset of 'Genocide.'" *Journal of Genocide Research*, 14(1), March 2012, 79–98.

14. France Diplomatie—French Ministry of Foreign Affairs and International Development, *Statement of Laurent Fabius, French Minister of Foreign Affairs and International Development, United Nations Security Council Debate*, March 27, 2015.

15. "Christians in the Middle East: Interview given by Laurent Fabius, French Minister of Foreign Affairs and International Development," *La Croix*, March 27, 2015.

16. France Diplomatie—French Ministry of Foreign Affairs and International Development, *International Conference on the Victims of Ethnic and Religious Violence in the Middle East: Co-Chairs' Conclusions*, Paris, September 8, 2015.

Foreword

The outcome document of the conference, otherwise known as the "Paris Action Plan," identified concrete measures grouped under core areas: humanitarian, political, and juridical.[17] The humanitarian aspect mentioned efforts to ensure protection and assistance of affected populations; to improve resilience of the same; and to support their return and reintegration. The legal aspect underlined the need to respect the rule of law as well as international criminal law, international humanitarian law, and international human rights, especially freedom of religion or belief. The political aspect emphasized the need to preserve the diversity and plurality of the Middle East; to promote inclusiveness in the political processes; to prevent and fight radicalization, violence extremism, and terrorism; to encourage universal ratification of major conventions and treaties; and to protect the cultural heritage of the communities concerned.

Then, according to certain investigations, Christians currently in asylum centers and refugee camps in Europe have shared their fears concerning violence and mistreatment at the hands of some of their fellow Muslim migrants as well as guards or security personnel.[18] One should keep in mind that while the number of Christians rose from about 43,000 in 2014 to 67,000 in 2015, they remain a minority in comparison to the number of applications of the Muslim faith, about 110,000 in 2014 to 355,000 in 2015.[19] As one report noted, the tone of these camps and facilities is set by the Muslim migrant majority.[20] The plight of Christians, and in particular converts to the faith, has been poignantly described: "It is sobering to hear persecuted Christians telling a Western Country that they recognize the very same persecution patterns . . . as in their home countries."[21]

---

17. France Diplomatie—French Ministry of Foreign Affairs and International Development, *The Paris Action Plan*, Paris, September 8, 2015.

18. See Observatory on Intolerance and Discrimination Against Christians in Europe, 2015 *Report: Special Focus on Christian Refugees in Europe*, released June 2016 (cf. Open Doors, *Report: Religious Motivated Attacks on Christian Refugees in Germany*, released May 2016); See also Soeren Kern, "Germany: Christian Refugees Persecuted by Muslims," *Gatestone Institute International Policy Council*, May 15, 2016 ("Incidents are deliberately downplayed and even covered up").

19. Observatory on Intolerance and Discrimination Against Christians in Europe, 9.

20. Ibid.

21. Ibid., 10.

In 2017, the U.N.'s Office of the High Commissioner for Refugees (UNHCR), charged with overseeing aid operations in the region, has been accused of religious discrimination in the marginalization of Christians, both within refugee camps in the region, and through its resettlement programs.[22] Unprotected from persecution by Muslims within the U.N. refugee camps, and unsure of the commitment of the U.N. for their resettlement, many Christians have opted to stay away from the camps.[23]

We should not be perplexed to learn that Pope Francis, as leader of the Catholic Church, has recently reclaimed the term "martyrdom" to describe what is happening to Christians in the Middle East.[24] Jesus forewarned his disciples of the persecution they would encounter when he said: "and you will be hated by all for my name's sake" (Matthew 10:22). This conflict between the mentality of the world and that of the Gospel, was recently underlined by Pope Francis when he argued the world "hates Christians for the same reason it hated Jesus because He brought the light of God and the world prefers the darkness to hide its wicked works."[25]

The first martyr, Saint Stephen, was stoned to death for bearing witness to the truth, thereby becoming a victim of the mystery of evil in the world.[26] According to the *Catechism of the Catholic Church*, this supreme witness to the truth of the faith and of Christian doctrine means that by bearing witness even unto death, the martyr has become a "witness to Christ who died and rose, to whom he is united by charity."[27] This ultimate gift of self was emphasized by Our Lord, when he asserted: "If a man wishes to come after me, he must deny his very self, take up his cross, and begin to follow in my footsteps. Whoever would save his life will lose it, but whoever loses his life for my sake will find it. What profit would a man show if he were to gain the whole world and destroy himself in the process?" (Matthew 16:24–26).

The witness of these martyrs is tied to the apocalyptic vision of the

---

22. Edmunds, "U.N., West, Accused of Ignoring Plight," 10.
23. Ibid.
24. Holy See Press Office Bulletin, Visit to Villa Nazareth, June 20, 2016.
25. Pope Francis, Angelus on St. Stephen's Day, December 26, 2016.
26. Ibid.
27. *Catechism of the Catholic Church*, No. 2473.

Foreword

Book of Revelation, where St. John sees the saints from every nation, people, and race, standing before the throne. St. John is told that "These are the ones who have survived the great period of trial; they have washed their robes and made them white in the blood of the Lamb" (cf. Revelation 7:9–17). In other words, they are blessed in the eyes of God and the eighth beatitude, in this regard, is particularly relevant: "Blest are those persecuted for holiness' sake; the reign of God is theirs" (Matthew 5:10).

Martyrdom also attests to the nature of the Church, which from its very beginnings has presented witnesses committed to the truth up to the martyrs of today. Saint Pope John Paul II emphasized that "by their eloquent and attractive example of a life completely transfigured by the splendor of moral truth, the martyrs and, in general, all the Church's saints, light up every period of history by reawakening its moral sense."[28] In this regard, the *Catechism* underlines that the Church "has painstakingly collected the records of those who persevered to the end in witnessing to their faith. These are the acts of the Martyrs. They form the archives of truth written in letters of blood."[29]

Pope Benedict XVI emphasized that martyrdom is not reserved only to a few, but is a realistic eventuality of every Christian.[30] Pope Francis made the distinction between "cruel" and "everyday" martyrdom;[31] the former concerns Christians and the bloodletting in the Middle East, while the latter regards Christians living in relatively peaceful circumstances, dying to themselves through, for example, faithful love of their spouses, patient education of their children, honest completion of their work, just treatment of others, and generous assistance to those in need.[32]

In brief, the Christian martyr narrative is correlated to the Passion of Christ, the courageous perseverance that is the path to everlasting life: "Be glad and rejoice, for your reward is great in Heaven" (cf. Matthew 5:10–12). The Christians killed in the Middle East and

---

28. Pope John Paul II, Encyclical Letter, *Veritatis Splendor* (Splendor of Truth), 6 August 1993, No. 93.
29. *Catechism of the Catholic Church* No. 2474.
30. Pope Benedict XVI, Angelus, October 28, 2007.
31. Holy See Press Office Bulletin, Visit to Villa Nazareth, June 20, 2016.
32. Ibid.

North Africa, therefore, are martyrs before they are victims of genocide.

With this in mind, an international expert meeting was organized under the auspices of the International Center on Law, Life, Faith and Family (ICOLF) on "The Persecution of Christians in the Middle East & North Africa: Reflections on Certain Legal Strategies through the Prism of Religious Freedom." It was inspired by the declaration of genocide by Pope Francis and the Paris Action Plan with its attention to legal aspects. The book publishes the acts of this meeting and includes three additional papers.

In regard to the meeting, the participants included academics, politicians, lawyers, theologians, journalists, and humanitarian relief workers. It commenced with the keynote address of Professor Robert George, former Chairman of the United States Commission for International Religious Freedom. Introductory comments followed, which included important background information concerning the responses of Christians to persecutions around the globe. In this regard, Mr. Al Kresta of Ave Maria Radio offered his reflections on an international conference entitled "Under Caesar's Sword: A Christian Response to Persecution," which he attended in Rome.[33]

The remainder of the meeting was comprised of a series of panel discussions. The first panel consisted of the following presenters: Dr. Robert Fastiggi of Sacred Heart Major Seminary on historical and theological considerations concerning the persecution of Christians; Mr. Edward F. Clancy of the Aid to the Church in Need on hot spots in the Middle East and North Africa; and Mr. John Klink, former president of the International Catholic Migration Commission, on the current crisis concerning refugees, displaced persons, and forced migrants.

The second panel commenced with legal scholar Mr. Geoffrey Strickland on Sharia Law and women's issues. My presentation followed on sexual violence against Christian women and girls, while Mr. John Klink finished with an overview on the problem of human trafficking.

---

33. This project is the result of a partnership of the Notre Dame Center for Ethics and Culture, the Religious Freedom Institute, and Georgetown University's Religious Freedom Project, with the support of the Templeton Religion Trust. More details are provided in chapter 13.

Foreword

The third panel was devoted to geopolitical issues as well as national security concerns and the importance of religious freedom. Professor Kevin Govern presented a paper on American National Security Concerns and Freedom of Religion; Mr. Luca Volontè of the Italian Foundation Novae Terrae considered geo-political issues and initiatives in Europe; Monsignor Piotr Mazurkiewicz of the University of Warsaw spoke on the importance of religious freedom; and Ms. Marcella Szymanski of Aid to the Church in Need described the nature and content of its working relationship with the European Union.

The fourth panel commenced with my brief overview of the legal issues. Professor Kevin Govern of the Ave Maria School of Law (AMSL) spoke to the question of International Humanitarian Law; President and Dean Kevin Cieply of AMSL addressed International Criminal Law; Professor Ron Rychlak of the University of Mississippi School of Law presented his reflections on the International Criminal Court; Professor Mark Bonner of AMSL spoke about the extraterritorial jurisdiction in the United States for punishing acts of torture; and Professor Brian Scarnecchia of AMSL raised pertinent issues facing the Association of Southeast Asian Nations, where Islam is the most widely practiced religion in the region.

A fifth panel considered practical concerns and considerations. Ms. Nina Shea, Director of the Center for Religious Freedom, Hudson Institute, opened the conversation with reflections regarding the importance of a genocide designation from the American government; Professor Ligia de Jesus of AMSL moderated a working group on the possible creation of an International Convention on the Elimination of All Forms of Discrimination, Intolerance, and Violence Based on Freedom of Religion. Another working group was led by Professors Cieply and Rychlak on practical issues concerning the prosecution of perpetrators of atrocity crimes.

The book also includes the contributions of Professor Bob Destro of Catholic University of America Columbus School of Law on political considerations regarding the designation of genocide; Professor John Czarnetzky of the University of Mississippi School of Law on the Holy See's diplomatic response to the crisis in Syria; and Professor Richard V. Myer of the University of Mississippi School of Law on the creation of an International Convention Prohibiting (Religious) Cultural Genocide.

Persecution & Genocide of Christians in the Middle East

The meeting would not have been possible without the moral support of Mr. Leonard Leo and his ability to raise the necessary funding for the project. I am also indebted to Professor Robert George, who agreed to give the keynote address, in the midst of his recovery from a rather grave medical condition. Finally, the Dean and President Kevin Cieply of Ave Maria School of Law, who permitted ICOLF to hold the meeting at the Florida campus, must also be thanked. In this regard, the expert meeting would not have been a success without the organizational assistance of Professor Ligia De Jesus and the Ave Maria staff, including members of the technology department, who worked so hard to make the meeting a success. Lastly, in regard to securing the publication agreement and their work as lead editors, I am especially indebted to Professor Ron Rychlak and his wife Claire.

Telsqof, Northern Iraq. Palm Sunday 2017 procession, first since 2014 when town was overrun by ISIS.

East Aleppo, Syria. A common scene in churches of liberated towns in Syria and Iraq: images of Christ Crucified were a favorite gun target for ISIS (January, 2016).

Preface

Ronald J. Rychlak

ONE NEED ONLY GLANCE at the daily news to realize that this era is the most violent for Christians in modern history. As detailed throughout this book, persecution of Christians in the Middle East has risen to a level akin to an ethnic cleansing. Military and diplomatic responses are contemplated and sometimes undertaken, but what about the legal system? Are there things we can or should be trying? That question animates this book.

The best, if not only, way to find an answer is to honestly look at the knowable facts, history, successes, and failures from efforts undertaken in the Middle East and elsewhere. By doing this, careful scholars, political figures, religious leaders, and private actors need to develop plans of action available to the legal community. That is the goal of this book, and each author has made a significant contribution to understanding and answering the difficulties that are faced on a daily basis.

While we are concerned about horrors faced by all people, the focus of this book is on Christian victims. Too frequently they are overlooked. For one example, there is an almost complete lack of Christians among the Syrian refugees admitted into the United States. As of the fall of 2016, the United States had exceeded its goal of resettling 10,000 Syrian refugees into the United States. However, of the nearly 11,000 refugees admitted, only 56 were Christian. In other words, while ten percent of the population of Syria is Christian, less than one-half of one percent of the admitted refugees were Christian.[1]

---

1. Perhaps things will change. In early 2017, President Trump said persecuted Christians would be given priority when it comes to applying for refugee status in the United States. "We are going to help them," he told CBN News. "They've been horribly treated. Do you know if you were a Christian in Syria it was impossible, at least very tough to get into the United States? If you were a Muslim you could come

Persecution & Genocide of Christians in the Middle East

As ISIS and other militant groups continue to target Christians throughout the Middle East, the need for legal responses to the outrages will only grow. I am particularly proud of the lineup that was assembled for this book. Many are leading thinkers, actors, and activists in their respective field, and they have met the challenge of thinking deeply about this topic. The options left are not many, and those that exist do not appear easy, but the authors in this book have identified the avenues that remain. In so doing, they provide a roadmap that could help lead to a brighter future.

One of the true highlights of my career has been the opportunity to work with the Holy See mission to the United Nations. My work on this book grows directly out of that mission, and I am indebted to His Excellency, Archbishop Bernardito Auza, Apostolic Nuncio and Permanent Observer of the Holy See to the United Nations, for permitting me to continue with the work that I began in 2000, under Archbishop (now cardinal) Renato Martino, who currently serves as President Emeritus of the Pontifical Council for Justice and Peace. I am grateful to Jane Adolphe for inviting me to take part in the original conference from which this book was developed, and to Ave Maria School of Law, which hosted that conference. I also appreciate Angelico Press for encouraging this process and dealing with the inevitable delays that come with a project like this. I am most indebted to my wife, who not only did her normal great work proofreading and checking citations, but also learned the Chicago Manual of Style and converted this work to conform to it.

---

in, but if you were a Christian, it was almost impossible." David Brody, "Brody File Exclusive: President Trump Says Persecuted Christians Will Be Given Priority As Refugees," *CBN News*, Jan. 27, 2017.

Aleppo, Syria. Maronite bishop Joseph Tobji in
St. Elias Cathedral (January, 2016).

Iraq. Destruction by ISIS of a Christian church in the Nineveh Plains.

1

ISIS Genocide of Christian Communities in Iraq and Syria

Nina Shea

> We strongly request [you] to recognize what happened to us—Christians of Iraq and particularly of Mosul and [the Plain] of Nineveh—as genocide. Many of our people [have] been killed, [an] enormous number of them [have] been forced to leave their lands,
> —Archbishop Amel Nona, Bishop of the Chaldean Catholic Church of Mosul, June 2014

Introduction and Background

ON MARCH 17, 2016, for only the second time in American history, the U.S. secretary of state officially designated an ongoing genocide. Reversing an announcement that the State Department had issued the day before, Secretary John Kerry announced the determination that ISIS (also known as ISIL, ISIS, DAESH and the Islamic State) is "responsible for genocide" against Christians, Yizidis and other vulnerable groups in areas under its control." A few days earlier, the House of Representatives had resolved to also condemn as genocide the violence against these Christians and other minorities. The Senate followed with a similar genocide resolution in July 2016.[1]

The U.S. designation was a hard-won fight and followed mounting public appeals, by the Catholic Church in particular. In July 2015, Pope Francis had been the first to bring world attention to the fact

---

1. Secretary of State John Kerry, "Remarks on Daesh and Genocide," Washington, DC, March 17, 2016, https://2009-2017.state.gov/secretary/remarks/2016/03/254782.htm; H.R. Res. 75, "Expressing the Sense of Congress That the Atrocities Perpetrated

that "our brothers and sisters are persecuted, tortured and killed for their faith in Jesus," and called it "genocide," emphasizing, "I insist on the word." In mid-February 2016, the Holy Father, in an historic joint statement with Russian Patriarch Kirill, asserted that Islamist extremists were waging a religious persecution so severe that "whole families, villages and cities of our brothers and sisters in Christ are being completely exterminated." The U.S. Catholic Conference of Bishops and key Catholics and Catholic lay groups, such as the Knights of Columbus, also played major roles in calling attention to this genocide.

Nowhere today does the term genocide apply more than in Iraq and Syria, where Christian communities have been devastated by targeted killing, hostage taking, rape, forcible conversion, deportation, and the systematic destruction of their churches and every trace of the two-millennia-old Christian presence. ISIS has not been the only persecutor of these countries' Christians. Iraqi Christians have been relentlessly targeted for death and brutality by al Qaeda in Iraq, the Islamic State of Iraq, Shi'a militants, and others since a coordinated bombing of their churches in Baghdad in 2004. Syria's Christians have been deliberately attacked, particularly by Jabhat al Nusra, the al Qaeda affiliate, since the early years of the Syrian conflict, which began in 2011. Some of the most infamous examples of this anti-Christian persecution—such as the kidnapping and disappearance of Aleppo's Greek and Syriac Orthodox archbishops, Boulos Yazigi and Gregorios Yohanna Ibrahim, and the 2010 suicide attack on a Baghdad Catholic church filled with worshippers—may have been perpetrated by others than ISIS or by ISIS's predecessor groups. Some of those attacks are also addressed in this chapter.

Of course, not all Muslims should be blamed or implicated in this genocide. The majority of Muslims, including those in Iraq and Syria, have lived side by side in peace and cooperation with Chris-

---

by ISIL against Religious and Ethnic Minorities in Iraq and Syria Include War Crimes, Crimes against Humanity, and Genocide," 114th Cong. (2015–2016), https://www.congress.gov/bill/114th-congress/house-concurrent-resolution/75/text; S. Res. 340, "A Resolution Expressing the Sense of the Senate That the Atrocities Perpetrated by the Islamic State of Iraq and the Levant (ISIL) against Religious and Ethnic Minorities in Iraq and Syria Include War Crimes, Crimes against Humanity, and Genocide," 114th Cong. (2015–2016), https://www.congress.gov/bill/114th-congress/senate-resolution/340.

ISIS Genocide of Christian Communities in Iraq and Syria

tians for centuries. In February 2016, several hundred Muslim leaders issued the Marrakesh Declaration, which was initiated by Morocco's King Mohammed VI. Some 250 major Muslim leaders from 120 countries participated. The declaration, entitled, "The Rights of Religious Minorities in Predominantly Muslim Majority Communities: Legal Framework and Call to Action," affirmed the understanding of Islam based on the example of the Prophet Muhammad making peace with the Christians and Jews, and not on the understanding of ISIS and its affiliates that these non-Muslims must be destroyed.

Christians belonging to the various Catholic, Orthodox, and Protestant churches are certainly not the only religious communities threatened in Iraq and Syria. Members of all religions—including Sunni Muslims who fail to conform to ISIS dictates—have been cruelly attacked and killed by members of the group. Overall casualties from conflict among Iraqis and Syrians of all religious backgrounds have reached staggering levels. Genocide, however, as the gravest of human rights crimes, demands specific attention.

The Secretary of State named the Yazidis and Shi'a Muslims, along with the Christian minority, in his designation. The congressional resolutions also include the Sabean-Mandeans and Kaka'i. Internationally, there is a growing consensus that the Yazidi community of Iraq's Nineveh province, in particular, has been targeted for genocide by ISIS. This report does not in any way deny or detract from those assessments. Both Yazidis and Christians, as well as other minorities, have suffered from ISIS atrocities that have intentionally and entirely eradicated those communities from ISIS-controlled territory and thus fit the international definition of genocide. Such attacks are religiously based.

This book focuses on the Christians, and their particular situation, as a compelling case study of this larger genocide and its implications for international and national law. A comprehensive, systematic, and professional documentation of ISIS's assaults against these Christians has yet to be undertaken. What we do know is substantial and has been pieced together from the testimony of the survivors and reported by local church leaders, Shlomo (a lawyers' group comprised of Christian survivors now displaced in Kurdistan), international journalists, the Christian media, the U.N., and Western nongovernmental organizations, including the Knights of Columbus.

In February 2015, the world awakened to a graphic demonstration of ISIS slaughtering Christians in a YouTube video. Made by ISIS, the video showed the terror group's militants methodically beheading a line of bound, kneeling men, all of whom were dressed in orange jumpsuits, on a Libyan beach. These ISIS victims were twenty-one Egyptian Coptic Orthodox Christians and a Christian from Ghana. They had worked in Libya as migrants and had been selectively seized from their dormitory after confessing their Christian faith. As they knelt on the beach awaiting their fate, the Lord's Prayer whispered with their last breath was audible from some of them.

This beheading video has become emblematic of the modern manifestation of anti-Christian genocide and an icon of the suffering under ISIS. Obscured by the region's conflicts, the scope and details of ISIS's genocide of Iraq and Syria's Christians within its self-proclaimed caliphate are less well known but no less brutal and no less specifically aimed at eradicating Christians for their faith.

Christian clergy have been killed or disappeared, including bishops. Lay persons, too, have been singled out for attack. They have been targeted for "unIslamic" dress, speech, behavior, and businesses. Many thousands of Christians have been taken hostage and tortured or killed. Some Christians have been forced to convert to Islam with swords to their or their children's throats. Some who refused have been crucified. Scores of Christian women and girls have been taken as sex slaves for ISIS jihadis, along with thousands of Yizidis. An occasional video or report of an ISIS demolition of a church or monastery has reached the international media, but few in the West understand that within ISIS-controlled territory, all churches have been shut, desecrated, or destroyed, all clergy have been assassinated or driven out, and no Christian community has been left intact.

Barely a decade ago, Iraq and Syria ranked among the four Middle Eastern countries with the most robust Christian populations—over a million Christians each. The genocidal toll taken by the rise of Islamist extremism within these two states is fully apparent from the demographics of Iraq's Christian community. Collectively numbering about 1.4 million before the U.S. invasion in 2003, Iraqi Christians now are said by Church leaders to amount to about 250,000. Most of them are in the Kurdistan region, and the majority are considered Internally Displaced Persons (IDPs) living as refugees. Between one million and one and a half million of Syria's two million

ISIS Genocide of Christian Communities in Iraq and Syria

Christians are said to remain in Syria, and two thirds of them are estimated to be displaced. Both Syrian and Iraqi Christian survivors can be found as refugees in surrounding areas of Jordan, Lebanon, and Turkey. In none of these places of refuge, not even in Iraqi Kurdistan, do the fleeing Christians have resettlement rights. They also have encountered discrimination and persecution by other refugees in United Nations camps in the region and, thus, eschew them. The Christians who escape ISIS depend on the Church and other private charity for their survival.

These are ancient communities with ties to the earliest Church. Some of them still pray in Aramaic, the language of Jesus of Nazareth, and trace their religion to St. Thomas the Apostle and to the Pentecost. Most of these Christians are Catholic or Orthodox, but Protestants are also represented. The Eastern Catholic Churches—the Chaldeans, the Syriacs, the Maronites, the Greek Melkites, and the Armenians—are in communion with the Roman Catholic Church. ISIS's attacks are aimed at destroying all these Christian church communities.

Such assaults are solely for religious reasons; these Christians are members of a small minority that lacks political power and has not taken up arms for any side in the region's conflicts. ISIS's own public statements frequently claim credit for the murder of Christians, exult in the enslavement of Christian women and girls, and express the intent to wholly eradicate Christian communities from its "Islamic State." ISIS threatened: "We will conquer your Rome, break your crosses, and enslave your women," in a recent issue of its propaganda magazine *Dabiq*, which also carried a cover photo of St. Peter's Basilica in Rome with a black flag replacing the cross atop its dome.[2]

Archbishop Jeanbart of Aleppo's Melkite Greek Catholic Church has also attested to the openness with which the Islamist militants, whether ISIS or a similar group, declare their intent to eradicate Christians and others they consider infidels. In 2013, he stated:

> Christians are terrified by the Islamist militias and fear that in the event of their victory they would no longer be able to practice their

---

2. Umberto Bacchi, "ISIS Magazine Dabiq Threatens 'Rome Crusaders' Flying Islamic State Flag at Vatican on Front Cover," *International Business Times* (October 13, 2014), http://www.ibtimes.co.uk/isis-magazine-dabiq-threatens-rome-crusaders-flying-islamic-state-flag-vatican-front-cover-1469712.

religion and that they would be forced to leave the country. As soon as they reached the city [of Aleppo], Islamist guerrillas, almost all of them from abroad, took over the mosques. Every Friday, an imam launches their messages of hate, calling on the population to kill anyone who does not practice the religion of the Prophet Muhammad. They use the courts to level charges of blasphemy. Who is contrary to their way of thinking pays with his life.[3]

ISIS stormed Mosul, Iraq's second largest city and the provincial capital, on June 9 and 10, 2014. It was from there that Abu Bakr al Baghdadi proclaimed the establishment of his so-called caliphate, the Islamic State, and himself as Caliph Ibrahim on June 29, 2014. The ISIS "caliphate" was intended to resonate among Muslims, as Iraq and Syria had been the sites of the seventh and eighth century caliphates established by the descendants of the Muslim Prophet Muhammad. At the peak of ISIS's power, its territory stretched from Raqqa, Syria, in the west, to Mosul, Iraq, in the east, with the Christian heartland of Nineveh lying strategically in between these two poles. To purify its caliphate, ISIS set out to conquer and eliminate the Christians, Yazidis, and other minorities who had ancestral ties to Nineveh, which was at that time the homeland for most of their members. ISIS achieved the total eradication of these communities from Nineveh in a murderous, blitzkrieg-like strike during the first two weeks of August 2014.

The relentless targeting of Christians in this area in this century, however, did not begin in 2014. In Iraq, it dates to 2004, the year al Qaeda in Iraq (AQI) surfaced and six Baghdad churches were targeted in coordinated bombing attacks. The attacks continued and intensified when AQI rebranded itself as the Islamic State in Iraq (ISI) in 2006, which came to be headed by al-Baghdadi in 2010 and changed its name to ISIS in 2011. By the time ISIS entered Nineveh, most of Iraq's Christians were settled there for security, having fled there in prior years to escape targeting by Islamist groups in Baghdad, Basra, and other southern towns. In Syria, the Christian community came under severe and deliberate attack in 2011 when Arab Spring protests turned violent and worsened after ISIS claimed Raqqa for its

---

3. Nina Shea, Testimony, June 25, 2013, http://www.hudson.org/content/research attachments/attachment/1114/shea_testimony_(house_foreign_affairs,_25_j un_13). pdf.

capital in 2013. In that year, Archdeacon Emanuel Youkhana of the Assyrian Church of the East observed: "Behind the daily reporting about bombs there is an ethno-religious cleansing taking place, and soon Syria can be emptied of its Christians."[4] The targeting of the Christian minority continues as this book goes to print.

ISIS's Intent

Publications and videos by ISIS repeatedly assert its intent to destroy the Christian church—that is, all Christians under its control—and its pattern of attacks evidences such intent. Nevertheless, ISIS claims to offer Christians in some areas of its self-proclaimed caliphate an option to pay a traditional Islamic tax, or jizya, as an alternative to death, deportation, and forcible conversion. Superficially, ISIS may appear to have revived the medieval Islamic practice that provided limited toleration for the Jewish and Christian "People of the Book" which was formally abandoned over a century and a half ago under the last Ottoman caliphate. Closer examination of ISIS's treatment of Christians, which includes all three major cases where jizya was claimed to have been offered as an option, however, reveals that these ISIS claims are a deception or propaganda ploy.[5] ISIS does not tolerate Christians. Its demands for payments from Christians, which it calls jizya, are actually extortion and ransom. ISIS has never given a traditional jizya option to Christians at any time. Even when it extorts payments and calls them jizya, this always, within a short time, results in dispossession, rape, murder, kidnapping, and enslavement of Christians—all acts evidencing the crime of genocide. Nowhere in ISIS-controlled territory are there intact Christian communities, only individuals, mostly elderly, who are forced to pay extortion and have no possibility of exercising their religious rights, as their churches are destroyed or closed and their clergy have been killed or forced to flee.

Genocide is a crime of intent, one that requires the deliberate aim of destroying a group, such as a religious one, "in whole or in part."

---

4. Shea, Testimony.
5. Nina Shea, "The ISIS Genocide of Middle Eastern Christian Minorities and Its Jizya Propaganda Ploy," The Hudson Institute, August 2016, https://s3.amazonaws.com/media.hudson.org/files/publications/20160721TheISISGenocideofMiddleEasternChristianMinoritiesandItsJizyaPropagandaPloy.pdf.

In a recent report, the Independent Commission of Inquiry on the Syrian Arab Republic (a body created by the U.N. Human Rights Council) denies that ISIS intends to destroy the Nineveh Christian community.[6] It points to ISIS claims to offer a jizya option while overlooking contrary evidence. It makes a summary conclusion, without citing any supporting evidence, that ISIS recognizes the "right to exist as Christians," including those within its territory, "as long as they pay the jizya tax." The Commission's conclusion is demonstrably false.

In the American debate leading up to the U.S. government's designation of genocide,[7] the issue of jizya first came to be a central rationale for those within and outside the Obama administration who argued Christians should be excluded from the designation.[8] Based on unsupported claims that jizya arrangements were being implemented, some erroneously concluded that ISIS lacked the intent—required by the international Genocide Convention—to destroy the Iraqi and Syrian Christian community. This argument, which ultimately did not prevail in the U.S. State Department's genocide designation decision, depended on taking selective ISIS assertions about jizya at face value; ignoring the evidence in the purported cases of jizya; overlooking the obligations of the Islamic authorities under traditional jizya theory and assuming that ISIS adheres to traditional Islamic rules and practices; and assuming that ISIS can be trusted to honor its agreements with non-Muslims.

This chapter presents the facts of ISIS's treatment of Christian communities under its control and analyzes them in conjunction

---

6. Office of the United Nations High Commissioner for Human Rights, Human Rights Council, "*They Came to Destroy*": *ISIS Crimes against the Yazidis*, June 15, 2016, http://www.ohchr.org/Documents/HRBodies/HRCouncil/CoISyria/A_HRC_32_CRP.2_en.pdf.

7. Nina Shea, "ISIS Genocide: Christians Killed and Enslaved as the State Department Looks the Other Way," Hudson Institute (originally published in *National Review Online* as "ISIS Genocide against 'People of the Book'—How Long Will Kerry Continue to Talk around It?" March 16, 2016), http://www.hudson.org/research/12320-isis-genocide-christians-killed-and-enslaved-as-the-state-department-looks-the-other-way.

8. Michael Isikoff, "U.S. Weighs 'Genocide' Label for IS in Iraq—And More Than a Word May Be at Stake," *Yahoo News*, November 12, 2015, https://www.yahoo.com/news/u-s-weighs-genocide-label-1298023405674550.html.

ISIS Genocide of Christian Communities in Iraq and Syria

with the terror group's claims regarding a jizya option for these Christians. These facts show beyond doubt that the Christians of Nineveh and of those areas of Syria under ISIS control have been among the religious minority groups facing ISIS genocide.

Jizya Payments

Jizya is mentioned once in the Qur'an (9:29, Surah al-Tawbah), although no payment amount or details are actually given. Under what is known as the Pact of Omar (named after a seventh-century caliph), jizya was an arrangement for coexistence with "People of the Book," *ahl al kitab*, meaning Jews and Christians, and even Sabean-Mandeans and Zoroastrians. A progressive tax was paid by men or their community in exchange for protection for their families, including protection of their lives and property and the right to worship, receive the sacraments, and practice their religious rites. They did not have full religious freedom, were harshly discriminated against, and were compelled to adhere to Muslim mores in ways that were deliberately humiliating and onerous and would be seen today as flagrant violations of international human rights law. Yet this arrangement at least allowed the protected non-Muslim communities to assemble inside their houses of worship for communal prayer led by their own religious leaders. For 1,300 years, from the region's Muslim conquest in the seventh century until the mid-nineteenth, Christianity was practiced and perpetuated in this region under such arrangements.

Those who conflate today's extortion and ransom payments demanded of Christians with a tax for jizya may lack knowledge about historical jizya and fail to understand the two obligations assumed by authorities in a jizya arrangement. The jizya payment was to be made in exchange for protection of persons and property and for the right to non-Muslim religious worship. A legal brief prepared for the Philos Project—drawing on such sources as *Encyclopedia of Islam*, *The Jews of Arab Lands: A History and Source Book*, and *The Oxford Encyclopedia of the Islamic World*—succinctly describes such obligations:

> Shortly after the founding of Islam, the Assyrian Christians came under Muslim rule. They were relegated to dhimmi status, and were required to pay the jizya. Under the historical Islamic caliphates, the

jizya was a tax levied on their non-Muslim subjects, referred to as dhimmis. Historically, dhimmis were "the non-Muslims who live within Islamdom [who] have a regulated and protected status." *In return for protection and the right to continue practicing their religion,* and as a mark of their obedience, dhimmis were required to pay the jizya. If the Muslim ruler failed to provide the dhimmis adequate security, he was obliged to return the money, as the Egyptian sultan Saladin did after withdrawing his army from Syria. [Emphasis added]⁹

By contrast, there is no evidence that ISIS has fulfilled the caliphate's obligations under a jizya agreement. In fact, irrespective of any payment made to it by a Christian, ISIS prevents and punishes Christian worship, attacks the Christian and his family members, and steals the Christian's property. What ISIS refers to as "jizya" taxes are simply extortion and ransom payments that at most provide temporary protection from ISIS attacks. Virtually every Christian who can, flees ISIS-controlled territory. The few aged, disabled, and other Christians who have stayed behind in ISIS-controlled areas have been forced to convert to Islam, become jihadi "brides," or been taken captive or killed. In invoking the term jizya, ISIS is providing a pretext to appear more authentically Islamic. Experts on ISIS have called this a "ploy" and a "publicity stunt." Both terms are accurate.

In March 2007, Abu Omar al-Baghdadi, the first leader of the Islamic State in Iraq, who took the title of commander of the faithful but did not claim the caliphate himself, proclaimed a policy to kill Christians and justified this in Islamist terms by declaring the contract for jizya to be null and void:

> We find that the sects of the People of the Book (Christians, Jews, or Sabians) in the State of Islam today are people of war who qualify for no protection, for they have transgressed against whatever they agreed to in many countless ways, and if they want peace and security then they must start a new era with the State of Islam according

---

9. Legal brief sent to U.S. Secretary of State John F. Kerry from Andrews Kurth LLP, counsel for the Philos Project, The American Mesopotamian Organization, The Assyrian Aid Society of America, and The Iraqi Christian Relief Council, March 8, 2016, https://www.andrewskurth.com/assets/htmldocuments/2016-03-08_Philos_Project_Letter.pdf.

ISIS Genocide of Christian Communities in Iraq and Syria

to (Caliph) Omar's stipulations [the historic "Covenant" of Caliph Omar with Christians] that they have annulled.[10]

In February 2014, a few months before ISIS declared its Islamic State caliphate, it publicized a jizya contract with the Christian community of Raqqa. In June 2014, during its assault on Mosul's Christian community, ISIS announced an offer of jizya. Subsequently, it announced jizya arrangements for Christian communities in several areas of Syria. These assertions misrepresented what actually occurred. As the 300-page *Genocide against Christians in the Middle East* report finds:

> As used by ISIS, [jizya] is almost always a term for extortion and a prelude or postscript to ISIS violence against Christians. In Nineveh, demands for so-called jizya payments were a prelude to killings, kidnappings, rapes and the dispossession of the Christian population.... In Raqqa, the offer was made after ISIS had already closed the churches, burned bibles and kidnapped the town's priests.[11]

The complete absence anywhere in ISIS-controlled territory of functioning churches, active clergy, and intact Christian communities is prime facie evidence that there is no jizya option for the Christians. Testimony and reports from the affected Christians reveal beyond doubt that there has been no jizya option, only lethally enforced demands for money, property, or women and girls as ransom and extortion payments, which ISIS calls "jizya." A review of the major cases where ISIS took over areas where Christian communities resided and in some instances claimed to offer a "jizya option" follows.

Mosul and Nineveh, Iraq

Soon after Saddam Hussein's overthrow, Sunni extremists made common cause with Hussein's military officers in Mosul. With their help, ISIS easily took control of the country's second largest-city and Nineveh's capital on June 10, 2014. It was from there that Abu Bakr

---

10. Alberto M. Fernandez, "The ISIS Caliphate and the Churches," MEMRI, Daily Brief No. 53, August 27, 2015, http://www.memri.org/report/en/print8721.htm.

11. Knights of Columbus and In Defense of Christians, *Genocide against Christians in the Middle East: A Report Submitted to Secretary of State John Kerry*, March 9, 2016, http://stopthechristiangenocide.org/scg/en/resources/Genocide-report.pdf.

al-Baghdadi announced the Islamic State caliphate a month later, on June 29. By late August 2014, Patriarch Ignatius Youssef III Younan of the Syriac Catholic Church, northern Iraq's largest church, had begun pronouncing the situation facing his now-displaced and brutalized flock to be "genocide."[12]

ISIS summoned Christian leaders to meet with its representatives on July 17, 2014, at an auditorium in Mosul for the purpose of announcing the jizya terms on which they could stay in the Islamic State's "caliphate." The Mosul Christians who did not respond were then given an ultimatum, announced from the loudspeakers of Mosul mosques, to leave by July 19 to avoid death or forced conversion to Islam. All but a few dozen fled or died trying. This terror-driven mass exodus of Christians was repeated three weeks later throughout the rest of Nineveh Province. Since Nineveh was the historical homeland of Iraqi Christianity and the place to which many Iraqis had gone to escape persecution in the south of the country, this meant that by late August 2014, only a small fraction of Iraqi Christians remained in Iraq, outside of Kurdistan, mostly in Baghdad.

The Christians who did not leave have been sometimes characterized as having chosen to live under ISIS and pay jizya. The major flaw in this description is that it overlooks the facts and omits the views of the Christian leaders most closely involved. The available evidence paints a much direr picture.

Rev. Emanuel Adelkello, the Syrian Catholic priest who directly dealt with ISIS over the fate of the one thousand Christians still in Mosul in late July 2014, wrote details about the "jizya option" in response to this author's inquiry. He related that ISIS demanded all remaining Christian leaders to gather at a Mosul civic center, purportedly to hear ISIS's jizya demand. After the Christian leaders throughout Nineveh consulted among themselves, they decided it

---

12. Doreen Abi Raad, "Syriac Patriarch Calls Islamic State Actions 'Attempted Genocide,'" *National Catholic Reporter*, August 27, 2014, https://www.ncronline.org/news/global/syriac-patriarch-calls-islamic-state-actions-attempted-genocide; Deborah Gyapong, "Syriac Patriarch Pleads for Help to Stop Christian Genocide in Middle East," *BC Catholic*, August 25, 2014, http://www.bccatholic.ca/component/content/article/1-latest-news/4138-syriac-patriarch-pleads-for-help-to-stop-christian-genocide-in-middle-east.

ISIS Genocide of Christian Communities in Iraq and Syria

was a "trap." As Father Adelkello explained, they feared that they were being rounded up for slaughter and that the women and girls would be jeopardized if their people remained under ISIS "protection." According to the priest's statement, which was recorded, translated, and sent on March 5, 2016, by the Chaldean Catholic Archdiocese of Erbil to this author:

> The collective belief was that this gathering was not an attempt to negotiate, it was only going to be a demand at best, and a trap at worst. The Christians mostly believed they would likely be killed if they showed up. At the appointed time, no Christians showed up. Angered, ISIS then gave them two choices, leave or be killed. The remaining Christians then all left. At checkpoints on the way out of town they were robbed of everything of value, had all their family and property documents taken from them, and their cars stolen as well. Thus stripped, they were allowed to walk to the border with the Kurdistan Region.[13]

Father Adelkello explained that Mosul's Christians had a deep dread of ISIS:

> [Jizya] was only put forward initially as a ploy from which ISIS could keep the Christians there to further take advantage of them and abuse them. There was specific concern that the intention was to keep women there so that they could be taken freely by the ISIS fighters. The ISIS fighters had made public statements that according to the Koran it was their right to take the Christian women as they pleased.[14]

An estimated twenty-five to fifty Christians remained behind in Mosul, a city of over a million residents, and church leaders are adamant that there is no jizya agreement for them and that they are badly treated. Some have been killed, while some of the elderly have reportedly died of neglect in their houses, been allowed to starve to death or deprived of medications, and left with no one to bury them. The others have been enslaved or forcibly converted to Islam.[15]

Mosul clergy, who had direct engagement with ISIS in July 2014, state that there was never a serious option for Nineveh's Christians to

---

13. Shea, "ISIS Genocide."
14. Ibid.
15. Knights of Columbus and In Defense of Christians, *Genocide against Christians in the Middle East*.

pay jizya to avoid ISIS atrocities. They believe that ISIS never had any intention of protecting Christians or of allowing Christian worship. Syriac Catholic Archbishop Yohanna Petros Moshi, for instance, writes that the Christians of northern Iraq determined they "can never trust Daesh [supporters] no matter how many good intentions they try to show."[16] It should be noted that Western policymakers mistrust ISIS, too. (The archbishop, along with virtually all of his flock, is now dispossessed and displaced.)

Archbishop Moshi states that the suspicions that ISIS was plotting against the Christians were confirmed on the second day after the failed meeting, when ISIS falsely publicized that a jizya agreement had been reached with him. He rejects the ISIS claims in no uncertain terms, calling them "lies" that were intended to trick the Christian laity into staying so that ISIS could kill the men and abduct the women. He writes:

> [ISIS] released a statement saying that the meeting has taken place between representatives of the Islamic State and Christian religious leaders, and the document has been signed by the Iraqi chief of priests [Archbishop Moshi]. [This] was a lie made up in order to encourage Christians to stay so they [could] take their revenge from their men and use the women [the] same as what happened to the Yazidis.

Archbishop Moshi states that after the Christians fled, ISIS representatives taunted them about the jihadis' desire for the Christian women, thus validating the Christians' fears: "One of them [called a] few of our sons to tell them: 'Unfortunately! You managed to run away! Because you have such beautiful daughters and women.'" The Chaldean Catholic patriarch Louis Raphael Sako, who was among the Mosul refugees, categorically states that no Christian community, or even family, remains in Mosul to pay jizya. He disputes Kurdish media reports that families in Mosul are paying an annual jizya of $170. In a May 11, 2016, letter to the international Catholic press, the Patriarchate asserted:

> There are no more Christian families in Mosul... only a few individuals who were unable to escape.... [In Mosul,] 50 disabled Christians were left at a medical facility because they were unable to

---

16. Shea, "ISIS Genocide."

escape ... [and] it has been impossible so far to rescue them. Some Christians abducted by Daesh are still being held, but no family.

Other diverse Christian voices are consistent on this point. The Assyrian Iraqi parliamentarian Yonadam Kanna reports that the Christians who remained in Mosul, largely due to old age or disabilities, were forced to convert to Islam. Father Douglas Bazi, an Iraqi Chaldean priest who ran a refugee camp in the Iraqi Kurdistan capital of Erbil, said that one Mosul family with disabled members was told they could remain Christian if each family member paid $8,000 each month. This was exorbitant, and thus they could not exercise this ISIS "option." Other church leaders, now in exile in Kurdistan, state that those Christians who were left behind in Mosul are indigent, starving, and dying from neglect. They do not pay jizya or attend church, since there are no churches or monasteries, ISIS having destroyed, closed, or repurposed all of them.

After the Nineveh Christian leadership made clear that it viewed the jizya offer as a ruse, ISIS showed no mercy to those Christians whom it encountered when it stormed the province in the first two weeks of August 2014. Christians who remained in Nineveh after ISIS arrived and did not convert to Islam met grim fates. Some were killed outright. Patriarch Younan estimates that ISIS killed over a thousand Christians in Syria and over five hundred Christians in Iraq. Using a questionnaire devised by the State Department for documenting the Darfur genocide a decade ago, the Knights of Columbus gathered information from several hundred of the Nineveh Christian survivors in Kurdistan in March 2016. In case after case, a son, two cousins, a father, or a brother was reported missing after being led away by ISIS jihadists. Based on relatives' testimony collected in Erbil, Knights of Columbus lawyer Scott Lloyd reported: "Dozens and perhaps hundreds of Christians, mostly men, were demanded as hostages in exchange for their families to leave. They haven't been seen since."[17]

The press reported, based on the account of a Sunni tribesman, that in May 2015, an 80-year-old Nineveh Christian woman was burned alive for not following ISIS sharia. His Eminence Theodore McCarrick, Washington, DC's archbishop emeritus cardinal, related

17. Ibid.

to this author that in early 2016, he spoke with an Iraqi Christian woman, now displaced in Kurdistan, who witnessed jihadists crucifying her husband to the front door of their home. This report was confirmed independently by Iraqi Catholic priest Father Denkha Joola, who aided the refugees and knows the woman. The parents and brothers of one girl fled by car but never reappeared, reported Georgina, their daughter who escaped with her grandmother in a separate car [statement to the American Foundation for Relief and Reconciliation]. They are presumed to have been murdered at a checkpoint by ISIS militants.

The Most Rev. Amel Nona, who was then Chaldean Catholic archbishop of Mosul, wrote an open letter stating that those who could not get out of Nineveh when ISIS stormed through it were either killed or enslaved. He gave an example of four children from a family in his diocese, from the city of Qaraqosh—ages four, six, eight, and fifteen—who were killed. He "confirmed" that a "huge number of Christians" from Mosul and the Nineveh Plain were also killed.

While ISIS sexual enslavement of women and girls has been mostly associated with the thousands of Yazidis who were captured, an unknown but smaller number of Christians were also enslaved. Another Nineveh family who did not leave before ISIS arrived, due to the father's blindness, had their three-year-old daughter, Christina Noah, taken from them by ISIS militants. From a cell phone call from another captured Christian woman, as reported in a *New York Times* magazine cover story, they learned that both were being detained in a holding pen with other women and girls and sold at a Mosul slave market.[18] In the following months, ISIS would publish a price list for the sale of specifically Christian and Yazidi female slaves in slave markets, with those aged one to nine being the most expensive. This price list was authenticated by the U.N. expert for sexual violence in conflict, Zainab Bangura. In another case, a mother relates that after her young daughter was told by ISIS to get into a separate vehicle, she never saw her again. After three months without word, in the refugee camp, she received a call from the daughter saying that she had "converted" to Islam and "married" a Muslim man.

Archbishop Nona states he knows of "many" young girls who were

---

18. Eliza Griswold, "Is This the End of Christianity in the Middle East?" *New York Times*, July 22, 2015.

ISIS Genocide of Christian Communities in Iraq and Syria

taken from Nineveh by ISIS and that their whereabouts are unknown. Syriac Catholic archbishop Moshi reports that over 20 Christian girls and women were captured and most have not been seen since, despite church ransom offers:

> Weeks after the displacement, we had indirect communication with Daesh members in order to save more than 20 women whom [sic] stayed and are hostages, they confirmed that they were in good conditions. A 3 years old girl, a 25 years old girl, a 30 years old young woman and other girls and women aging from 40 to 70 years old. We agreed to pay a ransom not a Jizya, which was 30 thousand dollars in exchange for their release, with the condition that we don't pay anything until we guarantee their arrival, at least the arrival of the small girl, the other girl and the young woman. But that didn't happen until this day. And today we know nothing about them or what happened to them.[19]

The horrific story of a Christian mother who escaped ISIS enslavement is recounted in *No Way Home: Iraq's Minorities on the Verge of Disappearance*, the June 2016 report of the UK-based Minority Rights Group International. She attests that as an ISIS captive she was brutally tortured and then taken to a sex slave detention center under the direction of an ISIS sheikh who performed "marriages" between the captive Christian and Yazidi girls and women and ISIS fighters, in accordance with strict ISIS religious rules. She explained:

> That night I was married to eight different men and divorced eight times. Each man raped me three or four times. When all this was over, we were taken back to the room where all the girls were being held. They made us walk naked through the big room where all the men were sitting. We were barely able to walk. This scenario was repeated every week—it was like a nightmare.[20]

World magazine editor Mindy Belz interviewed Christians from Nineveh who fled ISIS. In her book, *They Say We Are Infidels*, she wrote that in the major Christian city of Qaraqosh, some one hundred Christians, who were initially left behind, were held hostage in their homes. She related: "One father described being tortured while

---

19. Letter on file at the Hudson Institute.
20. Minority Rights Group et al., *No Way Home: Iraq's Minorities on the Verge of Disappearance*, July 2016, http://unpo.org/downloads/1895.pdf.

his wife and two children were threatened after the family refused to deny their faith."[21] In another Christian family, the mother and twelve-year-old daughter were raped by ISIS militants, causing the father, who was forced to watch, to commit suicide. Father Bazi says that many of the girls and women have been raped but shame prevents them from talking about it.

Some reported being tortured in attempts to force them to convert. Forced conversion to Islam was so prevalent that there are now special ministries by Iraqi churches and clergy in Kurdistan. They minister to those who escaped and are burdened by the guilt of having renounced their faith, even though they did so with a knife blade at their children's neck or their own.

In September 2014, a family of twelve Assyrian Christians, trapped in their Nineveh hometown of Bartella after ISIS swept in the previous month, escaped after being robbed and forcibly converted to Islam. The press told their story as follows:

> The Assyrians said for the first three days they were given food by ISIS but for the next 17 days after they were given nothing. They survived from whatever they had in the house. ISIS stole all their money and their papers. They were brought to an Islamic court in Mosul where they "converted" and were given an Islamic state ID and then returned to Bartella. They said they saw one Assyrian who had not converted and was badly beaten, his hands were tied behind his back and he was driven off in a truck. They assumed that he was killed.[22]

In another case a group of men reportedly converted when jihadists threatened to rape the girls:

> There was Khalia, a woman in her fifties, who was captured and held hostage along with 47 others. During her 15 days in captivity, she rebuffed demands to convert, despite a gun being put to her head and a sword to her neck. She literally fought off ISIS militants as they tried to rape the girls, and again later when they tried to take

---

21. Mindy Belz, *They Say We Are Infidels: On the Run from ISIS with Persecuted Christians in the Middle East* (Carol Stream, IL: Tyndale Momentum, 2016), 251.

22. "12 Assyrians Who Were Held By ISIS Escape by Faking Conversion," *Assyrian International News Agency*, September 15, 2014, http://www.aina.org/news/20140915144247.htm.

a 9-year-old as a bride. Because of the abuse, 14 men gave in to ISIS's demands and said they would convert to Islam. Khalia would not. Ultimately, the hostages were left in the desert to walk to Erbil. Others in Kurdistan affirmed without prompting that "she had saved many people."[23]

The vast majority of Nineveh's Christians, like the vast majority of Yazidis, fled to Iraq's Kurdistan region or neighboring countries. What few possessions and wealth the Christian families were able to pack were stolen from them by ISIS at checkpoints along the way out. A Sunni imam of Mosul protested their treatment and was killed by ISIS.

With cars and bus fare stolen by ISIS militants, many had to walk through miles of desert-like terrain in 120-degree temperatures without water or food. They carried the small children and pushed grandparents in wheelchairs. Those who glanced back could see armed groups looting their homes and loading the booty onto trucks. Some who were sick or weak did not survive. Church leaders told a Knights of Columbus researcher that the toll from this death march is not known and that those who fell dead along the way were left there in the panic. Others died from stress-related diseases shortly after becoming refugees. Iraqi Dominican sister Diana Momeka reported that a dozen of the elderly nuns from her convent died within the first year of exile from Nineveh. Those with cancers and other serious conditions now struggle to survive as destitute refugees in the face of grossly inadequate medical services.

Mosul's Christians (some 35,000, according to reports that quote Patriarch Sako,[24] though other estimates are lower) first fled in June, and then a second wave left in late July for the large Christian town of Qaraqosh, about eighteen miles away, and other Nineveh villages, where they doubled up with relatives or sought shelter in schools, churches, and monasteries. That summer, the ISIS leadership in Mosul turned off the water supply to some of these Christian places in Nineveh, explaining that they did not deserve to drink.

---

23. Knights of Columbus and In Defense of Christians, *Genocide against Christians in the Middle East*.

24. "Iraqi Christians Flee after ISIS Issue Mosul Ultimatum," *BBC*, July 18, 2014, http://www.bbc.com/news/world-middle-east-28381455.

Christian leaders, perceiving an impending ISIS offensive against the rest of Nineveh, pleaded for help. In late June 2014, Archbishop Moshi issued a dramatic appeal to the international community for urgent protection for his people in Qaraqosh:

> I appeal to the consciences of political leaders around the world, to international organizations and to all men of good will: it is necessary to intervene immediately to put a stop to the deterioration of the situation, working not only at a humanitarian level, but also politically and diplomatically. Every hour, every day lost, is likely to make all unrecoverable. Inaction becomes complicity with crime and abuse of power. The world cannot turn a blind eye to the tragedy of people who have fled from their homes in a few hours, taking with them only the clothes they are wearing.[25]

The archbishop's pleas went unheeded. By the second week of August, ISIS had confiscated Christian homes and businesses in Mosul, after marking them with the red letter nun, the Arabic equivalent of N, for Nazarene, and consolidated its control over all of Nineveh province. Virtually the entire Christian population, some one hundred twenty thousand recent exiles from Mosul and the residents of the Nineveh Plain, was forced to flee to Kurdistan, Jordan, Lebanon, and Turkey. Seeking shelter and aid, they flocked to the local churches, which were utterly unprepared to receive them. For months the exiled Christian families lived out in the open, under plastic tarps or in abandoned buildings. During that first winter in 2014, they were gradually moved into seven-foot-wide shipping containers, where thousands still remain.

Two years later the local churches and international aid groups continue to provide all their food, clothing, medicine and, to the extent it exists, education, since they lack resettlement rights even in Iraqi Kurdistan. Moreover, they find the U.N. camps to be too dangerous for them. Stephen Rasche, director of internally displaced persons resettlement programs for Erbil's Chaldean Catholic Archdiocese, testified to Congress that in Erbil "there are no Christians who

---

25. "Syrian Catholic Archbishop Moshe's Appeal to the International Community: Save Us!" *Voice of the Persecuted* (June 27, 2014), https://voiceofthepersecuted.wordpress.com/2014/06/27/syrian-catholic-archbishop-moshes-appeal-to-the-international-community-save-us/comment-page-1/.

ISIS Genocide of Christian Communities in Iraq and Syria

will enter the U.N. camps for fear of violence against them"—concerns that U.N. representatives told him are valid for Christians.[26]

ISIS treatment of the Christian community in Mosul and Nineveh is aptly described by Ambassador Alberto Fernandez, a former State Department counterterrorism expert, as an "extinction," with ISIS labeling Christians "polytheists" (representatives of *shirk*), not "People of the Book."[27]

Raqqa, Syria

What happened in Raqqa, the capital of the Islamic State, is upheld as the prime example of ISIS offering a jizya option to Christians. Only a few dozen Christian families remained in Raqqa at the time ISIS raised the jizya issue, it militants having captured the city from Jabhat al Nusra (al Qaeda) in mid-2013. In early 2014, ISIS gave Raqqa's Christians an ultimatum: they could either sign a written order to pay jizya and abide by a list of restrictions regarding the practice of their faith or be considered combatants and put to "the sword." The order was posted on the Internet, bearing the blurred-out signatures of some twenty Christians of that city, and it received wide international coverage.[28] It turned out to be a cover for an extortion racket against the few scattered and most elderly Christians remaining. The Raqqa Christians who have been paying ISIS, far from being protected, were used by ISIS as human shields and never had a chance to exercise their religious rights.

Under the purported jizya arrangement, Christian men were required to pay ISIS, in gold, amounts equivalent to one month of the average Raqqa salary, later raised to three months. In exchange, they were to receive the "protection of the Prophet" and would not be harmed. The written order, a purported dhimmi contract,[29] pre-

---

26. Stephen Rasche, Testimony, September 22, 2016, https://www.csce.gov/sites/helsinkicommission.house.gov/files/3_Steve%20Rasche_Testimony.pdf.

27. Fernandez, "The ISIS Caliphate and the Churches."

28. Nina Shea, "Syrian Jihadists Are Forcing Christians to Become Dhimmis Under Seventh-Century Rules," Hudson Institute (originally published in *National Review Online*, February 28th, 2014), http://www.hudson.org/research/10148-syrian-jihadists-are-forcing-christians-to-become-dhimmis-under-seventh-century-rules.

29. This was an agreement used under historical caliphates that gives protections and certain religious liberties to some non-Muslim groups but requires annual payment of a poll-tax (jizya).

sumed the existence of functioning churches, with its detailed list of things forbidden to the churches, such as ringing bells, displaying crosses, making repairs, and holding wedding and funeral processions outside church walls. In fact, ISIS quickly set about destroying and shutting down all the churches, and none remained open after the caliphate was announced in July 2014. The last cleric left when ISIS arrived. It was in Raqqa that the Italian Jesuit, Father Paolo Dall'Oglio, was presumably murdered by jihadis in July 2013.

As of this writing, only a few dozen older Christians remain in Raqqa, and without churches or priests, they have no ability to worship as Christians. They are not allowed to leave the city and are being kept under house arrest, according to reports in spring 2016.[30] Moreover, far from being provided "protection," these Christians are being used by ISIS as human shields as rebels and foreign forces strike the city.[31]

In an article on Armenians in Syria, *Voice of America* quotes Ara Sisserian, an advocate for Syrian Christian refugees in Armenia: "With the rise of extremists, being a non-Muslim minority is the last thing you want to be in Syria now." The article explains, "In areas under control of the Islamic State, Armenians face increased peril." It mentions purported jizya arrangements but then states: "IS has also confiscated their land and used them as human shields to deter international coalition and Syrian warplanes from hitting its positions in Raqqa and elsewhere."[32]

The touted "jizya" arrangement proved to be a deception: the Raqqa document was actually a protection contract for extortion, for there simply was no practical way for Christians to worship as Christians after being left without churches or priests. Rather than being protected, the two dozen or so elderly Christians were subjected to

---

30. Samuel Smith, "ISIS Holds Last Remaining Christian Families under House Arrest So They Can't Escape Raqqa," *Christian Post*, March 31, 2016, http://m.christianpost.com/news/isis-holds-last-remaining-christian-families-under-house-arrest-so-they-cant-escape-raqqa-160599/.

31. Jack Moore, "ISIS Preventing Remaining Christian Families From Leaving Raqqa," *Newsweek*, March 30, 2016, http://europe.newsweek.com/isis-preventing-remaining-christian-families-leaving-raqqa-442216?rm=eu.

32. Mehdi Jedinia and Sirwan Kajjo, "Fleeing Syrian Armenians Find Surer Path to Freedom," *Voice of America*, April 16, 2016, http://www.voanews.com/content/fleeing-syrian-armenians-find-surer-path-to-freedom/3288663.html.

ISIS Genocide of Christian Communities in Iraq and Syria

house arrest and used as human shields. Though the State Department acknowledged there were no churches left open, it too (prior to its finding of genocide) repeated the ISIS propaganda that Christians were given a jizya option: "Former residents of Raqqa estimated there were no more than 30 Christians left in Raqqa City, paying an unknown amount in protection taxes (jizya), and without access to public places of worship."[33] Ambassador Fernandez observed the following about Raqqa:

> After burning Christian books, destroying churches, and kidnapping priests in Raqqa in 2013, ISIS then publicized, in February 2014, a new dhimmi pact with Christians in Raqqa State. The announcement received considerable attention in international media, but there is little evidence that there was much of a Christian community to form the pact with. Although the agreement includes the standard language of "not building a church, monastery or monk's hermitage," there is no evidence that any existing churches actually remained open or in Christian hands, much less that anyone would want to build any. Indeed, there are no images whatsoever of what could be described as normal Christian life in ISIS-controlled territory—no functioning churches, no monasteries or working priests, and no Christian families or Christian schools—all of which had existed throughout Islamic history.[34]

Fernandez explains that ISIS may have raised the jizya issue as a "publicity stunt" in order to appear more Islamic:

> The pact seems more aspirational, and more about preparing the stage for Abu Bakr al-Baghdadi's assuming the mantle of the Caliph, which happened only four months later, than a real document regulating the life of an actual community. Just as the Caliph Omar in the 7th century produced an agreement to regulate the life of a protected minority, so would the Caliph-in-Waiting do the same. The only thing missing were actual Christians.[35]

The respected outlet "Raqqa is Being Slaughtered Silently," which monitors ISIS in Raqqa, also repeats the jizya term but makes clear

---

33. U.S. Department of State, Bureau of Democracy, Human Rights and Labor, *International Religious Freedom Report for 2014: Syria*, http://www.state.gov/j/drl/rls/irf/religiousfreedom/index.htm?year=2014&dlid=238478#.
34. Fernandez, "The ISIS Caliphate and the Churches."
35. Ibid.

that these payments did not spare the city's Christian minority from brutal ISIS bigotry. "Christians are the most vulnerable group in the country," said one member of the group.[36]

John, a college student, was one of the Christians who remained in Raqqa after ISIS seized it. After finally escaping in early 2016, he managed to survive for eighteen months by carrying an official ISIS protection document he obtained by making extortion payments to ISIS, which he mistakenly called a jizya tax. Despite the protection payments, he lived in "constant fear," was forced to conform to ISIS haircut and dress codes and behavior rules, and while he was able to meet socially with other Christians, he had no ability to go to church or receive the sacraments.

John related how he once watched a street demonstration with crowds shouting "Allahu Akbar" (Allah is the greatest): "I didn't shout it—I am a Christian. But when an IS [Islamic State] man saw me being silent, he stopped the car. I had to say '*Allahu Akbar*' too." Eventually one night in early 2016, John made his escape in secrecy. He said he was the last young Christian to leave Raqqa.[37]

Christian girls and women faced a much harder time than even John did in ISIS-controlled Raqqa. ISIS defectors report that the rape of Christian "infidels" was common and approved by the ISIS sharia court. Some were girls as young as twelve years old.[38]

Despite payments to ISIS, the two dozen older Christians remaining in Raqqa are reportedly under house arrest or serving ISIS as human shields at this writing. They have no freedom to practice their Christian faith.

Qaryatayn, Syria

In August 2015, ISIS captured Qaryatayn, a Syrian city where Christians and Muslims lived as neighbors. Another "jizya offer" was reported there, involving some three hundred Syriac Orthodox and Catholic men, women, and children who were immediately taken

---

36. Jedinia and Kajjo, "Fleeing Syrian Armenians Find Surer Path to Freedom."

37. "Living as a Christian in the Islamic State," *World Watch Monitor*, February 18, 2016, https://www.worldwatchmonitor.org/2016/02/4307204/.

38. Rozh Ahmad, "Exclusive: Q&A with Former Islamic State Member," *Your Middle East*, September 28, 2014, http://www.yourmiddleeast.com/culture/exclusive-qa-with-former-islamic-state-member_26696.

ISIS Genocide of Christian Communities in Iraq and Syria

hostage by ISIS. News reports announced that the following month they were "released," returned to their homes, and confined there under a jizya arrangement ordered by an Islamic State sharia court.[39] The terms were similar to those in Raqqa. The actual circumstances of the Christians under ISIS control there, however, were revealed after Qaryatayn's liberation in April 2016, and they sharply differed from those claimed by ISIS and repeated in the media.

The ISIS propaganda campaign surrounding the signing of a dhimmi contract in Qaryatayn was extensive, as detailed by Middle East Media Research Institute (MEMRI):

> In October 3, 2015, the information office of the Islamic State (ISIS) in Damascus Province posted a five-minute video titled "[Fight Those Who Do Not Believe In Allah] Until They Give The Jizya Willingly While They Are Humbled" (from Koran 9:29). The video, posted on Archive.org and disseminated via social media, including on Twitter under the Damascus Province hashtag, deals with ISIS's imposition of a dhimma contract and the jizya poll tax on the Christian residents of the city of Qaryatayn, Syria, which it recently conquered. The video is accompanied by footage of ISIS removing crosses from churches and destroying them, as well as video of the signing of the contract.[40]

In a translation by MEMRI, the narrator of the ISIS video explained:

> The Caliph of the Muslims displayed kindness and generosity, and agreed to accept their jizya tax, and to allow them to live under the rule of the Caliphate as part of the dhimma contract. He also gave the Christians who fled the town an opportunity to return to their homes and fields within a month from the signing of the dhimma contract.

He warned that if the Christians stayed and refused to make the payments to ISIS, the orders were for "the men to be killed and the women and children to be enslaved."

---

39. Jack Moore, "ISIS Forces Christians to Live Under Its Rules in Syrian Town after Release," *Newsweek*, September 4, 2015, http://europe.newsweek.com/isis-forces-christians-live-under-its-rules-syrian-town-after-release-332538?rx=us.

40. The quotations in the next three paragraphs are from "ISIS in New Video to Christians in Qaryatayn, Syria: Pay Jizya—Or You Will Be Executed and Your Wives Enslaved," *MEMRI, Special Dispatch*, No. 6178, October 9, 2015, http://www.memri.org/report/en/print8785.htm.

Apparently many of the Christians who were originally taken away were allowed to return to the town after being ransomed by their relatives, though some still remain missing. That fall, Syriac Orthodox archbishop Jean Kawak attested that the Christians who made the jizya payments were being treated like "slaves" and "third-class citizens." He said they were held there against their will in a form of house arrest.[41] The facts revealed in April 2016 following the liberation of the town by Russian-backed Syrian troops support the archbishop's assessment.

Syriac Orthodox patriarch Ignatius Aphrem II reported that ISIS subjected the town's Christians to abuse and violence from the start. He said that twenty-one were killed trying to escape or refusing to convert to Islam or submit to the "caliphate" rules.[42] All had been forced to sign the agreement to make payments to ISIS in order not to be killed. However, the community was never able to assemble and worship as Christians or live anything resembling a normal life. The Christians lived in constant fear and torment. Furthermore, the militants reportedly were plotting to take the Christian girls as "slaves."[43] In early September, three of the Christians were taken as hostages to Raqqa and, according to reports, were killed. On September 22, 2015, another Christian was murdered by jihadists on charges of blasphemy, allegedly because he was overheard cursing by Muslims while they were working together in a vineyard.

In October 2015, with the help of Muslim friends, the Christians set up an underground railroad and began escaping in small groups to areas under Syrian army control. The community decided to send out the young girls first, after being warned that jihadi leaders desired them as "wives."[44] The escaping Christians left on foot and used a farm along the way as a stop on the underground railroad. It was manned by five Christians and six Muslims, all of whom were killed in December by an armed group. After the first escape, the

---

41. Moore, "ISIS Forces Christians to Live Under Its Rules."

42. "Al-Qaryatayn: 21 Christians Killed by Islamic State, Others Still in the Hands of the Jihadists," AsiaNews, http://www.asianews.it/news-en/Al-Qaryatayn:-21-Christians-killed-by-Islamic-State,-others-still-in-the-hands-of-the-jihadists-37195.html.

43. Ibid.

44. "Syria war: IS Group Killed 21 Christians in Al-Qaryatain, Says Patriarch," *BBC*, April 10, 2016, http://www.bbc.com/news/world-middle-east-36011663.

jihadists seized ten young Christian men and threatened to kill them unless they converted to Islam, which they did.

Father Jacques Mourad, a Syriac Catholic priest, was the prior of the historic fifth-century Mar Elian monastery in Qaryatayn, where he led a Christian-Muslim dialogue and sheltered war refugees from both religions. In May 2015, he and Deacon Boulos were captured by ISIS. For five months, they were confined in a 19 x 10-foot bathroom where they had no electricity or contact with the outside world. The two prisoners were given rice and water twice daily. Three times during their captivity, they were given tea. They were threatened with beheading if they did not convert, and Father Mourad was beaten with a plastic hose.[45] On October 10, 2016, with the help of a Muslim friend and dressed as a Muslim, Father Mourad escaped on a motorcycle.

Qaryatayn, which once had thirty thousand inhabitants, of which up to two thousand were Christians, was long a symbol of religious coexistence. Today it is a ghost town, in ruins. Father Murad's 1,500-year-old monastery, which housed the relics of St. Elian, martyred by the Romans for refusing to renounce his faith, was bulldozed by ISIS jihadists. Soon after Qaryatayn's liberation, a Christian delegation visited the area and reported to AsiaNews.it.com on the "total devastation" of the church, monastery, and center for pilgrims. According to the local priest, Father Michel Noman, a group of the town's Christians was captured by ISIS and negotiations for their release were ongoing. "We do not even know for sure if they are still alive, or dead," the priest stressed.

In Qaryatayn, Christians received neither protection nor the right to worship in exchange for their payments. Some were killed, others taken captive, and others held in the town against their will. Others risked their own lives and the lives of those who helped them in order to escape impending sexual slavery. Yet ISIS insisted on calling their forced payments "jizya" and made a propaganda show of their signing a dhimmi contract.

---

45. Doreen Abi Raad, "Freed Syrian Priest Says Imprisonment Was Way to Carry Cross of Jesus," Catholic News Service, November 13, 2015, http://www.catholic-news.com/services/englishnews/2015/freed-syrian-priest-says-imprisonment-was-way-to-carry-cross-of-jesus.cfm.

Persecution & Genocide of Christians in the Middle East

Khabour River Valley, Syria

On February 23, 2015, ISIS stormed through some thirty-five Christian villages in the Khabour River Valley in Syria's Hassaka Province and abducted 230 Assyrian Christian men, women, and children.[46] They detained them in an undisclosed area, away from their villages, until millions of dollars were paid by their church. This, too, was deceptively framed by ISIS as an Islamic "tax" on Christians.

At first, the militants demanded the impossible sum of $23 million, later reduced to $10 million, from the Assyrian Church of the East for their release. After an undisclosed amount was handed over, the last forty-three surviving members of this group were freed on February 22, 2016. The captives had been released in small groups throughout the year, presumably after ransom money was raised and paid. During their captivity, the Christians were held incommunicado as prisoners and were deprived of basic religious and other human rights.

Three Christian men from this group, dressed in orange jumpsuits were shown in an ISIS video. They were made to kneel and identify themselves as Nazarenes or Christians. They were then executed at point-blank range by gunshot to the back of their heads. Three more men from this group of hostages, also dressed in orange jumpsuits, were then shown kneeling behind the three fallen bodies, identifying themselves as Nazarenes and stating they would be killed next unless payments were made.[47]

Eventually, as the Assyrian Human Rights Network reported, the surviving Khabour Christians gained their freedom following an order by an ISIS sharia court that they pay an amount of money "levied as a tax on non-Muslims."[48] Though this was labelled a religious "tax," this incident can only be understood as a large-scale hostage case.

---

46. "ISIS Release 43 Assyrian Hostages in Syria," Assyrian International News Agency, February 22, 2016, http://www.aina.org/news/20160222125248.htm.

47. These murders occurred on September 23, 2015. Nina Shea, "ISIS Genocide Mideast—U.S. Must Take Refugees," Hudson Institute (originally published in *National Review Online*, October 9, 2015), http://www.hudson.org/research/11765-isis-genocide-mideast-u-s-must-take-refugees.

48. "Islamic State Frees 19 of 220 Abducted Assyrian Christians," BBC, March 1, 2015, http://www.bbc.com/news/world-middle-east-31685931.

ISIS Genocide of Christian Communities in Iraq and Syria

Idlib, Syria

Various other actors demand "jizya" payments from members of the Christian minority in the Middle East. Some claim to represent ISIS and others do not, but their demands, like those of ISIS, come with no guarantees for either physical protection or respect for religious rights. For example, Iraqi Christian families living as refugees outside Amman, Jordan, periodically receive knocks on the door at night from men who say they are members of ISIS and demand a jizya tax for protection. If the family has no money (since ISIS in Iraq has already taken everything they own), these men then demand the daughters. In such cases, Canon Andrew White's American Foundation for Relief and Reconciliation in the Middle East, which supports refugee families, and local churches have helped to immediately relocate them within Jordan.

Another example occurred in Syria before ISIS surfaced. Syrian Christian refugees told Dutch blogger Martin Janssen that the thirty Christian families from their village near Idlib were confronted with so-called "jizya" demands in 2012. The sums demanded quickly increased and proved so ruinous that some of the Christians fled, leaving behind their property, while others converted to Islam in order to escape enslavement or death. There was no evidence they were ever allowed to worship as Christians from the time the protection payments were demanded. While this case preceded ISIS, it provides insight into the extortion system that ISIS and other jihadist groups call jizya.

One of Janssen's accounts, translated by the Rev. Mark Durie, the renowned Australian linguist, writer, and Anglican priest, follows:

> Jamil [an elderly man] lived in a village near Idlib where 30 Christian families had always lived peacefully alongside some 200 Sunni families. That changed dramatically in the summer of 2012. One Friday trucks appeared in the village with heavily armed and bearded strangers who did not know anyone in the village. They began to drive through the village with a loud speaker broadcasting the message that their village was now part of an Islamic emirate and Muslim women were henceforth to dress in accordance with the provisions of the Islamic Shariah. Christians were given four choices. They could convert to Islam and renounce their "idolatry." If they refused they were allowed to remain on condition that they

pay the jizya.... For Christians who refused there remained two choices: they could leave behind all their property or they would be slain. The word that was used for the latter in Arabic (dhabaha) refers to the ritual slaughter of sacrificial animals.[49]

The man told Janssen that his and a number of other families began making the payments, but the amount demanded kept increasing over several months, so the Christians fled, leaving behind their farms and property. Some who could not pay or escape were forced to convert to Islam. In the end, no Christians were able to survive as Christians.

Destroying Every Trace of Christianity

ISIS lost no time in eradicating all physical traces of the 2,000-year-old history of Christianity from the towns the faithful left behind. In Mosul, all forty-five churches and church facilities were seized and their crosses and religious symbols stripped off. Some were turned into mosques. One, the Mar (Saint) Ephraim Cathedral, the seat of the Syrian Orthodox Church, is now known as the Mosque of the Mujahideen and outfitted with loudspeakers that call Muslims to prayer. On July 6, 2015, ISIS blew up the 1,000 year old church in Mosul known as the church of the Mother of Perpetual Help. In February 2015, ISIS blew up Mosul's Virgin Mary Church. In mid-2015, Mosul's historic St. Joseph's Catholic Church was also converted into a mosque, with its cross removed and gold dome painted black. The three Syriac Orthodox churches in Sinjar were demolished by ISIS, as were other churches throughout the Nineveh Plain.

In March 2015, ISIS tweeted photos showing the group blowing up the fourth-century Mar Behnam Monastery in Qaraqosh, Nineveh. The monastery was known to contain one of the most valuable Syriac libraries in Iraq and wall inscriptions by thirteenth century Mongol pilgrims. Iraqi Catholic Dominican nun Sister Diana Momeka said that it was especially demoralizing to watch the destruction of their

---

49. Nina Shea, "Religious Minorities in Syria: Caught in the Middle," Hudson Institute (Testimony before the U.S. House Committee on Foreign Affairs, June 25, 2013), http://www.hudson.org/research/9643-religious-minorities-in-syria-caught-in-the-middle.

heritage in real time on YouTube. Photos also showed the bombing of the tombs of Saint Behnam and Saint Sarah, both thought to have been converted to Christianity by Saint Matthew. Other church facilities were turned into a women's prison and ISIS administrative offices. The fourth century Mar Behnam, a Syriac Catholic monastery outside Mosul, was captured and its monks expelled, leaving behind a library of early Christian manuscripts.

ISIS's destruction of churches in its Syrian territory was no less systematic. In July 2014, after declaring its caliphate, ISIS shut all churches in Raqqa, and a Christian who escaped witnessed them destroy the interior of three of them: "They broke everything inside—the icons, the altar, everything. One church building is now a centre" for ISIS. The fifth century Mar Elian monastery in Qaryatain, in Syria, was bulldozed by ISIS in August 2015. Upon invading the thirty-five Christian villages strung along Syria's Khabour River in February 2015, ISIS set about destroying and desecrating all the churches even though the population had been captured, killed, or had fled, and the villages had become ghost towns. When ISIS captured Raqqa from al Nusra in spring 2013, its militants destroyed several churches and their contents and shuttered the rest.

Christian and Shiite gravesites, deemed idolatrous by ISIS, were blown up and destroyed, including the tomb of the eighth century BC Old Testament Prophet Jonah and the Muslim shrine that enclosed it. Libraries of ancient Christian manuscripts and priceless artifacts were destroyed or sold on the international black market. Before fleeing, the Orthodox Christian community successfully spirited away the relics of Thomas the Apostle who, it is said, introduced Christianity to Nineveh.

In January 2016, satellite imagery brought to light the complete obliteration of Mosul's massive, stone-walled monastery of St. Elijah, dating from the sixth century and distinguished by an entryway etched by Christian monks with Chi Rho, the first Greek letters of the word Kristos, "Christ." From satellite photos of the isolated hill where it had stood, it was confirmed that the monastery was pulverized into a field of gray dust by ISIS fanatics, evidently using some determined application of sledgehammers, bulldozers, and explosives.

Built before Christianity's sectarian divisions and having gathered Christian worshipers for one and a half millennia, this ancient sacred edifice, now reduced to rubble, represents yet another irreparable loss to Christian patrimony at the hands of these Islamist extremists. Even more importantly, its destruction also symbolizes the genocide of Iraq's Christian people and their civilization. It gives shocking reminder that Nineveh has been inalterably changed. Its pluralistic cultural mosaic since antiquity has been shattered and putting it back together may prove impossible in this generation.

This eradication of Christian history continued with ISIS blowing up Mosul's Clock Church, named after its famous clock tower, in April 2016. The clock tower was paid for by Empress Eugenie of France, wife of the last Emperor Napoleon III, as a gift to the Dominican Fathers who were building the church in the 1870s.

As thorough as ISIS has been in erasing the historical memory of Christianity, it should be acknowledged that this practice of church destruction began by ISIS predecessor groups with coordinated church bombings in Baghdad, as early as 2004. From then until the Islamic State was established in June 2014, more than seventy Iraqi Christian churches were destroyed by such groups. The most catastrophic was the suicide attack on Baghdad's Our Lady of Perpetual Help Catholic Church during a Sunday Mass in October 2010, when virtually everyone inside was killed or wounded, including one of the priests, as he stood at the altar. As Bishop Angaelos of the UK Coptic Orthodox Church told the U.S. Congress in 2013, attacks by "radical elements" are not merely targeting individuals, but "the Christian and minority presence in its entirety."

Targeting Clergy

As described above, many Christians have been deliberately murdered by ISIS and affiliated Islamist groups solely for religious reasons in Iraq and Syria since AQI surfaced in 2004. The vast majority of such cases have not been documented or investigated, much less prosecuted. A partial roster of Christian leaders singled out for assassination there, however, can be made. Such a pattern of murders hold specific significance in evidencing the crime of genocide. While it is often difficult to determine the identity of the perpetrator, it is apparent that these leaders were killed for their Christianity by a stream of extremist groups that evolved into ISIS. For example, in Syria in 2013, two Orthodox bishops, Metropolitans Mar Gregorios Yohanna Ibrahim and Boulos Yazigi, were taken captive. Their fate remains unknown. That sent an unmistakable signal to all Syrian Christians: none were protected.

Also in Syria, two beloved European Jesuit priests were attacked by jihadists after they had devoted their entire adult lives, some 40 years each, to serve Syria's poor and oppressed. On April 7, 2014, Fr. Frans van der Lugt, who cared for disabled children of all faiths and refused to leave them when the war started, was dragged from his monastery, beaten, shot twice, and left to die in the street. Fr. Paolo Dall'Oglio had gone to negotiate a hostage release and a truce between Islamist rebels and local Kurds at ISIS headquarters in Raqqa when he disappeared in July 2013; it is thought that he was murdered by ISIS.

On June 23, 2013, Catholic Syrian priest Fr. François Murad was murdered by Islamist terrorists. Affiliated with the Franciscan order that was given custody of the Holy Land sites by Pope Clement VI in 1342, the forty-nine-year-old priest was killed in Gassanieh, in northern Syria, in the Convent of the Rosary where he had taken refuge after his monastery was bombed at the outset of the conflict, and where he had been giving support to the few remaining nuns. According to local sources, Fr. Murad's building was attacked by the jihadi group Jabhat al-Nusra, the Syrian al Qaeda franchise.

In February 2013, twenty-seven-year-old Father Michael Kayal, of Aleppo's Armenian Catholic Church, was pulled off a bus when Islamist gangs spotted his clerical garb. He is presumed dead. A similar fate befell the Greek Orthodox priest Maher Mahfouz around the same time. In December 2012, reports surfaced of the abduction of Syrian Orthodox priest Fadi Haddad, taken as he left his church in the town of Qatana to negotiate the release of one of his kidnapped parishioners. A week later, his mutilated corpse was found by the roadside, his eyes having been gouged out.

Iraq has also seen clerical assassinations. These occurred in the larger cities prior to the Islamic State's caliphate, when all clergy left along with the vast majority of the faithful. For instance, Maher Dakhil, pastor of Baghdad's St. George's Anglican Church, disappeared in 2005 and is thought to have been murdered, along with his deacons and staff. In November 2006, Father Boulous Iskander, a prominent Syriac Orthodox priest in Mosul, was kidnapped for ransom and three days later beheaded and dismembered. His captors left a message linking the murder to a papal speech critical of Islam. In November 2006, Father Mundhir al-Dayr was taken from his

Protestant church in Mosul and found later with a bullet in his head. As they went about their ministry in June 2007, Father Ragheed Ganni and three deacons were gunned down in their car, which was then rigged with explosives to prevent anybody from retrieving their bodies. They had refused jihadi demands to close their church. Anglican Canon Andrew White, who leads a Baghdad ecumenical congregation, reported in 2007: "All of my leadership were . . . taken and killed—all dead."

Also in Mosul, Paulos Faraj Rahho, a charismatic Chaldean Catholic archbishop, was abducted by extremists while he finished the Lenten Stations of the Cross at the Church of the Holy Spirit in 2008. The sixty-five-year-old prelate was found dead two weeks later in a shallow grave, his body marked by signs of torture. In October 2010, Our Lady of Perpetual Help Syriac Catholic Church in Baghdad was attacked during Mass, and two priests were killed along with dozens of worshippers.

A Syrian evangelical preacher and his twelve year old son were tortured and killed after they refused to renounce their Christianity, outside Aleppo on August 28, 2015. "All were badly brutalized and then crucified," according to the Christian Aid Mission, in Charlottesville, Virginia. The boy had his fingertips cut off, in an attempt to force his father to convert to Islam. Their bodies were left hanging on the crosses for two days, under signs reading "infidels." Their names were withheld to protect their family members.

Prominent laypersons are also marked for assassination. Pascale Warda, Iraq's minister of migration in 2004 and a Christian, survived four assassination attempts, including one that killed her four bodyguards. Iraq's lay Christians have been targeted for not abiding by Muslim dress or social codes. There are numerous documented reports of Christians killed by extremists for mingling with the opposite sex or for operating "un-Islamic" businesses, such as liquor stores, cinemas, and hair salons. In 2010, roadside bombs blew up a convoy of school buses organized by the Catholic diocese to transport university students from the Christian towns of the Nineveh Plain to the University of Mosul. The attack occurred despite an army escort. Sandy Shibib, a young woman studying biology, was killed from shrapnel wounds to her head; one hundred and sixty others were injured. After this episode, a thousand Christian students withdrew from the university, which was exactly the result the terrorists hoped for. Armenians in Syria, given away by their ethnic names or by the crosses around their necks, have been pulled off of buses by jihadis and beheaded.

In 2006, from Baghdad's Dora neighborhood, tens of thousands of Christian families fled seemingly overnight, never to return. One Dora resident said that when he was commanded to tell the terrorists that he had five children, they replied, "'Fine, three for you and two for us.' They wanted us to pay $10,000 a month as a kind of tax to staying in Dora, or they would take my children." Letters went to each Christian house, warning, "We know your house and we know your family. We will kill you one after the other. Depart the Muslim areas." They had bullets in them. One Christian resident of Dora who fled was the late Donny George, who, as Baghdad Museum director, had saved many of its artifacts from looting in 2003, during the U.S. invasion. As journalist Belz observed, "Sectarian violence was killing Muslims, but it was wiping out the city's Christian community. By 2008, the Islamic State of Iraq had terrorized much of the Christian population out of Mosul and everyplace in Iraq except Nineveh and Kurdistan. Many Christians got death threats, such as: 'Be informed that we will cut off your heads and leave your dead bodies with no organs and no heads in your stores and houses.'" Archbishop Rahho and Orthodox priest Boulous Iskander were among those murdered there at that time.

Hostage Taking Before ISIS

The eradication of Christians from Iraq began in earnest the decade before ISIS invaded Nineveh. Over those ten years, Iraq's Christian population declined by an estimated one million persons. By the time ISIS entered Mosul, it was no longer the religiously diverse city it had been; only a few thousand Christian families remained. While scores of church bombings and the assassinations of church leaders and brutality against ordinary Christians had taken a large toll and driven out Christians, there was another persecution that played a large role in the decade long exodus of Christians—hostage taking. By 2008, Christian kidnappings in Mosul were so common, author Mindy Belz reports, that "their ransom notes simply demanded *daftar*, slang which everyone knew meant $10,000."

Perhaps the biggest scourge against the Church in Iraq since the fall of the Hussein regime, and in Syria since the beginning of its conflict, has been hostage taking. In Iraq in particular, the kidnapping one by one of thousands of ordinary Christians has been an atrocity that has been largely invisible to the outside world. It is a phenomenon in which the victims and their families have no real voice and one that the churches have been loath to publicize for fear of exacerbating it and risking captives' lives.

As hostages, Christians frequently have been subject to torture, rape, and other abuse. They have even been killed. Interviews of Iraqi Christians indicate that many, if not most, have had a least one family member taken hostage by Islamists since 2004. This experience emotionally traumatized entire families and the ransoms paid to redeem loved ones were ruinous. These personal encounters with kidnapping—crimes that governments either could not or would not protect them from—pushed many Iraqi families to migrate to the more secure northern borders of Iraq or out of the country altogether. More than any other form of violence, the threat of kidnappings likely accounts for the fact that the Christian communities of Baghdad and Basra have been nearly extinguished in recent years.

Christians have been victimized by uniquely relentless kidnappings for ransom. Their ties to Western churches with deep pockets for ransom payments make them especially lucrative targets. Christian social structures, lacking tribal networks and militias of their own, render them especially vulnerable. Muslims are subject to kidnapping too, but, as the *Wall Street Journal* reported on June 11, 2013, often "their outcome is different" because they have armed defenders, whereas the Christians do not. The Journal told the story of a twenty-five-year-old cabdriver, Hafez al-Mohammed, who said he was kidnapped and tortured for seven hours by Sunni rebels in al-Waer, Syria, in late May that year. He was released after Alawites (a religious group centered in Syria that follows a highly controversial branch of Shia Islam) threatened to retaliate by kidnapping Sunni women.

Hostage taking is profitable to the Islamist kidnappers, but they also have less worldly motives. Thousands of Christian hostages have likely been killed—Aleppo's Melkite Catholic Archbishop says 1,000 there alone, including the two Orthodox bishops. Fr. Paolo Dall'Oglio is another example of a kidnapped Christian who has not been seen since. Other clerics, such as Fr. Fadi Haddad, have been kidnapped and killed while negotiating the release of kidnapped laity. Many hostages have been killed despite ransoms being paid. On July 10, 2015, the Vatican press *Fides* reported that, after their families paid ransoms of up to $50,000, Christian hostages in Baghdad were being killed instead of freed. Relatives have been murdered when paying ransoms for loved ones. The kidnappers' intent to "purify" the land for Islam is clear: Al Qaeda in Iraq (AQI) posted an Internet statement concerning a Christian hostage its militant killed in Mosul several years before ISIS. Belz describes it as "typical" at that time: "We eliminated him, because this impure crusader offended our noble prophet Muhammad."

Many of the kidnapped Christians, like Chaldean Catholic priest Douglas Bazi, are released for ransom but turn up more dead than alive, horribly tortured. Fr. Bazi, who ran a shelter for 500 ISIS survivors in Kurdistan has reported his ordeal by Shi'a Islamist militants in Baghdad in 2006:

> They destroyed my car, they blew up my church in front of me, I got shot by an AK-47 in my leg. The bullet is still in my leg. And I been kidnapped for nine days [sic]. They smash my nose and my teeth by hammer. And they broke one of my back discs.

He shared how the kidnappers withheld all food and water from him and kept him shackled on a filthy bathroom floor for four days. They released him only on the ninth day, when his church paid a ransom. Some of his family members left Iraq, but he stayed, moving to the Northern Kurdish territory where Christians are safer.

Due to their brutalization in captivity, Fr. Bazi and many others have required surgery and medical treatment upon release. One Iraqi Christian man told Belz that he was desperately seeking medical help for his son, who, after being kidnapped, suffered memory lapses, and post-traumatic stress disorder. Belz met an eight year old, now in a Christian camp in Kurdistan, who can no longer talk after his kidnapping. Another victim, a church worker, remains in hiding, perpetually afraid.

In Syria, large groups of Christians have been taken captive and held for ransom. An entire convent of Orthodox nuns from the Syrian Christian town of Maaloula was taken hostage by al Nusra extremists for three months in 2014 until a prisoner exchange was arranged with the Syrian government.

Conclusion

There is no functioning church, no Christian clergy, no Christian liturgies or sacraments, no intact Christian community—in short, no Christian life evident anywhere in ISIS territory. ISIS eradicated these communities and nearly every trace of their two-millennia-old history. These Christian communities were extremely fragile; they had suffered relentless persecution in Iraq for a decade before ISIS and in Syria for three years, at the hands of other Islamists, including those groups from which ISIS emerged. Many assassinations of clergy, cases of hostage taking, and targeted church bombings occurred in the immediate pre-ISIS period in both of these countries. ISIS finished off these Christian communities in areas under its control with a brutality that was both deliberate and systematic.

Far from respecting Christians as "People of the Book," the Islamic State has amply demonstrated its intent is to kill, enslave, and drive out this indigenous Middle Eastern Christian community. In many cases, ISIS did not bother to offer a jizya option before brutalizing and killing Christians. Even where ISIS claimed to offer a jizya option for Christians, though, it would not tolerate peaceful coexistence with them.

ISIS believes that the very presence of practicing Christians, whom it routinely calls unbelievers, infidels, polytheists, and Crusaders, defiles its caliphate. In 2015, in the seventh issue of its English-language magazine *Dabiq*, ISIS declared that "the truth is also clear regarding . . . jihad against the Jews, the Christians," and others, and directed the reader to "go forth for jihad and defend your Islam wherever you may be."

To be sure, ISIS routinely demanded money of Christians and took their property, and sometimes it called this "jizya." A review of those situations in Iraq and Syria, where the payment of jizya was claimed to have been offered as an option, reveals that ISIS does not allow Christians to live in security as Christians. The so-called jizya option is not the concept under traditional Islam that, in exchange for money, the caliph purported to undertake a two-fold obligation: respect for Christians as "People of the Book," and the assurance of peaceful coexistence. In every known case where ISIS uses the term "jizya," the Christian payments are clearly forms of ransom or extortion, as they do not allow a right to Christian "rites," which jizya traditionally purported to do.

ISIS Genocide of Christian Communities in Iraq and Syria

Virtually every Christian who can escape ISIS territory does so. From the available information, it appears that those few who have remained behind in the ISIS caliphate, mainly the elderly or disabled, have been killed, enslaved, brutalized, forcibly converted, detained, held under house arrest, used as human shields, and/or robbed of all their wealth. Syriac Catholic Patriarch Younan, whose church was Nineveh's largest, and Archbishop Nona, who headed the Chaldean Catholic Archdiocese in Mosul, have both described ISIS treatment of the Nineveh Christians as "genocide."

ISIS apparently invokes the jizya issue as religious propaganda to give its "caliphate" an aura of authenticity. In its elaborate recruitment videos, in glossy magazines, and in the blogosphere, the ISIS leadership attempts to portray itself as the standard bearer of authentic Islam. Alberto Fernandez, the State Department's former counter-terrorism coordinator, characterizes the ISIS jizya claims as a "Salafi Caliphate publicity stunt" undertaken to make the group's leader look more caliph-like.[50]

The fiction of an ISIS "jizya option" for Middle Eastern Christians has been uncritically repeated in the media, reporting by the widely-cited Syrian Observatory for Human Rights, the Kurdish press, and the "Our Generation is Gone" report of the Holocaust Museum's genocide prevention office, among others.[51] Most disappointing, in its June 2016 report, the U.N.-established International Commission of Inquiry on Syria errs in its summary conclusion that ISIS respects Christians as "People of the Book" and gives them a jizya option. In its scant one paragraph mention of Christians, the commission's report repeats ISIS's propaganda and fails to include any critical analysis of it or any citations, quotations, or other supporting evidence regarding Christians in ISIS-controlled territory. Some influential in policy making around the world are relying on such claims to assert that Yizidis were victims of ISIS genocide but Christians, respected as "People of the Book," were not since they were given a "jizya option." Thus, they conclude, this indicates that ISIS does not intend to destroy the Christian community and that the persecution

---

50. Fernandez, "The ISIS Caliphate and the Churches."
51. Nina Shea, "The ISIS Genocide of Middle Eastern Christian Minorities and Its Jizya Propaganda Ploy."

of Iraqi and Syrian Christians by the Islamic State does not meet the high bar of the Genocide Convention.

As this book shows, the crime of genocide—the most heinous of all human rights violations—has impacted Iraq and Syria's Christian communities, and there is an urgent need to explore legal strategies in response.

Sinjar, Iraq. When this Christian church was reduced to rubble, a Yezidi man fashioned a cross and placed it on top (October, 2016).

Still from video of 21 Coptic Christians being executed on a Libyan beach by ISIS (February, 2015).

2

Genocide, Statecraft, and Domestic Geopolitics

Robert A. Destro

"WHY SHOULD MY BOSS vote for a resolution condemning the genocide of Christians?" That question, posed by a congressional staffer in mid-September 2015, was innocent enough, but it left me speechless. By late summer 2015, the massacres of Christians and Yazidis in Northern Iraq had become "old news." On February 21, 2015, only seven months earlier, members of the criminal gang that calls itself "The Islamic State in Iraq and al-Sham" (ISIS or *Da'esh*)[1] organized the public beheading of twenty-one Coptic Christians on a beach in Libya and posted it to social media.[2] A month before that, in January, 2015, it killed a Paris police officer, attacked a Jewish supermarket in Porte de Vincennes where it killed four Jewish shoppers, killed twelve members of the staff of the satirical newspaper *Charlie Hebdo*, and murdered five additional people in the Île-de-France

---

1. *Da'esh* is the Arabic acronym for "*al-Dawla al-Islamiya al-Iraq wa-ash-Shaam*," the Islamic State of Iraq and Syria. The word "shaam" is used in Syrian dialect to refer to Damascus or to "Greater Syria" or "the Levant." ISIS rejects the use of the term Da'esh "[b]ecause they hear it, quite rightly, as a challenge to their legitimacy: a dismissal of their aspirations to define Islamic practice, to be 'a state for all Muslims' and—crucially—as a refusal *to acknowledge and address them as such.*" See Alice Guthrie, "Decoding Daesh: Why is the new name for ISIS so hard to understand?" (February 19, 2015), https://www.freewordcentre.com/blog/2015/02/daesh-isis-media-alice-guthrie/.
2. CNN Staff, "ISIS video appears to show beheadings of Egyptian Coptic Christians in Libya," *CNN World*, Monday, February 16, 2016, http://www.cnn.com/2015/02/15/middleeast/isis-video-beheadings-christians/.

Region.[3] Members of this extremist network also deliberately killed or claimed credit for killing Christians in Syria,[4] Iraq,[5] Egypt,[6] and Nigeria.[7] Not long after the staffer posed her question, ISIS would also take credit for the high-altitude bombing over Sinai of a Russian passenger jet that, according to an ISIS spokesman, "carried over 220 Crusader Russians."[8]

Armed with facts such as these, I thought that it would (or should) be relatively easy to use the framework of the laws defining genocide, war crimes, and crimes against humanity to accomplish several important goals.

1. To "connect the dots" among the many hundreds of incidents where people have been slaughtered because of their religion;

2. To highlight the connection between the criminals who commit these crimes and the toxic ideology that drives ISIS and its allies to

---

3. Heather Saul, "Paris attacks timeline: From *Charlie Hebdo* to a Jewish grocery store—how two hostage situations unfolded," *The Independent*, January 9, 2015.

4. BBC, "Syria's beleaguered Christians," BBC News, February 25, 2015, http://www.bbc.com/news/world-middle-east-22270455 ("Melkite Greek Catholic Patriarch Gregorios III Laham said last year that more than 1,000 Christians had been killed, entire villages cleared, and dozens of churches and Christian centres damaged or destroyed.").

5. Michael W. Chapman, "Vicar of Baghdad: ISIS Beheaded 4 Christian Children; They Said, 'We Love [Jesus],'" *CNS News.com*, December 15, 2014 3:45 PM, http://www.cnsnews.com/news/article/michael-w-chapman/vicar-baghdad-isis-beheaded-4-christian-children-they-said-we-love.

6. BBC World, "Islamic State: Egyptian Christians held in Libya 'killed,'" *BBC.com*, February 15, 2015, http://www.bbc.com/news/world-31481797.

7. Associated Press, "Extremist violence against Muslims, Christians sweeps Nigeria, 60 dead," July 6, 2015, http://www.foxnews.com/world/2015/07/06/bombs-at-mosque-restaurant-in-central-nigerian-city-kill-44/ (reporting attacks on and the destruction of 32 Christian churches and the targeted killings of Christians and Muslims).

8. Abul Taher, "Islamic State terrorists release sick video celebrating Sharm el-Sheikh atrocity titled: 'Satisfaction of souls by killing of Russians,'" *DailyMail.com*, November 7, 2015 at 18:18 GMT, http://www.dailymail.co.uk/news/article-3308706/Islamic-State-terrorists-release-sick-video-celebrating-Sharm-el-Sheikh-atrocity-titled-Satisfaction-souls-killing-Russians.html#ixzz3rV9ZYg16 ("By God's will, and strong efforts of our brothers and soldiers on the ground in the province of Sinai, they brought down a Russian airplane, which carried over 220 Crusader Russians. All of them have been killed, and thanks to God for that.").

Genocide, Statecraft, and Domestic Geopolitics

recruit and train thousands of young *jihadi-irhabis* to murder in name of God;[9]

3. To commit the resources of the United States Government to a long-term, concerted effort to prevent and punish not only the murderers, but as many of those involved in the *jihadi-irhabi* network's supply and money-laundering chains as can be discovered and brought to justice;[10] and

4. To encourage Congress and the State Department to work with friendly governments—especially those with Muslim majorities—to develop the means by which we can act jointly—and openly—against these killers to prevent and punish these crimes.

That, at least, was my thinking when Representatives Jeff Fortenberry (R-NE) and Anna Eshoo (D-CA) asked for volunteers to produce what became the first draft of the genocide resolution adopted by the U.S. House of Representatives on March 14, 2016, by a vote of 393-0: House Concurrent Resolution 75.

The pages that follow identify those goals which have been accomplished and highlight those that remain. Part I recounts the history of the House and Senate genocide resolutions and their relationship to Secretary of State John Kerry's genocide declaration. Part II discusses the geopolitics of genocide and the main arguments made against such declarations. Part III makes the case that U.S. Government policy is caught in a "perfect storm" where political correctness, Cold War thinking, and willful blindness about U.S. Government support for terrorist organizations is creating a poisonous human rights atmosphere at home and a feckless foreign policy abroad.

---

9. *Irhabi* إرهابي is the Arabic term for "terrorist." The term *Jihadi* has several meanings, which are discussed below. For present purposes, the term refers to those who practice "the Lesser Jihad" or "violent struggle on behalf of Islam." The jihadis then are literally "'those who struggle'..., and the expression is used by members of groups such as al-Qaeda to describe themselves. (Mujahideen, meaning 'holy warriors,' is another expression commonly used to refer to Muslims engaged in the Lesser Jihad)." Andrew Silke, "Holy Warriors: Exploring the Psychological Processes of Jihadi Radicalization," 5(1) *European Journal of Criminology*, 99–123 (2008) at 100.

10. See Mark Townsend, "Is Cosa Nostra now selling deadly assault weapons to Islamist terrorist groups?" *The Guardian*, July 23, 2016, https://www.theguardian.com/world/2016/jul/23/cosa-nostra-assault-weapons-islamist-terror-group.

The Congressional Genocide Resolutions and Secretary of State John Kerry's Genocide Declarations

Work on what was to become House Concurrent Resolution 75 (H. Con. Res. 75) began in late August, 2015.[11] What began as a small group of volunteers has now grown into an informal "Genocide Working Group" (GWG) that works closely with members, senators, and their staffs in an effort to make real, continuing progress on the genocide issue:

1. September 9, 2015: Mr. Fortenberry, Mrs. Eshoo, and four co-sponsors introduced H. Con. Res. 75.[12] It highlighted the massacres of "Christians and other ethnic and religious minorities, including Yezidis, Turkmen, Sabea-Mandeans, Kaka'e, and Kurds."[13]

2. December 18, 2016: Senators Bill Cassidy (R-LA) and Joe Manchin (D-WV) introduced Senate Resolution 340 with three (3) co-sponsors.[14] By the time it passed by unanimous consent in July 2016, it had 17 co-sponsors.[15]

3. March 14, 2016: The House of Representatives voted 393-0 to adopt an amended version of H. Con. Res. 75.[16] Before passage, it had 293 cosponsors.

4. July 7, 2016: Amended Senate Resolution 340 passed by unanimous consent.[17]

---

11. House Concurrent Resolution 75 (as introduced September 9, 2015 by Reps. Jeff Fortenberry and Anna Eshoo).

12. Mr. Fortenberry and Mrs. Eshoo were joined by Reps. Trent Franks (R-AZ), Daniel Lipinski (D-IL), Jeff Deham (R-CA), and Juan Vargas (D-CA). In all, there were 213 cosponsors.

13. House Concurrent Resolution 75.

14. Senate Resolution 340 (introduced December 18, 2015).

15. In addition to Senators Casey and Manchin, the original co-sponsors were Senators Marco Rubio (R-FL), Mark Kirk (R-IL), and Roger Wicker (R-MS). In all, there were seventeen (17) co-sponsors.

16. House Concurrent Resolution 75, "Expressing the sense of Congress that the atrocities perpetrated by ISIL against religious and ethnic minorities in Iraq and Syria include war crimes, crimes against humanity, and genocide," March 15, 2016 (as adopted).

17. Senate Resolution 340, "Expressing the Sense of Congress that the So-called Islamic State in Iraq and al-Sham (ISIS OR DA'ESH) is Committing Genocide, Crimes Against Humanity, and War Crimes," 162 Cong. Rec. S4920, 114th Congress, 2d Sess (July 7, 2016).

Genocide, Statecraft, and Domestic Geopolitics

5. Ongoing activities: Members of the GWG meet regularly in an effort to keep the United States, foreign governments, and international bodies focused on the effort to prevent future genocide and to punish that which has already occurred. To date, these activities include:

6. Proposing amendments to appropriations bills, developing a legislative agenda for the 115th Congress, and proposing initiatives for the incoming Trump Administration;[18]

7. Working with diplomatic missions at the United Nations to develop support for a Security Council Resolution creating an international hybrid tribunal with authority to try those whose crimes fit into the definition of one of the three international "atrocity" crimes: genocide, war crimes, and crimes against humanity;[19]

8. Providing U.S.-based support for forensic teams working in the field in Iraq, Syria, and elsewhere to document these crimes;

9. Collating information and analysis from observers in Syria, the newly-liberated areas of Iraq, Africa, and South Asia; and

10. Collaborating with advocates and legislators in Europe, Australia, Asia, the Middle East, and Africa to bring other governments and their human and financial resources into the effort.

The 393-0 House vote on H. Con. Res. 75 was a major political accomplishment for Mr. Fortenberry, Mrs. Eshoo, and all of those who were pushing the Obama Administration to make a formal genocide declaration. Supporters knew, however, that even a unani-

---

18. See, e.g., H.R. 5912, Department of State: Foreign Operations and Related Programs for the fiscal year ending September 30, 2017 (114th Cong. 2d Sess.) §7034 (b)(3) (appropriating $4 million for "forensic anthropology assistance related to the exhumation of mass graves and the identification of victims of war crimes, crimes against humanity, or genocide").

19. According to the United Nations:

> The term "atrocity crimes" refers to three legally defined international crimes: genocide, crimes against humanity, and war crimes. The definitions of the crimes can be found in the 1948 Convention on the Prevention and Punishment of the Crime of Genocide, the 1949 Geneva Conventions and their 1977 Additional Protocols, and the 1998 Rome Statute of the International Criminal Court, among other treaties.

United Nations, *Framework of Analysis for Atrocity Crimes: A Tool for Prevention*, at 1 (2014) (emphasis in original, footnotes omitted), http://www.un.org/en/preventgenocide/adviser/pdf/framework%20of%20analysis%20for%20atrocity%20crimes_ en.pdf.

mous vote in the House would not be enough. There was talk that, for weeks, there was considerable opposition from the State Department's Office of the Legal Adviser (OLA). Unless supporters could provide significant evidence *in addition to* the recurring news accounts of new atrocities, it was likely that the Secretary would defer to OLA.

Carl A. Anderson, Supreme Knight of the Knights of Columbus, had foreseen this scenario. The Knights had been running television ads for months that were designed to bring attention to the plight of those displaced by ISIS,[20] but the political feedback in Washington made it increasingly apparent that a public relations campaign would not be enough. For geopolitical reasons that will be explained in Part II, the State Department has long had an aversion to the use of the word "genocide" (the G-word). There was also the hard-to-prove-but-difficult-to-shake feeling that some in the Obama Administration suspected that Republicans would use genocide as a "wedge" political issue against them the upcoming presidential campaign.

In sum, "hard" evidence of criminal behavior would be needed to support the use of the G-word. In late February, GWC member, E. Scott Lloyd, an attorney with the Knights of Columbus, got on a plane, flew to Iraq, took witness statements, and worked with local church and human rights organizations to send the available documentation to the United States for processing. Dr. Gregory Stanton, founder and president of Genocide Watch, did superb work coordinating with experts in the field of genocide documentation. L. Martin Nussbaum and Ian Speir of the law firm Lewis, Roca, Rothgerber, and Christie also provided invaluable advice and assistance to the data collection effort on the ground in Iraq, database design and construction efforts here in the United States and editorial assistance on the final report. It was an extraordinary team effort.

On March 9, 2016, the Knights of Columbus and In Defense of Christians held a joint press conference to announce the publication and filing of a formal petition to Secretary of State John Kerry.[21]

---

20. See News Release, "New TV Ad Highlights Needs of Middle Eastern Christians Facing Genocide and Extinction," April 1, 2016, http://www.kofc.org/en/news/media/facing-genocide-extinction.html.

21. See http://www.stopthechristiangenocide.org/en/report-photos.html.

Genocide, Statecraft, and Domestic Geopolitics

They asked that the Obama Administration formally "[a]cknowledge the ongoing genocide of Christians, Yazidis, and other religious groups being targeted for extinction in the territories controlled or attacked by the ISIS and its affiliates."[22]

Congress also played a critical role in the process. On December 18, 2015, the same day that the Senate genocide resolution was introduced, Congress adopted the Consolidated Appropriations Act of 2016. It gave the Secretary of State until March 17, 2016, to provide Congress with:

> an evaluation of the persecution of, including attacks against, Christians and people of other religions in the Middle East by violent Islamic extremists and the Muslim Rohingya people in Burma by violent Buddhist extremists, including whether either situation constitutes mass atrocities or genocide (as defined in section 1091 of title 18, United States Code), and a detailed description of any proposed atrocities prevention response recommended by the [Atrocities Prevention Board].[23]

The Secretary announced his decision on schedule. On March 17, 2016, Secretary Kerry formally declared that ISIS and its affiliated organizations were committing genocide:

> My purpose in appearing before you today is to assert that, in my judgment, Daesh is responsible for genocide against groups in areas under its control, including Yezidis, Christians, and Shia Muslims. Daesh is genocidal by self-proclamation, by ideology, and by actions—in what it says, what it believes, and what it does. Daesh is also responsible for crimes against humanity and ethnic cleansing

---

22. Robert A. Destro, L. Martin Nussbaum, & Ian Speir, "Genocide Against Christians in the Middle East: A Report Submitted to Secretary of State John Kerry by the Knights of Columbus and In Defense of Christians" (March 9, 2016), http://www.stopthechristiangenocide.org/scg/en/resources/Genocide-report.pdf (footnotes omitted). The Petition notes that "[w]hile the focus of this Petition is the targeting of Christians, ISIS has targeted many other religious groups as well," including Yazidis, Shia and Sunni Muslims, Turkmen, Shabaks, Sabean-Mandeans, Kaka'e, Kurds, and Jews.

23. H.R. 2029, Consolidated Appropriations Act, 2016, Public Law No: 114-113 §7033(d). Deadlines such as these are critical to the advocacy process because they confine the discretion of the Executive Branch. While it is possible that an agency will miss a statutory deadline, tough questions about why the deadline was missed are certain.

directed at these same groups and in some cases also against Sunni Muslims, Kurds, and other minorities.

The fact is that Daesh kills Christians because they are Christians; Yezidis because they are Yezidis; Shia because they are Shia. This is the message it conveys to children under its control. Its entire worldview is based on eliminating those who do not subscribe to its perverse ideology. There is no question in my mind that if Daesh succeeded in establishing its so-called caliphate, it would seek to destroy what remains of ethnic and religious mosaic once thriving in the region.

I want to be clear. I am neither judge, nor prosecutor, nor jury with respect to the allegations of genocide, crimes against humanity, and ethnic cleansing by specific persons. Ultimately, the full facts must be brought to light by an independent investigation and through formal legal determination made by a competent court or tribunal. But the United States will strongly support efforts to collect, document, preserve, and analyze the evidence of atrocities, and we will do all we can to see that the perpetrators are held accountable.[24]

For reasons that will become clear, it was an extraordinary move.

The Geopolitics of Genocide

Students of the Holocaust and of the Ottoman government's involvement in the extermination of at least 1.5 million Armenians from 1915 to 1917 are all-too-familiar with the geopolitics of genocide. So too are modern-day advocates for the victims of the atrocities that have occurred (or are occurring) in Bosnia, Cambodia, Rwanda, Myanmar, Darfur, and other troubled areas of the world.[25]

In her masterful treatment of the political calculus of genocide declarations, *A Problem from Hell: America in the Age of Genocide*,[26]

---

24. Secretary of State, John Kerry, "Remarks on Daesh and Genocide," March 17, 2016, http://www.state.gov/secretary/remarks/2016/03/254782.htm.; https://www.youtube.com/watch?v=hrbeMwlBYLY

25. See Gregory H. Stanton, Ph.D., "Genocide Alert Map," https://www.click2map.com/v2/H3llo/Genocide_Prevention.

26. Samantha Power, *A Problem From Hell: America and the Age of Genocide* (Basic Books, 2002), Kindle Edition.

Genocide, Statecraft, and Domestic Geopolitics

Samantha Power, who served as U.S. ambassador to the United Nations during the Obama Administration, provided a sobering description of what happened when irrefutable evidence made it impossible for the Clinton Administration to deny that genocide was occurring in Bosnia and Rwanda: "American officials ... shunned the g-word. They were afraid that using it would have obliged the United States to act under the terms of the 1948 genocide convention. They also believed, rightly, that it would harm U.S. credibility to name the crime and then do nothing to stop it."[27]

Those arguing that the United States should use its resources and alliances to intervene to protect Christians and other religious minorities from ISIS's genocidal campaign to convert or exterminate them faced not only these arguments, but also several others unique to the forum (Congress) and targets (religious groups). The first such argument was that the Constitution's Bill of Attainder Clause makes Congress an inappropriate forum in which to debate the genocide issue.[28] This is so, say its proponents, because genocide is a crime under both American and international law.[29] Legislative declarations that connect identifiable crimes with their alleged perpetrators are both fundamentally unfair and constitutionally forbidden, or so the argument goes.

The argument is mistaken. A Bill of Attainder is "a legislative act which inflicts punishment without a judicial trial."[30] The House and Senate genocide resolutions do nothing more than allege that genocide, war crimes, and crimes against humanity are being committed—and that ISIS is committing them. They are analogous to legislative findings that there is probable cause to believe that these

---

27. Ibid., 359.
28. U.S. Const., Art. I §9 cl. 3 (1787) ("No bill of attainder ... shall be passed.") See United States v. Brown, 381 U.S. 437, 440 (1965) ("The Bill of Attainder Clause was intended not as a narrow, technical (and therefore soon to be outmoded) prohibition, but rather as an implementation of the separation of powers, a general safeguard against legislative exercise of the judicial function or more simply—trial by legislature.").
29. See 18 U.S.C. §1091, Genocide Convention Implementation Act of 1987, 18 U.S.C. §1093.78, and U.N.T.S. 277, entered into force Jan. 12, 1951, for the United States Feb. 23, 1989. See U.S. Dep't of State, *Treaties in Force* 345 (1994).
30. Cummings v. Missouri, 71 U.S. (4 Wall) 277, 323 (1867).

genocide crimes are being committed and that ISIS and its network are committing them.[31] The power of impeachment, which is expressly granted to the House of Representatives,[32] is just that: a finding of probable cause that a crime has been committed.[33]

A closely-related argument against *any* declaration of genocide by the legislative branch is the full scale denial that *neither* the legislative, *nor* the executive power of a national government has the power to declare genocide. Secretary Kerry's declaration addresses this argument as follows: "I want to be clear. I am neither judge, nor prosecutor, nor jury with respect to the allegations of genocide, crimes against humanity, and ethnic cleansing by specific persons."[34] Kerry's point is not simply a legal nicety. It reflects a major foreign policy concern of one of America's leading allies in the Middle East: Turkey.

Modern Turkey is the successor government to that of the Ottoman Empire. Its government and politicians are implacable opponents of any attempt by foreign governments to brand the massacres of Armenians and others between April 24, 1915–1917 "a genocide."[35]

---

31. See Robert A. Destro, L. Martin Nussbaum, and Ian Speir, *Genocide Against Christians in the Middle East: A Report Submitted to Secretary of State John Kerry by the Knights of Columbus and In Defense of Christians* (March 9, 2016), http://www.stopthechristiangenocide.org/scg/en/resources/Genocide-report.pdf [hereafter "KofC/IDC Genocide Petition"].

32. U.S. Const., Art. I §2, ¶4 (1787) ("The House of Representatives . . . shall have the sole power of impeachment.").

33. See, e.g., Akhil Reed Amar, "On Prosecuting Presidents," 27 *Hofstra L. Rev.* 671, 674–75 (1999) ("The President is elected by the entire nation, and should be judged by the entire nation. His true grand jury is the House, his true petit jury is the Senate, and the true indictment that he is subject to is called an impeachment.").

34. See Remarks of Secretary of State John Kerry.

35. See, e.g., Perìçek v. Switzerland, Application # 27410/08, ECHR (October 15, 2015), http://hudoc.echr.coe.int/eng?i=003-5199806-6438950 (holding that Mr. Perìçek, who is a lawyer and was Chairman of the Turkish Workers' Party, could not be prosecuted for calling "the allegations of the 'Armenian genocide' . . . an international lie," alleging that "[t]he Kurdish problem and the Armenian problem were therefore, above all, not a problem and, above all, did not even exist . . . ;" and "this is the truth, there was no genocide of the Armenians in 1915. It was a battle between peoples and we suffered many casualties . . . the Russian officers at the time were very disappointed because the Armenian troops carried out massacres of the Turks and Muslims. These truths were told by a Russian commander.").

Genocide, Statecraft, and Domestic Geopolitics

Its leading proponent of the position that the Armenian Genocide is not properly classified as a "genocide," Dr. Mustafa Serdar Palabiyik, argues:

> [G]enocide is first and foremost a crime and therefore a legal concept. According to the Genocide Convention, the only competent authority to define a particular event such as genocide is a competent tribunal of the state in the territory where the genocidal act was committed, or an international penal tribunal with jurisdiction with respect to those Contracting Parties, with its jurisdiction accepted. Without a clear decision by these legal authorities, an event can only be categorized politically as a genocide, not legally, and a purely political categorization, of course has no legal consequence.[36]

Two observations concerning the Armenian Genocide are in order here. First of all, the House and Senate Genocide Resolutions, as well as Secretary Kerry's Declaration of Genocide, assume that trials in a duly-constituted court having jurisdiction over the offenses and the persons accused are essential components of the prevention and punishment goals of the Genocide Convention. Certainly the Turkish argument that a formal conviction of the crime of genocide can be made only by a "competent tribunal of the state in the territory where the genocidal act was committed, or an international penal tribunal ... with its jurisdiction accepted" is legally unassailable. This argument, however, begs the question raised by those demanding formal recognition that a genocide occurred in 1915–1917. Some Turkish officials were tried in courts-martial, but the geopolitics of

---

36. Mustafa Serdar Palbiyik, *Understanding the Turkish-Armenian Controversy Over* 1915 (Ertem Ankara: Basim Yayin Dagitim San. Tic. Ltd. Şti 2015) at 102. The Turkish legal argument also rests on an argument that there was no "intent to destroy":

> There was no plan to destroy Armenians, but only the wartime necessity of relocating them for the sake of military security. Those deported ... were generally treated humanely and all necessary provisions were made for their safety and well-being (though, admittedly this broke down at times). Some Armenians were killed by criminals and roving tribes; others were killed as the result of the civil war they were waging against Turkey within a global war.

Roger W. Smith, "Denial of the Armenian Genocide," in *Genocide: A Critical Bibliographic Review* 2: 63, 6–68 (Israel W. Charny, ed. 1991), quoted in M. Cherif Bassiouni, "World War I: 'The War to End All Wars' and the Birth of a Handicapped International Criminal Justice System," 30 *Denv. J. Int'l L. & Pol'y* 244 (2002).

genocide aborted the more formal trials contemplated by the Treaties of Versailles and Sèvres.[37]

On July 5, 1919, a Turkish Military Tribunal entered a verdict sentencing Prime Minister Talaat Pasha, Minister of War Enver Effendi, Minister of the Navy Djemal Effendi, and Minister of Education Dr. Nazim to death *in absentia* for "the massacres which took place in the Kaza of Boghazlayan (Ankara), the Sanjak of Yozgat, and the Vilayet of Trebizond." The verdict recognized that these atrocities "were organized and perpetrated by the leaders of the *Ittihad* and *Terakki* [Union and Progress] Party."[38] Thus, while the crime of "genocide" as we know it today had yet to be defined, there were, in fact, convictions for massacres that occurred under Ottoman supervision.[39]

It is also undeniable that accountability requires documentation and a willingness to use the evidence to seek and obtain convictions in a properly-constituted court of competent jurisdiction. Early estimates put a price tag of over $100 million for the forensic documentation effort alone. Add the cost of trials, defense, and prosecution costs, and the price goes up exponentially,[40] to perhaps a billion dollars or more.[41] Among the choices of fora are: 1) the International Criminal Court (ICC), a forum that, for reasons amply discussed elsewhere, appears highly unlikely;[42] 2) a local court in the countries

---

37. Bassiouni observes that American Secretary of State Robert Lansing, who chaired the Commission on the Responsibility of the Authors of War and on Enforcement of Penalties established on January 25, 1919, during the Paris Peace Conference, argued "that the Europeans' plan to place the Kaiser on trial was nothing more than an exercise in political pandering" during Lloyd George's election campaign. Bassiouni, 250, quoting James F. Willis, *Prologue to Nuremberg: The Politics and Diplomacy of Punishing War Criminals of the First World War* (1982), 69.

38. Official Transcript of Verdict ("Kararname") of the Turkish Military Tribunal, published in the Official Gazette of Turkey (*Takvimi Vekayi*), No. 3604 (supplement), July 22, 1919. The transcript was translated into English by Haigazn K. Kazarian and published in the *Armenian Review*, vol. 24 (1971).

39. Whether those trials were fair is, of course, another question entirely and is a topic beyond the scope of this essay.

40. In 2003, The Economist reported that the costs were "running at more than $100m a year." "The Lesson of Slobodan Milosevic's Trial and Tribulation," *The Economist*, February 13, 2003, http://www.economist.com/node/1576821.

41. See Rupert Skilbeck, "Funding Justice: The Price of War Crimes Trials," https://www.wcl.american.edu/hrbrief/15/3skilbeck.pdf; David Wippman, "The Costs of International Justice," 100: 4 *Am. J. Int'l Law* 861 (2006).

42. See chapter eleven in this volume.

in which specific crimes were committed; or 3) a hybrid tribunal created to handle cases in which the defendants are alleged to have committed violations of international law.

By far, the most difficult—and frustrating—argument against the proposed genocide resolutions was the claim that ISIS could not be accused of the "genocide" of Christians because it offered them an option: convert to Islam or pay *jizya*—the Islamic tax imposed on non-Muslims as payment for protection by the Islamic community.[43] Most forcefully expressed in the U.S. Holocaust Memorial Museum's otherwise-excellent November, 2015 report: *Our Generation is Gone: The Islamic State's Targeting of Iraqi Minorities in Ninewa*, the argument is that:

> IS specifically notes that its treatment of the Yezidis differs from its treatment of *ahl al kitab*, the "people of the book," Christians and Jews, who had the option of paying the *jizya* (tax) to avoid conversion or death.²⁰ By refusing Yezidis any option to avoid death or forced conversion, IS demonstrates that its actions were calculated with the intent of destroying the community and thereby different from its attacks against other minorities, which were part of a campaign of ethnic cleansing.[44]

There are several problems here. The first is the report's uncritical acceptance of IS propaganda that there was, in fact, an actual choice. (There was not.) Even if there were, it would make no difference under the law of genocide. As Ambassador Samantha Power has observed:

> "Genocide," as defined in the U.N. treaty, suffered then (as it suffers now) from several inherent definitional problems. One is what might be called a numbers problem. On the question of how many individuals have to be killed and/or expelled from their homes in order for mass murder or ethnic cleansing to amount to genocide, there is—and can be—no consensus. If the law were to require a

---

43. M.A.S. Abdel Haleem, "The *jizya* Verse (Q. 9:29): Tax Enforcement on Non-Muslims in the First Muslim State," *Journal of Qur'anic Studies* 14.2 (2012) 72–89. See chapter one in this volume.

44. Naomi Kikoler, U.S. Holocaust Memorial Museum, Simon-Skjodt Ctr. for the Prevention of Genocide, *Our Generation is Gone: The Islamic State's Targeting of Iraqi Minorities in Ninewa* (Nov. 12, 2015), https://www.ushmm.org/m/pdfs/Iraq-Bearing-Witness-Report-111215.pdf.

pre-specified percentage of killings before outsiders responded, perpetrators would be granted a free reign up to a dastardly point. The law would be little use if it kicked in only when a group had been entirely or largely eliminated. By focusing on the perpetrators' intentions and whether they were attempting to destroy a collective, the law's drafters thought they might ensure that diagnosis of and action against genocide would not come too late.[45]

Even more important is the profound misunderstanding of the nature of the ideological and kinetic warfare being waged by the so-called "Islamic State." There are considerable differences of opinion between and among Islamic and non-Muslim scholars over the meaning of the Qur'an's *jizya* verse (Q: 9:29).[46]

Reproduced below are two translations of the verse:

قَاتِلُوا الَّذِينَ لَا يُؤْمِنُونَ بِاللَّهِ وَلَا بِالْيَوْمِ الْآخِرِ وَلَا يُحَرِّمُونَ مَا حَرَّمَ اللَّهُ وَرَسُولُهُ وَلَا يَدِينُونَ دِينَ الْحَقِّ مِنَ الَّذِينَ أُوتُوا الْكِتَابَ حَتَّى يُعْطُوا الْجِزْيَةَ عَنْ يَدٍ وَهُمْ صَاغِرُونَ.

THE KORAN INTERPRETED: *A Translation*, A.J. Arberry (Touchstone, 1995)	THE QUR'AN WITH REFERENCES TO THE BIBLE: *A Contemporary Understanding*, Safi Kaskas & David Hungerford (Bridges to Reconciliation, 2016)
Fight those who believe not in God[a] and the Last Day and do not forbid what God and His Messenger have forbidden—such men as practise not the religion of truth, being of those who have been given the Book— until they pay the tribute out of hand and have been humbled.	Fight those People of the Book[a] who do not believe in God and the Last Day, those who do not forbid that which has been forbidden by God and His Messenger, and do not follow the religion of Truth, until they pay the exemption tax after having been subdued. a. [Refers to "the Byzantine Empire and their Ghassanid allies . . . [who wished] to destroy Islam and the Muslims."]

---

45. Samantha Power, 65.
46. M.A.S. Abdel Haleem.

Genocide, Statecraft, and Domestic Geopolitics

Writing in the *Journal of Qur'anic Studies,* Abdel Haleem explains that:

> The root verb of jizya is *j-z-y,* "to reward somebody for something," "to pay what is due in return for something" and, as will be explained later, it has a positive connotation. The important question now is, "what was the *jizya* paid in return for?" Many exegetes and Western scholars take this to mean that it was in return for allowing Christians and Jews to live in the Muslim state, practising their religion and being protected. However, the Prophet's treaty with the Christians of Najrän stipulates that they should not be obliged to join the Muslim army (*lä yuhsharün*). From the practice of the early Muslim community, it is known that Christians and Jews were not obliged to join the Muslims in fighting to defend the state, and this was right, because military *jihäd* has an Islamic religious connotation and should not be imposed on them. As Muhammad 'Imära puts it, "those who did volunteer to fight with the Muslims against the Persians and Byzantines were exempted from the *jizya* and shared the battle gains with the Muslims." *Jizya* in this sense can be considered, as 'Imära states, "*badal jundiyya*" ("in exchange for military service"), not in exchange for the People of the Book being allowed to keep their own faith.[47]

Ahmad Ziauddin amplifies the point, and puts it into political context:

> A close study of the early history of *Jizya* particularly since its imposition by the Prophet till later in the period of *Khulafa' Rashidun* will reveal that it was a tax through the payment of which the non-Muslim subjects were expected to pay allegiance to the political authority of Islam. There is nothing to prove that it was imposed just to humiliate them or to make them socially degraded.
>
> As a matter of fact, *Jizya* or poll tax had been in vogue since before the advent of Islam. The Greeks are reported to have imposed a similar tax upon the inhabitants of the coastal regions of Asia Minor during 500 BC. The Romans imposed similar taxes upon the people they conquered, and the amount was much heavier than what was later imposed by the Muslims. The Persians are also reported to have introduced a similar tax upon their sub-

---

47. Ibid., 14.2; *Journal of Qur'anic Studies* at 76 (footnotes omitted).

jects. According to Shibli Nu'mani, the word *Jizya* itself is the Arabicised version of the word گزیت (*Kizyat*), meaning a levy which the Persian rulers used to employ in administering the affairs of war.[48]

Thus, even assuming that the "Islamic State" is, in fact, a "state" and exercises legitimate authority (which it most assuredly does not), the report's uncritical acceptance of ISIS propaganda is profoundly disturbing. It is bad enough to give credit to a group of *Salafi-jihadi-irhabi*-inspired criminals who—not surprisingly—interpret Islamic Law to justify their behavior. It even worse to add to the already-rampant confusion about the nature of the criminals who are committing these atrocities.

Willful Blindness: The Domestic Geopolitics of Religion, Ideology, and Political Correctness

Now that Congress and the Obama Administration have called the slaughter of innocents in the name of religion by its proper name, genocide, authorities can turn to the next item of urgent business on the agenda: developing a focused strategy to hunt the killers, roll up their networks, and bring them to justice. The longer-term goals of the House and Senate genocide resolutions are:

1. To "connect the dots" among the many hundreds of incidents where people have been slaughtered because of their religion;

2. To highlight the connection between the criminals who commit these crimes and the toxic ideology that drives ISIS and its allies to recruit and train thousands of young *jihadi-irhabis* to murder in the name of God.

Who *are* the men and women who invoke the name of God as they commit murder, rape, and engage in human trafficking? The answer is not easy to find. The concept of "Islamophobia" is well established in academic literature, the media, and in the self-perception of Mus-

---

48. Ahmad Ziauddin, "The Concept of Jizya in Early Islam," *Islamic Studies*, 14: 4 (Winter 1975), 293–305 at 294.

Genocide, Statecraft, and Domestic Geopolitics

lim communities worldwide.⁴⁹ The American Muslim community is particularly concerned in light of the debate during the 2016 presidential election campaign.⁵⁰ It is, therefore, critically important that the names used (or official "characterizations") of the individuals, groups, and behaviors condemned be carefully considered and take into account religious and political sensitivities of the persons who *hear* the message.

The easiest, most accurate, and least ideological way to describe the behavior of groups like ISIS and *Jema'ah Islamiyah* is to characterize the behavior as "criminal." Among other crimes, one can catalogue hundreds of thousands of murders, rapes, examples of pillage and mayhem, human and weapons trafficking, and money laundering. "Organized criminals" is an equally neutral characterization that focuses on the criminal behavior of the individuals committing these crimes, but adding the term "organized" recognizes that they are not isolated occurrences. All of the available evidence indicates that these criminals accused are engaged in a well-planned and well-coordinated program of action.

The term "terrorist" (Arabic: إرهابي "*irhabi*") is often used in the domestic and foreign press (including the Arabic language press) to describe those who commit the atrocity crimes that are the subject of this essay. While there is a general consensus that the term "terrorist"—"*irhabi*" refers to persons "who use violent and intimidating methods in the pursuit of political aims,"⁵¹ there is no universally-accepted definition of the term.⁵²

The United States Code contains several definitions of "terror-

---

49. Brian Klug, "Islamophobia: A Concept Comes of Age," 12:5 *Ethnicities* 665–682 (Sage Publications, 2012).

50. See, e.g., Bloomberg View, "Islamophobia is not a National Security Policy," *Chicago Tribune*, Nov. 22, 2016; Arsalan Iftikhar, "Commentary: Being Muslim in Trump's America," *Chicago Tribune*, Nov. 9, 2016.

51. "Terrorist, n. and adj," *OED Online*. September 2016, Oxford University Press. http://www.oed.com.proxycu.wrlc.org/view/Entry/199609?redirectedFrom=terrorist.

52. See, e.g., Andrew Silke, *Holy Warriors*, 100 ("The questions of what constitutes terrorism and who is a terrorist are deeply problematic. There is still no precise and agreed definition of terrorism, and some writers have concluded that 'it is unlikely that any definition will ever be generally agreed upon.'"), citing Shafritz, J.M., Gibbons, E.F., Jr and Scott, G.E.J., *Almanac of Modern Terrorism* (Oxford: Facts on File, 1991).

ism."[53] All track the common understanding. 18 U.S.C. §2331 (1, 3) provide:

(1)..."International terrorism" means activities that	3) ..."Domestic terrorism[54] means activities that"
A) involve violent acts or acts dangerous to human life that are a violation of the criminal laws of the United States or of any State, or that would be a criminal violation if committed within the jurisdiction of the United States or of any State;	(A) involve acts dangerous to human life that are a violation of the criminal laws of the United States or of any State;
(B) appear to be intended— (i) to intimidate or coerce a civilian population; (ii) to influence the policy of a government by intimidation or coercion; or (iii) to affect the conduct of a government by mass destruction, assassination, or kidnapping; and	(B) appear to be intended— (i) to intimidate or coerce a civilian population; (ii) to influence the policy of a government by intimidation or coercion; or (iii) to affect the conduct of a government by mass destruction, assassination, or kidnapping; and
(C) occur primarily outside the territorial jurisdiction of the United States, or transcend national boundaries in terms of the means by which they are accomplished, the persons they appear intended to intimidate or coerce, or the locale in which their perpetrators operate or seek asylum;	(C) occur primarily within the territorial jurisdiction of the United States.

What drives these criminals to commit unspeakable atrocities against such a broad spectrum of religious groups? Their victims

---

53. See, e.g., 8 U.S.C. §1182 (a)(1)(3)(B) (defining terrorism, terrorist activity, terrorist organization); 22 U.S.C. § 2656f (d).

54. The November 28, 2016, car and knife attacks on pedestrians at The Ohio State University by Abdul Razak Ali Artan certainly fit within this category. See Mitch Smith, Richard Pérez-Peña & Adam Goldman, "Suspect is Killed in Attack at Ohio State University that Injured 11," The New York Times, Nov. 28, 2016, http://www.nytimes.com/2016/11/28/us/active-shooter-ohio-state-university.html. While there is some confusion about whether Artan's acts were commanded, or simply "influenced," by ISIS, the statute does not differentiate. See, e.g., Mitch Smith, Richard Pérez-Peña, and Adam Goldman, "ISIS Calls Ohio State University Attacker a 'Soldier,'" The New York Times, Nov. 29, 2016.

Genocide, Statecraft, and Domestic Geopolitics

include Christians, like the elderly French priest beheaded at morning Mass[55] and hundreds of others killed while at worship.[56] Thousands of Shia and Sunni Muslims have been slaughtered across the Middle East and Africa. They have kidnapped more than 200 Nigerian women and girls and committed the "systematic" rape and abuse of "thousands of women and children, some as young as eight years of age."[57] Aside from the profit motive, why would they pillage and sell priceless historical artifacts and destroy some of the world's most important cultural treasures?[58]

The answer is the religious ideology of the killers. Because of that, one must attempt to describe that ideology in a way that is true to its claims to be the only authentic version of Islam, while still differentiating it from all contrary versions of Islamic theology, law, philosophy, or thought. There are several, plausible ways to do this:

The synonyms "*jihadi*" جهادي and "*mujāhid*" مجاهد are a good starting point for two reasons. First, those who pledge spiritual allegiance ("make *bay'at*" بَيْعَة)[59] to the leadership of ISIS and related groups

---

55. Peter Allen, Julian Robinson, and Imogen Calderwood, "'You Christians, you kill us': Nun reveals words of ISIS knifemen who forced elderly priest, 84, to kneel at altar as they slit his throat on camera after invading Mass—before police shot them," *Daily Mail.com*, July 26, 2016, http://www.dailymail.co.uk/news/article-3708394/Two-men-armed-knives-people-hostage-French-church.html#ixzz4RKukS2Kn.

56. See, e.g., Declan Walsh and Nour Youssef, "ISIS Claims Responsibility for Egypt Church Bombing and Warns of More to Come," *New York Times*, Dec. 13, 2016, http://www.nytimes.com/2016/12/13/world/middleeast/egypt-isis-bombing-coptic-christians.html (Cairo); Reuters, "Egypt church blast death toll rises to 23," Jan. 4, 2011, http:// www.reuters.com/articleus-egypt-church-idUSTRE7010M020110104 (Alexandria).

57. U.S. Department of State, Bureau of Counterterrorism and Countering Violent Extremism, "Country Report on Terrorism, 2015," chapter 6 in *Islamic State of Iraq and the Levant*, http://www.state.gov/j/ct/rls/crt/2015/257523.htm [hereafter Counterterrorism Country Report 2015], referencing U.S. Department of State, Office to Monitor and Combat Trafficking in Persons, *Trafficking in Persons Report 2015*, http://www.state.gov/documents/organization/245365.pdf, 39.

58. See Ben Taub, "The Real Value of the ISIS Antiquities Trade," *The New Yorker*, December 4, 2014, http://www.newyorker.com/news/news-desk/the-real-value-of-the-isis-antiquities-trade; Nasir Behzad and Daud Qarizadah, "The Man Who Helped Blow Up the Bamiyan Buddhas," BBC Afghan, March 12, 2015, http://www.bbc.com/news/world-asia-31813681.

59. See, e.g., AlHazrat.net, "The Meaning and Excellence of Bayat (Pledge)," http://www.alahazrat.net/islam/meaning-and-excellence-of-bayat-(pledge).php

refer to themselves as "mujahedeen;" that is "those who make *jihad*" ("strive in the cause of God as a religious duty"). Second, and more important, both terms convey the religious character of the perceived obligation.

As used in the West, the terms *jihadi* and *mujahedeen* almost always have a military connotation. If we focus only on *jihadi* organizations that have or claim an offensive military mission, we can begin to narrow the scope from Islam as a whole to organizations that display one or more aspects of the "the multifaceted Islamist belief system."[60] As Dr. Mary Habeck points out:

> the main difference between jihadis and other Islamists as the extremists' commitment to the violent overthrow of the existing international system and its replacement by an all-encompassing Islamic state. She believes that "only by understanding the elaborate ideology of the jihadist faction can the United States, as well as the rest of the world, determine how to contain and eventually defeat the threat they pose to stability and peace."[61]

The terms "radical Islam" or "radical Islamic terrorism" are catch-all descriptive terms. They are sometimes used as a form of shorthand to describe the belief system of those who commit crimes and terrorist activities in furtherance of their "Islamist" ideology. Dr. Quintan Wiktorowicz, for example, uses the phrase "Radical Islam" as the title of his study of why Muslims in the West are drawn to radical groups and how they are convinced to engage in what he calls "high-risk, high-cost activism."[62] President Donald Trump, by contrast, uses these terms in a more descriptive, popular sense.

("The meaning of Bay'at or pledging spiritual allegiance is to be totally sold, which means to surrender yourself totally to a Spiritual Master (Murshid) to guide you to Allah.")

60. Mary Habeck, *Knowing the Enemy: Jihadist Ideology and the War on Terror* (New Haven: Yale University Press, 2006) reviewed in Mohammad M. Amman, 15:2 *Domes* 137–139 (Fall 2006).

61. Ibid., 138.

62. Quintan Wiktorowicz, *Radical Islam Rising: Muslim Extremism in the West* (Lanham, MD: Rowman & Littlefield, 2005); Christine Fair, Book Review, Quintan Wiktorowicz, "Radical Islam Rising: Muslim Extremism in the West" (Lanham, MD: Rowman & Littlefield, 2005) in 39 *International Journal of Middle East Studies* 137–38 (2007).

Genocide, Statecraft, and Domestic Geopolitics

Today we begin a conversation about how to Make America Safe Again. In the twentieth century, the United States defeated Fascism, Nazism, and Communism. Now, a different threat challenges our world: Radical Islamic Terrorism.... We cannot let this evil continue. Nor can we let the hateful ideology of Radical Islam—its oppression of women, gays, children, and nonbelievers—be allowed to reside or spread within our own countries. We will defeat Radical Islamic Terrorism, just as we have defeated every threat we have faced in every age before. But we will not defeat it with closed eyes, or silenced voices. Anyone who cannot name our enemy, is not fit to lead this country. Anyone who cannot condemn the hatred, oppression, and violence of Radical Islam lacks the moral clarity to serve as our President.[63]

Both President Trump and Dr. Wiktorowicz use the term in a "broadly" descriptive sense, and are criticized for that reason. Former President Barak Obama, for example, has claimed that the terms are dangerously "loose language that appears to pose a civilizational conflict between the West and Islam, or the modern world and Islam," which "make[s] it harder, not easier, for our friends and allies and ordinary people to resist and push back against the worst impulses inside the Muslim world."[64]

An "Islamist" is an adherent of "an ideology that demands man's complete adherence to the sacred law of Islam and rejects as much as possible outside influences...and...a deep antagonism toward non-Muslims and has a particular hostility toward the West."[65] While the term "Islamist" is broadly descriptive, the connotation is often viewed (wrongly) as descriptive of a broader subset of Muslims. This is so because the Western media has yet to grapple with—or to report on—what it means to have a *religious* ideology.

The terms Salafi Islam and Salafist are terms "used as a self-designation by Muslims claiming authenticity, and [are] often used by

---

63. Donald J. Trump, Speech at Youngstown, Ohio, August 15, 2016, http://thehill.com/blogs/pundits-blog/presidential-campaign/291498-full-transcript-donald-trump-addresses-radical.
64. See, e.g., Uri Friedman, "The Coming War on 'Radical Islam': How Trump's Government Could Change America's Approach to Terrorism," *The Atlantic* (Nov. 29, 2016).
65. Daniel Pipes, "Distinguishing Between Islam and Islamism," *Daniel Pipes Middle East Forum*, June 30, 1998.

outsiders in a negative sense, designating reactionary and conservative Muslims, at times violently inclined."[66]

> Salafism is an ideology and reform movement calling for a return to traditional Islam as it was practiced and observed in the days of the Prophet Muhammad and his circle of Companions. In Arabic "*salaf*" means "predecessors; forebears, ancestors, forefathers." According to Kamran Bokhari, "From the Salafist perspective, non-Islamic thought has contaminated the message of 'true' Islam for centuries, and this excess must be jettisoned from the Islamic way of life." The Egyptian scholar and Islamist Muhammad 'Abduh (1849–1905) spearheaded the Salafist reform movement, which continues to inspire present-day Salafist movements. Salafists constitute both violent and nonviolent minorities (in terms of ideology) within Muslim populations worldwide. As Bokhari explains, "Unlike members of the Muslim Brotherhood, Salafists do not belong to a single, unified organization. Instead, the movement comprises a diffuse agglomeration of neighborhood preachers, societal groups and—only very recently—political parties, none of which are necessarily united in ideology."[67]

Susanne Olsson observes that while "most Salafis share a common creed (*'aqīda*), but the program for action (*manhaj*) differs." Quoting Wiktorowicz, she points out that "in spite of their common creed, Salafis' divergence 'lies in the inherently subjective nature of applying a creed to new issues and problems. This is a human enterprise and therefore subject to differing interpretations of context.'"[68] In her view,

> This implies that theology, or creed, are often similar among groups that can be designated as Salafi-oriented, but the program of action differs, including views on how they should relate to the surround-

---

66. Susanne Olsson, "Proselytizing Islam—Problematizing 'Salafism,'" 104(1–2) *The Muslim World* 171–97 (January/April 2014) at 176.

67. Hayat Alvi, "The Diffusion of Intra-Islamic Violence and Terrorism: The Impact of the Proliferation of Salafi/Wahhabi Ideologies," 18.2 *Middle East Review of International Affairs* (Online) 38–50 (Summer 2014) (footnotes omitted) at 39, quoting Kamran Bokhari, "Salafism and Arab Democratization," *Stratfor Global Intelligence*, October 2, 2012, http://www.stratfor.com/weekly/salafism-and-arab-democratization. See also Hans Wehr, *A Dictionary of Modern Written Arabic* (Ithaca: Spoken Language Services, Inc., 3rd ed. 1976), 423.

68. Olsson, 186.

ing society, to people of other faiths and to other people claiming to be Muslims but who do not share their view on what true Islam is or should be.[69]

The last of the terms proposed here—*Wahhabi*—points to the religious, geographic, and financial foundation of the ideology that drives ISIS and other organizations that share its worldview: The Kingdom of Saudi Arabia.

The Salafi/Wahhabi ideology has long enjoyed support in many forms from Saudi Arabia, especially in the case of the mujahidin fighting against the Soviets in Afghanistan. Today, we see other Gulf Cooperation Council (GCC) states, like Qatar, Kuwait, and the United Arab Emirates (UAE), also joining the game. However, unlike in previous incarnations, the primary targets of today's Salafi jihadists have become fellow Muslims, especially Shi'a, but even fellow Sunnis are not spared.[70]

Writing in the February, 2008 edition of the journal of the Combatting Terrorism Center at West Point, Dr. Assaf Moghadam advised that:

> Accurately labeling the nature of Salafi-jihadist doctrine as a religious ideology is not merely an exercise in academic theorizing, but has important policy implications. Most importantly, it should be obvious that the United States and its allies are not facing a religion—Islam—as their main enemy, but an ideology, namely the Salafi-jihad. The fact that the Salafi-jihad is no ordinary secular ideology, but a religious one, however, is of additional significance because it renders the attempt to challenge that ideology far more complex.[71]

"Far more complex" is, if anything, an understatement. Muslim scholars recognize that:

> the broader ideology name[d] "Wahhabism" represents a serious challenge to the theology and practice of the mainstream Sunni Islam.... Should this radicalized understanding of Islam continue to spread unchecked, radical interpretations could threaten social

---

69. Ibid.
70. Alvi, 38.
71. Assaf Moghadam, Ph.D., "The Salafi-Jihad as a Religious Ideology," *CTC Sentinel* 1:3 (Combating Terrorism Center at West Point, February 2008).

stability at the local, national and regional levels and create serious geopolitical dangers to which neighboring powers, as well as the U.S. and Europe, would have to react.[72]

Writing on behalf of the Islamic Supreme Council of America, Shaykh Muhammad Hisham Kabbani has stated:

> In truth, there is no clash between Islam and the West, which is another way of saying a clash between Islam and Christianity. If that were the case, Muslims would be attacking the Christian communities in their own nations. While there are isolated conflicts along these lines, they have never been widespread, nor have they ever been a focus of the jihadist movement.
>
> What we are witnessing instead is a clash between people with power and those without it. It is a conflict rooted in the history of colonialism and the perception of present-day imperialism. It is a conflict in which religion is simply a means to an end. We must recognize this if we are to understand the true nature of this so-called "jihad" and its increasingly global character....
>
> Make no mistake: The aim of the jihadists is to extend their power not only through Afghanistan, Kazakhstan and Pakistan, but also through "Francistan," "Londistan," "Italistan," "Switzeristan," "Hollandistan" and even "Americastan." That is the globalization of jihad.[73]

ISIS is an outgrowth of *al Qaeda*. The U.S. State Department's "Country Reports on Terrorism, 2015" reports that "[i]n October 2006, AQI [Al-Qa'ida in Iraq] publicly re-named itself the Islamic State in Iraq and in 2013 it adopted the moniker Islamic State of Iraq and the Levant (ISIL) to express its regional ambitions as it expanded its operations to include the Syrian conflict."[74] Richard Allen Green and Nick Thompson of CNN report that "It was an ally of—and had

---

72. The Islamic Supreme Council of America [ISCA], "Islamic Radicalism: Its Wahhabi Roots and Current Representation," *Understanding Islam, Anti-Extremism*, http://islamicsupremecouncil.org/understanding-islam/anti-extremism/7-islamic-radicalism-its-wahhabi-roots-and-current-representation.html.

73. Shaykh Muhammad Hisham Kabbani, "The Globalization of Jihad: From Islamist Resistance to War Against the West—A Clash of Civilizations" in Islamic Supreme Council of America [ISCA], *Understanding Islam: Anti-Extremism*, http://islamicsupremecouncil.org/understanding-islam/anti-extremism/56-the-globalization-of-jihad-from-islamist-resistance-to-war-against-the-west.html.

74. Counterterrorism Country Report 2015.

similarities with—Osama bin Laden's *al Qaeda*: both were radical anti-Western militant groups devoted to establishing an independent Islamic state in the region."[75]

Like other *Salafi-jihadi* groups, the leadership of ISIS shares the view that "Westerners are . . . infidels, while moderate Muslims and Arabs are labeled apostates. To the most extreme Salafi-jihadists, Muslims who reject the tenets of Salafi-jihad are tantamount to infidels, thus deserving of death."[76] Along with other organizations that share its ideology, it is but one member of a global *Salafi-jihadi* network that is (or should be considered to be) the centerpiece of the current malevolent threat matrix.[77] In sum, the enemy is the global *Salafi-jihadi* movement and all of the organizations that support and carry out its desire to conquer and hold territory.

Reconceptualizing the Malevolent Threat Matrix

The term "threat matrix" is used to avoid many of the assumptions that have complicated—and hobbled—American policy-making and political discourse. Unless and until it is possible to have an honest conversation about the true nature of the threat, use of this term may help. The goal is to create a framework in which it is possible to have an honest conversation about the true nature of the threat posed by the spread of Salafi-jihadi ideology around the world. Without a clear understanding of the breadth and depth of the threat, it will not be possible to mount an effective counter-strategy.

> The reason for [building and using a generic threat matrix] is a combination of historical aspects and the significance of the problem being faced today. Although the "threat of the day" is important to understand, it is not the only issue in place. While looking at only

---

75. See generally Richard Allen Green & Nick Thompson, "ISIS: Everything you need to know," *CNN*, August 11, 2016, http://www.cnn.com/2015/01/14/world/isis-everything-you-need-to-know/.

76. Moghadam, "The Salafi-Jihad as a Religious Ideology."

77. David P. Duggan, Sherry R. Thomas, Cynthia K. K. Veitch, and Laura Woodard, "Categorizing Threat: Building and Using a Generic Threat Matrix," *Sandia Report*, SAND2007-5791 (Sandia National Laboratories) ("Malevolent Threat: A manmade event or condition; for example, a bombing of a federal facility or the use of chemical and biological agents in terrorist attacks"), http://energy.gov/sites/prod/files/oeprod/DocumentsandMedia/14-Categorizing_Threat.pdf, 9.

the current threat, the entire picture can become skewed based on assumptions that follow names of organizations due to statements of the media and personal opinion. These assumptions do not allow for the objective differentiation of threats. Creating a generic threat matrix not only removes the assumptions that come with names, but also includes those types of organizations that are not the primary focus of a day, month, year, or decade.[78]

Let us consider, for example, the assumptions built into the United States Government's understanding of the threat matrix. The Introduction to the State Department's 2014 Human Rights Report begins by noting that "the year 2014 will be remembered as much for atrocities committed by non-state actors,"[79] including:

> Terrorist organizations like ISIL, *al-Qa'ida* in the Arabian Peninsula (AQAP), *al-Qa'ida* in the Islamic Maghreb (AQIM), *Boko Haram*, *al-Shabaab*, *Jabhat al-Nusra*, and others perpetrated human rights abuses and violations of international humanitarian law against innocent non-combatants. Often, they sought to eliminate those who did not conform to their extreme views, including other Sunni Muslims. Some governments committed violations and abuses in response; such reactions to violent extremism often undermined efforts to contain it.[80]

The same organization-by-organization and country-by-country focus is seen in the "Strategic Assessment" contained in chapter one of the State Department's *Country Reports on Terrorism* 2015.[81] After recounting ISIS/ISIL's fortunes in Iraq and Syria, it reports on its activities in Egypt, Pakistan, Afghanistan, and notes that:

> ISIL-aligned groups have also emerged in other parts of the Middle East, Africa, the Russian North Caucasus, Southeast Asia, and South Asia, although the relationship between most of these groups and ISIL's leadership remained symbolic in most cases. Many of

---

78. Ibid., 14.
79. U.S. Department of State, 2014 Human Rights Report Introduction, 1 (2015), http://www.state.gov/documents/organization/236534.pdf; see also Priyanka Boghani, "What a Pledge of Allegiance to ISIS Means," *PBS Frontline*, Nov. 12, 2014.
80. 2014 Human Rights Report, Introduction, 1.
81. To be fair, the State Department is providing "Country Reports," but a Strategic Assessment requires a more broadly-based analysis.

Genocide, Statecraft, and Domestic Geopolitics

these groups are made up of pre-existing terrorist networks with their own local goals and lesser capabilities than ISIL.

In March, the Nigeria-based terrorist group Boko Haram declared its affiliation to ISIL.... Beyond affiliated groups, ISIL was able to inspire attacks in 2015 by individuals or small groups of self-radicalized individuals in several cities around the world. ISIL's propaganda and its use of social media have created new challenges for counterterrorism efforts. Private sector entities took proactive steps to deny ISIL the use of social media platforms by aggressive enforcement of violations to companies' terms of service. Twitter reported in 2015 that it had begun suspending accounts for threatening or promoting terrorist attacks, primarily related to support for ISIL.[82]

While it is true that "[m]any of these groups are made up of pre-existing terrorist networks with their own local goals and lesser capabilities than ISIL," and that most are properly classified as "non-state actors," there is no attempt to "connect the dots" or to unpack the assumptions on which these narratives are based.

As a result, *both* analyses miss the connections between the groups, their supporters, and the ideology that spawns and unites them. Using a "generic threat matrix" is helpful under these circumstances because the cultural, religious, and geopolitical assumptions on display in the State Department reports quoted above "do not allow for the objective differentiation of threats." For example:

> 1. It is undisputed that these seemingly distinct groups are united by their adherence to a common *Salafi-jihadi* ideology. It is at least plausible to argue that what the State Department views as a "symbolic" relationship among them that the "enemy" is best understood as a transnational, *ideological movement* "rooted in the history of colonialism and the perception of present-day imperialism" in which "religion is simply a means to an end."[83] If this is, in fact, the case, the use of military and financial weapons will be necessary, but not sufficient to disrupt its growth.
>
> 2. It is also undisputed that the *Salafi-jihadi* ideology common to these groups is rooted in the teaching of Saudi Arabia's Abd al-Wahhab, which views "all Shiites ... as *kufr* and *rafida* (rejection-

---

82. Counterterrorism Country Report 2015, chapter 1.
83. Kabbani, "The Globalization of Jihad," 6.

ists)."84 As a practical matter, this means that the Islamic Republic of Iran, whose population is over 90% Shia Muslim, is both a *target* of the *Salafi-jihadi* movement and a potential ally of those fighting to eliminate it.85

3. *Salafi-jihadi* ideology also rests on "interpretations of the Qur'an and Sunna that declare the *ahl al-kitab* [People of the Book: Jews, Christians, and Zoroastrians] and contemporary Christians and Jews to be unbelievers."86 Partly in response, Russian President Vladimir Putin "has presented himself in a new role—as the potential saviour of Middle Eastern Christians. And even his critics wonder whether he may, in fact, have a point."87 A binary approach to Russia's actions in the region obscures the importance of religion and of the role of the Russian Orthodox Church in President Putin's political calculations.

4. There is considerable evidence that certain nation states, including Saudi Arabia, Qatar, and Turkey—as well as private and quasi-public actors within those nation states—provide both material and logistical support for the *Salafi-jihadi* cause.

Rethinking the malevolent threat matrix should involve reconsideration of each assumption and relationship within that matrix and reveal that the movement against which the United States seeks to do battle includes not only the terrorist *Salafi-jihadis* ("soldiers," "sleep-

---

84. Aylin Ünver Noi, *A Clash of Islamic Models: 15 Current Trends in Islamic Ideology*, 92–116.

85. Abbas Milani of the Hoover Institute suggests that Iran's Islamic Revolutionary Guard Corps—*The Army of Guardians* سپاه پاسداران انقلاب اسلامی / *Sepāh-e Pāsdārān-e Enqelāb-e Eslāmi*, or *Sepāh*—shares some of the characteristics of *Salafist-jihadi* ideology. See Abbas Milani, Lecture, "ISIS, Iran, and Saudi Arabia," *Hoover Institution*, April 18, 2016, http://www.hoover.org/research/abbas-milani-isis-iran-and-saudi-arabia. This is a subject worthy of extended discussion, but at first glance, Milani's thesis appears to confuse alliances of convenience between those who view the West as enemies and the profoundly incompatible religious world views of the Shia and the *Salafi-jihadis* who consider them to be *kufr* and *rafida*.

86. Aysha Hidayatullah, "Review of Adis Duderija, Constructing a Religiously Ideal 'Believer' and 'Woman' in Islam: Neo-traditional Salafi and Progressive Muslims' Methods of Interpretation," *Contemporary Islam* 8:75–78, 76 (2014).

87. Robert Wargas, "Vladimir Putin's Holy War," *The Catholic Herald*, Dec. 10, 2015.

ers," and recruits) who commit the crimes and the ex-military commanders who direct their actions, but also a network of *Salafi-jihadi* businesses, bankers and money brokers, social media experts, clerics, academics, madrassas, prison chaplains, charities, and donors that make its work and spread possible.

Disrupting and dismantling the global support network that makes it possible for these *Salafi-jihadi* organizations to take and control territory, to travel freely, to recruit globally and to spread the war to Paris, Brussels, Amman, Florida, and Ohio is going to require creative thinking on many levels. Especially important will be a frank discussion of two issues that are—for a myriad of reasons—mentioned only in hushed tones: 1. The important role that religion plays in the geopolitics of terrorism; 2. The uniquely important roles that America's Christians, Jews, and Muslims will need to play in the fight against it.

With significant ties to organized crime and the international banking sector, as well as to the substantial resources of petro-wealthy *Salafist* individuals, entities, and governments in the Middle East, the United States is watching helplessly as the global *Salafi-jihadi movement* expands its reach, recruitment efforts, influence, and violence across the globe. There is considerable evidence that private individuals, particularly in places such as Qatar, Saudi Arabia, Turkey, and Kuwait, have contributed hundreds of millions of dollars—perhaps more—to the *Salafi-jihadi* cause.[88] Even more launder funds; engage in human trafficking; trade oil, diamonds, and other natural resources; and trade in priceless artifacts. Some are smuggling themselves across America's southern border.[89]

At a private meeting in Tehran in May, 2014, Dr. Ali Larijani, the Speaker of the Iranian Parliament (*Majlis*), observed that "the United States does not think strategically" about either the Middle East or about how to grapple with the problem of international terrorism. In his view, the major powers have neither a sense of history, nor an appreciation of the roles that they have played in it. Because their focus has long been the protection of immediate interests, their

---

88. See, e.g., Email from Hillary Rodham Clinton to John Podesta, August 17, 2014, https://wikileaks.org/podesta-emails/emailid/3774.

89. Bill Gertz, "Southern Command Warns Sunni Extremists Infiltrating from the South," *The Washington Free Beacon*, August 22, 2016.

approaches have been "purely tactical, with no sense of the long term."[90]

America's efforts to destroy ISIS/*Da'esh* and other groups that share its *Salafi-jihadi* ideology, such as Indonesia's *Jema'ah Islamiyah* and Nigeria's *Boko Haram*, are reactive. Because the current rules of military, political, financial, and religious engagement are not rooted in a clear vision of what a long-term "good outcome" would look like for the United States, they are doomed to failure. Unless and until the American rules of engagement take adequate account of the ideological nature of the enemy and its efforts to recruit disaffected Muslims here in the United States and abroad, kinetic and financial warfare will not be sufficient. Like sharks' teeth, new leaders will arise to replace the fallen because Western leaders have no strategy to counter the *Salafi-jihadi* narrative that the *jihadis* are being be martyred on the front lines of a "war against Muslims and Islam."

In sum, the ultimate measure of success for American and other nations' efforts to destroy the *Salafi-jihadi* movement of which ISIS is a part will be found in the answers to three empirical questions: 1. Is the number of *Salafi-jihadi* terrorist incidents increasing or decreasing? 2. Is the *Salafi-jihadi* ideology that drives ISIS and other groups spreading? 3. Are the financial and human resources needed to support *Salafi-jihadi* terrorist groups readily available through sympathetic businesses, bankers, clerics, academics, media, and charities?

As these words are written, the number of incidents is increasing, the ideology is spreading, and resources are readily available from both State-sponsored and private sources. The West is losing. Consideration must be given to taking a hard, strategic look at what a long-term "good relationship" with each of the countries in the Middle East would look *for the United States*. Of necessity, such an exercise should re-examine *all* assumptions regarding: 1. The economic needs, cultures, religious traditions, regional interests, and behavior of the countries in the Middle East/North Africa (MENA) region: Israel, Iran, Iraq, Saudi Arabia, Yemen, Turkey, Lebanon, Syria, Jordan, the Gulf States, Egypt, Libya, Tunisia, Algeria, Morocco, Ethiopia, and Sudan; 2. The behavior of the great powers in addition to

---

90. Compare, Peter Frankopan, *The Silk Roads: A New History of the World* (Knopf: Reprint edition, 2016).

the United States (Russia, Germany, the UK, and France) that have so long viewed the countries of the region as "the pieces on a chessboard upon which is being played out a game for the dominion of the world."[91]

All of these issues come together in the fight against ISIS or *Da'esh*. In the space of less than two years, these *Salafi-jihadis* have erased many of the post-World War borders in the region and forced over seven million people to flee their homes. Over 3.5 million Iraqis have been displaced, and another 3.5 million Syrians are refugees.[92] Nearly one million more have fled the scourges of Taliban and are internally displaced in Afghanistan or refugees in Iran and Pakistan.[93] Another two million have fled the depredations of *Boko Haram* in northeastern Nigeria,[94] and the list goes on with victims in Yemen, Russia, Chechnya, Sinai, Jordan, Western Europe, the United States, and Canada.

Conclusion

This chapter began with a question posed by a Congressional staffer in September 2015: "*Why should my boss vote for a resolution condemning the genocide of Christians?*" Although the question seemed crass at the time, with study, it can be appreciated not only for its simplicity, but also for its practical political significance. An experienced Hill staffer knows that a resolution condemning "the atrocities perpetrated by ISIL against Christians, Yezidis, and other religious and ethnic minorities [as] war crimes, crimes against humanity, and genocide" is serious business.[95] For starters, it is a commitment to a long-term legislative and appropriations agenda with very real political and fiscal consequences at home and abroad.

---

91. George N. Curzon, *Persia and the Persian Question* (London: Frank Cass & Co., Ltd. 1892), 4–5.

92. United Nations High Commissioner for Refugees, Population Statistics: "Persons of Concern," http://popstats.unhcr.org/en/persons_of_concern.

93. Ibid. The search engine calculates that over 950,000 Afghan refugees were living in Iran in 2014.

94. United Nations Office for the Coordination of Humanitarian Affairs (OCHA), Nigeria, "About the Crisis," http://www.unocha.org/nigeria/about-ocha-nigeria/about-crisis.

95. H. Con. Res. 75, ¶ 1.

Persecution & Genocide of Christians in the Middle East

Such an agenda will include, at a minimum, efforts to prod the Executive Branch to use its diplomatic and intelligence resources to confirm reports from the field;[96] to develop bipartisan and multilateral strategies to prevent such murderers in the future;[97] and to seek out and punish as many of those involved in the *Salafi jihadi* network's supply and money-laundering chains as can be discovered and brought to justice.[98] That is no small agenda. To date, the price in blood and treasure is already enormous. Unless we act strategically—and recognize the enemy's ideology for what it is, it will grow exponentially.

Such a vote should not be taken lightly. No wonder she asked that question.

---

96. See, e.g., H.R. 2029, Consolidated Appropriations Act, 2016, Public Law No: 114–113 §7033(d):

> Not later than 90 days after the enactment of this Act, the Secretary of State, after consultation with the heads of other United States Government agencies represented on the Atrocities Prevention Board (APB) and representatives of human rights organizations, as appropriate, shall submit to the appropriate congressional committees an evaluation of the persecution of, including attacks against, Christians and people of other religions in the Middle East by violent Islamic extremists and the Muslim Rohingya people in Burma by violent Buddhist extremists, including whether either situation constitutes mass atrocities or genocide (as defined in section 1091 of title 18, United States Code), and a detailed description of any proposed atrocities prevention response recommended by the APB: Provided, that such evaluation and response may include a classified annex, if necessary.

97. H. Con. Res. 75, ¶3.

98. See, e.g., P.L. 104–208 §555, Omnibus Consolidated Appropriations Act, 1997 (September 30, 1996) (from the LIS summary, this section permits "the President to provide a specified amount of commodities and services to the U.N. War Crimes Tribunal if doing so will contribute to a resolution of charges regarding genocide or other violations of international law in the former Yugoslavia.").

Karamles, Iraq. Fr. Thabet Habeb Mansur in the Mar Addai church days after the town was liberated from ISIS (August, 2016).

Girl at entrance to home, Christian IDP camp, 2016.

3

Historical and Theological Reflections on the Persecution of Christians

Robert Fastiggi

CHRISTIANITY has its roots in Judaism, and the Jews suffered persecution at the hands of the Greeks.[1] The New Testament testifies to the persecution of Christians,[2] and Jesus warned his disciples: "They will hand you over to persecution, and they will kill you. You will be hated by all nations because of my name" (Mt 24:6).[3] This predication came true. During the first four centuries of the Christian era, the followers of Christ were persecuted at various times by both the Roman and the Persian empires. The Roman persecutions are better known, but persecutions under the Sassanian Persian dynasty were no less brutal. In the late fourth century, the Persians executed hundreds of Eastern Christian bishops and priests, and they "killed sixteen thousand Christian believers in a forty-year period."[4]

Although some have tried to minimize the persecution of Chris-

---

1. The Old Testament books of 1 and 2 Maccabees detail the persecution of the Jews by the Hellenistic Seleucid kings.
2. This persecution was initially experienced at the hands of the Jewish authorities (cf. Acts 4: 5–21; 5:17–41; 9:1–2).
3. All biblical references are from the 1986 New American Bible.
4. Philip Jenkins, *The Lost History of Christianity* (New York: HarperCollins, 2008), 57. Some argue that the Zoroastrian Persians only seriously began persecuting Christians after the rival Roman Empire began to favor Christianity in the fourth century. The Persian persecutions began to end in the fifth century. After losing a critical battle to the Romans in 422, the Persian emperor, Varahran (Bahram) V, was

tians during Roman times,[5] there is ample documentary evidence that Christians suffered periods of severe persecution at the hands of Roman emperors.[6] The main persecutions were those carried out during the imperial reigns of Nero (54–68), Domitian (81–96), Marcus Aurelius (161–180), Maximin (235–236), Decius (249–251), and Diocletian (284–305).[7] These persecutions resulted in the deaths of thousands of Christians. According to one estimate, there were 3000–3500 Christian martyrs during the height of the Diocletian persecution of 303–305.[8]

Why were Christians persecuted by the Romans? The Roman senator and historian Tacitus (c. 56–120) relates that Nero accused the Christians of "hatred of the human race" and considered them followers of a "pernicious superstition."[9] In a similar vein, the Roman historian Suetonius (c. 69–122) describes Christians as those "adhering to a novel and mischievous superstition."[10] It seems that Christians were perceived by the Romans as followers of a foreign sect that forbade worship of the Roman gods. According to Diocletian, the emperor ruled with the consent of the gods.[11] If the gods were not honored then the Roman Empire would suffer. Indeed, many ancient Romans believed that, because of the Christian neglect of the gods, "floods, plagues, famines, earthquakes were sent by angry spirit-powers who had not been placated with customary offerings."[12]

---

forced to concede freedom of worship to the Christians. See R. N. Fryre, "Persia," in B. L. Marthaler, OFM Conv. ed, *New Catholic Encyclopedia* Second Edition, vol. 11 (Detroit: Thomas Gale, 2003), 138.

5. See Candida Moss, *The Myth of Persecution: How Early Christians Invented a Dangerous Legacy* (San Francisco: HarperOne, 2013).

6. This evidence is not only provided by Christian accounts but also by Roman authors such as Tacitus and Pliny the Younger. See Henry Bettenson & Chris Maunder eds. *Documents of the Christian Church* 3rd ed. (Oxford: Oxford University Press, 1999), 1–5.

7. See W. H. C. Frend, *Martyrdom & Persecution in the Early Church* (Garden City, NY: Doubleday & Company, 1967).

8. Frend, *Martyrdom*, 394.

9. Tacitus, *Annales*, xv, 44; cited in Bettenson & Maunder, 2.

10. Suetonius, *Vita Neronis*, xvi; cited in Bettenson & Maunder, 3.

11. Frend, *Martyrdom*, 352.

12. Henry Chadwick, "The Early Christian Community" in *The Oxford History of Christianity* ed. John McManners (Oxford and New York: Oxford University Press, 1993), 47.

Reflections on the Persecution of Christians

Christians were also accused of having nocturnal meetings where "they indulged in cannibalism and incest."[13] Such false accusations led to persecutions of Christians by "mob violence" in addition to state-sponsored repressions.[14]

The Roman persecutions of Christians came to an end (for the most part) during the reign of Emperor Constantine I (r. 306–337). According to the Church historian Eusebius (263–339), Constantine had a vision of either the cross or the *chi-ro* (the first two letters of Christ's name) on the eve of the critical Battle of the Milvian Bridge.[15] In the vision he also read the words, "In this sign you shall conquer."[16] Constantine ordered his soldiers to put the *chi-ro* on their armor and their battle standards. When his army was victorious using this sign, Constantine saw the need to give protection to the Christians. This he did by means of the Edict of Milan of 313, which recognized that "freedom of religion ought not to be denied, but that to each man's judgment and will the right should be given to care for sacred things according to each man's free choice."[17] Constantine himself became a Christian, although the depth and quality of his faith has been challenged by some.[18]

During his brief reign of 361–363, the Emperor Julian "the Apostate" tried to restore the worship of the pagan gods. By the end of the fourth century, however, Theodosius I (r. 379–395) had made Christianity not only a legal religion but the favored religion of the empire. As one historian notes, Theodosius I "forbade all pagan worship and closed the temples, although pagans continued to hold public office until the time of Justinian I (r. 527–565), who closed the school of philosophy at Athens, the final sign of Christianity's victory."[19]

The Christian Roman Empire had its center in Constantinople beginning in 330 when Constantine I moved the capital from the "old

---

13. Ibid., 48. Such charges were perhaps due to misconceptions of Eucharistic celebrations.
14. Ibid., 47.
15. James Hitchcock, *History of the Catholic Church* (San Francisco: Ignatius Press, 2012), 56.
16. Ibid.
17. Constantine I, *Edict of Milan* (313): cited in Frend, *Martyrdom*, 389.
18. Hitchcock, *History*, 56.
19. Ibid., 59.

Rome" to the "new Rome" of Byzantium in Asia Minor (present day Istanbul).[20] This is why the Roman Empire after the time of Constantine I came to be called the Byzantine Empire. The Byzantine Empire, however, understood itself as the continuation of the ancient Roman Empire in Christian form. Indeed, the sixth century emperor Justinian (r. 527–565) saw himself as *reestablishing* Roman rule when he conquered the various Germanic tribes who had assumed control over parts of the ancient Roman Empire. He opened his celebrated *Institutes* with these words:

> In the Name of Our Lord Jesus Christ
> The Emperor Caesar Flavius Justinian
> Conqueror of the Alamani, Goths, Franks,
> Germans, Antes, Alani, Vandals, Africans
> Devout, Fortunate, Renowned
> Victorious and Triumphant
> Forever Augustus
> To
> Young Enthusiasts for Law[21]

The political vision of Justinian was one of Christian imperialism. He told the "young enthusiasts" how "long hours of work and careful planning" and "God's help" have enabled "Africa and countless other provinces" to be "restored to Roman jurisdiction."[22]

The earlier political-theological vision of Augustine (354–430), however, was quite different than that of Justinian. Living during a time when barbarian invasions were threatening the survival of the Roman Empire, Augustine, like the Psalmist, placed no trust in earthly princes who were "mere mortals powerless to save" (Psalm 146:3). Instead he saw human history as divided between two cities formed by two loves, "the earthly by the love of self, even to the contempt of God," and "the heavenly by the love of God, even to the contempt of self."[23] According to Augustine, the Church on earth cannot

---

20. Ibid., 58.
21. Justinian, *Institutes*, trans. Peter Birks & Grant McCleod (Ithaca, NY: Cornell University Press, 1987), 33.
22. Ibid.
23. Augustine, *The City of God*, Book 14, chapter 28 in Saint Augustine, *On the Two Cities: Selections from the City of God*, ed. F. W. Strothman (New York: Frederick Ungar, 1957), 63.

simply be equated with the City of God because within the visible Church there are those who are actually citizens of the earthly city.

Etienne Gilson noted that "when St. Augustine speaks of a 'City,' it is a figurative sense, or, as he himself states, a mystical sense."[24] The City of God, nevertheless, can be understood as the Church destined for glory because it is "the society or city of all men, who, loving God in Christ, are predestined to reign eternally with God."[25] The earthly city, on the other hand, "is the city of all those men who do not love God, and who are to suffer eternal punishment along with the demons."[26] These two cities co-exist throughout human history; it is only in the eschaton that they reach finality.

The political visions of Justinian and Augustine have both influenced Christian history. During her long history, the Catholic Church has needed protection from invading forces—whether barbarian, Persian, or Muslim. It is clear, though, that Jesus did not intend to set up an earthly kingdom. He told Pontius Pilate that his kingdom "does not belong to this world" (Jn 18:36).

The mission of the Church is religious and not political. As Vatican II teaches, "The Church, by reason of her role and competence, is not identified in any way with the political community nor bound to any political system. She is at once a sign and a safeguard of the transcendent character of the human person."[27] The mission of the Church, therefore, cannot be tied to the destiny of the Roman Empire or any other empire. While Justinian's vision of a Christian Roman Empire has a certain appeal, Augustine's view of the two cities is more enduring. This is because "the Church has a saving and an eschatological purpose which can be fully attained only in the future world."[28] Throughout her 2,000 year history, the Church has survived as a persecuted religion and flourished in political regimes more supportive of her mission. Vatican II is correct when it observes that the manner in which "the earthly and the heavenly city penetrate each other is a fact accessible to faith alone; it remains a mystery of

---

24. Etienne Gilson, Foreword to *St. Augustine: City of God*, trans. Gerald G. Walsh, SJ et al. (Garden City, NY: Image Books, 1958), 26.
25. Ibid.
26. Ibid.
27. Vatican II, *Gaudium et Spes*, 76.
28. Ibid., 40.

human history, which sin will keep in great disarray until the splendor of God's sons is fully revealed."[29]

The Rise of Islam: The Challenge of a New Religious Imperialism

Muhammad (570–632) was born in Arabia five years after the death of Justinian. When he was around twenty-five, he entered into the service of a wealthy widow named Khadijah, whom he subsequently married. According to Islamic tradition, Muhammad began to receive "revelations" from God when he was around forty years old (circa AD 610). These revelations would continue until his death some twenty-two years later. They constitute the content of the Qur'an, the sacred book of Islam.

Those who accepted the authenticity of Muhammad's revelations formed the initial Islamic community or *ummah*. They believed that Muhammad was affirming the truths of the original religion, which went back to the prophet Adam. All of the prophets since Adam, including Moses and Jesus, affirmed the basic truths of the unity of God; the reality of angels and demons; the Day of Judgment; and the resurrection of the body.[30] Muhammad and his followers were driven out of the Arabian city of Mecca in 622, but eight years later they were able to return and gain control of the city.

Although Muhammad preached the truths of the Islamic faith, military conquest was part of the Islamic *modus operandi* from the beginning. According to Fr. Samir Khalil Samir, SJ, violence and conquest were characteristic of the culture of Muhammad's time: "Violence was definitely a part of the rapid rise and expansion of Islam. At that time, no one found anything blameworthy in Muhammad's military actions since wars were part of the Arab Bedouin culture."[31]

In spite of claims to the contrary, Islam *did* spread by military conquests. Those who were conquered were not forced to convert to

---

29. Ibid.
30. Robert L. Fastiggi, "Islam," in Michael L. Coulter et al., eds. *The Encyclopedia of Catholic Social Thought, Social Science, and Social Policy*, vol. 1 (Lanham, MD: The Scarecrow Press, 2007), 567.
31. Samir Khalil Samir, SJ, 111 *Questions on Islam*, trans. Fr. Wafik Nasry, SJ and Claudia Castellani (San Francisco: Ignatius Press, 2008), question 24, 66.

Reflections on the Persecution of Christians

Islam. If, however, they chose not to convert, they were obliged to pay the *jizya* or poll tax and live as *dhimmis* (non-Muslims who were protected yet subject to Islamic governance).[32] Within 100 years after the death of Muhammad, Islamic rule spread throughout the Middle East, Africa, and Spain. Muslims took control of Damascus in 636; Jerusalem in 638; Egypt in 642; the Persian Empire in 651; Carthage in 698; and Spain in 711.[33] The Muslims, however, did suffer some setbacks. Their efforts to conquer Constantinople in 674–677 and 717 failed.[34] In 732, the invading Muslims were defeated by Charles Martel in Tours, France [also called the Battle of Poitiers].[35]

How did Christians fare under Islamic rule? Karen Armstrong and others argue that Christians were allowed full religious freedom under Islamic rule, and they try to contrast the alleged Muslim toleration with Christian bigotry.[36] Many scholars, though, dispute such a claim. Philip Jenkins, for example, points out that the historical record of Christian persecutions under Islamic rule would "surprise many Americans who derive their view of Muslim tolerance from the widely seen PBS documentary, *Empires of Faith*, or the film *Kingdom of Heaven*, about the First Crusade."[37] He goes on to say that "even in the most optimistic view, Armstrong's reference to Christians possessing 'full religious freedom' in Muslim Spain or elsewhere beggars belief."[38]

The history of Christians living under Islamic rule is only beginning to be written. As Bat Ye'or notes: "Whereas there are innumerable studies on Islamic civilization, those devoted to the *dhimmi* people are few."[39] At present, the scholarly consensus seems to be

---

32. See the documents on "The Theory of Jihad" in Bat Ye'or, *The Decline of Eastern Christianity under Islam: From Jihad to Dhimmitude* (Madison, N.J.: Fairleigh Dickinson University Press, 1996), 295–302.

33. See Jenkins, *The Lost History*, 101–2 and John Vidmar, OP, *The Catholic Church Through the Ages: A History* (New York/Mahwah, NJ: Paulist Press, 2005), 93–95.

34. Jenkins, *The Lost History*, 102.

35. Vidmar, *The Catholic Church*, 94.

36. See Karen Armstrong, *Muhammad* (San Francisco: HarperOne, 1992), 22.

37. Jenkins, *The Lost History*, 99.

38. Ibid.

39. Bat Ye'or, *The Decline of Eastern Christianity*, 257.

that systematic persecution of Christians under Muslim rule did not really begin until the 996–1021 reign of the Caliph Hakim. For unknown reasons, he began a sustained persecution of Christians and Jews culminating in the destruction of the Christian Church of the Holy Sepulcher in 1009.[40] Prior to the reign of Hakim, Christians and Jews under Islamic rule "were assured freedom of person, property, and worship," even if they "were treated as second-class citizens and suffered inequality before the law, penal taxation, and a variety of other discomforts, humiliations, and indignities."[41] There is also evidence that "many Eastern Christians—Nestorians, Jacobites, and others—were not sorry to witness the fall of the Byzantine authorities who had so persecuted them over the decades, and the followers of the Arab prophet would not necessarily be more heavy-handed as rulers."[42] After Muslim rule was established in Syria, some Christians even rose to prominent positions. St. John of Damascus (c. 675–749), for example, served as an official of the Caliph in Damascus.[43]

Scholars such as Bat Ye'or, however, believe that the theoretical principle of religious tolerance by Islam was never respected.[44] As she writes:

> The *jihad*, or rather the alternative forced on the Peoples of the Book—namely, payment of tribute and submission to Islamic law or the massacre and enslavement of survivors—is, in its very terms, a contravention of the principle of religious freedom. The constant aggression by Muslim armies against the *dar-al harb*, the razzias [raids] on non-Muslim populations condemned to slavery for their religion, the piracy on the seas in order to ransom travelers, the regional deportation of the conquered, the destruction of towns and villages—all these recurrent acts of aggression in a compulsory

---

40. Jenkins, *The Lost History*, 109.
41. Jeremy Johns, "Christianity and Islam" in John McManners, ed. *The Oxford History of Christianity* (Oxford: Oxford University Press, 1993), 180.
42. Jenkins, *The Lost History*, 104.
43. Hitchcock, *History*, 200. See also Hugh Goddard, *A History of Christian-Muslim Relations* (Chicago: New Amsterdam Publications, 2000), 38. Enzo Lodi identifies St. John of Damascus as "the finance minister for Muslim caliph;" see Enzo Lodi, *Saints of the Roman Calendar*, trans. Jordan Aumann, OP (New York: Society of St. Paul, 1992), 379.
44. Bat Ye'or, *The Decline of Eastern Christianity*, 88.

Reflections on the Persecution of Christians

jihad, repeated over the centuries, constituted permanent violations of religious freedom.[45]

Bat Ye'or also provides examples of Christians and Jews being tortured and killed by Muslim rulers in Syria, Armenia, and Andalusia in the eighth and ninth centuries, way before the 996–1021 reign of Hakim.[46]

Muslim rulers justified certain acts of violence against Christians and Jews on the basis of various Qur'anic texts that allow for war against those who resist the reign of Islam (e.g., 8:38–39). As Fr. Samir explains:

> The Muslim has the duty to announce to his enemy his intention of declaring war on him. If he refuses to submit, war is unavoidable, and the Muslim has the right to kill him because he has not surrendered. If, on the contrary, the other would be ready to surrender, the Muslim would no longer have the right to kill him but only to occupy his land.[47]

The extent of Christian persecution before the reign of Caliph Hakim is a matter of scholarly debate. It is certainly clear that those areas that had large and influential Christian populations before Islamic control became increasingly Muslim. Prior to Islamic rule, North Africa had been a great center of Christian learning with scholars such as Tertullian (d. 220), Cyprian (d. 258), and Augustine (d. 430) among the best known. By the twelfth century, however, North Africa had become almost completely Muslim.[48] The rate of conversion to Islam was not as dramatic in other countries and regions, but the Christian populations of Egypt, Syria, Mesopotamia, and Persia definitely decreased under Muslim rule. By the tenth century, the majority of the population of Egypt had become Muslim.[49] The same was true for Syria and Mesopotamia, and Persia (Iran) had become a largely Muslim country by the beginning of the ninth cen-

---

45. See Ibid. *Dar-al harb* is defined as "The 'domain of war': the non-Muslim world where Islamic law does not rule." Ibid., 472.
46. Ibid., 88–89.
47. Samir, 111 *Questions on Islam*, 74–75.
48. Goddard, *A History of Christian-Muslim Relations*, 70.
49. Ibid., 72.

tury.[50] In the Middle East, only Lebanon retained a Christian majority—though that is no longer the case.[51]

Bat Ye'or and others believe these conversions were due to either direct or indirect coercion.[52] Even if Christians were not forced to convert, many opted to become Muslims because of the burdens of life under *dhimmitude*, viz., heavy taxation, segregation, and humiliation.[53] Some scholars, such as Hugh Goddard, believe there were multiple factors for Christian converts to Islam, including disunity among competing Christian groups and economic hardships.[54]

While Christian populations suffered many hardships under Islamic rule from 650–1000, the situation grew worse during and after Caliph Hakim's reign of 996–1021. Hakim's destruction of the Church of the Holy Sepulcher in 1009 was understood as a direct assault against Christian civilization. This act of destruction along with the Muslim victory over the Byzantine Christians at Manzikert in 1071 set in motion the conditions for Pope Urban II's 1095 call for a Crusade in defense of the Christian churches of Jerusalem and the East.[55] Some scholars believe that the Crusades "had less to do with the relationship between Christianity and Islam than with the internal stresses and strains of Christian Europe."[56] As Fr. Samir observes:

> The Crusades were not considered wars of religion, not even by the Muslim historians of those times. The Muslims never called them "Crusades" as they do today, in imitation of the West. The new Muslim expression, *al hurūb-al salībiyya* (the wars of those who hold the Cross), dates back only to the nineteenth century. Earlier, the Crusades were called *hurūb al-Faranj* (the wars of the Franks), which signified wars with the West in general.[57]

The anti-Christian reign of Hakim, the Muslim aggression against the Byzantine Empire, and the subsequent Crusades all led to increased Muslim persecution of Christians during the Middle Ages.

---

50. Ibid., 72–73.
51. Ibid., 72.
52. See Bat Ye'or, *The Decline of Eastern Christianity*, 88–89.
53. Ibid., 91–99.
54. Goddard, *A History of Christian-Muslim Relations*, 70–71.
55. Johns, 175–77.
56. Ibid., 175.
57. Samir, 111 *Questions on Islam*, 73–74.

Reflections on the Persecution of Christians

During the first three centuries of Muslim rule over formerly Christian lands, the Christian and Jewish communities were kept intact—even if they suffered second-class status as *dhimmis* and occasional slaughters. All this changed during the period from 1200 to 1500. As Jenkins notes, "According to one estimate, the number of Asian Christians fell, between 1200 and 1500, from 21 million to 3.4 million. In the same years, the proportion of the world's Christian population living in Africa and Asia fell from 34 percent to just 6 percent."[58] The Muslims themselves, however, suffered persecutions at the hands of the invading Mongols between 1219 and 1303.[59] The Mongols at first showed favor to Christians and Buddhists over Muslims, but they began to persecute Christians, especially when the Khan Oljeitu (r. 1304–1316) became Muslim.[60] The Christians now "found themselves under the control of a Muslim superstate," and they "were now subject to intense persecution."[61]

The Islamic Abbasid Caliphate held power over most of the Muslim world from 750 until 1258 (with Baghdad as its capital since 762). By the thirteenth century, however, "the Abbasid empire was a sprawling, fragmented, deteriorating commonwealth of semiautonomous states, sultanates, governed by military commanders."[62] After Baghdad fell to invading Mongols in 1258, political power in the Muslim world came to exist in "a chain of dynamic sultanates ... which eventually spread from Africa to Southeast Asia."[63] The Abbasid Caliphate moved from Baghdad to Cairo, Egypt, and it lasted (at least in name) from 1260 to 1517. Islamic power, however, shifted in the thirteenth century from the Abbasid Caliphate to the various Turkish sultanates of the Seljuks and the Ottomans. After the Mongols became Muslim in the fourteenth century, the Ottomans grew in power. The Islamic scholar, John L. Esposito wrote:

> The Ottoman Empire was the heir to the Mongol-Turkish legacy of Genghis Khan. The fall of Constantinople (Istanbul) in 1453 to the

---

58. Jenkins, *The Lost History*, 24.
59. Ibid., 121–23.
60. Ibid., 123–24.
61. Ibid., 124.
62. John L. Esposito, *Islam: The Straight Path* (Oxford and New York: Oxford University Press, 1998), 60.
63. Ibid.

Ottoman sultan Mehmet II and the conquest of Byzantium realized the cherished dream of Muslim rulers and armies since the seventh century.... The Ottomans drew on their Mongol-Turkish and Islamic roots and traditions, combining a warrior heritage with an Islamic tradition that believed in Islam's universal mission and sacred struggle [jihad], to establish themselves as worldwide propagators and defenders of Islam. They became the great warriors of Islamic expansion through military conquest.[64]

Only in 1517 did the Caliphate officially come under Turkish-Ottoman control, but the Turks had become the *de facto* leaders of the Islamic world in the late thirteenth century. The Arab Muslims had tried to conquer Europe from the west (Spain and France) in the eighth century and from the south (Sicily and Malta) in the ninth century. After the Ottoman Empire came into existence around 1300,[65] Muslim invasions came more frequently from the east. From the fourteenth through the sixteenth centuries, the Ottomans attacked and conquered Bulgaria (1396); Constantinople (1453); Serbia (1459); Herzegovina (1483); Moldavia (1538); Hungary (1541); and Cyprus (1570).[66]

Christians suffered many persecutions under Ottoman rule. According to Philip Jenkins, "the Ottomans were more aggressively anti-Christian than were the original Arab conquerors of the Middle East."[67] The first Ottoman Caliph, Selim I (r. 1517–1520) "ordered the confiscation of all churches, many of which were razed and Ottoman authorities forced many thousands to accept Islam."[68] Christians "were placed in a situation of permanent inferiority."[69] They were forced to pay heavy taxes and to wear distinctive dress. Moreover, "their children could be seized to serve in the sultan's court or in the

---

64. Esposito, *Islam*, 61.

65. The term Ottoman comes from the name of the founder of the empire, Osman I; see https://www.britannica.com/place/Ottoman-Empire.

66. See Bat Ye'or, *The Decline of Eastern Christianity*, 55, Esposito, *Islam*, 61, and Goddard, *A History of Christian-Muslim Relations*, 109–111.

67. Jenkins, *The Lost History*, 142.

68. Ibid.

69. Kallistos Ware, "Eastern Christianity" in John McManners, ed. *The Oxford History of Christianity* (Oxford: Oxford University Press, 1993), 161.

Reflections on the Persecution of Christians

janizary guard."[70] Often Christian families "were required to give a proportionate number of their sons to be raised by the state as slaves."[71] The Bulgarians referred to this practice as the "Blood Tax."[72] The Ottomans also placed heavy restrictions on the practice of the Christian faith. They forbade religious processions and the ringing of bells. Christians who tried to convert Muslims could be sentenced to death.[73]

The Ottomans, as noted above, were from a warrior culture, and their manner of war "drew heavily on methods that stemmed from the Turkish heritage of central Asia."[74] They "carried out notorious massacres against Christian populations" and practiced "such gruesome techniques as impaling, crucifixion, and flaying."[75] When the Ottomans would conquer a city, they would take Christian women and children as hostages, but they would promise their freedom if the defeated Christian men would convert to Islam. This is what occurred in the southern Italian city of Otranto in 1480. After the Turks beheaded the archbishop and a priest who refused to convert to Islam, "all the male citizens of Otranto between the ages of fifteen and fifty were bound in pairs and brought before Gedik Ahmet Pasha [the Ottoman general], who promised the prisoners their lives, their freedom, and the return of their captive families in exchange for their conversion to Islam."[76] One of the bound men, a tailor named Antonio Primaldo, urged the Catholic men not to deny their faith in Christ. His words had an effect. None of the 800 men agreed to convert to Islam, and all were beheaded on August 14, 1480.[77] The cause for the beatification of the 800 men began in 1539. Pope John Paul II

---

70. Ibid. (The word "janizary" means "new soldier." The Janissaries under Ottoman rule were mostly kidnapped Christian boys forced into the military service of the Sultan.)

71. Jenkins, *The Lost History*, 143.

72. Ibid.

73. Ware, "Eastern Christianity," 161.

74. Jenkins, *The Lost History*, 143.

75. Ibid. Impaling was also employed by the Hungarian-Romanian prince, Vlad "the Impaler" (1431–1477), who resisted the Turks in Hungary. The tales of Count Dracula are based on Prince Vlad's life.

76. Elizabeth Lev, "Otranto (Italy), Martyrs of" in *New Catholic Encyclopedia Supplement* 2010, ed. Robert L. Fastiggi (Detroit: Gale Cengage Learning, 2010), 872.

77. Ibid., 872–73.

visited the tomb of the slain men in 1980, and on July 6, 2007, Benedict XVI declared the validity of their martyrdom.[78] Pope Francis canonized Antonio Primaldo and the martyrs of Otranto on May 12, 2013. In his homily for the Mass on Canonization, the Holy Father used the Martyrs of Otranto as a reason to pray for all Christians who still suffer violence:

> Today the Church holds up for our veneration an array of martyrs who in 1480 were called to bear the highest witness to the Gospel together. About 800 people, who had survived the siege and invasion of Otranto, were beheaded in the environs of that city. They refused to deny their faith and died professing the Risen Christ.... Dear friends, let us keep the faith we have received and which is our true treasure, let us renew our faithfulness to the Lord, even in the midst of obstacles and misunderstanding. God will never let us lack strength and calmness. While we venerate the Martyrs of Otranto, let us ask God to sustain all the Christians who still suffer violence today in these very times and in so many parts of the world and to give them the courage to stay faithful and to respond to evil with goodness.[79]

The Ottoman Empire reached the height of its power in the 1500s and 1600s, and "a besieged Europe struggled for its existence."[80] Various popes encouraged Catholic rulers to respond with military force "to the alarming expansion of the power of the Ottomans."[81] Pope Pius V asked Catholics to pray the rosary to turn back the Ottoman fleet during the 1571 Battle of Lepanto. The outnumbered Catholic fleet, aided by a sudden shift of winds, defeated the Turkish fleet. Pius V was so grateful that he established the Feast of Our Lady of Victory. This feast, later renamed Our Lady of the Rosary, is still celebrated on October 7.[82]

The Christian resistance to the expansion of the Ottoman Empire was hindered by the religious and political divisions among Christian nations in Europe and the Middle East. King Francis I of France

---

78. Ibid., 873.
79. Pope Francis, Homily for the Mass of Canonizations (May 12, 2013), http://w2.vatican.va/content/francesco/en/homilies/2013/documents/papa-francesco_20130512_omelia-canonizzazioni.html.
80. Esposito, *Islam*, 61.
81. Hitchcock, *History*, 205–6.
82. Lodi, *Saints of the Roman Calendar*, 302.

Reflections on the Persecution of Christians

natural outcome of a policy inherent in the political-religious structure of *dhimmitude*."[98] As she writes:

> The genocide of the Armenians was a *jihad*. No *rayas* took part in it. Despite the disapproval of many Muslim Turks and Arabs and their refusal to collaborate in the crime, these massacres were perpetuated solely by Muslims and they alone profited from the booty; the victims' property, houses, and lands granted to the *muhajirun*, and the allocation to them of women and child slaves.[99]

While political and social upheavals certainly were a factor, the religious motivation cannot be ignored. Even Muslim sources understood the suppression of Christian uprisings during the early twentieth century as a "war between the Crescent and the Cross" and a fight against the "unbelievers and infidels."[100]

The collapse of the Ottoman Empire after World War I, the rise of the secular Turkish state in 1923, and the 1924 termination of the Caliphate by Mustafa Kemal Atatürk in 1924 all contributed to a growing reaction on the part of more traditionally-minded Muslims. There was a desire for "a new Islamic world, one free from all Western influence."[101] The Muslim Brotherhood was founded in Egypt in 1928.[102] In Arabia and elsewhere, there was a revival of Wahabism, the form of Islamic fundamentalism associated with the theologian Muhammad bin 'Abdil-Wahhāb (1703–1787).[103]

The rise of Islamic radicalism in the twentieth and early twenty-first century can be understood as a reaction to the rise of the western political superiority that began to be evident in the eighteenth and nineteenth centuries. The Muslim world had been nurtured for centuries by a mindset of religious and cultural superiority. When this attitude of superiority became challenged by the political realities of the twentieth century, the turn to more radical forms of Islam became attractive.[104] The current rise of Islamic terrorism repre-

---

98. Bat Ye'or, *The Decline of Eastern Christianity*, 197.
99. Ibid.
100. Jenkins, *The Lost History*, 163.
101. Samir, 111 *Questions on Islam*, 84.
102. Ibid.
103. Ibid., 239.
104. See Bernard Lewis, *What Went Wrong? The Clash Between Islam and Modernity in the Middle East* (New York: Oxford University Press, 2002).

Persecution & Genocide of Christians in the Middle East

sented by groups such as ISIS can be understood, therefore, as the manifestation of a movement of de-Christianization in the Middle East that began in the twentieth century. In 1900, Christians constituted ten percent of the population of the Middle East, but by the end of the twentieth century this figure was down to three percent.[105] While some of this change can be explained by Christian migration and a booming Muslim birthrate, there can be little doubt that systematic massacres of Christians (such as the 1915–1916 genocide of the Armenians) have been a major factor.

Christian Persecutions under Secular Regimes from the French Revolution to the Present

This chapter has spent considerable space examining the history of Christian persecution under Islamic rule. It is equally important, though, to understand that Christians have also endured persecutions and killings under secular regimes, which began to emerge in the West in the late eighteenth century. Space does not permit a thorough exposition of the reasons for these persecutions, but the more prominent deserve mention.

The first major persecution of Christians during the rise of secularism occurred during the 1793–1794 "Reign of Terror" of the French Revolution. Inspired by forms of new thinking and anti-clericalism, the leaders of the revolution exiled or executed those Catholics who did not support the revolution. About 30,000 priests were exiled, and hundreds if not thousands were killed.[106] Some 17,000 Catholics were executed and 10,000 others died in jails.[107]

The nineteenth century restored religious freedom for Catholics in France, but anti-clericalism and secularism, often linked to Freemasonry, led to other persecutions of Catholics in Europe. Freemasonry and anti-clericalism inspired many within the *Risorgimento*, the Italian unification movement of the nineteenth century.[108] Free-

---

105. Jenkins, *The Lost History*, 108.
106. Vidmar, *The Catholic Church*, 106. In his book, *Triumph: The Power and the Glory of the Catholic Church: A 2,000 Year History* (New York: Three Rivers Press, 2001), H.W. Crocker states that "thousands" of priests were killed during the Reign of Terror (346).
107. Vidmar, *The Catholic Church*, 272.
108. Hitchcock, *History*, 350.

Reflections on the Persecution of Christians

masonry also was a major inspiration behind anti-Catholic persecutions in Mexico in the early twentieth century. As James Hitchcock wrote:

> Following a revolution in 1910, Mexico became one of the fiercest anti-religious regimes in the world, virtually outlawing the practice of the faith. Priests who continued to minister to their people were systematically hunted down and killed, notably the Jesuit martyr, Bl. Miguel-Agostino Pro, who was shot by a firing squad in 1927, his arms outstretched in the form of a cross.[109]

Beginning with the Bolshevik Revolution of 1917, Marxist-inspired regimes have systematically persecuted Christians and still do in places like China.[110] In the 1920s, Communist Russia began a systematic persecution of the Orthodox Church which extended also to Catholics, Protestants, and also Muslims.[111] The Communist persecution of Christians moved from Russia to counties like Poland and the Ukraine, which came under Soviet domination. In the early 1930s millions of Ukrainian Catholics were systematically starved to death by the Soviet government.[112] Other socialist movements of the twentieth century saw the Catholic Church as an enemy to be eliminated. This was clearly the case with communists during the Spanish civil war of the 1930s.[113]

The fascist regimes of Mussolini and Hitler also persecuted the Catholic Church. Catholics could be useful if they supported the state; otherwise they were the enemy. Mussolini sought to associate his regime with the pagan Romans, and "the Nazis invoked the old Norse gods as appropriate deities for a warlike people."[114] Hitler's effort to exterminate the Jewish people is well-known; less well-known is his murder of millions of Catholics, especially in Poland. In Dachau, 2,000 Catholic priests were executed, and of the 10,000

---

109. Ibid., 375.
110. On ongoing persecution of Christians in China, see John L. Allen, Jr. *The Global War on Christians* (New York: Image, 2013), 69–74.
111. See Stéphanie Courtois et al. *The Black Book of Communism: Crimes, Terror, Repression* trans. J. Murphy and M. Kramer (Cambridge, MA: Harvard University Press, 1999), 172–74.
112. Hitchcock, *History*, 374.
113. Ibid., 379–80.
114. Ibid., 380.

priests in Poland during the Nazi occupation, 3,700 were imprisoned and 2,700 executed.[115]

Christianity and Religious Toleration from the Late Patristic Age to the 1700s

Those who try to bring attention to the genocide against Christians today are sometimes challenged by secularists and progressive Christians who argue that Christianity has been the most intolerant religion throughout history.[116] There can be no doubt that Jews, Muslims, and people of other faiths have sometimes suffered persecutions and violence at the hands of Christians. For Catholics at least, there has always been an effort to condemn forced conversions. Moreover, religious freedom—even if linked with various restrictions—has been part of Catholic teaching from the early centuries of Church history.

The following magisterial interventions deserve special mention. In 602, Pope Gregory I defended the religious liberty of Jews in Naples, Italy, noting that "they should have complete freedom to observe and celebrate all of their feasts and holy days as up till now . . . they have possessed."[117] The Second Council of Nicaea (787) decreed that Jews should not be forced to convert or pretend to convert. Rather, they should be allowed to practice their religion openly.[118] In 1065 Pope Alexander condemned bringing people into the Christian faith by violence.[119] In 1199, Innocent III in his constitution, *Licet perfidia Iudaeorum*, forbad compelling Jews to become Christian by violence.[120]

---

115. Vidmar, *The Catholic Church*, 329; see Ronald J. Rychlak, *Hitler, the War, and the Pope* (Huntington, Indiana: Our Sunday Visitor, 2010), 195.

116. See Jenkins, *The Lost History*, 43. Past failures of Christians are no reason to ignore the very real persecution of Christians today.

117. Heinrich Denzinger and Peter Hünermann, eds. *Compendium of Creeds, Definitions, and Declarations on Matters of Faith and Morals* 43rd ed. (San Francisco: Ignatius Press, 2012) [henceforth D-H], n. 480.

118. Norman Tanner, SJ, ed. *Decrees of the Ecumenical Councils Volume One: Nicaea I to Lateran V* (Washington, DC and London: Sheed & Ward and Georgetown University Press, 1990), Nicaea II, canon 8, 145–46.

119. D-H, 698.

120. Ibid. 772–73.

Reflections on the Persecution of Christians

In 1215 the Fourth Lateran Council required Jews (and Muslims) to wear special clothing. Moreover, Jews were not to hold public office, and they were to be prevented from charging excessive interest in loans (usury).[121] In spite of these restrictions, the previous condemnations of forced conversions were upheld. These condemnations were made by Pope Innocent III himself who presided over Lateran IV.[122] Later magisterial interventions warned about baptizing Jewish children against the wishes of their parents, even to the point of imposing a penalty of 1000 ducats and suspension "on those who baptize the children of Hebrews against their parents' wishes."[123] In 1747, Pope Benedict XIV, in agreement with St. Thomas Aquinas, made it clear that baptism against the wishes of the child's parents would violate natural justice.[124]

As is well-known, there have been Christian actions and words that seem to violate the principle of religious freedom as articulated by Vatican II. We can recall the expulsion of Jews and Muslims from Spain in 1492; the establishment of the Jewish ghetto in Venice in 1516; and the migration of numerous Jews from Western Europe because of intolerant attitudes they endured. Many of these Jews went to Poland during the 1500s because Poland manifested a more tolerant policy toward them.

Even though there have been actions, words, and policies of Christian people and governments that have violated the religious freedom of those of other faiths, it has never been the teaching of the Catholic Church that those of other religions are to be forcibly converted or killed because they reject the Catholic faith.[125] Even when restrictions were placed on Jews and Muslims living in Catho-

---

121. See Lateran IV, canons 67–70 in Tanner, *Decrees*, 265–67.

122. See D-H.

123. See Decree of the Holy Office of July 23, 1639 in D-H, 1998. In danger of death, children could be baptized licitly and validly even if their parents do not give consent. See D-H, 2555 and the 1983 *Codex Iuris Canonici*, canon 868 § 3.

124. D-H, 2552.

125. Some people might object that the various Catholic inquisitions violated the prohibition of forced conversion. The tribunals of the Inquisition, however, were aimed at Christian heretics, not non-Christians. The Jews and Muslims brought before the Spanish Inquisition were those who had accepted baptism. See Vidmar, *The Catholic Church*, 150–52.

lic countries during the Middle Ages, Catholics were forbidden to baptize them against their will or kill them for belonging to another faith.

The Catholic Commitment to Religious Liberty

The concept of religious freedom became a major issue of concern during the Second Vatican Council (1962–1965). By the mid-twentieth century, fewer countries in the world could claim to be Catholic, and many Catholics were living under regimes that were hostile to Christianity and/or Catholicism. The bishops of Vatican II saw the need to pursue peace in the world by promoting a more positive approach to those of other faiths and by upholding religious freedom. Positive statements about Jews and Muslims are found in Vatican II's 1964 *Dogmatic Constitution on the Church, Lumen Gentium*. More detailed statements about Jews and Muslims and other Non-Christian religions are found in Vatican II's 1965 *Declaration on the Relation of the Catholic Church to Non-Christian Religions, Nostra Aetate*. The key document of Vatican II concerning religious freedom, however, is its 1965 *Declaration on Religious Liberty, Dignitatis Humanae*. While upholding the duty of all human beings to seek the truth, *Dignitatis Humanae* affirms religious liberty as a fundamental human right:

> This Vatican Council declares that the human person has a right to religious freedom. This freedom means that all men are to be immune from coercion on the part of individuals or of social groups and of any human power, in such wise that no one is to be forced to act in a manner contrary to his own beliefs, whether privately or publicly, whether alone or in association with others, within due limits.
>
> The council further declares that the right to religious freedom has its foundation in the very dignity of the human person as this dignity is known through the revealed word of God and by reason itself. This right of the human person to religious freedom is to be recognized in the constitutional law whereby society is governed and thus it is to become a civil right. It is in accordance with their dignity as persons—that is, beings endowed with reason and free will and therefore privileged to bear personal responsibility—that

Reflections on the Persecution of Christians

all men should be at once impelled by nature and also bound by a moral obligation to seek the truth, especially religious truth.[126]

The Council did not wish to specify how exactly civil governments were to enact laws respecting religious freedom, but it upheld the principle that civil governments were not to promote or tolerate persecution of people because of their religion. The Council was not teaching religious indifferentism or religious relativism because *Dignitatis Humanae* made it quite clear that it left untouched "the traditional Catholic doctrine on the moral duty of men and societies toward the true religion and toward the one Church of Christ."[127]

Religious freedom "has to do with freedom from coercion in civil society" in which "the truth cannot impose itself except by virtue of its own truth."[128] The Catholic Church believes that religious freedom is rooted in Sacred Scripture and the natural law. Moreover, this is a freedom that should be respected in civil constitutions and international law.

In light of the persecution of Christians in the world today, the principle of religious freedom affirmed by Vatican II is more important than ever. According to the Italian scholar Massimo Introvigne, over 100,000 people a year are now being killed simply because of their faith as Christians.[129] As we have seen, Christians have been persecuted over the centuries by different groups and for different reasons. We have now reached a critical point in human history. When speaking to the religious leaders in Ankara, Turkey, Pope Francis addressed the need for Christians, Muslims, and all people of goodwill to work together to end violence in the name of religion:

> Especially tragic is the situation in the Middle East, above all in Iraq and Syria.... Particular concern arises from the fact that, owing mainly to an extremist and fundamentalist group, entire communities, especially—though not exclusively—Christians and Yazidis, have suffered and continue to suffer barbaric violence simply because of their ethnic and religious identity. They have been forcibly evicted from their homes, having to leave behind everything to

---

126. Vatican II, *Dignitatis Humanae* (Dec. 7, 1965), n. 2; D-H, 4240.
127. Ibid., n. 1.
128. Ibid.
129. http://www.christianpost.com/news/every-5-minutes-a-christian-is-martyred-for-their-faith-persecution-watchdog-group-warns-145451/.

save their lives and preserve their faith. This violence has also brought damage to sacred buildings, monuments, religious symbols and cultural patrimony, as if trying to erase every trace, every memory of the other.

As religious leaders, we are obliged to denounce all violations against human dignity and human rights. Human life, a gift of God the Creator, possesses a sacred character. As such, any violence which seeks religious justification warrants the strongest condemnation because the Omnipotent is the God of life and peace. The world expects those who claim to adore God to be men and women of peace who are capable of living as brothers and sisters, regardless of ethnic, religious, cultural or ideological differences.

As well as denouncing such violations, we must also work together to find adequate solutions. This requires the cooperation of all: governments, political and religious leaders, representatives of civil society, and all men and women of goodwill.[130]

The approach of Pope Francis makes sense. We need to condemn religious persecution wherever we find it, and we need to alert the world to the genocide being carried out against Christians across the globe today. We need, though, to appeal to the people of different faiths to help end this violence. We cannot appeal to past models of Christian monarchs and emperors defeating the enemies of the Church. Jesus predicted persecution for his followers, but he also preached hope. He told his disciples: "If the world hates you, realize that it hated me first" (Jn 15:18), and he also said: "In the world you will have trouble, but take courage. I have conquered the world" (Jn 16:33).

---

130. Pope Francis, Address before the President of the Dyanet at the Department of Religious Affairs, Ankara, Turkey (Nov. 28, 2014): http://w2.vatican.va/content/francesco/en/speeches/2014/november/documents/papa-francesco_20141128_turchia-presidenza-diyanet.html.

Erbil, Iraq. Christian IDP camp, 2016.

Batnaya, Iraq. Children after Easter Sunday Mass, April, 2017, the first held since 2014, when the church was overtaken and used by ISIS as a training center.

4

International Humanitarian Law (IHL): Five Key Dynamics Shaping the Global Landscape, Security, and Freedom of Religion and the Way Ahead

Kevin H. Govern

THE TWENTY-FIRST CENTURY has experienced unprecedented international security challenges in which criminal and national security threats arise in the domains of land, sea, air, space, and cyberspace, with ever-increasing scope, complexity, and gravity.[1] In particular, religious intolerance and acts of violence between religions and against specific religions has gained great notoriety and infamy; the Open Doors USA watchdog group advocating for Christians found that "more than 7,100 Christians were killed in 2015 for 'faith-related reasons,' up 3,000 from the previous year, according to the group's analysis of media reports and other public information as well as external experts."[2] This comes despite a trend wherein "[w]orldwide, both government restrictions on religion and social

---

1. Federal Bureau of Investigation, "Ten Years After: The FBI Since 9/11," https://www.fbi.gov/about-us/ten-years-after-the-fbi-since-9-11/just-the-facts-1/cyber-1.
2. William J. Cadigan, "Christian persecution reached record high in 2015, report says," *CNN.com*, January 17, 2016, http://www.cnn.com/2016/01/17/world/christian-persecution-2015/. For the 2016 Watch List from Open Doors USA, see https://www.opendoorsusa.org/christian-persecution/world-watch-list/.

hostilities involving religion decreased modestly from 2013 to 2014 despite a rise in religion-related terrorism."[3]

This chapter addresses five key dynamics shaping the global landscape with regard to security, religious freedom, and belief. It surveys freedom of religion impacted by and impacting upon international law, specifically, International Human Rights Law (IHRL) and International Humanitarian Law (IHL), comparing and contrasting each as sources of prescriptive rights and proscriptive responsibilities among nations and peoples. In particular, it looks at the Universal Declaration of Human Rights (UDHR) as the centerpiece of international concurrence on human rights, and the successor treaties that are being used to preserve, protect, and defend Christians' religious freedom and belief, as well as the rights of other religious groups subject to oppression. In so doing, this chapter shows how and why ongoing recognition and respect can be accomplished for human rights of all citizens of the world, especially with respect to religious freedom and belief.

Five Key Dynamics Shaping the Landscape

In 2014, Brian Katulis from the Center for American Progress presciently noted five key national security issues that were relevant to religious freedom and belief or the lack thereof.[4] The first was cyber security. According to Katulis, "[c]yber security became a new front in the messy battle lines involving states, corporations, and non-state actors. Cyber attacks have featured in Syria's conflict,[5] in covert

---

3. "Trends in Global Restrictions on Religion," Pew Research Center, June 23, 2016, http://www.pewforum.org/2016/06/23/trends-in-global-restrictions-on-religion/. The report goes on to summarize that "[o]f the 198 countries included in the study, 24 percent had high or very high levels of government restrictions in 2014 (the most recent year for which data are available), down from 28 percent in 2013." It also states that "[t]here was a similar decline in the share of countries with high or very high social hostilities involving religion, which dropped from 27 percent to 23 percent. This decline comes over a two year span, after three years of steady increases."

4. Brian Katulis, "5 National Security Issues to Watch in 2015," *WSJ.com*, December 31, 2014, http://blogs.wsj.com/washwire/2014/12/31/5-national-security-issues-to-watch-in-2015/.

5. "Western media websites hacked by Syrian Electronic Army," *Reuters.com*, November 24, 2014, http://www.reuters.com/article/2014/11/27/us-syria-crisis-hack-idUSKCN0JB1HM20141127.

International Humanitarian Law: Five Key Dynamics

attacks on Iran's nuclear infrastructure,[6] and in Russia's invasion of Ukraine.[7] At its September 2014 summit in Wales, NATO expanded its pledge of collective defense to include a large-scale cyber attack."[8] Katulis opined that "[T]he opaque nature of this threat and the blurry lines of authorities and capacities to respond present major complications for U.S. foreign policy."[9]

According to the independent watchdog group, Freedom House, twenty out of forty-seven countries surveyed since January 2011 have had declining freedom of speech and internet freedom, "with authorities in forty of sixty-five countries imprisoning people in 2015 for sharing information concerning politics, religion or society through digital networks."[10] As Fox News assessed the role of cyber censorship on freedom of speech and religion, "[f]ar from leading to the spread of democracy and freedom online, the events of the 2011 Arab Spring led many authoritarian countries to clamp down more tightly, fearful of rebellious citizens inciting and organizing online."[11] In other cases, such as that of Pakistan, "religious restrictions were the reason for censoring so-called blasphemous speech online."[12] From China to the Middle East, "[t]he ways and means of blocking political discussion,

---

6. David E. Sanger, "Obama Order Sped Up Wave of Cyberattacks Against Iran," *NYT.com*, June 1, 2012, http://www.nytimes.com/2012/06/01/world/middleeast/obama-ordered-wave-of-cyberattacks-against-iran.html, cited with authority in Katulis.

7. Peter Bergen and Tim Maurer, "Cyberwar hits Ukraine," *CNN.com*, March 7, 2014, http://www.cnn.com/2014/03/07/opinion/bergen-ukraine-cyber-attacks/.

8. David E. Sanger, "NATO Set to Ratify Pledge on Joint Defense in Case of Major Cyberattack," *NYT.com*, August 31, 2014, http://www.nytimes.com/2014/09/01/world/europe/nato-set-to-ratify-pledge-on-joint-defense-in-case-of-major-cyberattack.html.

9. Katulis, supra note 4.

10. Freedom House, "Freedom on the Net 2015–Key Findings," *freedomhouse.org*, October 2015, https://freedomhouse.org/report/freedom-net/freedom-net-2015. The complete 972-page report is available at https://freedomhouse.org/sites/default/files/FOTN%202015%20Full%20Report.pdf.

11. John R. Quain, "Special report: censorship in cyberspace," *Foxnews.com*, February 13, 2013, http://www.foxnews.com/tech/2013/02/13/special-report-censorship-in-cyberspace.html.

12. Ibid. See also Asad Hashim, "Surveilling and censoring the internet in Pakistan," *Aljazeera.com*, May 13, 2015, http://www.aljazeera.com/indepth/features/2015/05/pakistan-internet-censorship-150506124129138.html.

religious freedom and reports of institutional corruption are getting more invidious."[13]

The second issue identified by Katulis was the fragmentation of states. He noted that "[i]n key parts of the world, particularly the Middle East, state structures are being eroded in power struggles fueled in part by conflicts over identity and Islamic State (IS) and other non-state actor power expansion."[14] He further observed that "Syria's civil war, the battles in Iraq, and Libya's conflict continue, with the spillover of millions of refugees and displaced persons straining the surrounding region."[15] Furthermore, "[i]n most of the world, the nation-state system of international order remains stable, but the fragmentation of key states has global security implications, with terrorist networks recruiting thousands from myriad Middle Eastern nations and governments seeking continued military backing from the U.S. and others."[16]

The Center for American Progress's extensive 2015 study entitled *The Plight of Christians in the Middle East* notes that "[s]ome of the oldest Christian communities in the world are disappearing in the very lands where their faith was born and first took root."[17] In particular, "during the past decade, Christians around the Middle East have been subject to vicious murders at the hands of vicious terrorist groups, forced out of their ancestral lands by civil wars, suffered societal intolerance fomented by Islamist groups, and subjected to institutional discrimination found in the legal codes and official practices of many Middle Eastern countries."[18]

---

13. Quain, "Special report." See Beina Xu, "CFR Backgrounders–Media Censorship in China," *cfr.org*, April 7, 2015, http://www.cfr.org/china/media-censorship-china/p11515 (China); Rana Asfour, "Fighting censorship in the Middle East is nothing new—but the battleground has changed," *theguardian*.com, October 19, 2014, http://www.theguardian.com/world/she-said/2014/oct/19/fighting-censorship-in-the-middle-east-is-nothing-new-but-the-battleground-has-changed (Middle-East).

14. "Islamic State Conflict," *BBC.com*, http://www.bbc.com/news/24758587.

15. Ibid.

16. Ibid.

17. Brian Katulis, Rudy deLeon, and John B. Craig, "The Plight of Christians in the Middle East—Supporting Religious Freedom, Pluralism, and Tolerance During a Time of Turmoil," americanprogress.org, March 12, 2015, https://cdn.americanprogress.org/wp-content/uploads/2015/03/ChristiansMiddleEast-report.pdf.

18. Ibid., 1.

International Humanitarian Law: Five Key Dynamics

The year 2015 saw brutal atrocities committed against Christians,[19] Yazidis,[20] and others because of their religious identity by terrorist groups such as the Islamic State (IS).[21] They have also moved to safe havens within the Middle East, and the Christian presence has become more concentrated in places such as Jordan,[22] the area controlled by the Kurdistan Regional Government in Iraq, and Lebanon.[23]

The third issue relevant to religious freedom relates to massive waves of migration. Katulis quoted the Office of the U.N. High Commissioner for Refugees (UNHCR) in its study showing that "nearly 60 million people have been driven from their homes by war and persecution," or nearly "one in every 122 humans is now either a refugee, internally displaced, or seeking asylum."[24] A statement accompanying the report said that this is "an unprecedented global exodus that has burdened fragile countries with waves of newcomers and littered deserts and seas with the bodies of those who died trying to reach safety."[25] Also included in this flight from risk and danger is "[a] surge of undocumented children and families from Central America detained at the U.S. border [that] could trigger a 2016

---

19. See, e.g., Justen Charters, "ISIS Declares War on 'The Cross': 21 Christians Beheaded in Barbaric New Video from the Islamic State," February 25, 2015, http://www.ijreview.com/2015/02/251741-isis-terrorists/.

20. See, e.g., Nina Shea, "ISIS Genocide Victims Do Not Include Christians, the State Department is Poised to Rule," *nationalreview.com*, http://www.nationalreview.com/article/427044/isis-genocide-victims-do-not-include-christians-state-department-poised-rule-nina.

21. See, e.g., BBC, "Islamic State Conflict," *bbc.com*, http://www.bbc.com/news/24758587.

22. Katulis, deLeon, and Craig, "The Plight of Christians," 1, 19.

23. Ibid., 1, 9, 14, and see, e.g., Al Monitor, "Syria Pulse," *al-monitor.com*, March 2015, http://www.al-monitor.com/pulse/originals/2015/03/iraq-christians-refugees-jordan-hopeless-islamic-state.html. See, e.g., Maria abi-Habib and Dana Ballout, "Lebanon Takes in Fleeing Christians," *wsj.com,* March 19, 2015, http://www.wsj.com/articles/lebanon-takes-in-fleeing-christians-1426807082.

24. UNHCR, "Worldwide displacement hits all-time high as war and persecution increase," *UNHCR.org*, June 18, 2015, http://www.unhcr.org/558193896.html.

25. Somini Sengupta, "60 Million People Fleeing Chaotic Lands, U.N. Says," *NYT.com*, June 18, 2015, http://www.nytimes.com/2015/06/18/world/60-million-people-fleeing-chaotic-lands-un-says.html, cited with authority in Katulis.

repeat of the 2014 migrant crisis just as the presidential campaign gathers pace."[26]

U.S. border agents detained 19,035 people traveling in family groups during April, May, and June 2016, somewhat higher than in Fiscal Year (FY) 2015, but "significantly lower than FY 2014 and FY 2013," according to Borders and Customs Protection.[27] By way of perspective, at least 62,000 unaccompanied children from Central America came across the U.S.–Mexico border from the fall of 2013 up through August 2014, more than twice the number that came the previous year.[28]

The level and quality of freedom, religious and otherwise, in the world has been eroding steadily over the past decade, with 2015 marking the sharpest decline yet, as revealed in the 2016 report from Freedom House on *Freedom in the World: Anxious Dictators, Wavering Democracies: Global Freedom under Pressure*.[29] Freedom House extensively chronicles that "[p]olitical rights and civil liberties can be affected by both state and non-state actors, including insurgents and other armed groups," including but not limited to acts by and against religious groups.[30]

Worldwide, of 7.3 billion people, only 40 percent live in countries judged "free," down from 46 percent a decade ago.[31] Of 195 countries, only 86 are rated "free."[32] Even in countries rated "free," the report

---

26. Nina Lakhani, "Surge in Central American migrants at U.S. border threatens repeat of 2014 crisis," *theguardian*.com, January 12, 2016, https://www.theguardian.com/us-news/2016/jan/13/central-american-migration-family-children-detention-at-us-border.

27. "United States Border Patrol Southwest Family Unit Subject and Unaccompanied Alien Children Apprehensions Fiscal Year 2016," cbp.gov, June 2016, https://t.co/y3j6bekljd.

28. Michael De Yoanna, "Top U.S. General Says Border Kids Fleeing Gangs," *CPR.org*, August 6, 2014, http://www.cpr.org/news/story/top-us-general-says-border-kids-fleeing-gangs. See Kevin Govern, Chapter 23: *Defense Support of Civil Authorities Responding to Natural and Man-Made Disasters*, U.S. Military Operations Law, Policy, and Practice (Oxford 2015), 27–28.

29. Freedom House, "Freedom in the World 2016: Anxious Dictators, Wavering Democracies: Global Freedom under Pressure," https://freedomhouse.org/sites/default/files/FH_FITW_Report_2016.pdf.

30. Ibid., 2.

31. Ibid., 8.

32. Ibid., 9.

notes, leading democracies that include the United States are experiencing a crisis of confidence.[33] Instead of leading the way and encouraging democratic progress, "they have grown divided and ineffectual on the world stage, unwilling to inspire and unable to develop a coherent, united policy to tackle many of these global challenges."[34]

The fourth issue to look for relates to global economic strains. Concurring with The Economist's assessments,[35] Katulis opined that "U.S. economic fundamentals appear fairly strong, but continuing economic weaknesses among other global powers—including parts of Europe, China, and Japan—have raised concerns about a global economic imbalance and possible troubles ahead."[36] Katulis's perspective on this was such that "[g]lobal economic crises in the late 1990s and in 2008 had a major impact on overall U.S. foreign policy and foreign engagement."[37]

Why is this relevant to freedom of religion and belief? Freedom of belief is one of three factors significantly associated with global economic growth, according to a recent study by researchers at Georgetown University and Brigham Young University, looking at the GDP growth of 173 countries in 2011 controlled for two-dozen financial, social, and regulatory influences.[38] The same study finds a positive relationship between religious freedom and ten of the twelve pillars of global competitiveness, as measured by the World Economic Forum's Global Competitiveness Index.[39] That latter research indicates that when freedom of religion or belief is put to practice, it

33. Ibid., 2.
34. Frida Ghitis, "Freedom going into reverse," *cnn.com*, January 30, 2016, http://www.cnn.com/2016/01/30/opinions/freedom-world-reverse/, citing with authority id.
35. "Past and Future Tense: The world economy in 2015 will carry troubling echoes of the late 1990s," *economist.com*, http://www.economist.com/news/leaders/21636742-world-economy-2015-will-carry-troubling-echoes-late-1990s-past-and-future-tense.
36. Katulis, supra note 4.
37. Ibid.
38. Brian J. Grim, Greg Clark, and Robert Edward Snyder, "Is Religious Freedom Good For Business? A Conceptual and Empirical Analysis," *Interdisciplinary Journal of Research on Religion*, 10:4 (2014), http://www.religjournal.com/pdf/ijrr10004.pdf.
39. World Economic Forum, "The Global Competitiveness Report 2013–2014," http://www3.weforum.org/docs/WEF_GlobalCompetitivenessReport_2013-14.pdf.

leads to reduced corruption. Conversely, "laws and practices burdening religion are related to higher levels of corruption."[40] That conclusion was borne out by a simple comparison between the Pew Research Center's Government Restrictions on Religion Index and the Transparency International Corruption Perceptions Index.[41]

Finally, Katulis looked at enduring human development challenges. He persuasively asserted that "[g]lobal poverty and basic human development challenges are part of the environment shaping overall U.S. foreign policy,"[42] but much the same thing holds true for each nation around the globe. The annual U.N. General Assembly meeting in September 2015 "sought to adopt the 2030 Agenda for Sustainable Development to replace the 2000 Millennium Development Goals that expired in 2015," to meet the demand for "leadership on poverty, inequality and climate change."[43]

In the context of U.S. legislation defining religious freedom and belief, and protecting persons suffering from persecution in foreign countries on account of religion, the International Religious Freedom Act of 1998 (IRF Act)[44] defines five types of violations of religious freedom: arbitrary prohibitions on, restrictions of, or punishment for (i) assembling for peaceful religious activities, such as worship, preaching, and prayer, including arbitrary registration requirements; (ii) speaking freely about one's religious beliefs; (iii) changing one's religious beliefs and affiliation; (iv) possession and distribution of religious literature, including Bibles and other sacred texts; and (v) raising one's children in the religious teachings and practices of one's choice.[45] The Act was passed to promote religious

---

40. Grim, Clark, and Snyder, "Is Religious Freedom," 5.

41. Compare Pew Research Forum, "Government Restrictions Index 2014," http://www.pewforum.org/files/2014/01/RestrictionsV-GRI.pdf, 8 with "Transparency International, Corruptions Perceptions Index 2011," http://files.transparency.org/content/download/101/407/file/2011_CPI_EN.pdf.

42. Katulis, supra, note 4.

43. United Nations Development Programme, "A new sustainable development agenda, undp.org." September 2015, http://www.undp.org/content/undp/en/home/sdgoverview.html.

44. 22 U.S. Code §§ 6401–6481, International Religious Freedom policy, https://www.gpo.gov/fdsys/pkg/PLAW-105publ292/pdf/PLAW-105publ292.pdf.

45. Ibid.

freedom as a foreign policy of the United States and to advocate on behalf of the individuals viewed as persecuted in foreign countries on account of religion.[46] The legislation also established the United States Commission on International Religious Freedom (USCIRF),[47] and provided the President with a number of options to use in addressing "Countries of Particular Concern,"[48] those being countries that have committed or allowed the commission of particularly severe violations of religious freedom. All of this was done in the context of international relations as prescribed and proscribed by domestic and international law.

Freedom of Religion Impacted by and Impacting Upon International Law

Proclaimed by the United Nations General Assembly in Paris on December 10, 1948, as General Assembly Resolution 217A, the Universal Declaration of Human Rights (UDHR) is the cornerstone of an International Bill of Human Rights, considered together with two International Covenants on Human Rights: the International Covenant on Economic, Social and Cultural Rights, and the International Covenant on Civil and Political Rights, adopted by the United Nations General Assembly on December 16, 1966. This International Bill of Human Rights is the birthright of all human beings with respect to civil, political, cultural, economic, and social rights.

International Human Rights Law (IHRL) refers to a small core of basic individual rights embraced by the international community as reflected in various declarations, treaties, and other international provisions beginning with the United Nations (U.N.) Charter and UDHR. These agreements include, but are not limited to:

- International Convention on the Elimination of All Forms of Racial Discrimination;

- International Covenant on Civil and Political Rights;

---

46. Ibid., Preamble.
47. See, e.g., Website, United States Commission on International Religious Freedom, http://www.uscirf.gov/.
48. U.S. Department of State, Countries of Particular Concern, http://www.state.gov/g/drl/irf/c13281.htm.

- International Covenant on Economic, Social and Cultural Rights;

- Convention on the Elimination of All Forms of Discrimination against Women;

- Convention against Torture and Other Cruel, Inhuman or Degrading Treatment or Punishment;

- Convention on the Rights of the Child;

- International Convention on the Protection of the Rights of All Migrant Workers and Members of Their Families;

- International Convention for the Protection of All Persons from Enforced Disappearance;

- Optional Protocol to the Covenant on Economic, Social and Cultural Rights;

- Optional Protocol to the International Covenant on Civil and Political Rights;

- Second Optional Protocol to the International Covenant on Civil and Political Rights, aiming at the abolition of the death penalty;

- Optional Protocol to the Convention on the Elimination of Discrimination against Women;

- Optional Protocol to the Convention on the Rights of the Child on the involvement of children in armed conflict;

- Optional Protocol to the Convention on the Rights of the Child on the sale of children, child prostitution and child pornography;

- Optional Protocol to the Convention on the Rights of the Child on a communications procedure;

- Optional Protocol to the Convention against Torture and Other Cruel, Inhuman or Degrading Treatment or Punishment; and

- Optional Protocol to the Convention on the Rights of Persons with Disabilities.[49]

---

49. See, e.g., United Nations Human Rights Office of the High Commissioner, "International Human Rights Law," http://www.ohchr.org/EN/ProfessionalInterest/Pages/InternationalLaw.aspx. To access these and other core instruments, see http://www.ohchr.org/EN/ProfessionalInterest/Pages/CoreInstruments.aspx.

International Humanitarian Law: Five Key Dynamics

International Humanitarian Law (IHL), also known as the Law of War or the Law of Armed Conflict, refers to those conventions from the law of war that protect the victims of war, along with customary IHL. A major part of IHL is contained in the four Geneva Conventions of 1949. Nearly every State in the world has agreed to be bound by them. The Conventions have been developed and supplemented by two further agreements: the Additional Protocols of 1977 relating to the protection of victims of armed conflicts. Other agreements prohibit the use of certain weapons and military tactics and protect certain categories of people and goods. These agreements include, but are not limited to:

- Convention for the Protection of Cultural Property in the Event of Armed Conflict, plus its two protocols;
- Biological Weapons Convention;
- Conventional Weapons Convention and its five protocols;
- Chemical Weapons Convention;
- Ottawa Convention on anti-personnel mines;
- Optional Protocol to the Convention on the Rights of the Child on the involvement of children in armed conflict.[50]

The IHL regulates the conduct of state *vis-à-vis* state, whereas IHRL regulates the conduct of state *vis-à-vis* individual.[51] IHL applies only to armed conflict; it does not cover internal tensions or disturbances such as isolated acts of violence. The law applies only once a conflict has begun, and then equally to all sides regardless of who started the fighting. The right to protection under IHL is vested not in the individual, but in the state. Under IHRL, the protection flows to the individual directly, and theoretically protects individuals from their own state, which was a radical transition of international law. The IHRL obligates states to recognize and respect basic rights of the individual generally. The IHL obligates states to recognize and

---

50. International Committee of the Red Cross, "What is International Humanitarian Law?" July 2004, https://www.icrc.org/eng/assets/files/other/what_is_ihl.pdf. To access these and other core instruments, see, e.g., http://www.ijrcenter.org/international-humanitarian-law/.

51. See, e.g., *International Humanitarian Law and International Human Rights Law*, Oma Ben-Naftali ed. (2011), 206.

respect certain rights in times of armed conflict. Precepts of IHRL should be respected in all circumstances but may be abrogated in emergencies; IHL precepts may not be abrogated under any circumstances. IHRL covers rights that are outside the scope of IHL (e.g., political rights) and IHL rules may not have equivalencies in IHRL (e.g., rules for conduct of hostilities/use of weapons).[52]

In January 1941, President Franklin D. Roosevelt proclaimed the following in his Message to Congress:

> We look forward to a world founded upon four essential human freedoms. The first is freedom of speech and expression—everywhere in the world. The second is freedom of every person to worship God in his own way—everywhere in the world. The third is freedom from want ... everywhere in the world. The fourth is freedom from fear... anywhere in the world.[53]

The *Four Freedoms* were long-range peace objectives articulated by President Roosevelt as Western Europe faced Nazi domination, and the U.S. faced the likelihood of war and accompanying sacrifices. Roosevelt would not live to see the end of what came to be known as the Second World War, but his wife Eleanor Roosevelt was appointed by Roosevelt's successor Harry S. Truman as a delegate to the then-newly established U.N. Human Rights Commission on February 16, 1946 and was then elected chair of the Commission by its members.[54]

On December 10, 1948, the U.N. General Assembly adopted a resolution endorsing the Universal Declaration of Human Rights; forty-eight nations voted in favor of it, eight countries abstained from vot-

---

52. *The Judge Advocate General's Legal Center & School, Operational Law Handbook* (2012), 45 et. seq.

53. *Speeches in World History*, Suzanne McIntire and William E. Burns eds. (2010), 355.

54. See, e.g., "Eleanor Roosevelt and the Universal Declaration of Human Rights," *FDR Library*, https://fdrlibrary.org/documents/356632/390886/sears.pdf/c30 0e130-b6e6-4580-8bf1-07b72195b370. The French jurist René Cassin was originally recognized as the principal author of the UDHR. Cassin would later go on to win the Nobel Peace Prize in the field of Human Rights for his role as President of the European Court for Human Rights. See, e.g., "The Nobel Peace Prize 1968: René Cassin—Biographical," *nobelprize.org*, 2016, http://www.nobelprize.org/nobel_prizes/peace/laureates/1968/cassin-bio.html. The lead in authoring the UDHR's first drafts is generally credited to John Humphrey, a Canadian professor of law and the U.N.

ing, and no countries dissented or directly opposed the UDHR when it was adopted.[55] In her speech to that assembly, Eleanor Roosevelt said:

> We stand today at the threshold of a great event both in the life of the United Nations and in the life of mankind. This declaration may well become the international Magna Carta for all men everywhere. We hope its proclamation by the General Assembly will be an event comparable to the proclamation in 1789 [the French Declaration of the Rights of Citizens], the adoption of the Bill of Rights by the people of the U.S., and the adoption of comparable declarations at different times in other countries.[56]

The UDHR's Preamble and thirty articles set forth a common standard of achievements for all peoples and all nations with respect to fundamental rights to be universally protected and held.[57] Many of the IHRL and IHL documents are successor treaties inspired by, or influenced by the UDHR, with a legion of international instruments advancing human rights since the UDHR has been adopted. A few notable conventions emanated between the 1960s and 1980s. For instance, the International Convention on the Elimination of All Forms of Racial Discrimination (1965) considered the UDHR's proclamation that all human beings are equal in dignity and rights, and

---

Secretariat's Human Rights Director. See, e.g., "Biography—John Peters Humphrey: Father of the Modern Human Rights System," *humphreyhampton.org*, 2016, http://humphreyhampton.org/biography.html. Also instrumental in the drafting of the UDHR were Chang Peng-chun, a Chinese playwright, philosopher, and diplomat, and Charles Habib Malik, a Lebanese philosopher and diplomat. Lengthy debates led to the evolution of the draft language, with a discussion and approval process in eighty-one meetings, one hundred and sixty-eight amendments, and nearly one thousand, four hundred votes over a two-year span. See, e.g., Dag Hammarskjöld Library, "Drafting of the Universal Declaration of Human Rights," updated May 9, 2016, http://research.un.org/en/undhr/draftingcommittee.

55. Ibid.

56. The Eleanor Roosevelt Papers Project, "Statement to the United Nations' General Assembly on the Universal Declaration of Human Rights 9 December 1948," https://www.gwu.edu/~erpapers/documents/displaydoc.cfm?_t=speeches&_docid=spc057137.

57. United Nations, "The Universal Declaration of Human Rights," http://www.un.org/en/universal-declaration-human-rights/.

reflected upon how all humans are equal to the law, while condemning racial discrimination.[58]

The International Covenant on Economic, Social, and Cultural Rights (1966) recognized that, in accordance with the UDHR, "the ideal of free human beings enjoying freedom from fear and want can only be achieved if conditions are created whereby everyone may enjoy his economic, social and cultural rights, as well as his civil and political rights."[59]

The Convention on the Elimination of All Forms of Discrimination Against Women (1979) noted that "the Universal Declaration of Human Rights affirms the principle of the inadmissibility of discrimination and proclaims that all human beings are born free and equal in dignity and rights and that everyone is entitled to all the rights and freedoms set forth therein, without distinction of any kind, including distinction based on sex." It further proscribed discrimination against women if there were "any distinction, exclusion or restriction made on the basis of sex which has the effect or purpose of impairing or nullifying the recognition, enjoyment or exercise by women, irrespective of their marital status, on a basis of equality of men and women, of human rights and fundamental freedoms in the political, economic, social, cultural, civil or any other field."[60]

The Convention Against Torture and Other Cruel, Inhuman, or Degrading Treatment or Punishment (1984), "having regard to article 5 of the Universal Declaration of Human Rights and article 7 of the International Covenant on Civil and Political Rights," noted "both of those instruments provided that no one shall be subjected to torture or to cruel, inhuman or degrading treatment or punishment."[61]

---

58. International Convention on the Elimination of All Forms of Racial Discrimination, December 21, 1965, http://www.ohchr.org/EN/ProfessionalInterest/Pages/CERD.aspx.

59. International Covenant on Economic, Social and Cultural Rights, December 16, 1966, http://www.ohchr.org/EN/ProfessionalInterest/Pages/CESCR.aspx.

60. Convention on the Elimination of All Forms of Discrimination against Women, December 19, 1979, http://www.ohchr.org/Documents/ProfessionalInterest/cedaw.pdf.

61. Convention against Torture and Other Cruel, Inhuman, or Degrading Treatment or Punishment, December 10, 1984, http://www.ohchr.org/EN/ProfessionalInterest/Pages/CAT.aspx.

International Humanitarian Law: Five Key Dynamics

The Convention on the Rights of the Child, which entered into force in 1989, recognized that the U.N. has "proclaimed and agreed that everyone is entitled to all the rights and freedoms set forth therein, without distinction of any kind, such as race, colour, sex, language, religion, political or other opinion, national or social origin, property, birth or other status."[62]

Article 7 of the UDHR provides that "[a]ll are entitled to equal protection against any discrimination in violation of this Declaration and against any incitement to such discrimination."[63] Article 8 provides that "[e]veryone has the right to an effective remedy by the competent national tribunals for acts violating the fundamental rights granted him by the constitution or by law."[64] While there is no specified, direct international enforcement mechanism for violations of the UDHR, requests may go to the United Nations and its Office of the High Commissioner for Human Rights office to act for humanity with respect to a finding that violation of international human rights law and the disregard for human rights has taken place.[65] States may provide remedies for gross human rights violations, especially those established by the status of *Jus Cogens* or obligations *Erga Omnes*; failing that, the universal human rights set forth in the UDHR, and as amplified and clarified in other treaties and conventions, and in custom, become universally enforceable and protectable by states individually or collectively through the U.N. Security Council, the European Union, and other regional and global alliances to promote human rights and sanction violations.[66]

On December 10, 2004, the General Assembly of the United Nations "proclaimed the World Programme for Human Rights Education (2005–ongoing) to advance the implementation of human

---

62. Convention on the Rights of the Child, November 20, 1989, http://www.ohchr.org/en/professionalinterest/pages/crc.aspx.
63. The Universal Declaration of Human Rights, http://www.un.org/en/universal-declaration-human-rights/.
64. Ibid.
65. United Nations Human Rights Office of the High Commissioner, "Human Rights Council Complaint Procedure," http://www.ohchr.org/EN/HRBodies/HRC/ComplaintProcedure/Pages/HRCComplaintProcedureIndex.aspx.
66. See, e.g., M. Cherif Bassiouni, "International Crimes: Jus Cogens and Obligation Erga Omnes," *Law and Contemporary Problems* 59:4 (1966).

rights education programmes in all sectors."[67] This was done to meet both the spirit of the UDHR Preamble and the letter of Article 26 regarding the role of education in developing the person spiritually as well as intellectually. "Everyone has the right to education . . . free, at least in the elementary and fundamental stages" and "[e]ducation shall be directed to the full development of the human personality and to the strengthening of respect for human rights and fundamental freedoms," such that "[p]arents have a prior right to choose the kind of education that shall be given to their children."[68]

The right to food is set forth in Article 25's statement that "[e]veryone has the right to a standard of living adequate for the health and well-being of himself and of his family, including food, clothing, housing and medical care and necessary social services, and the right to security in the event of unemployment, sickness, disability, widowhood, old age or other lack of livelihood in circumstances beyond his control."[69] In the spirit of the UDHR, the Universal Declaration on the Eradication of Hunger and Malnutrition (1974) solemnly proclaimed that:

> Every man, woman and child has the inalienable right to be free from hunger and malnutrition in order to develop fully and maintain their physical and mental faculties. Society today already possesses sufficient resources, organizational ability and technology and hence the competence to achieve this objective. Accordingly, the eradication of hunger is a common objective of all the countries of the international community, especially of the developed countries and others in a position to help.[70]

Where there is no meaningful spiritual or intellectual growth possible without basic human needs being met, there are new challenges to freedom of faith and religion. The world's ever-increasing population challenged by natural and man-made constraints and imped-

---

67. United Nations Human Rights Office of the High Commissioner, "World Programme for Human Rights Education (2005–ongoing)," http://www.ohchr.org/EN/Issues/Education/Training/Pages/Programme.aspx.

68. UDHR.

69. Ibid.

70. Universal Declaration on the Eradication of Hunger and Malnutrition, December 17, 1973, http://www.ohchr.org/EN/ProfessionalInterest/Pages/EradicationOfHungerAndMalnutrition.aspx.

International Humanitarian Law: Five Key Dynamics

iments to the production, distribution, and consumption of nutritionally adequate foodstuffs and clean water, may well cause individuals and groups to challenge others' and nations' actions affecting food and nutrition as fundamental human rights violations.

The scourge of human trafficking continues even in the twenty-first century, and amongst other agreements and conventions proscribing human trafficking, especially but not exclusively are those related to trafficking for purposes of sex. The Protocol to Prevent, Suppress and Punish Trafficking in Persons, Especially Women and Children, supplementing the United Nations Convention against Transnational Organized Crime (2000), exhorted that human trafficking violates women's and children's right to life, liberty and security of person,[71] where such a fundamental individual right to life, liberty, and security of person is reflected in Article 3 of the UDHR[72] and Article 6 of the International Covenant on Civil and Political Rights (ICCPR).[73] Notwithstanding that one hundred and thirty-four countries and territories have criminalized trafficking under the Protocol, according to the latest Global Report on Trafficking in Persons, the most common form of human trafficking (58 percent) is sexual exploitation, and women make up the largest proportion of trafficking victims (55–60 percent globally, with women and girls together accounting for 75 percent).[74] The second most common form of human trafficking is forced labor (36 percent). It also reports that 27 percent of all trafficking victims are children.

The Office of the High Commissioner for U.N. Human Rights recognizes that persons with disabilities face discrimination and barriers that restrict them from participating in society on an equal basis with others every day. The Convention on the Rights of Persons with

---

71. Protocol to Prevent, Suppress and Punish Trafficking in Persons, Especially Women and Children, supplementing the United Nations Convention against Transnational Organized Crime, November 15, 2000, https://www.unodc.org/unodc/treaties/CTOC/.

72. UDHR.

73. International Covenant on Civil and Political Rights, December 16, 1966, http://www.ohchr.org/en/professionalinterest/pages/ccpr.aspx.

74. United Nations, "Global Report on Trafficking in Persons" (2012), 9, 35, https://www.unodc.org/documents/data-and-analysis/glotip/Trafficking_in_Persons_2012_web.pdf.

Disabilities[75] signaled a "'paradigm shift' from traditional charity-oriented, medical-based approaches to disability to one based on human rights"[76] and offered "sufficient standards of protection for the civil, cultural, economic, political and social rights of persons with disabilities on the basis of inclusion, equality and non-discrimination."[77] Additionally, the Optional Protocol on the Convention came into force at the same time as the Convention.[78] It gave the Committee of experts additional capacities to advance the UDHR's Article 25 recognitions that "[e]veryone has the right to a standard of living adequate for the health and well-being of himself and of his family, including food, clothing, housing and medical care and necessary social services, and the right to security in the event of unemployment, sickness, disability, widowhood, old age or other lack of livelihood in circumstances beyond his control."[79]

Most directly on point with regards to religious freedom and belief, or the lack thereof, under Article 18 of the UDHR, "[e]veryone has the right to freedom of thought, conscience and religion; this right includes freedom to change his religion or belief, either alone or in community with others and in public or private, to manifest his religion or belief in teaching, practice, worship and observance."[80] Some secular humanists and atheists may object in principle or practice to the UDHR's Article 18 principles, but a more clearly defined religious tension resulted in a parallel declaration with religious influence. On June 30, 2000, members of the Organisation of the Islamic Conference (now the Organisation of Islamic Cooperation) officially resolved to support the Cairo Declaration on Human Rights in Islam (CDHRI), wherein persons have "freedom and right to a dignified life in accordance with the Islamic Shari'ah," without any discrimination on grounds of "race, colour, language, sex, reli-

---

75. Convention on the Rights of Persons with Disabilities, December 13, 2006, https://www.un.org/development/desa/disabilities/convention-on-the-rights-of-persons-with-disabilities.html.

76. United Nations Human Rights Office of the High Commissioner, "Human rights of persons with disabilities," http://www.ohchr.org/EN/Issues/Disability/Pages/DisabilityIndex.aspx.

77. Ibid.
78. Ibid.
79. UDHR.
80. Ibid.

International Humanitarian Law: Five Key Dynamics

gious belief, political affiliation, social status or other considerations."[81] In addition to the fact that non-state criminal, terrorist actors often flaunt national and international standards of human rights, the CDHRI has been criticized for being implemented by a set of states with widely disparate religious policies and practices who had "a shared interest in disarming international criticism of their domestic human rights record."[82]

Conclusion

The August 26, 1789, Declaration of the Rights of Man and of the Citizen, a fundamental document of the French Revolution, affirmed that all men possess certain universal rights, valid at all times and in every place.[83] Just over 159 years later, George C. Marshall recalled the impact of that document and exhorted the United Nations General Assembly to "adopt approval of a new Declaration of Human Rights for free men in a free world."[84]

Translated into 369 languages and dialects from Abkhaz to Zulu, the UDHR set a world record in 2009 for being the most translated document in the world. At the time of this chapter's writing, a new report by the Global Citizenship Commission (GCC), under the leadership of former British Prime Minister Gordon Brown, affirmed the continuing relevance and inspirational force of the UDHR, and sought further recognition and respect for human rights for all citizens of the world today.[85] The legal precedents outlined above in this

---

81. The Cairo Declaration on Human Rights in Islam, August 5, 1990, http://www.ohchr.org/EN/Issues/Education/Training/Compilation/Pages/2TheCairoDeclarationonHumanRightsinIslam(1990).aspx.

82. Eva Brems, *Human Rights: Universality and Diversity* (2001), 259.

83. Declaration of the Rights of Man, August 26, 1789, http://avalon.law.yale.edu/18th_century/rightsof.asp.

84. George C. Marshall, Speech to the United Nations General Assembly, September 23, 1948, https://www.google.com/url?sa=t&rct=j&q=&esrc=s&source=web&cd=1&ved=0ahUKEwimq5DO8aDOAhUGKx4KHQUIADIQFggeMAA&url=http%3A%2F%2Fmarshallfoundation.org%2Flibrary%2Fwp-content%2Fuploads%2Fsites%2F16%2F2015%2F01%2F48.09.23-Spee ch-to-UN-GA.doc&usg=AFQjCNER7dd RqlvX3lKevdZRoNAM_Ta7Eg&sig2 =4UN vpiPhf3RwAjeblm5w1g.

85. Kevin Govern, "Human rights and security in U.S. history," oupblog.com, December 9, 2015, http://blog.oup.com/2015/12/human-rights-and-security-in-us-hi story/.

chapter hopefully will continue to be used as a shield to preserve, protect, and defend the rights of people everywhere for religious freedom and belief, including but not limited to Christians, and as a sword against restriction and oppression. In the words of Marshall, toward this end:

> In the modern world the association of free men within a free state is based upon the obligation of citizens to respect the rights of their fellow citizens. And the association of free nations in a free world is based upon the obligation of all states to respect the rights of other nations.[86]

---

86. Marshall, supra note 84.

Erbil, Iraq. Christian IDP camp, 2017. This woman was without family and in process of moving from her fourth resettlement site in 18 months.

Qaraqosh, Iraq. Church of the Immaculate Conception, Iraq's largest church (January, 2017).

5

Sexual Violence as a Tactic of Terror: The Plight of Christian Women and Girls

Jane F. Adolphe

THE PURPOSE of this chapter is to give an overview of key problems and legal issues concerning possible responses to the systematic sexual violence against Christian women and children, in armed conflicts, by Islamic extremists. This chapter concentrates on legal and policy responses. It is beyond the scope of this chapter to give an exhaustive study of the issues, but the author hopes that it complements the work of other authors in this book who deal with related topics. The chapter is divided into five parts. Part I gives a brief overview of how sexual violence has become a tactic of terror. Part II discusses the misconception that Christian women and children have been virtually free from sexual violence due to the special status in the Islamic religion preserved for Jewish and Christian communities, who are otherwise known as People of the Book. Part III presents a case study concerning the abductions of Christian girls in Nigeria, namely the Chibok schoolgirls, by an extremist Islamic group known as Boko Haram. Part IV gives an overview of the International Policy Framework regarding sexual violence and the United Nations (U.N.) Security Council resolutions on the thematic issue of women, peace, and security. It then discusses what the Nigerian government has done in this regard. Part V discusses sexual violence and the International Legal Framework in relation to three areas of international law: international humanitarian law, international human rights law, and international criminal law and then considers the efforts of the Nigerian government.

Sexual Violence as a Tactic of Terror

Sexual violence is a term that can refer to different types of crimes including rape, sexual enslavement, forced pregnancy, forced prostitution, and so forth. These crimes are motivated in times of armed conflict for a number of reasons (e.g., a spoils of war mentality, troop mollification, and humiliation of enemy fighters). This chapter deals with sexual violence as a means to inflict terror upon a population forcing them to flee, including any genocidal strategy that inflicts life-threatening bodily and mental harm imposed to bring about, in whole or in part, the destruction of a group of people.

In June 2016, the Special Representative of the U.N. Secretary-General on Sexual Violence before the United Nations Security Council underlined that sexual violence may not only be a tactic of war, but also of terror. In her written statement, the Special Representative stated: "[I]slamic extremists know that to populate a territory, and control a population, you must first control the bodies of women."[1] In other words, their bodies are virtually converted into "biological weapons."[2] She continued: "Sexual violence is not merely incidental, but integral, to their ideology and strategic objectives. They are using sexual violence as a means of advancing political, military, and economic ends," and in some cases, as a tool of genocide.[3]

According to a "theology of rape,"[4] the capture and enslavement of the "infidel" woman and child comes with the conquest of new territory, where systematic rape, enslavement, and trafficking in them are religiously justified, codified, and regulated.[5] The Report of the Special Representative concluded that the mere threats of sexual violence

---

1. Statement of Zainab Hawa Bangura, Special Representative of the Secretary-General on Sexual Violence in Conflict, Security Council Open Debate on Sexual Violence in Conflict, June 2, 2016.

2. Security Council, Report of the Secretary-General on conflict-related sexual violence, S/2016/361 April 20, 2016, para. 14.

3. Ibid.

4. See e.g., Rukmini Callimachi, "ISIS Enshrines a Theology of Rape," *New York Times*, August 14, 2015.

5. S/2016/361, para. 21.

Sexual Violence as a Tactic of Terror

can push people to flee, culminating in forced displacement, while the offer of wives as sex slaves can attract men and boys, resulting in an effective recruitment strategy for fighters.[6] Moreover, millions of dollars can be generated to finance the ongoing conflict through the trafficking of women and girls in open slave markets and on on-line forums, according to price-lists that regulate their sale.[7] Lastly, in countries in which men, not women, confer nationality and religion upon their children, women can "alter the demography of a region" and "unravel existing kinship ties."[8] All of this, in turn, has not only negative effects on the victim, who suffers from medical and psychological problems if she lives through the ordeal, but the children born as a result of rape also suffer since they are usually left unregistered and stateless, viewed as the enemy, a future threat, or a terrible memory.[9] In addition, due to "stigma and religious norms," most victims of sexual violence are reluctant to speak out and to return to their communities for fear they will be rejected as a "source of dishonor." Moreover, the life situation of internally displaced persons in camps, in countries such as Nigeria, is particularly grim due to the lack of essentials (e.g., food, water, shelter, basic medical care) and human trafficking concerns.[10]

The Specific Problem Facing Christian Women and Girls

Although the number of persecuted Christians continues to rise, with estimates over 150 million,[11] the word "Christian" has been notably absent from many regional and international discussions concerning radical Islam and the atrocities committed against women and chil-

---

6. Ibid., para. 19.
7. Ibid.
8. Ibid., para. 14.
9. Ibid., para. 16.
10. Ibid., para. 86; See also International Organization for Migration, "Over 1.4 Million now Displaced in Six States in Northeast Nigeria," May 1, 2015, https://www.iom.int/news/iom-over-14-million-now-displaced-six-states-northeast-nigeria; *see also* Lauren Jekowsky, Oliver Kaplan, "Beyond Boko Haram: Nigeria's Human Trafficking Problem," *The National Interest*, May 19, 2014.
11. Jean-Michel di Falco, Timothy Radcliffe, Andrea Riccardi, *Il Libro Nero Della Condizione Dei Christiani Nel Mondo* (Mandadori: 2014), 3.

dren of religious minorities. Pope Francis changed the tone of the conversation when, on November 25, 2014, he underlined the atrocities committed against Christians in his Address to the European Parliament, wherein he stated:

> Here I cannot fail to recall the many instances of injustice and persecution which daily afflict religious minorities and Christians in particular, in various parts of our world. Communities and individuals today find themselves subjected to barbaric acts of violence: they are evicted from their homes and native lands, sold as slaves, killed, beheaded, crucified or burned alive, under the shameful and complicit silence of so many.[12]

The moment was short-lived, however. In the hours and days following the address, this particularly colorful description, which oozed with violence, usually a selling point for the secular media, did not feature in the press. If little has been said about the plight of Christians *per se*, even less has been mentioned concerning the legal issues associated with widespread and systematic sexual violence.

The deadly calm, in some quarters, is of considerable importance for consideration of legal issues surrounding Christian persecution. After all, any attempt to respond to a problem through legal means, requires the prior acknowledgement that the particular problem exists. Such indifference to the sufferings of Christian communities, in general, and Christian women and girls, in particular, is due to a number of reasons. One among them is the misconception that Christians have special protections associated with the possibility of paying an Islamic tax, known as the *jizya*. For example, in a *New York Times* article devoted to the "theology of rape" as a justification for systematic rape of women and children by the terrorist group Islamic State of Iraq and Al-Sham (ISIS), the authors focused only on Yazidi women and girls and emphasized that unlike Jews and Christians, "People of the Book," the Yazidis have no possibility of paying a tax to be freed from their captors since they are viewed as polytheists with an oral tradition as opposed to a written one.[13] But is this analysis of the ISIS tax accurate?

---

12. Pope Francis, "Address to The European Parliament," Strasbourg, France, November 25, 2014.

13. See e.g., Callimachi, "ISIS Enshrines a Theology of Rape."

Sexual Violence as a Tactic of Terror

As explained in chapter one of this book, Nina Shea, Director of Hudson Institute's Center for Religious Freedom, sees the ISIS *jizya* as a "fiction." She describes any payment to ISIS under the rubric of *jizya* as a form of "ransom or extortion" because Christians are not afforded the basic guarantees under the traditional *jizya* arrangement, namely those associated with protection of their lives, property, and right to Christian religious observance. She laments that media attention has focused largely on the enslavement of the Yazidis, when many Christian women and girls have also been taken as sex slaves by ISIS, in accordance with ISIS rules allowing sexual enslavement of Christians. In support of this proposition she points to "Dabiq," the magazine published by ISIS, which explicitly approved the enslavement of Christian girls in Nigeria.

In terms of the plight of Christian women, Shea underlines the problem of unreported cases and the general lack of evidence in determining the numbers of Christian women and girls who are victims of sexual violence. On the other hand, an incontrovertible situation that demonstrates systematic sexual violence against them concerns the kidnapping and sexual enslavement of 276 Christian schoolgirls in Nigeria by Boko Haram, a terrorist organization that collaborates with ISIS[14] and shares its "tactics, techniques, and procedures."[15] Since this incident clearly shows the attacks on Christian women and children, it will be used as a case study.

Case Study: The Enslavement of Christian Schoolgirls in Nigeria

During the night of April 14, 2014, about 276 schoolgirls were ripped from their dormitory beds at gunpoint, loaded into trucks, and taken away as their school and village were torched.[16] Around 53 children

---

14. Jim Muir, "Nigeria's Boko Haram Pledges Allegiance to the Islamic State," *BBC News*, March 7, 2015 ("The step came as no surprise, given evidence in Boko Haram's propaganda output of growing IS influence on the Nigerian movement, whose ideology and harsh practices mirror those of IS itself."); See also "Islamic State 'accepts' Boko Haram's Allegiance Pledge," *BBC News*, March 13, 2015.

15. Helene Cooper, "Boko Haram and ISIS Are Collaborating More, U.S. Military Says," *New York Times*, April 20, 2016.

16. Aminu Abubakar, Factsheet: "How many schoolgirls did Boko Haram abduct and how many are still missing?" *Premium Timesng.com,* June 4, 2016.

escaped, some by jumping from the trucks.[17] They had previously gathered together to attend final exams at the government high school, in Chibok, Borno State, located in Northeastern Nigeria.[18] The majority of the girls were Christian.[19]

On May 5, 2014, the leader of Boko Haram, an Islamic jihadist and terrorist organization, based in northeast Nigeria, claimed responsibility for the abductions.[20] The phrase "Boko Haram," loosely translated as "Western education is forbidden," deliberately targets Christians.[21] For example, in 2012, a spokesperson for Boko Haram reportedly stated: "We will create so much effort to end the Christian presence in our push to have a proper Islamic State that Christians won't be able to stay."[22] In specific regard to women and girls, one journalist has explained the twisted logic of Boko Haram in the following terms: "Women are the property of Allah and [Boko Haram] is waging [its] campaign on behalf of Allah. Therefore, when women fall into [Boko Haram's] grip, they become [its] property to dispose of as [it] thinks Allah would wish. The Chibok girls had offended Allah by (a) being Christian and (b) going to school."[23] One might

---

17. Ibid.
18. Opening Statement by Zeid Ra'ad Al Hussein, United Nations High Commissioner for Human Rights, at the 23rd Special Session of the Human Rights Council, April 1, 2015.
19. Adam Nossiter, "Tales of Escapees in Nigeria Add to Worries About Other Kidnapped Girls," *The New York Times*, May 15, 2014 ("Most of the Chibok residents are Christians of a small minority group who speak Kibaku, another of Nigeria's myriad languages."); David Smith, "Military operation launched to locate kidnapped Nigerian girls," *The Guardian*, May 14, 2014 ("Although most of the abducted girls are Christian, all were wearing Muslim dress and two were singled out to say they had converted to Islam."); "Nigeria abduction video: Schoolgirls 'recognised,'" BBC, May 13, 2014 ("The girls' families have said that most of those seized are Christians, although there are a number of Muslims among them.").
20. "Boko Haram 'to sell' Nigeria girls abducted from Chibok," *BBC News*, May 5, 2014.
21. Deacon Keith Fournier, "Majority of Kidnapped Girls in Nigeria Christians: Is Boko Haram Engaged in a War Against Christians?" Catholic Online, May 11, 2014.
22. Ibid.
23. David Blair, "Nigeria's Boko Haram isn't just kidnapping girls: it's enslaving them," *Telegraph*, January 13, 2015. See also "Boko Haram 'to sell' Nigeria girls abducted from Chibok," *BBC News*, May 5, 2014; Tim Lister, "Boko Haram: The essence of terror," CNN, May 6, 2014.

also offer a third reason, namely that the girls were over the age of nine and unmarried.

Frequently, the Boko Haram leader talks about finding husbands for the girls or marrying them off. But clearly, the term "marriage" in such circumstances is a "euphemism for systematic rape."[24] As one prominent Catholic nun pointed out in a recent interview, "This is not marriage. They are being given in sex slavery. This is human trafficking. We should call evil by its name."[25] Indeed, the brutal reality was fully exposed when two of the girls were found "defiled and bloody, tethered to a tree," left to die in the sweltering heat, after being beaten and raped.[26] Another four were shot for being uncooperative and were buried in shallow graves.[27] Other girls are now pregnant, while most, if not all of them, suffer from psychological and physical injuries.[28]

At least two weeks passed in the United States before any real media attention focused on the tragedy;[29] the social media campaign was eventually commenced and, while helpful, had little success in pushing governments to act.[30] Indeed, one hundred days after the capture, Emmanuel Ogebe, a human rights lawyer was quoted as saying: "Boko Haram is waging a relentless war against Nigeria's Christians and the world is doing nothing to stop it. The abduction of these innocent schoolgirls is a tragedy that has upset millions across the globe, and yet our governments are incapable of rescuing them."[31]

---

24. Charlotte Alter, "How We Failed the Lost Girls Kidnapped by Boko Haram," *Time.com*, May 2, 2014.

25. Ibid., See also Forest Whitaker, "Sister Rosemary Nyirumbe," *Time.com*, April 23, 2014.

26. Barbara Jones, "Defiled and bloody, tethered to a tree, school uniforms ripped: The moment I rescued two girls from Boko Haram," *Daily Mail*, May 17, 2014.

27. Ibid.

28. Ibid.

29. Mary Elizabeth Williams, "Why is the media ignoring 200 missing girls?" *Salon.com*, April 30, 2014; Charlotte Alter, "How We Failed the Lost Girls Kidnapped by Boko Haram," *Time.com*, May 2, 2014.

30. Adam Taylor, "Is #BringBackOurGirls helping?" *Washington Post*, May 6, 2014.

31. Katie Gorka, "100 Days a Slave: The Christian Girls Kidnapped by Boko Haram," *Breitbart.com*, July 24, 2014.

Persecution & Genocide of Christians in the Middle East

On April 1, 2015, at a special session convened by the United Nations Human Rights Council to address the terrorist attacks, human rights abuses, and other violations committed by Boko Haram, the United Nations Office of High Commissioner for Human Rights (OHCHR) underlined the following points. Since 2009, at least 15,000 individuals have been killed by Boko Haram, including women and children who "have been targeted for particularly horrific abuse, including sexual enslavement," forced labor, and compulsory conversion.[32] Entire villages and towns have been destroyed, and "Boko Haram has a specific animus against schools—particularly the education of girls—and its attacks have destroyed or severely damaged at least 300 schools, killed numerous students, and ended with the abduction of hundreds of schoolgirls."[33] Most importantly, the OHCHR emphasized that the "extremist and totalitarian ideology of Boko Haram targeted Christian communities."[34]

After a surprising delay on the part of its president, Nigeria fully engaged its governmental forces and eventually began working in collaboration with other governments as well as regional and international institutions.[35] However, the terrorist activities continued and the government and its allies have been ineffective in stopping similar atrocities or finding the girls.[36]

Key officials of the United Nations have continued to make statements and call for reports. In April 2015, the United Nations Secretary-General Ban Ki-moon reiterated a call for the girls' "immediate release and safe return to their families" after emphasizing that "going to school should not have to be an act of bravery."[37] The pres-

32. Zeid Ra'ad Al Hussein, United Nations High Commissioner for Human Rights.
33. Ibid.
34. Ibid.
35. Afolabi Sotunde. See the Opening Statement by Al Hussein ("In recent weeks, military offensives by Nigeria, Cameroon, Chad and Niger have led to the recapture of several towns in northeast Nigeria."); see also the United Nations Security Council, Presidential Statement of the United Nations Security Council, S/P RST/2015/4, January 19, 2015.
36. Adam Nossiter, "Boko Haram Abducted Nigerian Girls One Year Ago," *The New York Times*, April 14, 2015.
37. Statement by the United Nations Secretary-General, "On the One-Year Anniversary of the Abduction of Schoolgirls in Chibok, North-eastern Nigeria," New York, April 14, 2015.

Sexual Violence as a Tactic of Terror

ident of the United Nations Security Council also renewed a demand for their "immediate and unconditional release."[38] In June 2016, Ban Ki-moon described the abductions as the "most horrific examples of the use of sexual violence as a tactic of terrorism."[39]

The Special Representative of the United Nations Secretary-General on Sexual Violence in Conflict warned against a "culture of denial and silence"[40] that failed to denounce sexual violence as a tactic of terror specifically waged against religious and ethnic minorities.[41] She contended that "[s]exual violence in conflict represents a great moral issue of our time, and it merits the concerted focus of the Security Council."[42] The report concluded that the year under review was "marked by harrowing accounts of rape, sexual slavery, and forced marriage being used by extremist groups, including as a tactic of terror."[43] The recommendations for the Nigerian government included suggestions to implement its national action plan regarding Security Council Resolution 1325 (2000),[44] guarantee security of internally

---

38. "Presidential Statement of the United Nations Security Council," supra note 35.

39. Secretary-General, "Other speakers in Security Council Voice Concern over Evolution of Sexual Violence into Tactics of Terrorism," United Nations Meetings Coverage and News, 7704th Meeting (AM), Security Council, June 2, 2016, SC/12386.

40. "Emerging Threats Demand Renewed Fight Against Sexual Violence in Conflict: U.N. Envoy," *UN News*, April 14, 2015.

41. Interview with Zainab Hawa Bangura, Special Representative of the Secretary-General, on "Sexual Violence in Conflict," *UN News*, April 14, 2015; see also United Nations Security Council, "Report of the Secretary-General on Conflict-Related Sexual Violence" (S/2015/203) March 23, 2015.

42. "Fight against Sexual Violence in Conflict Reaches 'New Juncture,' Security Council Told," *UN News*, April 15, 2015; See also ibid., "Report of the Secretary-General on Conflict-related Sexual Violence," 2 ("The term 'conflict-related sexual violence', which appears throughout the present report, refers to rape, sexual slavery, forced prostitution, forced pregnancy, enforced sterilization and other forms of sexual violence of comparable gravity perpetrated against women, men, girls or boys that is linked, directly or indirectly (temporally, geographically or causally) to a conflict. This link may be evident in the profile of the perpetrator; the profile of the victim; in a climate of impunity or State collapse; in the cross-border dimensions; and/or in violations of the terms of a ceasefire agreement").

43. Ibid., "Report of the Secretary-General on Conflict-related sexual violence," 1.

44. Ibid., 81.

displaced persons in camps, and extend medical and psychosocial services.⁴⁵

Upon the request of the Permanent Representative of Algeria, on behalf of the African Group, the Human Rights Council convened a special session "in light of the terrorist attacks and human rights abuses and violations committed by the terrorist group Boko Haram."⁴⁶ The Algerian submission was originally supported by eighteen States Members of the Council as well as four Observer States.⁴⁷ The Special Session culminated in the Human Rights Council Resolution on the "Atrocities committed by the terrorist group Boko Haram and its effects on human rights in the affected States."⁴⁸ It strongly condemned the "cowardly abduction by Boko Haram" of the schoolgirls in the city of Chibok and demanded their release.⁴⁹ In addition, it condemned "the gross abuses of international human rights law and violations of international humanitarian law" and called for the "the perpetrators of the heinous crimes" to be brought to justice before the "competent courts of the affected States."⁵⁰ It also requested that the OHCHR collect information in order to prepare a report on the said violations and abuses for the purposes of legal accountability. In addition, it called for "increased collaboration of the international community . . . to monitor and dry up all possi-

---

45. Ibid.

46. Letter dated March 26, 2015 from the Permanent Representative of Algeria to the United Nations Office at Geneva addressed to the President of the Human Rights Council, A.HRC.S-23/1. See also Note Verbale sent by the Secretariat of the Human Rights Council on March 26, 2015, giving notice of the Twenty-third special session of the Human Rights Council, Geneva, April 1, 2015 (wherein it states that the Special Session was held on Wednesday, April 1, 2015, after meeting the requirements for a special session to be convened in accordance with operative paragraph 10 of General Assembly resolution 60/251, which necessitates the support of one-third of the membership of the Council, that is, sixteen members or more).

47. Ibid., Botswana, Brazil, Congo, Côte d'Ivoire, Ethiopia, France, Gabon, Ghana, Kenya, Morocco, Namibia, Nigeria, Pakistan, Paraguay, Russian Federation, Sierra Leone, South Africa, and Bolivarian Republic of Venezuela. The observer states were Cameroon, Central African Republic, Djibouti, and Mozambique.

48. Human Rights Council Resolution on Atrocities committed by the terrorist group Boko Haram and its effects on human rights in the affected States, A/HRC/Res/S-23/1 May 21, 2015.

49. Ibid., preamble para. 20.

50. Ibid., paras. 1 and 7.

Sexual Violence as a Tactic of Terror

ble sources of financing."[51] Lastly, it entreated the OHCHR to remain engaged with the matter to provide oral and written updates in subsequent sessions of the Human Rights Council.[52] It also requested a report from the OHCHR "on violations and abuses of human rights and atrocities . . . with a view towards [legal] accountability."[53]

Six different Special Rapporteurs gave a joint statement deploring the abduction of the schoolchildren.[54] They emphasized that many had "been forced to convert, [and] suffer horrifying abuse during their captivity ranging from forced labour to forced marriage, rape, slavery, trafficking, torture, and killings."[55] They also warned that such acts "could amount to crimes against humanity."[56] The statement did not mention that the girls were Christian, and the participation of the Special Rapporteur on Freedom of Religion and Belief is conspicuously missing.[57]

The United Nations Children Fund (UNICEF) released a brief or report entitled "Missing Childhoods: The impact of armed conflict on children in Nigeria and beyond," which repeated what the international community has long known: that "children have become deliberate targets, often subjected to extreme violence—from sexual abuse and forced marriage to brutal killings."[58]

---

51. "Human Rights Council Condemns Gross Abuse Perpetrated by Terrorist Group Boko Haram," *UN News*, April 1, 2015.

52. Ibid., operative para. 9 (the oral update was to be given as part of an interactive dialogue to be held at the twenty-ninth session of the Human Rights Council, and the written report was to be submitted for consideration at the thirtieth session).

53. Ibid.

54. Office of High Commission for Human Rights, "Nigeria: One Year on, UN and African experts call for decisive steps to bring back abducted children." Geneva, *UN News*, April 13, 2015. (The joint statement was given by the following experts: 1) Special Rapporteur on the sale of children, child prostitution, and child pornography; 2) Special Rapporteur on contemporary forms of slavery, including its causes and consequences; 3) Special Rapporteur on violence against women, its causes and consequences; 4) Special Rapporteur on trafficking in persons, especially women and children; 5) Chair-Rapporteur of the Working Group on the issue of discrimination against women in law and in practice; and 6) Special Rapporteur on Rights of Women in Africa of the African Commission on Human and Peoples' Rights.)

55. Ibid.

56. Ibid.

57. Ibid.

58. UNICEF, "Missing Childhoods: The impact of armed conflict on children in Nigeria and beyond" (April 2015).

By April 2015, many feared that the majority of girls were dead. The head of the United Nations Office of High Commissioner for Human Rights reported to the Human Rights Council on the "gruesome scenes of mass graves and further evident signs of slaughter by Boko Haram,"[59] and emphasized the "multiple reports" that retreating Boko Haram fighters had "murdered their so-called 'wives'—[that is], women and girls held in slavery."[60] Later, the High Commissioner expressed pessimism about finding the Christian schoolgirls alive.[61] In May 2015, the Nigerian military released about 700 persons held in captivity by the militants, but none of the girls were among this group.[62] One year later, in April 2016, news reports lamented the failure to find the girls.[63] The next month, one Chibok victim was rescued.[64] The rest were purportedly still alive, "somewhere in the Sambisa forest where Boko Haram members have been hiding out"; then, in October 2016, twenty-one girls were freed, and in May 2017, about another eighty-two of the schoolgirls were released in exchange for detained members of Boko Haram.[65] As this book goes to press, about 250 schoolgirls remain missing.

International Policy Framework

U.N. Security Council Resolutions on Women, Peace, & Security

The year 2015 marked the fifteenth anniversary year of Resolution

---

59. Opening Statement by Zeid Ra'ad Al Hussein, United Nations High Commissioner for Human Rights, at the 23rd Special Session of the Human Rights Council, April 1, 2015; see also Hortensia Honorati, "Nigeria, Boko Haram Kidnapped 200 Girl students in Chibok: Slaughter feared," *In Terris*, April 9, 2015.

60. Opening Statement by Zeid Ra'ad Al Hussein.

61. Ibid.

62. "Nigeria: Hundreds of Boko Haram Captives Freed," *R&E*, May 8, 2015.

63. CRUX staff, "Two Years on, fate of Nigeria's Chibok Girls remains a Mystery," *CRUX*, April 15, 2016.

64. Chris Stein and Dionne Stearcey, "Another Chibok Victim kidnapped by Boko Haram is found, Nigeria Says," *New York Times*, May 19, 2016; see also Chris Stein, "A Girl rescued in Nigeria was not taken in Chibok Kidnapping," *New York Times*, May 20, 2016. (Two victims were reported to have been rescued, but Stein later corrected his report, explaining that only one of the victims was at the Chibok school when the kidnapping occurred.)

65. Stein and Stearcey, "Another Chibok Victim"; Chris Stein and Dionne Stearcey, "Boko Haram frees 21 schoolgirls from group abducted in Chibok," *Guardian*, October 13, 2016; "Boko Haram releases…," *Guardian*, May 16, 2017.

Sexual Violence as a Tactic of Terror

1325, the first resolution devoted to women, peace, and security adopted by the United Nations (U.N.) Security Council. Resolution 1325 was adopted during the same year that the U.N. General Assembly was conducting a five-year review process of the strategic objectives adopted at the 1995 Fourth World Conference on Women in Beijing, which produced the non-binding outcome document: The Beijing Platform for Action.[66] By way of background, the Platform for Action underlined, among other things, that women and girls are particularly affected in situations of armed conflict due to their "status in society and their sex"; it also lamented that parties to the conflict often rape women "with impunity, sometimes using systematic rape as a tactic of war and terrorism."[67] The Platform for Action also emphasized that: sexual violence against refugees and displaced persons had been employed as a "method of persecution in systematic campaigns of terror and intimidation ... forcing members of a particular ethnic, cultural or religious group to flee their homes."[68] On a positive note, it was acknowledged that during times of armed conflict women worked to preserve social order and made "important but often unrecognized contribution as peace educators both in their families and in their societies."[69] As a response, the Platform of Action promoted a number of objectives and actions,[70] which included efforts: to increase participation of women in conflict resolution at decision making levels;[71] to reduce incidence of human rights abuse and breaches of humanitarian law in conflict situations;[72]

---

66. Fourth World Conference on Women on Action for Equality, "Development and Peace, Beijing, China 4–15 September 1995," *Report of the Fourth World Conference on Women*, A/CONF./177/20/Rev.1, Annex I: Beijing Declaration and Annex II: Beijing Platform of Action.

67. Platform of Action, 135.

68. Ibid., 136.

69. Ibid., 139.

70. Ibid., 142–49 (In total, the strategic objectives recommended by the report are six-fold: (1) increase the protection of women in situations of armed conflict and promote their participation in the peace process; (2) reduce excessive military spending and control the availability of armaments; (3) promote peaceful resolution of disputes; (4) promote women's contribution to fostering a culture of peace; (5) provide protection, assistance, and training to refugee and displaced women; and (6) provide assistance to women of colonies and non-self-governing territories).

71. Ibid., Strategic Objective E.1, 142.

72. Ibid., Strategic Objective E.3, 144–45.

and to give protection, assistance, education, and training opportunities to women and children, who had become refugees or otherwise displaced.[73]

Resolution 1325 addresses the unique impact of armed conflict on women and children, and stresses the need for women's full and equal participation in all stages of the peace process. It consists of ten preamble paragraphs and eighteen operative paragraphs and makes four key points: (1) *Difference*: women and children are impacted differently than men and boys and have different needs; they constitute the vast majority of those adversely affected by war, as civilian targets, refugees, and internally displaced persons; (2) *Protection*: women and children must be protected through the full implementation of international humanitarian law and international human rights law; (3) *Participation*: women should participate in all aspects of the peace process and ought to have an increased role in decision making; and (4) *Promotion*: gender mainstreaming should be promoted as the tool to bring about increased participation.

In addition, the Resolution calls to action five main target groups: the Security Council, the Secretary-General, member states, all parties to armed conflicts, and all actors involved in any other aspect of the peace process. In particular, the Security Council was expected to incorporate a gender perspective into peacekeeping operations and missions and when exercising its power under Article 41 of the U.N. Charter. The Secretary-General was to prepare a study and implement a plan to increase women's participation at decision-making levels (e.g., as special representatives, envoys to pursue good offices and field-based operations, humanitarian and human rights personnel, civilian police, and military observers).[74] The Secretary-General was also to provide member states with educational materials for peacekeeping operations on the protection of women and children.[75]

Since Resolution 1325 (2000), the Security Council has adopted seven additional resolutions on the thematic issues of "Women, Peace and Security."[76] Each concentrates on a related theme and five

---

73. Ibid., Strategic Objective E.5, 147–48.
74. Ibid., 13–15.
75. Ibid., 17.
76. S/RES/1820 (2008); S/RES/1888 (2009); S/RES/1889 (2009); S/RES/1960 (2010); S/RES/2106 (2013); S/RES/2122 (2013); and S/RES/2242 (2015).

Sexual Violence as a Tactic of Terror

of them treat the specific issue of sexual violence.[77] An article common to four of the five resolutions emphasizes that sexual violence,

> when used or commissioned as a tactic of war in order to deliberately target civilians or as a part of a widespread or systematic attack against civilian populations, can significantly exacerbate situations of armed conflict and may impede the restoration of international peace and security, affirms in this regard that effective steps to prevent and respond to such acts of sexual violence can significantly contribute to the maintenance of international peace and security, and expresses its readiness, when considering situations on the agenda of the Council, to, where necessary, adopt appropriate steps to address widespread or systematic sexual violence.[78]

Articles 3 of Security Council Resolution 1820: "Demands that all parties to armed conflict immediately take appropriate measures to protect civilians, including women and girls, from all forms of sexual violence." Article 4 underlines that rape and other forms of sexual violence can "constitute a war crime, a crime against humanity, or a constitutive act with respect to genocide." Security Council Resolution 2242 focuses on terrorism and sexual violence and emphasizes, in its preamble, the differential impact of terrorism and violent extremism on the human rights of women and girls. It also underlines that women and girls are often the target of terrorist groups, who use acts of sexual violence as part of their strategic objectives and ideology in an effort to increase their power through the financing, recruitment, and destruction of communities.

The resolutions cover a broad range of topics relevant to sexual violence in armed conflict and its aftermath, including the following points: 1) *Prohibition*: all violations against women and girls should be condemned,[79] especially sexual violence,[80] as a tactic of war[81] as well as sexual exploitation and abuse of them by U.N. peacekeep-

---

77. S/RES/1820 (2008); S/RES/1888 (2009); S/RES/1960 (2010); S/RES/2106 (2013); and S/RES/2242 (2015).

78. S/RES/1820 (2008), Art. 1; S/RES/1888 (2009), Art. 1; S/RES/1960 (2010), Art. 1; S/RES/2106 (2013), Art.1.

79. S/RES/2122 (2013); S/RES/1960 (2010); S/RES/1820 (2008).

80. S/RES/2106 (2013); S/RES/1888 (2009); S/RES/1960 (2010).

81. S/RES/2242 (2015); S/RES/2106 (2013); S/RES/1960 (2010); S/RES/1820/(2008); S/RES/1888 (2009).

ers;[82] 2) *Promotion*: U.N. entities should promote gender issues in post-conflict situations,[83] with the assistance of Gender Advisors;[84] 3) *Respect*: international law should be respected;[85] 4) *Participation*: women should participate in conflict prevention, management, and resolution,[86] and in post-conflict electoral processes as well as in United Nations missions,[87] especially as "women protection advisors" (WPAs);[88] 5) *Sanctions*: parties who commit rape should be punished;[89] 6) *Protection*: civilians should be protected by parties to the armed conflict, who bear this primary responsibility;[90] 7) *Prevention*: sexual violence should be prevented through comprehensive strategies, time-bound commitments,[91] and training of peacekeeping personnel;[92] 8) *Reports*: sexual violence should be investigated;[93] 9) *Prosecution*: perpetrators of sexual violence should be prosecuted;[94] 10) *Rehabilitation and reintegration*: women and children should have access to socio-economic and legal assistance as well as medical and psychological care,[95] health care services, including *sexual and reproductive health*,[96] *sexual and reproductive health services*,[97] and *sexual and reproductive health and reproductive rights*;[98]

---

82. S/RES/2106 (2013); S/RES/1960 (2010); S/RES/1820 (2008).
83. S/RES/1888 (2009); S/RES/1889 (2009).
84. S/RES/2122 (2013); S/RES/2106 (2013); S/RES/ 1888 (2009).
85. S/RES/2242 (2015); S/RES/2122 (2013); S/RES/2106 (2013); S/RES/1960 (2010); S/RES/1889 (2009); S/RES/1888(2009).
86. S/RES/2122 (2013); S/RES/2106 (2013); S/RES/1960 (2010); S/RES/1889 (2009); S/RES/1888 (2009); S/RES/1325 (2000).
87. S/RES/2122 (2013); S/RES/2106 (2013); S/RES/1960 (2010); S/RES/1889 (2009); S/RES/1888 (2009); S/RES/1820 (2008); S/RES/1325 (2000).
88. S/RES/1960 (2010); S/RES/1888 (2009)12; S/RES/1889 (2009).
89. S/RES/2242 (2015); S/RES/2106 (2013); S/RES/1960 (2010); S/RES/1888 (2009); S/RES/1820 (2008).
90. S/RES/2122 (2013); S/RES/ 2106 (2013); S/RES/1960 (2010); S/RES/1820 (2008); S/RES/1888 (2009).
91. S/RES/2242 (2015); S/RES/2106 (2013); S/RES/1960 (2010); S/RES/1889 (2009).
92. S/RES/2106 (2013); S/RES/1960 (2010); S/RES/1820 (2008); S/RES/1325 (2000).
93. S/RES/2242 (2015); S/RES/1888 (2009).
94. S/RES/2242 (2015); S/RES/2122 (2013); S/RES/2106 (2013); S/RES/1960 (2010); S/RES/1889 (2009); S/RES/1820 (2008); S/RES/1325 (2000).
95. S/RES/2122 (2013); S/RES/1960 (2010); S/RES/1888 (2009); S/RES/1325 (2000).
96. S/RES/2106 (2013) (emphasis added).
97. S/RES/2122 (2013) (emphasis added).
98. S/RES/1889 (2009) (emphasis added).

11) *Reparations*: victims of violations of international human rights should receive reparations;[99] and 12) *National Plans of Action*: governments should develop policies to implement SCR 1325.[100]

There are many points with which one might agree. On the other hand, States have expressed concern as to the meaning of certain terms (e.g., sexual and reproductive health services and rights) and whether these terms include access to abortion or abortifacients.[101] It is worth noting that such debates are ongoing in the field of international human rights law and international humanitarian law.[102] Perhaps the clearest statement underlining one side of the debate concerning the points of law was made at the World Humanitarian Summit, in 2016, when the Holy See contended that "there is no right to abortion under international human rights law or international humanitarian law."[103] The Holy See also repeated the exhortation of the Secretary-General that States "refrain from expansive and contentious" interpretations of international law. As an alternative to abortion, the Holy See has encouraged "religious institutions and Catholic organizations to accompany victims of rape in crisis situations, who, in turn, need effective and ongoing psychological, spiritual, and material assistance for themselves as well as their children, conceived and born of rape."[104]

With the support of the United Nations organ, U.N. Women, and

---

99. S/RES/2122 (2013).

100. S/RES/2242 (2015); S/RES/2122 (2013).

101. See, for example, Jane Adolphe and Robert L. Fastiggi, "Reproduction and Reproductive Rights (International and Catholic Perspectives)," *New Catholic Encyclopedia Supplement* 2012–13: *Ethics and Philosophy*. ed. Robert L. Fastiggi. 4 vols. Detroit: Gale (2013).

102. See, e.g., the non-binding "San Jose Articles on Abortion and the Unborn Child in International Law," http://www.sanjosearticles.com/?page_id=2; Stéphane Kolanowski, "Protection of Women under International Humanitarian Law," in *Women & War, Women & Armed Conflicts and the Issue of Sexual Violence*, Report of the Colloquium ICRC-EUISS, (September 30, 2014), 21–22; see also Susan Yoshihara, "Abortion and the Laws of War: Suffering Humanitarianism by Executive Edict," *University of St. Thomas Journal of Law and Public Policy*, Vol. IX, No. 1 (Fall 2014).

103. Statement of the Secretary of State of the Holy See, at the Roundtable: "Uphold the norms that safeguard humanity," The World Humanitarian Summit, Istanbul, 24 May 2016, http://www.worldhumanitariansummit.org/roundtable-statements.

104. Ibid.

the non-governmental organization Nigeria Stability and Reconciliation Programme, Nigeria developed its National Action Plan on Women, Peace and Security (NAP).[105] It is a non-binding policy document based upon five pillars: prevention, protection, promotion, participation, and prosecution, each of which is analyzed according to the following criteria: associated activities, progress indicators, expected outcomes, and key governmental actors, which in turn, consider various legal and policy initiatives. For example, NAP underlines that the government enacted the Violence Against Persons (Prohibition) Act, in 2015, which is a comprehensive piece of legislation dealing with violence against women and girls.

Non-governmental networks devoted to women, peace, and security issues have been involved on the domestic level. These groups monitor governmental implementation of NAP and are actively involved in advocacy, in particular regarding the abductions in Chibok. In countries such as Nigeria, where there is much poverty and political corruption as well as inadequate infrastructures and limited access to basic health and education,[106] the implementation of Women, Peace, and Security resolutions are seen as a necessary part of security sector reform and ought to be integrated into defense, police, justice, and military reforms.[107] Finally, were the Nigerian government to enact the bill giving effect to the provisions of the Rome Statute, then, this legislative action would also be in line with the Women, Peace, and Security Resolutions.

According to the 2015 Report of the United Nations High Commissioner for Human Rights, the Nigerian government accomplished a series of objectives such as: setting up committees to study the root causes of the violence and security challenges; commencing an inquiry into alleged international human rights violations by the army and the Civilian Joint Task Force in their counter-terrorism efforts; launching a support fund for victims and an initiative for

---

105. "National Action Plan for the Implementation of UNSCR 1325" (and related resolutions in Nigeria), Nigerian Stability and Reconciliation Stability Programme, http://www.peacewomen.org/assets/file/NationalActionPlans/nigeria_nationalactionplan_2013.pdf.

106. Curbing Violence in Nigeria II: The Boko Haram Insurgency, *International Crisis Group*, Africa Report No. 216, 3 April 2014.

107. See e.g., Megan Bastick, Daniel de Torres, *Implementing the Women, Peace and Security Resolutions in Security Sector Reform*, 2010.

Sexual Violence as a Tactic of Terror

reconstruction, recovery, and economic development; creating a specialized section to handle terrorism-related cases to expedite the handling of prosecutions. The report notes, however, that "prosecutions have not been commensurate with the large number of detained Boko Haram suspects."[108] Nigeria has also welcomed bilateral and multilateral partners to enhance the operational capacity of the Multinational Joint Task Force with financial and logistical assistance, relevant equipment, and intelligence-sharing to combat Boko Haram. The same report recommends that Nigeria implement its national action plan regarding Security Council resolution 1325 (2000),[109] guarantee security of internally displaced persons in camps, and extend medical and psychosocial services to include, controversial "sexual and reproductive health services" encompassing "safe abortion services at a minimum in cases of rape."[110]

International Legal Framework

International Humanitarian Law, Terrorism, and International Human Rights

Acts of sexual violence, including rape are prohibited by the four Geneva Conventions of 1949 (GC),[111] two Additional Protocols of 1977 (AP I-II),[112] and customary international law. These particular laws form part of an international body of law that regulates hostilities in situations of armed conflict, otherwise known as International Humanitarian Law (IHL), the law of armed conflict, or *jus in bello*. It

---

108. General Assembly, Human Rights Council, thirtieth Session, Agenda item 2, Annual Report of the United Nations High Commissioner for Human Rights, Violations and abuses committed by Boko Haram and the impact on human rights in the countries affected, A/HRC/30/67, December 9, 2015.

109. Ibid., 81.

110. Ibid.

111. Geneva Convention (I) on Wounded and Sick in Armed Forces in the Field, 1949 (2.08); Geneva Convention (II) on Wounded, Sick and Shipwrecked of Armed Forces at Sea, 1949 (12.08); Geneva Convention (III) on Prisoners of War, 1949 (12.08); Geneva Convention (IV) on Civilians, 1949 (12.08).

112. Additional Protocol (I) to the Geneva Conventions, 1977 (08.06); Annex (I) Additional Protocol (I), as amended in 1993 (30.11); Annex (I) Additional Protocol (I), 1977 (08.06); Annex (II) Additional Protocol (I), 1977 (08.06); Additional Protocol (II) to the Geneva Conventions, 1977 (08.06).

is an area of International Law separate and distinct from, but related to International Human Rights Law (IHRL) and international laws and policies relating to terrorism and counter-terrorism strategies.

The Geneva Conventions and Additional Protocols bind State Parties to those treaties while customary international law binds all States. ICRC underlines that IHL applies in the absence of a formal declaration of war and makes a distinction between International Armed Conflicts (IACs) and Non-international Armed Conflicts (NIACs), and it signifies armed conflicts between one or more States on opposing sides, while the latter expression generally denotes armed conflicts between one State and one or more organized non-State armed groups (e.g., rebel groups or militia), and so fewer rules apply. All parties to armed conflict must respect the rules of IHL, in particular those regarding civilians, who cannot be targeted. In specific regard to certain groups committing acts of violence described as "terrorist," a determination must be made whether they are armed groups within the meaning of IHL. For example, such a determination might exclude loosely organized groups or individuals that merely share a common ideology.

The International Committee of the Red Cross (ICRC), a predominant expert in the field of IHL, fleshes out the crucial differences between the legal framework of IHL and that of terrorism and counterterrorism measures.[113] IHL applies to armed conflicts where certain acts of violence are lawful and others are unlawful as parties to an armed conflict seek to prevail over one another. In contrast, there is no similar dichotomy in the legal framework that governs terrorism. Once an act is legally classified as terrorism, it is penalized as criminal under domestic or international law. Moreover, in IHL the principle of equality of belligerents means that parties to an armed

---

113. International Committee of the Red Cross (ICRC), "International Humanitarian Law and the Challenges of Contemporary Armed Conflicts," 28th International Conference of the Red Cross and Red Crescent, December 2–6, 2003, 17–19; ICRC, "International Humanitarian Law and the Challenges of Contemporary Armed Conflicts," 32nd International Conference of the Red Cross and Red Crescent, December 8–10, 2015, 16–2; ICRC, "The Applicability of IHL to Terrorism and Counterterrorism," October 1, 2015; ICRC, "International Humanitarian Law and Terrorism: Questions and Answers," January 1, 2011 (all of the aforementioned documents are available on the ICRC website at www.icrc.org).

Sexual Violence as a Tactic of Terror

conflict have the same rights and duties under IHL. The aim of IHL is not to determine the lawfulness of the cause pursued or confer legitimacy on non-State armed groups, as underlined in common article 3 of the Geneva Conventions and article 3 of AP II. Rather, IHL sets out the equal rights and obligations of parties in the conduct of hostilities and the treatment of persons under control of the same.

Having said that, there are overlaps between the two regimes since IHL, in situations of armed conflicts, prohibits acts of terrorism and a range of other acts of violence, as war crimes, when they are directly committed against civilians or civilian targets. The foundation of IHL is the "principle of distinction," namely, that those fighting in armed conflict must distinguish between civilians and combatants and between civilian and military objects. Other rules derive from this principle such as those directed at protecting civilians, for example, the prohibition of deliberate or direct attacks against civilians and civilian objects as well as the prohibition of using civilians as "human shields" or of taking hostages. Based on this principle, the ICRC underlines that in situations of armed conflict, "there is no legal significance in describing deliberate acts of violence against civilians or civilian objects as 'terrorist' because such acts would already constitute war crimes."[114] IHL prohibits acts specifically aimed at spreading terror among the civilian populations.[115]

As a general matter, it appears that ICRC would rather not have armed groups labeled as terrorists, if it all possible, since that could compromise efforts for convincing those groups to gain credibility in the international community by showing a willingness to adhere to IHL. In specific regard to Boko Haram, however, the U.N. Special Representative on Sexual Violence in Armed Conflict, Zainab Hawa Bangura of Sierra Leone, promotes the full employment of counter-terrorism measures. She believes it is critical "to deepen the understanding of sexual violence as a tactic of terrorism and to formally recognize victims of sexual violence as victims of terrorism in order to build counter-narratives and counter-strategies and pave the way

---

114. Ibid.
115. Geneva Convention (IV), Arts. 3; 4.2.d; Additional Protocol (I), Art. 51.2; Additional Protocol (II), Art. 13.2.

for reparations and redress."[116] She also suggests working with religious leaders to ensure that rape and sexual violence is not justified with religious reasons.

ICRC, in regard to ISIS and its affiliates, does not take the view that there is a unitary non-State party opposing one or more States, the prerequisite for finding an armed conflict of global dimensions that might justify the expression "war on terror." From a legal perspective, the ICRC adopts a case-by-case legal analysis of various situations of violence. When an NIAC that is confined to a certain territory reaches into another territory, the ICRC employs the pertinent IHL criteria once again to determine whether a NIAC has arisen in the new territory. The ICRC argues that listing a non-State armed group party to an NIAC as "terrorist" means that it is included on a list of terrorist organizations and others are prohibited from association with them. This, in turn, according to ICRC, could criminalize core activities of humanitarian actors, which by definition are considered neutral, independent, and impartial, but who need to work with such groups in order to meet the needs of victims and detainees of armed conflicts.

Various criteria have been considered with a view to categorizing conflicts such as the intensity of the violence or hostilities, the involvement and organizational element of the non-State actor, control of territory by a State of a dissident armed group, and so forth.[117] Additionally, a number of norms contained in the Geneva Conventions of 1949 and Additional Protocols I and II of 1977 have reached the status of customary international law, meaning that they are binding on all parties involved in armed conflicts, international or non-international, even if the State has not acceded to the relevant convention.

Some situations can be classified as IAC, others as NIAC, while others may fall outside any notion of armed conflict. Many argue that situations falling outside IHL are governed by IHRL. They argue

---

116. Security Council, "Report of the Secretary-General on Conflict-related Sexual Violence," S/2016/361, April 20, 2016, para. 22.

117. See e.g., Louise Arimatsu and Mohbuba Choudhury, "The Legal Classifications of the Armed Conflicts in Syria, Yemen and Libya," *Chatham House: International Law PP* 2014/01, March 2014.

that IHRL is displaced by IHL in times of armed conflict based on the principle of *lex specialis*. Others, on the other hand, argue that IHRL continues to apply during armed conflict as a complementary legal regime to IHL.

IHRL is largely based on a series of multilateral treaties entered into by State Parties negotiated within the United Nations system. There is an important distinction between treaties negotiated within the U.N. system, on the one hand, versus other treaties drafted within the European System, African System, or the Inter-American system. The former are commonly referred to as international human rights treaties, while the latter are referred to as regional human rights treaties. In specific regard to IHRL, due to the complexities of these instruments and the number of States involved in their drafting, State Parties usually enter reservations that can modify their respective legal obligations under the treaties. In addition, only core international treaties have monitoring mechanisms or Committees with mandates to receive State reports, complaints between State parties, individual communications, or to conduct inquires. The conclusions of such Committees are not binding, and their opinions are treaty-specific, related to the subject matters of the respective conventions (e.g., civil and political rights; economic, social, and cultural rights; the rights of children; elimination of discrimination against women; the rights of persons with disabilities; freedom from torture; elimination of racial discrimination; rights of migrants and their families; and freedom from enforced disappearance). Other sources of international human rights include those that bind each State based on customary international law and/or general principles of law, for example, freedom from slavery, torture, and genocide. In the field of international human rights there are ongoing debates within the United Nations systems over a number of issues including the source of human rights, the nature and meaning of certain rights, the role of treaty bodies, and so forth.

Assuming without deciding that international human rights law is applicable in cases of armed conflict, in 2005 scholar Noam Lubell underlined significant challenges and obstacles, namely: a) the extraterritorial applicability of human rights obligations; b) the mandate and expertise of human rights bodies; c) the different purposes, techniques, and expressions of the two legal regimes; d) the possible clashes between IHL and IHRL in NIACs; and e) applicability of economic, social, and cultural rights during armed conflicts.[118] In an attempt to clarify some of the issues, in 2011 the U.N. Human Rights Office of High Commissioner took up the challenge in a non-binding publication wherein the case for concurrent applicability of IHRL and IHL in armed conflict was made with heavy reliance on non-binding sources of international law.[119]

In terms of what the issue may mean for the prosecution of sexual violence in armed conflict, Patricia Viseur Sellers argues that international human rights can be used as means of interpretation for international humanitarian law and international criminal law.[120] Her central argument is that prosecution of offenders for rape during armed conflicts by international *ad hoc* tribunals has provoked different interpretations of the definitions of rape, in particular regard to the necessity of consent (see the discussion *infra*). Unfortunately, her exhaustive study gives little clarity on the complementarity of IHRL and IHL, when she concludes: "the jurisprudence of [regional] human rights law [tribunals] cannot offer definitive responses about the requirement of the lack of consent element under international criminal law."[121] Notwithstanding this conclusion, she contends that the notion of "sexual autonomy" is a core human rights value and should be advanced as a helpful tool in overcoming the difficulties regarding the definition of rape in international criminal law.

Amnesty International takes up the argument and explains that

---

118. Noam Lubell, "Challenges in Applying Human Rights Law to Armed Conflict," *International Review of the Red Cross*, vol. 87 No. 869 December 2005; see also Alexander Orkhelashvili, "The Interaction between Human Rights and Humanitarian Law: Fragmentation, Conflict, Parallelism, or Convergence?" *The European Journal of International Law*, vol. 19 no 1 (2008), 161–82; see also Francoise Hampson and Daragh Murray, "ESIL-International Human Rights Law Symposium: Operationalising the Relationship Between the Law of Armed Conflict and International Human Rights Law," *EJIL: Talk! Blog of the European Journal of International Law* (February 2016).

119. United Nations Human Rights Office of High Commissioner, "International Legal Protection of Human Rights in Armed Conflict," 2011.

120. Patricia Viseur Sellers, "The Prosecution of Sexual Violence in Conflict: The Importance of Human Rights as Means of Interpretation," available on the website of the United Nations Office of High Commission of Human Rights at http://www.ohchr.org/Documents/Issues/Women/WRGS/Paper_Prosecution_of_Sexual_Violence.pdf.

121. Ibid., 33.

Sexual Violence as a Tactic of Terror

"sexual autonomy" is different than consent in that it takes into account the environmental dynamics of the situation and the impact on women to make a genuine choice.[122] In addition, so the argument goes, the principle of equality would be respected because the starting point would not be the mistrust of a woman's complaint, as implied in the starting point of most rape cases in domestic law, when the question is framed as to whether the woman said "no," as opposed to whether she said "yes."[123] Amnesty International links the proposition that sexual autonomy is a key value in international human rights law with the non-binding 1995 Beijing Platform of Action wherein it states: "[t]he human rights of women include their right to have control over and decide freely and responsibly on matters related to their sexuality, including sexual and reproductive health."[124] Needless to say, this statement is loaded and implies that a woman can trump the right to life of her unborn child by resorting to abortion, which is not accordance with the ordinary meaning of the words in the binding treaty, the 1989 Convention on the Rights of the Child and its protection of children "before as well as after birth" (preamble para. 9).

In regard to those parties to an armed conflict that can be characterized as "armed groups" subject to IHL, the question raised is how does one ensure that such groups respect IHL? A number of methods has been discussed by scholars.[125] One way is to encourage the parties of the armed conflict to enter into special agreements. Another method is to disseminate international humanitarian law and meet with members of any armed group to educate them about the relevant provisions. An additional technique is for armed groups to make a declaration stating their commitment to respect IHL. Armed groups can also be encouraged to apply disciplinary sanctions for violations to prevent further abuses. On the other hand, some armed groups might be unwilling to comply based on ideologies that they

---

122. Amnesty International, "Rape and Sexual Violence: Human Rights Law and Standards in the International Criminal Court" (2011), 13.
123. Ibid.
124. Ibid., 17.
125. See, for example, Anne-Marie La Rosa, Carolin Wuerzner, "Armed Group Sanctions and Implementation of International Humanitarian Law," *International Review of the Red Cross*, Vol. 90, No. 870, June 2008.

have specifically developed to encourage flagrant violations of international humanitarian law. In such cases, the only non-military solution seems to be post-conflict criminal prosecution and punishment by States in domestic courts or by international or hybrid tribunals.

The four Geneva Conventions and Additional Protocol I create a "grave breaches" system of particularly serious violations of war crimes. While acts of sexual violence including rape are not specifically listed as "grave breaches" or war crimes, such acts form part of the "grave breaches" of torture or inhumane treatment or willfully causing great suffering or serious injury to body or health. These grave breaches are subject to universal jurisdiction. States must enact legislation to facilitate the prosecution of offenders, to search and arrest accused persons alleged to have committed acts of sexual violence or alleged to have ordered others to commit them, and to prosecute or extradite them to other countries for prosecution.

Rape is specifically prohibited under the Fourth Geneva Convention regarding the protection of civilian persons, which provides that "[w]omen shall be especially protected against any attack on their honour, in particular against rape, enforced prostitution, or any form of indecent assault."[126] Under Additional Protocol I, on the protection of victims in international conflicts, rape once again does not constitute a grave breach, but it is mentioned with respect to the protection of women: they "shall be the object of special respect and shall be protected in particular against rape, forced prostitution and any other form of indecent assault."[127] As regards children, rape is not mentioned but included since children "shall be the object of special respect and shall be protected against any form of indecent assault."[128] Finally, the prohibition against "outrages upon personal dignity, in particular humiliating and degrading treatment, enforced prostitution and any form of indecent assault,"[129] could be interpreted to include rape.

Article 3, common to all four Geneva Conventions of 1949, demands that any person not taking active part in hostilities or no longer taking part, be treated humanely. This common article does

126. Geneva Convention (IV), Art. 27.2.
127. Additional Protocol (I), Art. 76.1.
128. Ibid., Art. 77.1.
129. Ibid., Art.75.2.b.

Sexual Violence as a Tactic of Terror

not explicitly prohibit rape or other forms of sexual violence, but it condemns violence including cruel treatment and torture and outrages upon personal dignity, especially humiliating and degrading treatment. Additional Protocol II was created to extend the key rules pertaining to IACs to also cover NIACs, which were formerly governed only by common article 3. Rape is specifically mentioned in Additional Protocol II which prohibits "[o]utrages upon personal dignity, in particular humiliating and degrading treatment, rape, enforced prostitution and any form of indecent assault" on persons not taking active part in hostilities or no longer taking part in them (APII, Art. 4.2.e).[130]

In specific regard to the Chibok schoolgirls, Nigeria is a party to the Four Geneva Conventions of 1949 and Additional Protocol II. All parties to the conflict are bound by the relevant rules of treaty and customary law applicable to non-international armed conflicts, in particular Article 3 common to the Four Geneva Conventions of 1949 and Additional Protocol II. Nigeria must abide by all of the international treaties that it has ratified, as well as principles of customary international law.

The situation in Nigeria has been categorized as a non-international armed conflict that involves the non-state actor Boko Haram. The 2013 Report of the International Criminal Court on Preliminary Examination Activities, opined that the ongoing confrontations between the Nigerian security forces and Boko Haram reached the threshold of a non-international armed conflict, and thus international humanitarian law applied. In addition, a 2015 Report of the United Nations OHCHR argued that: "[t]he nature and intensity of the armed violence, its protracted nature and the level of organization of Boko Haram as an armed group attest to the existence of a

---

130. In terms of customary international humanitarian law, in situations of both IACs and NIACs, according to the research conducted by the International Committee of the Red Cross, rape and other forms of sexual violence are prohibited under Rule 93 of this study. International Committee of the Red Cross, *Customary International Humanitarian law*, https://www.icrc.org/customary-ihl/eng/docs/home. This study, however, is not free from criticism. See John B. Bellinger III and William J. Haynes II, "A U.S. government response to the International Committee of the Red Cross Study Customary International Humanitarian Law" in *International Review of the Red Cross*, vol. 89, No. 866, June 2007.

non-international armed conflict in northern Nigeria."[131] The applicability of international humanitarian law toward such groups is disputed by some, but Common Article 3 and Additional Protocol II of the Geneva Conventions declare that non-state actors are bound by international humanitarian law when they act on the territory of a Contracting Party to the Geneva Conventions.

Pursuant to obligations under IHL, in 2016, various training sessions on the implementation of IHL were held in Abuja, Nigeria. In one meeting, the ICRC held a workshop for university professors, representatives of non-governmental organizations, and IHL experts. Later in the month, ICRC met with members of the Economic Community of West African States (ECOWAS).[132]

Boko Haram has shown no interest in respecting IHL. Therefore, the key legal recourse seems to be the prosecution of offenders who have committed acts of sexual violence as a constitutive element of the crime of genocide, war crimes, or crimes against humanity. Accused members of Boko Haram could only be held accountable under domestic law for similar crimes if Nigerian penal law were amended to ensure prosecution of these crimes. It is noteworthy that while Boko Haram has also been accused of serious violations of international human rights,[133] Nigeria, which has ratified several international human rights instruments,[134] has equally been criticized for violations of IHRL committed by its security forces during

---

131. A/HRC/30/67, para.19.

132. Nigeria: ECOWAS member states discuss implementation of international humanitarian law, ICRC News Release, June 28, 2016, https://www.icrc.org/en/document/nigeria-ecowas-member-states-discuss-implementation-international-humanitarian-law: Nigeria: ICRC expands the scope of IHL exchange among university teachers, ICRC News Release, June 23, 2016, https://www.icrc.org/en/document/nigeria-icrc-expands-scope-ihl-exchange-among-university-teachers.

133. A/HRC/30/67, paras.20–52.

134. For example, the International Covenant on Civil and Political Rights; the International Covenant on Economic, Social and Cultural Rights; the Convention on the Elimination of All Forms of Racial Discrimination; the Convention against Torture and Other Cruel Inhuman or Degrading Treatment or Punishment; the Convention on the Elimination of All Forms of Discrimination against Women; the Convention on the Rights of the Child; the Convention on the Rights of Persons with Disabilities; the Convention on the Protection of the Rights of All Migrant Workers and Members of Their Families; and the Convention for the Protection of All Persons from Enforced Disappearance.

Sexual Violence as a Tactic of Terror

the conduct of counter-insurgency measures.[135] In 2016, the United States government, which had been assisting Nigeria in a number of ways, contended that the Nigerian government needed to address the roots of extremism that gave rise to Boko Haram, including "weak, ineffective governance, corruption, lack of education, and lack of economic opportunities."[136]

International Criminal Law
Crimes and Tribunals

In cases where accusations of genocide, war crimes, or crimes against humanity exist, arguments in favor of post-conflict trials are commonly based on consideration of individual responsibility to respect international humanitarian law. Other principles at play include those pertaining to deterrence, retribution, and rehabilitation.

Theoretically, the prosecution of atrocity crimes should be done at the local level, where the crimes occurred. This might not be possible, however, due to the protracted nature of the conflict, government corruption, rule of law concerns, or political considerations. In brief, State authorities might demonstrate an unwillingness or inability to prosecute accused persons at the local level. In such cases since World War II, international criminal tribunals such as the Nuremberg and Tokyo trials sometimes have been established to respond to atrocities committed during armed conflicts. In the mid-nineties, the United Nations Security Council created two *ad hoc* tribunals to prosecute persons responsible for atrocity crimes, that is, serious violations of international humanitarian law in armed conflicts. In this regard, the International Criminal Tribunal for the former Yugoslavia (ICTY) and the International Criminal Tribunal for Rwanda (ICTR) were created to deal with specific situations in certain geographical locations during a limited time period. In addition, hybrid tribunals have been established such as the Special Court of Sierra Leone (SCSL) established in 2002, the year the International Criminal Court

---

135. See e.g., A/HRC/30/67, paras. 55–56, 60, 65, 70.
136. "Boko Haram and Its Regional Impact," Remarks by Linda Thomas-Greenfield, Assistant Secretary, Bureau of African Affairs, The Capitol Visitor Center, U.S. House of Representatives, Washington, DC, February 9, 2016, http://www.state.gov/p/af/rls/rm/2016/252357.htm.

entered into force. In 1998, member States of the United Nations negotiated the Statute of the International Criminal Court (ICC) where offenders can be charged for acts of "sexual and gender-based" crimes within the subject matter jurisdiction of the court.[137]

To understand how a special tribunal might be established and operate in regard to the crimes committed by members of Boko Haram, consider the ICTY in The Hague and the ICTR in Arusha, Tanzania (with offices in Kigali, Rwanda, and an Appellate Chamber in The Hague). These courts were established to deal with specific armed conflict during a certain period of time, concerning the international crimes of genocide, crimes against humanity, and grave breaches (or war crimes). Both of the tribunals are considered concrete contributions to the restoration and maintenance of international peace and security and were created as subsidiary bodies of the United Nations Security Council. They do not deal with civil suits or other crimes ordinarily prosecuted under national law. Nor do they handle less grave crimes under international law cases. Therefore, the main focus has been high-ranking officials who play a leadership role in the commission of crimes.[138] Needless to say, prosecutors are very selective and charge only some accused for only a few crimes taking into consideration the prospects of conviction. Consequently, the judgments of these courts "cannot be said to reflect the totality of sexual-violence crimes—whether they amount to atrocity crimes or not—committed against civilians," including women and girls.[139] Finally, it is noteworthy that the Security Council established a residual mechanism to conclude the tasks of the ICTY and ICTR and guarantee the closure of their mandates.[140]

In 1993, the preamble of Security Council Resolution 827 that established the ICTY "expressed its grave alarm at continuing reports of widespread and flagrant violations of international humanitarian law occurring within the territory of the former Yugoslavia, and

---

137. See chapter eleven in this text.
138. United Nations Department of Peacekeeping Operations, "Review of the Sexual Violence Elements of the Judgments of the International Criminal Tribunal for the Former Yugoslavia, the International Criminal Tribunal for Rwanda, and the Special Court for Sierra Leone in the Light of Security Council Resolution 1820," (2009), 18.
139. Ibid., 19.
140. S/RES/1966, December 22, 2010.

Sexual Violence as a Tactic of Terror

especially in the Republic of Bosnia and Herzegovina, including reports of mass killings, and massive, organized, and systematic detention and rape of women."[141] Article 5 of the ICTY Statute expressly lists the crime of rape as a crime against humanity.[142] Rape can also constitute a crime against humanity as an element of other crimes, such as that of "torture," "enslavement," or "persecution on national, political, ethnic, racial or religious grounds." Under Article 3, rape could also implicitly constitute a war crime as a form of "torture or inhuman treatment," on the one hand, or by being an act causing "great suffering or serious injury to body or health," on the other.[143] In addition, according to Article 4, rape could constitute an act of genocide, namely an act causing "serious bodily or mental harm" to members of a group.[144] The crime of genocide differs from the other atrocity crimes because it requires specific intent to "destroy, in whole or in part, a national, ethnic, racial or religious group" through the commission of enumerated acts: 1) killing members of the group; 2) causing serious bodily or mental harm to members of the group; 3) deliberately inflicting on the group conditions of life calculated to bring about its physical destruction in whole or in part; 4) imposing measures intended to prevent births within the group; and 5) forcibly transferring children of the group to another

---

141. S/RES/827, May 25, 1993, preamble para. 3.

142. Updated Statute of the International Criminal Tribunal for the Former Yugoslavia, adopted May 25, 1993 as last amended July 7, 2009 by resolution 1877, Art. 5 (Crimes against humanity: "The International Tribunal shall have the power to prosecute persons responsible for the following crimes when committed in armed conflict, whether international or internal in character, and directed against any civilian population: (a) murder; (b) extermination; (c) enslavement; (d) deportation; (e) imprisonment; (f) torture; (g) rape; (h) persecutions on political, racial and religious grounds; (i) other inhumane acts").

143. Ibid., Art. 2 (Grave Breaches of the Geneva Conventions of 1949):

> The International Tribunal shall have the power to prosecute persons committing or ordering to be committed grave breaches of the Geneva Conventions of 12 August 1949, namely the following acts against persons or property protected under the provisions of the relevant Geneva Convention: (a) willful killing; (b) torture or inhuman treatment, including biological experiments; (c) willfully causing great suffering or serious injury to body or health; (d) extensive destruction and appropriation of property, not justified by military necessity and carried out unlawfully and wantonly; (e) compelling a prisoner of war or a civilian to serve in the forces of a hostile power; (f) willfully depriving a prisoner of war or a civilian of the rights of fair and regular trial; (g) unlawful deportation or transfer or unlawful confinement of a civilian; (h) taking civilians as hostage.

group. The specific intent requirement may be deduced from oral or written statements, orders, or repeated and continuous patterns.[145] Depending upon the fact situation in question, acts of sexual violence, including rape, could amount to: acts causing serious bodily and mental harm; acts deliberately inflicted knowing that victims will be expelled from the community or flee from the community thereby causing disunity and ultimately destroying the community; acts intended to sexual mutilate the victims rendering them unable to have births in the future; and acts done with a view to impregnating the victim for the purpose of changing the ethnic composition of the community.

In 1994, Security Council Resolution 955 established the ICTR to prosecute persons responsible for serious violations of international humanitarian law.[146] Like the Statute of the ICTY, the Statute of the ICTR explicitly recognizes the crime of rape as a crime against humanity, and rape can also be the constituent element of the crimes of torture, enslavement, or "persecution on national, political, ethnic, racial or religious grounds." In addition, rape can constitute a war crime; it is expressly listed as a specific example of an "outrage upon personal dignity."[147] Similar to the Statute of the ICTY, rape

---

144. Ibid., Art. 4 (Genocide):

1. The International Tribunal shall have the power to prosecute persons committing genocide as defined in paragraph 2 of this article or of committing any of the other acts enumerated in paragraph 3 of this article.
2. Genocide means any of the following acts committed with intent to destroy, in whole or in part, a national, ethnical, racial or religious group, as such: (a) killing members of the group; (b) causing serious bodily or mental harm to members of the group; (c) deliberately inflicting on the group conditions of life calculated to bring about its physical destruction in whole or in part; (d) imposing measures intended to prevent births within the group; (e) forcibly transferring children of the group to another group.
3. The following acts shall be punishable: (a) genocide; (b) conspiracy to commit genocide; (c) direct and public incitement to commit genocide; (d) attempt to commit genocide; (e) complicity in genocide.

145. Gregory H. Stanton, "On legal interpretation of intent in the Genocide Convention," available on the website of Genocide Watch at http://www.genocidewatch.org/rapeasgenocide.html.

146. S/RES/955, November 8, 1994, para. 1.

147. Ibid., Art. 4 (Violations of Article 3 common to the Geneva Conventions and of Additional Protocol II):

The International Tribunal for Rwanda shall have the power to prosecute persons committing or ordering to be committed serious violations of Article 3 common to the Geneva Conventions of 12 August 1949 for the Protection of War Victims, and of Additional Proto-

Sexual Violence as a Tactic of Terror

can also constitute an act that causes "serious bodily or mental harm," under the crime of genocide.[148]

Both of the tribunals have convicted perpetrators of sexual violence that were civilians and non-civilian leaders in positions of authority at various governmental levels or in detention camps or police units. Some were convicted on the basis of personal responsibility, while others on the basis of their responsibility as superiors. The victims included women, men, girls, and boys. Both of the tribunals have struggled with important issues such as how rape should be defined, including 1) whether specific body orifices have to be penetrated or whether any physical invasion of a sexual nature is sufficient; or 2) whether lack of consent is a relevant element of rape or whether it is presumed, if the accused person used coercion, force, or threat of force or took advantage of coercive circumstances.[149] In specific regard to children, it is noteworthy that where the definition of sexual violence, including rape, is based on coercion rather than

---

col II thereto of 8 June 1977. These violations shall include, but shall not be limited to: (a) Violence to life, health and physical or mental well-being of persons, in particular murder as well as cruel treatment such as torture, mutilation or any form of corporal punishment; (b) Collective punishments; (c) Taking of hostages; (d) Acts of terrorism; (e) Outrages upon personal dignity, in particular humiliating and regrading treatment, rape, enforced prostitution and any form of indecent assault; (f) Pillage; (g) The passing of sentences and the carrying out of executions without previous judgement pronounced by a regularly constituted court, affording all the judicial guarantees which are recognized as indispensable by civilized peoples; (h) Threats to commit any of the foregoing acts.

148. Ibid., Art. 2 (Genocide):

1. The International Tribunal for Rwanda shall have the power to prosecute persons committing genocide as defined in paragraph 2 of this article or of committing any of the other acts enumerated in paragraph 3 of this article.

2. Genocide means any of the following acts committed with intent to destroy, in whole or in part, a national, ethnical, racial or religious group, as such: (a) Killing members of the group; (b) Causing serious bodily or mental harm to members of the group; (c) Deliberately inflicting on the group conditions of life calculated to bring about its physical destruction in whole or in part; (d) Imposing measures intended to prevent births within the group; (e) Forcibly transferring children of the group to another group.

3. The following acts shall be punishable: (a) Genocide; (b) Conspiracy to commit genocide; (c) Direct and public incitement to commit genocide; (d) Attempt to commit genocide; (e) Complicity in genocide.

149. See e.g., Prosecutor v. Akayesu, ICTR-96-4-T, (2 September 1998); Prosecutor v. Furundžija, ICTY-95-17/1-T (December 10, 1998); ICTY-95-17/A (July 21, 2000); Prosecutor v Kunarac et al., ICTY-96-23-T & IT-98-30/1-T (February 22, 2001) & IT-96-23; ICTY-96-23 & IT-96-23/1-A (June 12, 2002); Prosecutor v. Gacumbitsi, ICTR-2001-64-A (July 7, 2006); Prosecutor v. Laurent Semanza, ICTR-97-20 (May 15, 2003).

consent, there is no need for statutory rape provisions based on a particular age limit.

Finally, both of the tribunals have produced important decisions in regard to sexual violence as crimes of humanity, war crimes, and the crime of genocide. For example, the ICTY in the *Mućic* case held that the rape of two women was a form of torture, and as such, was both a war crime (grave breach of the Geneva Conventions) and a violation of international customary humanitarian law.[150] The tribunal found that the women had been detained in a camp and raped by soldiers during interrogation in order to obtain information as well as to punish, coerce, and intimate them. In the *Kunarac* case, when women were gathered into detention centers, hotels, and private homes run as brothels; the ICTY entered convictions including rape and sexual enslavement as a crimes against humanity.[151] In the context of a widespread and systematic attack on civilians, rape was said to have been used as a strategy of "expulsion through terror," that is, forced displacement from the region.[152] In the *Akayesu* case, the ICTR found the accused Akayesu, the Major for the Taba community, guilty of genocide and rape as a crime against humanity.[153] In that case, the tribunal held that the accused ordered, instigated, and otherwise aided and abetted multiple acts of rape committed by militia against women on and near the communal premises by virtue of his presence and encouragement during their commission. In addition, the court found that Akayesu's comments during some of the rapes graphically depicted Tutsi women in way that provoked sexual violence against them because they were Tutsi. The court went on to conclude that sexual violence was one step in the process of destruction of the Tutsi group and, that in most cases, rapes accompanied an intent to kill the victim.

To understand how a hybrid tribunal might be established and operate in regard to the crimes committed by members of Boko Haram, let us now turn to the Special Court for Sierra Leone (SCSL) as a case study, which was established by agreement between the host

---

150. Prosecutor v. Mućic et al., ICTY-96-21 (16 November 1998); Prosecutor v. Mućic et al., ICTY-96-21-A (February 20, 2001).

151. Kunarac.

152. Ibid.

153. Akayesu.

Sexual Violence as a Tactic of Terror

State and the United Nations.[154] In general, the hybrid tribunal usually incorporates both international and domestic elements, such as a combined a) composition of staff consisting of both international and local persons as judges, prosecutors, and administrative assistants; and b) combined application of substantial and procedural law from both the international and domestic levels.

The SCSL has competence to try serious violations of international humanitarian law and of certain Sierra Leonean law committed in the territory of Sierra Leone according to a specific time frame.[155] It has subject matter jurisdiction over crimes against humanity committed against civilians; war crimes or violations of Article 3 common to the Geneva Conventions and of Additional Protocol II; other serious violations of international humanitarian law; and certain crimes under Sierra Leonean law.[156] The SCSL has no jurisdiction to try genocide. The special court has concurrent jurisdiction with the domestic courts of Sierra Leone, but the SCSL takes primacy over the domestic courts and may ask the domestic courts to defer to its competence.[157] A Residual Special Court for Sierra Leone was established by legislative enactment, in 2011, according to an agreement between Sierra Leone and the United Nations, in anticipation of completion of the judicial activities.[158]

"Rape, sexual slavery, enforced prostitution, forced pregnancy, and any other form of sexual violence" constitute crimes against humanity.[159] In addition, "[o]utrages upon personal dignity, in particular humiliating and degrading treatment, rape, enforced prostitution, and any form of indecent assault" may constitute war crimes.[160] Lastly, acts of sexual violence can be prosecuted under the category "other violations against international humanitarian law" when such attacks have been intentionally directed "against the civilian population as such or against individual civilians not taking

---

154. See e.g., the website of International Crimes Database available at http://www.internationalcrimesdatabase.org/Courts/Hybrid.
155. Statute of SCSL, Art. 1.
156. Ibid., Arts. 2–5.
157. Ibid., Art. 8.
158. The Residual Special Court for Sierra Leone Agreement (Ratification) Act, 2011, Supplement to the Sierra Leone Gazette vol. CXLIII, No. 6, February 9, 2012.
159. Statute of SCSL, Art. 2.g.
160. Ibid., Art.3.e.

direct part in hostilities."[161] In regard to domestic offenses, they include those relating to the abuse of girls under the Prevention of Cruelty to Children Act, 1926.[162]

In the AFRC case, the tribunal entered convictions for rape as a crime against humanity: part of a widespread or systematic attack directed against the civilian population of Sierra Leone targeting women and children, as well as for war crimes as outrages upon personal dignity, and various others acts of sexual violence, including rape and sexual slavery.[163] In that case, three leaders were held responsible on the basis of their personal and superior responsibility. The trial chamber heard accounts of sexual violence including incidences of public rape, sexual enslavement, sexual mutilations, sexual threats, and forced marriages (thousands of women referred to as "bush wives" were forcibly living with fighters as slaves after being kidnapped and raped).

Another possibility concerns the Rome Statute of the International Criminal Court ("Rome Statute"), which was adopted, on July 17, 1988, at an international diplomatic conference that gathered 120 State representatives, in Rome, for a period of six weeks. It provides for a treaty-based criminal court to try individuals for specific atrocity offenses committed after the treaty entered into force on July 1, 2002. The court, located in The Hague, The Netherlands, unlike the *ad hoc* tribunals established by the U.N. Security Council, is an independent and permanent court. It is not a body of the United Nations, although the U.N. Security Council can refer cases to the ICC for investigation. Persons can be prosecuted before the ICC if they have committed genocide, crimes against humanity, and war crimes on the territory of a State that has ratified the Rome Statute or if they have the nationality of a State Party. Otherwise, the State concerned would need to accept the jurisdiction by the ICC by filing a declaration. The crime of aggression can also be prosecuted in accordance with the Rome Statute and the relevant amendment thereto.[164]

---

161. Ibid., Art. 4.a.
162. Ibid., Art. 5.a.
163. Prosecutor v. Alex Tamba Brima, Brima Bazzy Kamera, Santigie Borbor Kanu, SCSL-04-16-T, June 20, 2007 (AFRC case).
164. (ICC, Art. 8-bis inserted by resolution RC/Res.6 of June 11, 2010). See chapter eleven in this volume.

Sexual Violence as a Tactic of Terror

Notwithstanding the paucity of pertinent convictions,[165] according to the 2014 "Policy Paper of the ICC on Sexual and Gender-based Crimes," the court acknowledges that sexual and gender-based crimes are amongst the severest under the Statute, as a result they are given importance in all stages of the work.[166] Indeed, the Rome Statute explicitly acknowledges various forms of sexual violence as types of war crimes, or in other words, as grave breaches of the Geneva Conventions or a serious violation of common article 3 of the Geneva Conventions, committed during international and non-international armed conflicts, respectively. Unlike the ICTR and the ICTY, rape is specifically mentioned as a war crime as well as "sexual slavery, enforced prostitution, forced pregnancy, as defined in article 7, paragraph 2 (f), enforced sterilization, and any other form of sexual violence."[167] Moreover, the ICC has jurisdiction over the crime of genocide and rape, along with other acts of sexual violence, which can constitute genocide when such acts are "committed with intent to destroy, in whole or in part, a national, ethnical, racial, or religious group."[168] Like the Statutes of the ICTY and the ICTR, under the Rome Statute the crime of rape is a distinct type of crime against humanity, yet the ICC expands the list to include "sexual slavery, enforced prostitution, forced pregnancy, enforced sterilization, or

---

165. See, for example, Blake Evans-Pritchard, "ICC Restates Commitment on Crimes of Sexual Violence, Hague Court Says It Is Serious about Gender-based Crimes. But It Is Yet to Secure a Conviction," *ACR Issue* 392, June 10, 2014.

166. International Criminal Court, "Policy Paper on Sexual and Gender Based Crimes" (June 2014).

167. Arts. 8.2.b.xxii and 8.2.e.vi of the Rome Statute of the International Criminal Court (hereinafter the "Rome Statute") originally circulated as document A/CONF.183/9 of July 17, 1998 and corrected by procès-verbaux of November 10, 1998, July 12, 1999, November 30, 1999, May 8, 2000, January 17, 2001, and January 16, 2002 entered into force July 1, 2002. (It is noteworthy that the term "forced pregnancy" was the matter of much debate during the ICC negotiations, some States believed that the expression could be used as a vehicle to promote an international right to abortion. To resolve the debate, the term was defined as to mean "the unlawful confinement of a woman forcibly made pregnant, with the intent of affecting the ethnic composition of any population or carrying out other grave violations of international law. This definition shall not in any way be interpreted as affecting national laws relating to pregnancy.")

168. Rome Statute, Art. 6.

any other form of sexual violence of comparable gravity."[169] Furthermore, the Statute criminalizes persecution on the basis of gender, as defined in the Rome Statute, as a crime against humanity.[170]

In terms of what all of this means for the prosecution of crimes committed by Boko Haram, Nigeria deposited its instrument of ratification to the Rome Statute on September 27, 2001. Therefore, the ICC has jurisdiction over crimes recognized in the Rome Statute committed on the territory of Nigeria or by its nationals since July 1, 2002, when the Rome Statute entered into force. The Office of the Prosecutor has published preliminary examination reports on the activities of Boko Haram in Nigeria from 2010 to 2015 and has found subject matter jurisdiction concluding that there is a reasonable basis to believe that in the context of a non-international armed conflict, Boko Haram has been committing crimes against humanity and war crimes. In conformity with the principle of complementarity, the Office is assessing pertinent national proceedings as regards the capability and willingness of Nigerian authorities to investigate and prosecute the alleged offenders. The latest report includes a discussion of the crimes committed against the Chibok girls, as including abduction and forced marriage entailing "repeated rapes or violence and death threats in cases of refusal."[171] The Office also noted that "[m]any of the attacks have specifically targeted Christian women."[172]

Since the jurisdiction of the ICC is merely complementary, Nigeria is primarily responsible for investigating and prosecuting atrocity crimes as the ICC will only intervene if Nigeria is shown to be unwilling or genuinely unable to act. The question is whether this domestic system can effectively prosecute the crimes recognized

---

169. Ibid., Art.7.1.g.

170. Ibid., Art. 7.1.h. The term "gender" provoked much debate during negotiations of the Rome Statue. Some States argued that the expression could be interpreted in a way that denied the biological relevance of male and female in favor of a subjective understanding of one's sexuality. In an effort to resolve the issue for the purpose of the Statute, the word was defined and "refers to the two sexes, male and female, within the context of society. The term 'gender' does not indicate any meaning different from the above." Ibid., Art. 7.3.

171. International Criminal Court Office of the Prosecutor, "Report on Preliminary Examination Activities," November 12, 2015, para. 206.

172. Ibid.

Sexual Violence as a Tactic of Terror

under the Rome Statute. In 2015, a Report of the United Nations OHCHR on Boko Haram concluded that "[t]he apparent systematic targeting of civilians and the widespread nature of the violations committed in territories where Boko Haram is active may, if established in a court of law, amount to crimes against humanity and war crimes if committed in connection with the armed conflict."[173] The Report, among other things, urged Nigeria to investigate all those responsible and to take special measures to protect victims and to ensure psychosocial support.[174]

A step in the right direction has been the development of "A Bill for an Act to Provide for the Enforcement and Punishment of Crimes Against Humanity, War Crimes, Genocide and Related Offences and to Give Effect to Certain Provisions of the Rome Statute of the International Criminal Court in Nigeria, 2013," which was designed to implement the Rome Statute and make the offenses therein punishable under Nigerian law.[175] Without the enactment of such a law, Nigeria does not have anything in place to prosecute international crimes recognized under the Rome Statute. It would have to default to traditional criminal charges like rape, kidnapping, and assault.[176]

Charles Adeogun, an international criminal lawyer, has been calling for a "localized" international court consisting of an international crimes division as part of the Federal High Court which sits in the capital city of Abuja.[177] He contends that this is a better solution because it would involve the Nigerian people, build expertise, and bolster the national criminal system and the rule of law. It would include local judges and prosecutors trained in prosecuting such cases balanced with international observers to monitor the trials. He

---

173. A/HRC/30/67, 78.
174. Ibid.
175. See the website of the Parliamentarians for Global Actions and their campaign for the effectiveness and universality of the Rome Statute at http://www.pgaction.org/campaigns/icc/africa/nigeria.html.
176. In August 2014, the Nigerian Coalition for the International Criminal Court (NCICC) continued to call for the Bill to be enacted into law. See the website of the Nigerian Coalition for the International Criminal Court (NCICC) available at http://www.iccnow.org/documents/NCICC_calls_on_Nigeria_to_pass_International_Crimes_Bill.pdf.
177. Charles Adeogun, "Nigeria: Boko Harm/JTF Justice must be done and seen by all Nigerians that Justice is Done," *AllAfrica.com*, August 21, 2014.

considers the approach as being similar to that established as part of the completion process of the ICTY and ICTR. In particular regard to the prosecution of offenders for sexual violence, Adeogun recommends the development of a mechanism to protect witnesses and permit them to testify through alternative methods to that of direct testimony in open court.

Conclusion

The purpose of this chapter is to provide an overview of key problems and legal issues concerning the plight of Christian women and children in armed conflict, as victims of sexual violence by Islamic extremists. The emphasis on Christian victims is not to suggest that in some way sexual violence against them is more egregious than sexual attacks on other groups, but rather to underline their plight given certain misconceptions regarding them coupled with the fact that in many incidents Christians have deeper roots in a specific region than their criminal oppressors. Sexual violence has become a tactic of terror, and it is a mistake to believe that Christian women and children enjoy special protection. The Chibok incident demonstrates a clear attack on Christian students and how the international community, in particular the various organs of the United Nations System and certain member States, have pulled together to offer analysis, support, and assistance to the government of Nigeria. Negotiated releases have led to the recovery of more than one hundred girls. On a more positive note, the Nigerian government has accepted assistance to train its forces and create policies and programs in line, for example, with the international policy framework of the U.N. Security Council on the topic of Women, Peace and Security (WPS). In particular, the Nigerian National Plan of Action (NAP) on WPS is based on the five pillars of prevention, protection, promotion, participation, and prosecution. However, the NAP will require commitment, time and money to implement. In terms of the prosecution of offenders under the international legal framework, preliminary investigations by the International Criminal Court have been ongoing for the past six years, and to date, legislation in Nigeria to implement ICC obligations has not yet been signed into law by the President. In response, one international lawyer has suggested that a local tribunal akin to those that have been established to bring an

Sexual Violence as a Tactic of Terror

end to the prosecutions of the ICTR and ICTY should be established, while others, aware of the substantial case law on crimes of sexual violence during armed conflict, especially by international *ad hoc* tribunals, might suggest that the U.N. Security Council establish a similar tribunal for the crimes committed by Boko Haram, in Nigeria. Given the current involvement of the ICC, however, and the analysis offered by Professor Rychlak in his chapter on the ICC,[178] serious problems for bringing the perpetrators to justice remain. In the end, the author shares the conclusion that "[t]oday, although we know more about the cases of conflict-related sexual violence, its magnitude and human cost, this knowledge has yet to be translated into effective prevention and response activities."[179]

---

178. See chapter eleven in this volume.
179. Vincent Bernard, Helen Durham, "Editorial: Sexual Violence in Armed Conflict: From Breaking the Silence to Breaking the Cycle," *International Review of the Red Cross, Sexual Violence in Armed Conflict* (2014).

Still from October, 2016 Boko Haram video showing some of the 276 missing Christian schoolgirls kidnapped from Chibok, Nigeria.

6

Sharia Law, the "Islamic" State, and the Persecution of Christians: Moving Past Phobia and Neologisms

Geoffrey Strickland

AS CHRISTIANS FACE annihilation in the Middle East and North Africa at the hands of the Islamic State and its interpretation of Sharia law, many people of good will—Christian and Muslim alike—have condemned these atrocities. International condemnation is acutely necessary, but the condemnation of these acts alone is not enough: we must move forward to confront those ideologies that underlie and motivate them. This chapter seeks to identify and discuss some of these difficult issues and in so doing is divided into the following sections. Part one offers a brief and general overview of Sharia law so as to give structure to the interpretations of the Islamic State. Part two considers the Islamic State and the interpretations of Sharia law used to justify the persecution of Christians. Part three then evaluates these issues. Finally, a brief conclusion is offered.

Sharia Law

The extensive chronological, cultural, and geographic development of Islam has contributed to a great variety in the understanding and articulation of Sharia law. Generally speaking, Sharia law is the comprehensive set of rules and regulations that govern Muslims in their daily lives. As Islam is understood to be an all-encompassing blueprint for society and thus more expansive than a religion in the western sense, Sharia law is thus more expansive than a religious or canonical law in the western understanding.[1] This comprehensive nature of Sharia law is important to highlight, as it covers all aspects of a Muslim's life including the religious, social, and political.[2] Sharia law for Muslims is the law of God, which serves as the "way."[3] Muslims believe that this "way" comes directly from God via the sacred book of the *Qur'an*, with the *Sunna* (traditions given by the words and actions of the Prophet), *Legal Reasoning, Legal Analogy,* and *Consensus* all playing important roles as well.[4]

The name Qur'an comes from the Arabic stem Qara'a, "to read," "to recite," and means the "Reading," the "Recitation," i.e., the "Book."[5] It is the primary and first source of Islamic law. Muslims consider the Qur'an to be the *literal and exact* word of God given to Muhammad by God through the Angel Gabriel. Muslims believe that these words were memorized by Muhammad (570–632), passed onto his companions, and then compiled in written form following his death.[6]

This secondary source of Islamic law, the *Sunna*, denotes a tradition or practice generally accepted as traceable back to Muhammad's behavior during his lifetime.[7] The term *Hadith* denotes an oral account of these Sunna, conveying what Muhammad "said, did, or tacitly approved with regard to a particular matter."[8] There are manifold collections of Hadith with varying levels of acceptance amongst Muslims.[9] Every Hadith is composed of both the chain of transmitters and the narrative itself.[10] Issues related to authenticity, veracity,

---

1. See Jonathan Berkey, *The Formation of Islam* (Cambridge: Cambridge University Press, 2003); Fred Donner, *Muhammad and the Believers at the Origins of Islam* (London, Belknap Press, 2010); Jamal J. Nasir, *The Status of Women under Islamic Law and Modern Islamic Legislation* (Leiden: Brill, 2009).

2. Ibid.

3. Giorgio Paolucci, Camille Eid, and Samir Khalil Samir, *Cento Domande Sull'islam: Intervista a Samir Khalil Samir* (Genova: Marietti, 2002), 216–217.

4. See generally Sami A. Aldeeb Abu-Sahlieh, *Il Diritto Islamico: Fondamenti, Fonti, Istituzioni* (Roma: Carocci, 2008); Wael B. Hallaq, *The Origins and Evolution of Islamic Law* (Cambridge: Cambridge University Press, 2005); Wael B. Hallaq, *An Introduction to Islamic Law* (New York: Cambridge University Press, 2011).

5. Abu-Sahlieh, *Il Diritto Islamico*, 93–100.

6. John L. Esposito, *The Oxford Dictionary of Islam* (New York: Oxford University Press, 2003), 256.

7. Abu-Sahlieh, *Il Diritto Islamico*, 167–68.

8. Hallaq, *An Introduction to Islamic Law*, 173.

9. Abu-Sahlieh, *Il Diritto Islamico*, 167–97.

10. Ibid., 171–72.

and reliability have given rise to controversy through the centuries regarding the content and collection of Hadith.[11]

The general idea in Sharia law is that new norms are not to be created—as God is the only legislator—but deduced through recourse to the Qur'an and Sunna.[12] *Ijtihad* refers to the personal discernment involved in applying the Qur'an and Sunna to a concrete situation.[13] *Qiyas*, or the deduction and articulation of a juridical solution through *legal analogy*, is a tool utilized in this respect.[14] *Ijma*, or Consensus, is the agreement on a particular issue by the Muslim community.[15] The debate on the proper understanding and utilization of these terms is longstanding and complex. Questions range, for example, from the role and limits of individual reasoning in the interpretation of the Sharia with regard to *Qiyas* and *Ijtihad* to the scope and nature of consensus in *Ijma*.[16]

The fundamental division between Sunni and Shia Muslims is foundational and impacts the modes of interpretation and understanding Sharia law. Sunni Muslims are estimated to be 85 percent of the world's 1.5 billion Muslims, comprising 90 percent or more of the populations of Egypt, Jordan, and Saudi Arabia.[17] Shia Muslims for their part are estimated to be around 10 percent of the overall global Muslim population, notably present in Iran, Iraq, and Lebanon.[18] This division has its roots in a dispute over who would lead the Muslims after the death of Muhammad.[19] "Sunnis," basing themselves in "tradition" as the Arabic word signifies, desired that the tradition of

---

11. Ibid., 167–97.
12. Ibid., 219.
13. Ibid., 219–34.
14. Ibid., 263–72.
15. Ibid., 255–62.
16. For some important aspects of the discussion, see for example, Wael B. Hallaq, "Was the Gate of Ijtihād Closed," *International Journal of Middle East Studies* 16 (1984): 3–41; Wael B. Hallaq, *Sharīa: Theory, Practice, Transformations* (Cambridge: Cambridge University Press, 2009); Robert R. Reilly, *The Closing of the Muslim Mind: How Intellectual Suicide Created the Modern Islamist Crisis* (Wilmington, DE: ISI Books, 2010).
17. See "Sunnis and Shia: Islam's ancient schism," BBC News, January 4, 2016, http://www.bbc.com/news/world-middle-east-16047709; Paolucci, *Cento Domande*, 216–17.
18. Ibid.
19. John L. Esposito, *The Future of Islam* (New York: Oxford University Press, 2010), 52.

consultation by tribal leaders decide who would lead the Muslim community.[20] Those who became known as the Shia argued that leadership should follow familial lines of Muhammad himself through the "party of Ali."[21]

Within both Sunni and Shia Islam, juridical schools of thought developed throughout the centuries with each varying in certain respects from one another.[22] It is beyond the scope of the present discussion to consider the schools in depth. It is important to note, however, that in the span of its vast territorial and cultural conquests a certain plurality of legal thought became an inevitable aspect of Islamic evolution.[23] This plurality has coalesced into schools of thought over time with geographic, cultural, and sociological factors all influencing them.[24] Traditionally, the predominant schools for the Sunni are the Hanbali, Maliki, Shafi'i, and Hanafi; and for the Shiites it is the Ja'fari.[25]

Notably, the Hanbali school is known for its conservative approach and is found in Saudi Arabia.[26] The Hanafi school is found in Central Asia, Egypt, Pakistan, India, China, Turkey, the Balkans, and the Caucasus.[27] The Maliki school is dominant in North Africa and the Shafi'i school in Indonesia, Malaysia, Brunei Darussalam, and Yemen.[28] For Shia Muslims, the Ja'fari school is prominent in Iran and Lebanon.[29]

Reform movements can impact the understanding and articulation of Sharia law as well, intensifying religious practice and thus the implementation of Sharia law. As will be discussed later, two examples often mentioned in the media are "Salafism" and "Wahhabism." The general idea behind these movements is to practice a more pure or authentic form of Islam that is cleansed of anything contrary to its

---

20. Abu-Sahlieh, *Il Diritto Islamico*, 50–51.
21. Esposito, *The Future of Islam*, 52.
22. Abu-Sahlieh, *Il Diritto Islamico*, 49–82.
23. Ibid.
24. Ibid.
25. Ibid.
26. Ibid., 57–59.
27. Ibid., 51–54.
28. Ibid., 54–57.
29. Ibid., 59–62.

original spirit and practice. For example, Salafism in its most general sense is a neo-orthodox reform movement striving to live according to the practices of the "pious forefathers" of early Islam.[30] Wahhabism concerns a particular current of Salafism that is well known for the adherence and global promulgation of Saudi Arabia.[31]

There is a broad spectrum regarding the degree of Sharia law integration into overall national legal systems. Saudi Arabia is perhaps the most well-known example of a modern nation applying its vision of Sharia law in a relatively comprehensive and literal manner.[32] Other examples where Sharia law is a primary source of the legal system are Kuwait, Bahrain, Yemen, and the United Arab Emirates.[33] Most Muslim majority countries, however, include aspects of Sharia law to varying degrees within their larger system, particularly with regard to issues of family and financial law. Some examples of this type of system are Jordan and Lebanon among others.[34]

Terrorist groups such as Al-Qaeda seek to violently impose a literal and fundamentalist interpretation of Sharia law in areas under their control. With the goal of establishing their vision of Islamic society at whatever the cost, Sharia law is often used as both the justification and goal of their actions. A common theme is that of seeking to expand their version of Islam through violent combat for the sake of their religious views, or *jihad*.[35]

The Islamic State on Sharia Law and Christian Persecution

The Islamic State is emblematic of this latter categorization.[36] Within the vastness of Sharia law, there is a complex grouping of ideological currents from which the Islamic State has flowed. The Islamic State

---

30. Esposito, *The Oxford Dictionary of Islam*, 274–75.
31. Ibid., 123.
32. "The World Factbook," Central Intelligence Agency, https://www.cia.gov/library/publications/the-world-factbook/fields/2100.html.
33. Ibid.
34. Ibid.
35. See, for example, George Weigel, *Faith, Reason, and the War against Jihadism: A Call to Action* (New York: Doubleday), 2007.
36. In the case of the Islamic State, it is generally accepted that a true nation-state according to International law has not been established. The traditional criteria of

ascribes to Sunni Islam, with an extreme Salafist-jihadist orientation routinely attributed to it.[37] The ideological progression that has led to what is now seen in the Islamic State is nuanced, but some important key figures and markers along the way can be identified.

Emerging from the Sunni tradition of Islam was Ahmad Ibn Hanbal (780–855), from which the Hanbali legal school, prominent in Saudi Arabia, takes its name.[38] Ibn Hanbal advocated for a literalist reading of the Qur'an and notably for the role of Islamic scholars to assist the ruling class in their religious adherence.[39] Ibn Taymiyya (1263–1328) continued in this tradition by emphasizing textual literalism, a desire to return to the example of the righteous early Muslim community and a stark delineation between believer and unbeliever.[40] These two figures and their ideological legacies would ultimately go on to influence later Salafist reformers and ultimately the creation of the Kingdom of Saudi Arabia itself.

Serving as a catalyst in this regard was Muhammad Ibn Abd al-Wahhab (1703–1792),[41] who emphasized textual literalism and sought the Islamic experience of the righteous early Muslims.[42] His 1744 alli-

---

statehood according to the Montevideo Convention includes a permanent population, a defined territory, a government, and a capacity to enter into relations with other states. All of these elements can be called into question in this case. See Joe Boyle, "Islamic State and the Idea of Statehood," BBC News, January 6, 2015, http://www.bbc.com/news/world-middle-east-30150681.

37. See generally, Cole Bunzel, "From Paper State to Caliphate: The Ideology of the Islamic State" (Analysis Paper, The Brookings Project on U.S. Relations with the Islamic World, March, 2015), http://www.brookings.edu/research/papers/2015/03/ideology-of-islamic-state; Elliot Friedland, "Islamic State" (Special Report, The Clarion Project, May 10, 2015), https://www.clarionproject.org/sites/default/files/islamic-state-isis-isil-factsheet-1.pdf; William McCants, *The ISIS Apocalypse: The History, Strategy, and Doomsday Vision of the Islamic State* (New York: St. Martin's Press, 2015); Michael Weiss and Hassan Hassan, *ISIS: Inside the Army of Terror* (New York: Reagan Arts, 2015); Jessica Stern and J. M. Berger, *ISIS: The State of Terror* (New York: HarperCollins, 2016); Jim Muir, "The Islamic State Group: The Full Story," *BBC News*, March 11, 2016, http://www.bbc.com/news/world-middle-east-35695648.

38. Bunzel, "From Paper State to Caliphate," 8; Muir, "The Islamic State Group: The Full Story."

39. Esposito, *The Oxford Dictionary of Islam*, 126–27.

40. Ibid., 130.

41. Ibid., 123; Friedland, *Islamic State*, 14.

42. Esposito, *The Oxford Dictionary of Islam*, 123; Friedland, *Islamic State*, 14; Muir, "The Islamic State Group: The Full Story."

ance with Muhammad Ibn al-Saud formed the basis for the modern Kingdom of Saudi Arabia.[43] The agreement effectively provided for the socio-religious reform as envisioned by al-Wahhab to serve as the foundation for the geopolitical conquests of Al-Saud.[44] These conquests in turn served to promulgate the strict vision of Islamic reform of al-Wahhab.[45] Egyptian activist and reformer Sayyid Qutb (1906–1966) is understood by many to then have "translated" these ideas of strict reform to a modern generation in emphasizing the corruption of Western secularism and the lapse of Islamic practice in modern Muslim societies.[46] Qutb proposed jihad, both in a defensive and offensive sense, to achieve the return to a pure Islam, which he deemed necessary for the flourishing of society.[47]

These ideological influences swirled into vacuums created by conflict and post-war destabilization. They found particular re-articulation in late twentieth-century jihadist terror organizations such as the Taliban and Al-Qaeda. The Afghan Taliban (literally, "students") arose following the anti-Soviet jihad and sought to create an Islamic State free from un-Islamic influence.[48] Led by Osama bin Laden, Al-Qaeda al-Jihad (literally, "the base of holy war") emerged as a network facilitating the jihad of Arab volunteers in the Soviet-Afghan conflict.[49] Upon the successful campaign against the Soviets, Al-Qaeda broadened its jihadist efforts against un-Islamic influences at large, with American presence and interests being a primary focus.[50]

Following the attacks of September 11, 2001, and the subsequent invasions of Afghanistan and Iraq by American coalitions, the socio-political situation of the region continued to destabilize. The Taliban

43. Muir, "The Islamic State Group: The Full Story"; Kingdom of Saudi Arabia Ministry of Foreign Affairs, "History of the Kingdom," March 12, 2013, 2016, http://www.mofa.gov.sa/sites/mofaen/ServicesAndInformation/aboutKingDom/Pages/CountryDevelopment36143.aspx.

44. Ibid.

45. Ibid.

46. Friedland, *Islamic State*, 14; Muir, "The Islamic State Group: The Full Story."

47. Muir, "The Islamic State Group: The Full Story."

48. "Who are the Taliban?" *BBC News*, September 29, 2015, http://www.bbc.com/news/world-south-asia-11451718.

49. Bunzel, *From Paper State to Caliphate*, 13–35; Jayshree Bajoria, and Greg Bruno, "Al-Qaeda," *Council on Foreign Relations*, June 6, 2012, http://www.cfr.org/terrorist-organizations-and-networks/al-qaeda-k-al-qaida-al-qaida/p9126.

50. Bunzel, *From Paper State to Caliphate*, 13–16.

was removed from power in Afghanistan, Al-Qaeda was hunted relentlessly, and the Baathist regime of Saddam Hussein was overthrown in Iraq.[51] The *Arab Spring* uprisings against longstanding governmental regimes further destabilized the region, with the Syrian population enduring vicious civil conflict.[52]

All of these factors, among others, set the stage for the onset of the Islamic State. A branch of Al-Qaeda formed in Iraq in 2004 with the related goals of expelling the American presence there and eventually founding an Islamic state enforcing Sharia law.[53] The Islamic State of Iraq was proclaimed in 2006, which in turn exploited tensions in Syria to expand its influence there under the name of the Islamic State of Iraq and Sham "ISIS" (Greater Syria) in 2013.[54] With a brutality and manner of operation seemingly too much even for Al-Qaeda, formal affiliation between the two entities was disavowed by Al-Qaeda in early 2014.[55] After sweeping conquests in Iraq, a caliphate (formal Islamic ruling institution in succession of the prophet Muhammad) was declared in mid-2014, with the understanding that Christians were "a people of war not enjoying a status of protection."[56]

Pursuant to this status of Christians, Issue 9 (May 2015) of the Islamic State's *Dabiq* propaganda magazine featured an article celebrating the slavery of Christian women and children.[57] The article, "Slave-Girls or Prostitutes?" praised the Islamic State practice of slavery, sexual and otherwise, as compared to the corruption of prostitution found in the West. The following verses from the Qur'an were given as justification for their views:

> And if you fear that you will not deal justly with the orphan girls, then marry those that please you of other women, two or three or four. But if you fear that you will not be just, then marry only one or those your right hand possesses.[58] An-Nisā': 3

51. Ibid.
52. Stern and Berger, *ISIS: The State of Terror*, 39–44.
53. Bunzel, *From Paper State to Caliphate*, 13–35.
54. See Chapter 1 and 2 of Stern and Berger, *ISIS: The State of Terror*.
55. Ibid.
56. Bunzel, *From Paper State to Caliphate*, 40.
57. Umm Sumayyah Al-Muhajirah, "Slave-Girls or Prostitutes?" *Dabiq*, May 2015.
58. Ibid. "The right hand's possession" (mulk al-yamīn) refers to female captives of war who were separated from their husbands by enslavement.

Moving Past Phobia and Neologisms

> And marry onto the unmarried among you and the righteous among your male slaves and female slaves. An-Nūr: 32
>
> And they who guard their private parts, except from their wives or those their right hands possess, for indeed, they will not be blamed. Al-Mu'minūn: 5–6
>
> And a believing slave-girl is better than a polytheist, even though she might please you. Al-Baqarah: 221

The outspoken proclamation of these practices as virtuous is haunting. For example, quotes such as the following fill the Islamic State's *Dabiq* propaganda magazine:

> As for the slave-girl that was taken by the swords of men following the cheerful warrior (Muhammad—sallallāhu 'alayhiwa sallam), then her enslavement is in opposition to human rights and copulation with her is rape?! What is wrong with you? How do you make such a judgment? What is your religion? What is your law?[59]

Their explanation, as illustrated in their official guidelines on the practice, is as follows.[60] For the Islamic State, it is the "unbelief" of the woman that makes it permissible to take a woman captive.[61] According to the guidelines of the Islamic State, there is no dispute among scholars that it is permissible to capture unbelieving women such as Christians.[62] It is permissible to have sexual intercourse with the female captive, even if she has not reached puberty and is deemed "fit for intercourse."[63] If she is not deemed "fit for intercourse" then one can "enjoy her without intercourse."[64] Female captives and slaves can be purchased, sold, and gifted as they are considered property.[65]

The tax, known as the *jizya*, is the tax Christians historically paid according to Sharia law to live in territories under Islamic rule. Through paying the *jizya* the life of the Christian is spared and the

---

59. Al-Muhajirah, "Slave-Girls or Prostitutes?" 49.
60. "Sex Slavery In The Islamic State—Practices, Social Media Discourse, And Justifications," The Middle East Media Research Institute, http://www.memrijttm.org/sex-slavery-in-the-islamic-state-practices-social-media-discourse-and-just ifications-jabhat-al-nusra-isis-is-taking-our-women-as-sex-slaves-too.html.
61. Ibid.
62. Ibid.
63. Ibid.
64. Ibid.
65. Ibid.

Christian is allowed to remain in the Islamic territory, though the Christian is relegated to the extremely restricted sociopolitical and theological category of *dhimma* ("protected" person).[66] Christians traditionally are presented with three options: convert to Islam, pay the tax, or death.[67] The justification given by the Islamic State from the Qur'an is the following:

> Fight those who do not believe in Allah or in the Last Day, and who do not consider unlawful what Allah and His Messenger have made unlawful, and who do not adopt the religion of Truth from those who were given the Scripture. [Fight them] until they give the jizya willingly in submission. At-Tawbaw: 29

In a video from October 2015, entitled, "Fight Those Who Do Not Believe in Allah Until They Give the Jizya Willingly While They Are Humbled," the Islamic State explains their interpretation. The Islamic State proclaimed that "this is a message to all the Christians in the East and West, and to America, the defender of the cross: Convert to Islam, and no harm will befall you. But if you refuse, you will have to pay the jizya tax."[68]

A *dhimma* contract of the Islamic State, in following traditional formulations of the agreement, contained the following stipulations.[69] Christians may not build churches or the like in the city or in

---

66. The term *dhimma* refers to the status of being "protected" as a Christian or Jew upon the signing of the contract and payment of the tax. See Paolucci, *Cento Domande*, 212.

67. "ISIS Message To France And World's 'Infidels': Convert To Islam Or Pay Jizya Poll Tax," The Middle East Media Research Institute, http://www.memrijttm.org/isis-message-to-france-and-worlds-infidels-convert-to-islam-or-pay-jizya-poll-tax.html; Kelly Phillips Erb, "Islamic State Warns Christians: Convert, Pay Tax, Leave Or Die," *Forbes*, July 19, 2014, http://www.forbes.com/sites/kellyphillipserb/2014/07/19/islamic-state-warns-christians-convert-pay-tax-leave-or-die/#266c59c63718.

68. "ISIS In New Video To Christians In Qaryatayn, Syria: Pay Jizya—Or You Will Be Executed And Your Wives Enslaved," The Middle East Media Research Institute, http://www.memrijttm.org/isis-in-new-video-to-christians-in-qaryatayn-syria-pay-jizya-or-you-will-be-executed-and-your-wives-enslaved-.html.

69. The origins can be traced back to the reportedly seventh century Pact of Umar, during the caliphate of Umar Ibn Khattab. See Norman Stillman, *The Jews of Arab Lands: A History and Source Book* (Philadelphia: Jewish Publication Society of America, 1979), 157–58.

Moving Past Phobia and Neologisms

the surrounding areas.[70] They may not display religious symbols nor recite their books such that Muslims may hear.[71] They may not own guns nor carry out any act of aggression against the Islamic State.[72] They must respect Muslims and not criticize their religion.[73] They must abide by the Islamic State's rules of dress and commerce. Christians considered wealthy must pay four gold dinars annually (approximately 715 USD), middle-class Christians two gold dinars (approximately 375 USD), and one for those considered poor (approximately 178 USD).[74]

From Issue 10 of *Dabiq*, entitled "The Laws of Allah or the Laws of Men,"[75] the Islamic State cites the following verses from the Qur'an:

> And when the sacred months have passed, then kill the polytheists (mushrikīn) wherever you find them and capture them and besiege them and sit in wait for them at every place of ambush. But if they should repent, establish prayer, and give zakah, let them [go] on their way. Indeed, Allah is Forgiving and Merciful. (At-Tawbah: 5)
>
> And fight them until there is no fitnah and until the religion, all of it, is for Allah. (Al-Anfāl: 39–40)
>
> So when you meet those who disbelieve strike their necks. (Muhammad: 4)
>
> Fight them; Allah will punish them by your hands and will disgrace them and give you victory over them. (At-Tawbah: 14)

From the aforementioned issue of *Dabiq*, the following passage below introduces the citation of the previous verses from the Qur'an:

> We will rub the noses of the kufār[76] in dirt, shed their blood, and

---

70. "ISIS Issues Dhimma Contract For Christians To Sign, Orders Them To Pay Jizyah," The Middle East Media Research Institute, http://www.memrijttm.org/isis-issues-dhimma-contract-for-christians-to-sign-orders-them-to-pay-jizyah.html.
71. Ibid.
72. Ibid.
73. Ibid.
74. "The Islamic State's Treatment Of Christians," The Middle East Media Research Institute, https://www.memri.org/reports/islamic-states-treatment-christians.
75. "The Law of Allah or the Laws of Men," *Dabiq*, July 2015, 61–62.
76. This derogatory term denotes "irreligious, unbeliever, infidel, atheist, ungrateful" and is associated with non-Muslims. See كافر and كفر in the *Hans Wehr Arabic English Dictionary*, 4th edition and Paolucci, *Cento Domande*, 214.

take their wealth as ghanīmah[77] by the might and power of Allah. And we do all that in emulation of the Prophet, not innovating anything. We do it in obedience to Allah and His Messenger, and to come closer to Allah. And we hope to attain abundant rewards by this deed, as per His statement.[78]

From Issue 7, in the article "Islam is the Religion of the Sword Not Pacifism," the Islamic State explains that:

"Islam is the religion of peace," and they mean pacifism by the word peace. They have repeated this slogan so much to the extent that some of them alleged that Islam calls to permanent peace with kufr and the kāfirīn. How far is their claim from the truth, for Allah has revealed Islam to be the religion of the sword, and the evidence for this is so profuse that only a zindīq (heretic) would argue otherwise.[79]

Discussion regarding the actions of the Islamic State has navigated toward condemning their inhumane conduct as not properly representative of Muslims universally nor Islam as such. Political and Religious leaders from around the world, Muslim and Non-Muslim alike, have issued sweeping condemnations of the actions of the Islamic State.[80] Pope Francis, for example, cautioned that "faced with disconcerting episodes of violent fundamentalism, our respect for true followers of Islam should lead us to avoid hateful generaliza-

---

77. This means the treasure or goods taken from war. See *The Encyclopedia of Islam*, ed. C.E. Bosworth, E. Van Donzel, W.P. Heinrichs, and G. Lecomte (Leiden: Brill, 1997), s.v. "Ghanima."

78. "The Law of Allah or the Laws of Men," *Dabiq*, July 2015, 61–62.

79. "Islam is the Religion of the Sword Not Pacifism," *Dabiq*, February 2015, 20.

80. See Asma Alsharif, "Egypt's top religious authority condemns Islamic State," *Reuters Africa*, August 12, 2014, http://af.reuters.com/article/egyptNews/idAFL6No Q I3DS20140812; Nash Jenkins, "Muslims Around the World Speak Out Against Terrorist Attacks in Paris," *Time*, November 14, 2015, http://time.com/4112830/muslims-paris-terror-attacks-islam-condemn/; Carol E. Lee, Julian E. Barnes, and Adam Entous, "World Leaders Pledge Strong Response to Paris Attacks," *Wall Street Journal*, November 15, 2015, http://www.wsj.com/articles/obama-erdogan-pledge-joint-respo nse-to-islamic-state-menace-1447587892; Ella Landau-Tasseron, *Delegitimizing ISIS on Islamic Grounds: Criticism of Abu Bakr Al-Baghdadi by Muslim Scholars* (Washington, DC: The Middle East Media Research Institute, 2015).

Moving Past Phobia and Neologisms

tions, for authentic Islam and the proper reading of the Qu'ran are opposed to every form of violence."[81] The Organization of Islamic Cooperation (OIC), which is composed of fifty-seven nations and describes itself as "the collective voice of the Muslim world," officially stated that the actions of the Islamic State "have nothing to do with Islam and its principles that call for justice, kindness, fairness, freedom of faith, and coexistence."[82]

The most well-known university in Sunni Islam, *Al-Azhar*, for its part called the Islamic State a "Satanic, terrorist" group.[83] However, in condemning the Islamic State, Al-Azhar has refrained from denouncing its militants as heretics, a nuanced proclamation that would essentially carry a death sentence.[84] Al-Azhar's refusal to proclaim heresy has, however, provoked questioning from Muslims and non-Muslims alike who have argued that the discrepancy is counterintuitive.[85]

Apparent discrepancies such as the aforementioned one have fueled discussion amongst critics as to whether ideological currents

---

81. Francis, "*Evangelii Gaudium*: Apostolic Exhortation on the Proclamation of the Gospel in Today's World," Vatican Website, November 24, 2013, http://w2.vatican.va/content/francesco/en/apost_exhortations/documents/papa-francesco_esortazione-ap_20131124_evangelii-gaudium.html, sec. 253.

82. "History," The Organization for Islamic Cooperation, http://www.oic-oci.org/oicv2/page/?p_id=52&p_ref=26&lan=en; "Ambassador Gokcen Addresses the Security Council," Organization of Islamic Cooperation Permanent Observer Mission to the United Nations in New York, http://www.oicun.org/9/2015033004080 2468.html.

83. Anne Barnard and Rob Nordland, "Militants' Killing of Jordanian Pilot Unites the Arab World in Anger," *New York Times*, February 4, 2015, http://www.nytimes.com/2015/02/05/world/middleeast/arab-world-unites-in-anger-after-burning-of-jordanian-pilot.html.

84. The pronouncement of a Muslim as an apostate, or *Takfir*, entails proclaiming the individual as an unbeliever (kafir) and thus sanctions violence against him. Militant groups, drawing upon the thought of Sayyid Qutb and Ibn Taymiyyah among others, utilize this concept as a justification for their actions. See Esposito, *The Oxford Dictionary of Islam*, 312; Stern and Berger, *ISIS: The State of Terror*, 269. "Al-Azhar: The Islamic State (ISIS) is a Terrorist Organization, but it Must not be Accused of Heresy," The Middle East Media Research Institute, http://www.memri.org/report/en/print8343.htm.

85. Ahmed Fouad, "Al-Azhar Refuses to Consider the Islamic State an Apostate," *Al-Monitor*, February 12, 2015, http://www.al-monitor.com/pulse/en/originals/2015/02/azhar-egypt-radicals-islamic-state-apostates.html.

Persecution & Genocide of Christians in the Middle East

of violence, seen in their extreme form in the Islamic State, pervade other movements within the larger corpus of Islam itself.[86] In other words, it is argued that the Islamic State practices what some other widely accepted Muslim entities preach.[87] The Kingdom of Saudi Arabia, one of the more prominent members of the OIC and the location of the permanent secretariat of the OIC (Jeddah), is commonly offered as an example.

Though the Kingdom has publicly denounced the Islamic State,[88] critics note that Islam is the official religion in Saudi Arabia with no protection of religious freedom.[89] To this effect, despite having an estimated 1.5 million Christian "guest workers," no churches are allowed in the country.[90] The example is often cited of the Saudi Grand Mufti, who as the highest religious official in the country, recently called for the destruction of all churches in the Arabian pen-

---

86. Fr. Samir Khalil Samir offers his opinion that,

> we hear, very often, Muslims say: "This has nothing to do with Islam." This is a spontaneous reaction of Muslims on the street. But, in fact, it's a false reaction. This is a part of Islam, and we can find it in the Qur'an itself and much more in the life of Mohammed, who had a very strong and violent attitude toward unbelievers. The main thing to note is that violence is an element of Islam. Violence is not an element of Christianity. When Christians were using violence in wars and so on, they were not following the Gospel, nor the life of Christ. When Muslims are using it, they are following the Quran and the sunnah and Mohammed's model. This is a very important point.

See Edward Pentin, "Father Samir on ISIS: 'What They Are Doing Is Diabolical,'" *National Catholic Register*, September 2, 2014, http://www.ncregister.com/daily-news/father-samir-on-isis-what-they-are-doing-is-diabolical/#ixzz42oYvOpZ6.

87. See "Egyptian TV Host Ibrahim Issa: Nobody Dares to Admit That ISIS Crimes Are Based on Islamic Sources," The Middle East Media Research Institute, http://www.memritv.org/clip_transcript/en/4773.htm; "Kuwaiti Researcher Abdulazziz Al-Qattan: ISIS Is the Product of Islamic Heritage," The Middle East Media Research Institute, http://www.memritv.org/clip_transcript/en/4821.htm; The Middle East Media Research Institute, "Egyptian Researcher Ahmad Abdou Maher: ISIS Implements Islamic Heritage Taught by Al-Azhar," http://www.memritv.org/clip_transcript/en/5234.htm.

88. Nawaf Obaid, "Only Saudi Arabia Can Defeat Isis," *The Guardian*, December 22, 2015, http://www.theguardian.com/commentisfree/2015/dec/22/saudi-arabia-isis-us-terrorists-coalition.

89. John Allen, *The Global War on Christians* (New York: Crown, 2013), 138–42.

90. Ibid.; Nina Shea, "Obama and the Churches of Saudi Arabia," *New York Times*, February 13, 2015, http://www.wsj.com/articles/SB10001424052702303563304579443534070918824.

insula region.⁹¹ Reports of state-approved primary and secondary school textbooks repeatedly containing references to discrimination and violence only serve to fuel these arguments.⁹² These textbooks are distributed throughout the Saudi public school system, including to the academies it runs in many capitals of nations throughout the world, and to other Islamic schools globally.⁹³ Examples of the violence in the textbooks include: teaching that Christians are enemies of the Muslims and that there is perpetual clash with them; that the Crusades have not ended and the "Crusader Threat" continues; that the life of a Christian is worth a fraction of that of a free Muslim male; that Christians are swine; and that Muslims are to hate Christians.⁹⁴

From Movements and Labels to Ideas: The Battle for Critical Inquiry

Due to the complexities involved, at times there has been a general reluctance to adequately examine and appreciate the difficult intertwining of issues related to violent interpretations of Sharia law. Questions touching upon Islam as such or Muslims in general can quickly lead to allegations of bigotry, discrimination, and phobia under the nebulous moniker of Islamophobia. Just as easily, the response of Christianophobia is similarly asserted when Christians and Christian converts lack churches and face taxation, slavery, rape, or death in Muslim dominated societies. Finger pointing and silencing ensue to the detriment of dialogue and reason while the capacity for critical assessment of oneself and the other—for all parties to the discussion—evaporates.

Is there a way to move forward to rediscover the capacity for critical assessment, first of all regarding one's own actions, and thus

---

91. See, for example, http://www.mcndirect.com/showsubject_ar.aspx?id=32143; Tom Heneghan, "Europe Bishops Slam Saudi Fatwa Against Gulf Churches," *Reuters*, March 23, 2012, http://www.reuters.com/article/us-saudi-christians-fatwa-idUSBRE82M1D720120323.

92. Available through the Hudson Institute's Center for Religious Freedom: https://wwwhudson.org/research/8089-saudi-arabia-s-curriculum-intolerance#.VOEFSXYhzV0.

93. Ibid., 15–17.

94. Ibid., 23–30.

move past reflexive reactions and labeling? Can people truly work against discrimination and persecution and those ideas that foster it, wherever and however it occurs in the global socio-religious context? In a way, it seems that the first step has already been taken, in identifying the shared common experience of perceiving one's humanity—common to us all—rejected by the "other" through "phobia."

Enlightening is the approach displayed by Pope Francis during his November 2014 in-flight press conference from Turkey. A Turkish journalist asked the Pope to comment upon the aforementioned neologisms of Islamophobia, Christianophobia, and what more can be done to address the ideas that underlie them.[95] Pope Francis began his response by addressing the notion of Islamophobia. He stated that:

> It's true that there has been a reaction to these acts of terrorism, not just in this region but in Africa as well: "If this is Islam it makes me angry!" So many Muslims feel offended, they say: "But that is not what we are. The Qur'an is a prophetic book of peace. This is not Islam." I can understand this. And I sincerely believe that we cannot say all Muslims are terrorists, just as we cannot say that all Christians are fundamentalists—we also have fundamentalists among us, all religions have these small groups.[96]

Pope Francis seems to say that a "small group" of "fundamentalists," specifically "fundamentalists" who carry out "acts of terrorism" in the name of Islam, perpetuate the association of Islam to violence. The Holy Father identifies this linking of Islam to violence as a major contributor to the phenomena described as Islamophobia.

The words "Islam" and "phobia" are combined to form the neolo-

---

95. The full question, posed by Yasemin Taskin, of Turkish television, is as follows: "President Erdogan spoke about 'Islamophobia'. Naturally, you reflected more on the current 'Christianophobia' in the Middle East, which is affecting both Christians and minorities. Taking interreligious dialogue into consideration as well, what more can be done? That is, is interreligious dialogue enough? Can more be done? And in your opinion, what must world leaders do? As you are not only the spiritual leader of Catholics, but also a moral leader on a global scale, what can be done concretely, is it possible to go further?"

96. Pope Francis, "In-flight Press Conference of His Holiness Pope Francis From Istanbul to Rome," Vatican Website, November 30, 2014, https://w2.vatican.va/content/francesco/en/speeches/2014/november/documents/papa-francesco_20141130_turchia-conferenza-stampa.html.

Moving Past Phobia and Neologisms

gism of Islamophobia. Islam, of course, denotes the religion of Muslims, literally meaning submission, resignation, or reconciliation to the will of God coming from the root "Salam," or a notion of "peace," as the fruit of this submission.[97] Phobia is generally understood as "an exaggerated usually inexplicable and illogical fear of a particular object, class of objects, or situation," as opposed to a rational fear.[98] Thus, literally, Islamophobia indicates the irrational fear of Islam.

Regarding Islamophobia in the international arena, the OIC is arguably the most vocal entity in defining and advocating against it. With a membership of fifty-seven states in the Middle East and North Africa (MENA) Region and beyond, the OIC is the second largest inter-governmental organization after the United Nations.[99] Through its "Islamophobia Observatory," the OIC has published yearly reports since 2008 to raise international awareness of Islamophobia "as harmful to global efforts for peaceful coexistence, harmonious and multicultural societies."[100] The OIC has recently offered the following definition of Islamophobia:

> Islamophobia is a contemporary form of racism and xenophobia motivated by unfounded fear, mistrust, and hatred of Muslims and Islam. Islamophobia is also manifested through intolerance, discrimination, unequal treatment, prejudice, stereotyping, hostility, and adverse public discourse. Differentiating from classical racism and xenophobia, Islamophobia is mainly based on stigmatization of a religion and its followers. As such, Islamophobia is an affront to the human rights and dignity of Muslims.[101]

The OIC concludes that the prevalent attitude in the West is that "being Muslim should be confined to the private space, as the perceived fashions or societal behavior linked to Islam are seen as a

---

97. See سلم and اسلام in the *Hans Wehr Arabic English Dictionary* (4th edition).
98. See "phobia" in the Merriam Webster Online Dictionary, http://www.merriam-webster.com.
99. The Organization for Islamic Cooperation, "History," http://www.oic-oci.org/oicv2/page/?p_id=52&p_ref=26&lan=en.
100. Islamophobia Observatory of the Organization of Islamic Cooperation, *Seventh OIC Observatory Report on Islamophobia*, Jeddah: Organization of Islamic Cooperation, June 2014 http://www.oic-oci.org/upload/islamophobia/2014/en/reports/islamophoba_7th_report_2014.pdf, 10.
101. Ibid.

threat to the established way of being in those societies."[102] In response, the OIC has dedicated special attention "to local Muslim communities living in the West, as these are the main victims."[103]

Generally, the situation "confirms the OIC's concerns and apprehensions that in some Western societies Islam was being increasingly misperceived as a religion of intolerance."[104] The OIC noted that Western media "continued to play a key role in promoting and disseminating an anti-Muslim culture," with a "continuous focus on the issue of 'Islamic extremism'" that "steadily consolidated negative stereotyping of Muslims."[105] However, a key question is both raised and answered in the OIC Report: "What accounts for this trend toward more negative views of Islam and Muslims? Surely this trend is due in part to the drumbeat of alarming news linking Muslims with violent events."[106]

After briefly discussing Islamophobia, Pope Francis then turned to Christianophobia. He explained:

> It's true, I'm not going to soften my words, no. We Christians are being chased out of the Middle East. In some cases, as we have seen in Iraq, in the Mosul area, they have to leave or pay a tax which then makes no sense. And other times they push us out wearing white gloves.... It's as if they wished that there were no more Christians, that nothing remain of Christianity. In that region this is happening. It's true, it's first of all a result of terrorism, but when it's done diplomatically with white gloves, it's because there's something behind it. This is not good.[107]

Essentially here the Holy Father links Christianophobia to the desire for the eradication of Christians and of Christianity and to the subsequent exodus of Christians from the region. Among the causes of this exodus of Christians alluded to by Pope Francis are terrorism and then policy, or acts done "diplomatically with white gloves," with this latter category being noteworthy "because there is something behind it."

102. Ibid.
103. Ibid., 7.
104. Ibid., 4.
105. Ibid., 5.
106. Ibid., 15.
107. Francis, "In-flight Press Conference From Istanbul to Rome."

Moving Past Phobia and Neologisms

The Holy See has not issued an official definition of the term Christianophobia, though both Pope Benedict and Pope Francis have spoken in reference to it.[108] However, the former Vatican Secretary for Relations with States, H.E. Dominique Mamberti, has described Christianophobia as a phenomenon understood in three aspects: erroneous education or disinformation regarding Christians and Christianity, intolerance and discrimination against Christian citizens through legislation and administrative decrees, and actual violence and persecution.[109]

The *Observatory on Intolerance and Discrimination against Christians* offers a similar explanation.[110] The *Observatory* explains that Christianophobia describes "the phenomenon of intolerance and discrimination against Christians." Consisting of the "words 'Christian' or 'Christ' and 'phobos,' the term means, therefore, an irrational animosity towards Christ, Christians, or Christianity as a whole."[111]

With regard to the phenomena generally, in the Middle East the Christian population has dropped from 20 percent of the total population to 5 percent and falling.[112] In Egypt, thousands upon thousands of Coptic Christians continue to experience persecution, violence, and massacres.[113] In Iraq, countless churches have been destroyed and numerous Christians persecuted, violated, and killed, causing hundreds of thousands of Christians to flee.[114] The situations in Syria, Iran, Pakistan, and elsewhere remain tragic.[115]

Regarding what should be done, Pope Francis said the following:

---

108. For example, see Benedict XVI, "Address On The Occasion Of Christmas Greetings to the Roman Curia," Vatican Website, December 20, 2010, http://w2.vatican.va/content/benedict-xvi/en/speeches/2010/december/documents/hf_ben-xvi_spe_20101220_curia-auguri.html.

109. "Combattere la cristianofobia, l'islamofobia e l'antisemitismo," *L'Osservatore Romano*, January 11, 2008, http://news.pusc.it/rassegna/geno8.pdf.

110. See Intolerance Against Christians, "About Us," http://www.intoleranceagainstchristians.eu/about/about-us.html.

111. For information on the history of the term, see Intolerance Against Christians, "Terminology," http://www.intoleranceagainstchristians.eu/about/terminology.html.

112. Allen, *The Global War*, 116.

113. Ibid., 120–24.

114. Ibid., 134–39.

115. Ibid., see generally Chapters 3 and 5.

I told the President [Erdogan] that it would be good to issue a clear condemnation against these kinds of groups. All religious leaders, scholars, clerics, intellectuals and politicians should do this. This way they hear it from their leaders' mouth. There needs to be international condemnation from Muslims across the world. It must be said, "no, this is not what the Qur'an is about!"

[W]hen the new Turkish Ambassador to the Holy See came to deliver his Letters of Credence, over a month and a half ago, I saw an exceptional man before me, a man of profound piety. The President of that office was of the same school. They said something beautiful. They said: "Right now it seems like interreligious dialogue has come to an end. We need to take a qualitative leap, so that interreligious dialogue is not merely: 'What do you think about this?' We need to take this qualitative leap, we need to bring about a dialogue between religious figures of different faiths."[116]

It seems that the Holy Father is calling for clear international condemnation from the International Muslim community and, in agreement with the Turkish officials, a "qualitative leap" in interreligious dialogue.

In this regard, the Holy Father's recent address to the Pontifical Academy of Arabic and Islamic Studies (PISAI) is poignant.[117] He noted that: "One needs to pay attention to avoid falling into the snare of a facile syncretism which would ultimately be an empty harbinger of a valueless totalitarianism, as a soft and accommodating approach, which says 'yes' to everything in order to avoid problems ends up being 'a way of deceiving others.'"[118] The Holy Father issued the invitation to "return to the basics" of the "encounter" with the other.[119] As such, if "one begins from the premise of the common affiliation in human nature, one can go beyond prejudices and fallacies and begin to understand the other according to a new perspective."[120]

Thus, double standards in the international consideration of dis-

---

116. Francis, "In-flight Press Conference From Istanbul to Rome."

117. Francis, *Address to Participants in the Meeting Sponsored by the Pontifical Institute for Arabic and Islamic Studies*, Vatican Website, January 24, 2015, http://w2.vatican.va/content/francesco/en/speeches/2015/january/documents/papa-francesco_20150124_pisai.html.

118. Ibid.

119. Ibid.

120. Ibid.

Moving Past Phobia and Neologisms

crimination and violence perpetuated against Christians in MENA Region—and the ideas that foster these phenomena—are unacceptable.[121] For example, imagine if the Pope today called for the destruction of all the mosques in Europe? Even more absurdly, imagine if the Vatican today issued official educational materials teaching that the life of a Muslim is worth a fraction of that of a free Christian male, Muslims are swine, and Christians are to hate Muslims?

This returning to the basics of encounter would take us to the point that, as described in the words of the Grand Mufti of Lebanon during the recent Synod for the Church in the Middle East, "when Christians are wounded, we ourselves are wounded."[122] Stated another way, in the words of Benedict XVI, "whatever damage is done to another in any one place, ends up damaging everyone."[123] It was thus that the words and ideas of that Synod were meant to be a "clarion call, addressed to all people with political or religious responsibility, to put a stop to Christianophobia; to rise up in defense of refugees and all who are suffering, and to revitalize the spirit of reconciliation."[124]

This way of thinking is beneficial to all parties involved. Violence and the proliferation of violence against Christians in the MENA Region perpetuate the linking of Islam to violence in the Western Media. Through an outspoken defense of the rights of Christians in the MENA Region, bearing the fruit of concrete and concerted action on their behalf, the OIC and similar groups could make greater strides in their mission to uproot what they term as Islamophobia

---

121. The Holy Father had this to say in his address to the President of Turkey:

> To this end, it is essential that all citizens—Muslim, Jewish, and Christian—both in the provision and practice of the law, enjoy the same rights and respect the same duties. They will then find it easier to see each other as brothers and sisters who are travelling the same path, seeking always to reject misunderstandings while promoting cooperation and concord. Freedom of religion and freedom of expression, when truly guaranteed to each person, will help friendship to flourish and thus become an eloquent sign of peace.

Pope Francis, Vatican Website, "Meeting With the President, Prime Minister and Civil Authorities," November 28, 2014, https://w2.vatican.va/content/francesco/en/speeches/2014/november/documents/papa-francesco_20141128_turchia-incontro-autorita.html.

122. Benedict XVI, "Address On The Occasion Of Christmas Greetings."
123. Ibid.
124. Ibid.

from Western Society.[125] As Fr. Samir Khalil Samir points out, perhaps the fear of Islam in the West is more accurately described as "fear of the aggression" associated with Islam.[126]

It is precisely this process of questioning and discussion that is crucial to the discernment of modern modalities of coexistence, at the personal, confessional, and societal level. The diversity of responses to these questions can be disconcerting, but in this tension of encountering the other, the imperfection of one's humanity is truly evident. From this shared humanity the bonds of unity are recognized, and the common fragility of man's existence is seen through the lens of our capacity to appreciate the goodness of life and ugliness of violence and death both individually and collectively. Transcending thus the limits of both that which we had previously conceived possible in ourselves and in our conception of the other, and that which we perceived to be possible in the other and their conception of us, this "qualitative leap" can occur. This leap takes us from speaking of tolerance for a tolerated entity toward an equality and non-discrimination that sees not Christian, Jew, or Muslim but rather, a human being.

The words of the Egyptian President Abdel Fattah Al-Sisi are noteworthy here. In contending that a "religious revolution" is necessary, and one which "the entire world" awaits, he says:

> It's inconceivable that the thinking that we hold most sacred should cause the entire Islamic world to be a source of anxiety, danger, killing and destruction for the rest of the world. Impossible! That thinking—I am not saying "religion" but "thinking"—that corpus of texts and ideas that we have sacralized over the centuries, to the

---

125. In this regard, Pope Francis in his "Address to President Erdogan" also noted during his trip to Turkey,

> Fanaticism and fundamentalism, as well as irrational fears which foster misunderstanding and discrimination, need to be countered by the solidarity of all believers. This solidarity must rest on the following pillars: respect for human life and for religious freedom, that is the freedom to worship and to live according to the moral teachings of one's religion; commitment to ensuring what each person requires for a dignified life; and care for the natural environment. The peoples and the states of the Middle East stand in urgent need of such solidarity, so that they can "reverse the trend" and successfully advance a peace process, repudiating war and violence and pursuing dialogue, the rule of law, and justice.

126. Edward Pentin, "Paris Terror Attacks: What They Did Is in the Name of Islam," *National Catholic Register*, January 13, 2015, http://www.ncregister.com/daily-news/paris-terror-attacks-what-they-did-is-in-the-name-of-islam#ixzz3RBspFpI6.

point that departing from them has become almost impossible, is antagonizing the entire world. It's antagonizing the entire world! Is it possible that 1.6 billion people should want to kill the rest of the world's inhabitants—that is 7 billion—so that they themselves may live? Impossible![127]

The assessment by Pope Benedict XVI with regard to those voices wishing to unify Christians and Muslims is equally applicable here: "this and similar voices of reason, for which we are profoundly grateful, are too weak."[128] There is much to be done. Research and critical analysis must support these "voices of reason" in both the East and West, of both Christians and Muslims, in seeking reformation of what "behind it" is "not good."

Conclusion

International condemnation of atrocities committed against Christians is acutely necessary, but this condemnation alone is not enough: we must move forward to confront the violent ideologies that underlie and motivate the persecution of Christians. In giving a brief overview of Sharia law generally, an initial structure was given to consider the interpretations of the Islamic State. By examining the Islamic State and some specific examples of its interpretation of Sharia law, a violent ideology behind the persecution of Christians was seen. An approach to considering these complicated issues followed, arguing that together people must confront and work against the discrimination and persecution of Christians and those ideas behind it, wherever and however they occur in the global socio-religious context. With Christians working as well to counter discrimination against Muslims, this approach would assist in breaking the association of Islam with violence and thus benefit Christians and Muslims alike in the common quest for peace.

---

127. John Hayward, "Egyptian President Al-Sisi Calls for an Islamic Reformation," *Breitbart News*, January 9, 2015, http://www.breitbart.com/national-security/2015/01/09/egyptian-president-al-sisi-calls-for-an-islamic-reformation/; Dana Ford, Salma Abdelaziz and Ian Lee, "Egypt's President Calls For a 'Religious Revolution,'" *CNN*, January 6, 2015, http://edition.cnn.com/2015/01/06/africa/egypt-president-speech/.

128. Benedict XVI, "Address On The Occasion Of Christmas Greetings."

Erbil, Iraq. Christian IDP camp, 2016.

7

The Theory of Religious Freedom

Fr. Piotr Mazurkiewicz

IN ORDER TO sensibly speak about freedom, one must assume that the world is not completely determined in its course. At least from time to time a local irregularity appears, a small miracle that cannot be explained away solely by reference to the chain of cause and effect. A *novum*, capable of changing the course of history even to a minimal degree, is introduced by man. Man possesses the inherent capacity to undertake or forsake certain action, to act one way or another. Action is understood as the ability to initiate or the power to generate certain acts that are not determined by factors external to the person. The power to initiate (the Latin *initium* is attributed to Man, whereas the word *principium* refers to of the rest of the created world)— writes Hannah Arendt—appeared in the world with the creation of Man, who alone is endowed with the capacity to determine the run of events in the physical world, to initiate and rupture causal chains.[1] This means that the future is a time open to human activity. By no coincidence does the reflection on man's freedom appear in St. Augustine in the context of his objection to the cyclical concept of time, which he simply labels as nonsense.[2] A unique experience in the capacity to rupture the causal chains and to begin something completely new is the act of forgiveness through which man frees

---

1. See H. Arendt, *The Life of the Mind: II. Willing* (Harcourt Brace Jovanovich: 1978), 185; J. Tischner, *Spór o istnienie człowieka* (The Dispute over the Existence of Man) (Wydawnictwo Znak, Kraków 1998), 307.
2. See St. Augustine, *De Civitate Dei*, XII, 21, http://www.thelatinlibrary.com/augustine/civ12.shtml.

himself and others from decisions and actions performed in the past.[3]

In order for freedom to exist, the absence of determinism is a necessary, but insufficient condition. "To be free," writes Robert Spaemann, "one must be able to do what one wills."[4] Consequently, one needs to be free from an external obstacle. No one and nothing from the outside may interfere with a person's actions. The more independence one has in setting out the objectives of one's actions and the more effectively one executes one's will in the world, the more one is master of oneself. This emancipative dimension of freedom signifies that a person's life can very well be the fruit of implementing a self-made design, a deliberate activity, even if in pursuit of a chosen goal the person has to, more than once, diverge from the set path, acknowledging the supremacy of some sort of past and the necessity to give way to encountered obstacles.

The Freedom of the Ancients

Antiquity divided people into free men and slaves; those who of their very nature were made to give out orders, and those who out of their very nature were born to follow them.[5] Hence freedom is not the outcome of the willed activity of an interested party, but the consequence of a natural hierarchy in the universe. The possibility of liberation means that the hierarchy does not hold absolute power over human society. The freedom of a freedman is essentially negative: owing to emancipation (*manumissio*) the freedman is no longer a slave. His status acquires meaning only by reference to the previous state of enslavement. Liberation does not occur based of the interested party's decision, but derives from the action of the authority that introduced the distinction between free men and slaves. The act of manumission itself could be subjected to certain conditions in

---

3. See H. Arendt, *The Human Condition* (The University of Chicago Press: 1998), 241.

4. R. Spaemann, Persons, "The Difference between 'Someone' and 'Something,'" *Oxford Studies in Theological Ethics*: 2006, 198.

5. "He then is by nature formed a slave who is qualified to become the chattel of another person, and on that account is so, and who has just reason enough to know that there is such a faculty, without being indued with the use of it" (Aristotle, *Politics: A Treatise on Government*, 1254b, iBooks. https://itun.es/pl/fS4Kx.l).

The Theory of Religious Freedom

favor of the former owner and revoked if they were not met. A freedman was therefore burdened with responsibility for his own freedom in so far as he could possibly lose it once again.[6]

We owe to Plato the discovery that external freedom is insufficient to call someone free. A person may well be enslaved not only by another person, but also by his/her own disorderly passions of lust and wrath. It is, however, of no significant importance whether one is the victim of one's own or another's nature. One can, therefore, be free in the outside world and yet internally enslaved. The fact that the impediment preventing one from doing what one wants is external does not make it less real.[7] Freedom, therefore, turns not only outside, achieving something in the world, but also inside, removing the impediments that linger within the individual. The notion of internal enslavement implies the existence of a hierarchy in the psychological order, which is based on the urge to subordinate emotions to the power of reason. Internal freedom is the consequence of liberating oneself from the inferior areas of one's personality. "The experiences of internal freedom," according to Hannah Arendt, "are derivative in that they always presuppose a retreat from the world where freedom was denied, into an inwardness to which no other has access."[8]

In societies built according to the liberal paradigm, freedom is usually associated with negative freedom, a freedom *from* obstacle and external interference. Ironically, claims Nicolas Berdyaev, "negative freedom, completely unknown to the ancient world, and also in a form unknown in the Jewish world, was first revealed to the world by Christianity."[9] The Greeks knew rational, positive freedom resulting from the knowledge of truth.[10] Being free is finding one's place in

---

6. See Z. Bauman, *Freedom* (Open University Press: 1998), 31.

7. "We are well aware—wrote later on St. Paul—that the Law is spiritual: but I am a creature of flesh and blood sold as a slave to sin. I do not understand my own behaviour; I do not act as I mean to, but I do things that I hate" (Letter to the Romans 7:14–15).

8. See H. Arendt, *Between Past and Future: Eight Exercises in Political Thought* (Penguin Classics: 2006), 145.

9. "It is interesting, that only Epicurus acknowledged freedom, as an indeterminism, and he connected it with Chance." N. Berdyaev, "The Metaphysical Problem of Freedom," http://www.berdyaev.com/berdiaev/berd_lib/1928_329.html.

10. See ibid.

the harmony of the world, freeing oneself, thanks to reason, from the threat of irrationality and chaos, of which the Greeks were terrified.[11] To this world of positive freedom, Christianity introduced the principle of negative freedom, understood as *indeterminism*.[12] It is freedom toward good and evil as well. The Greeks assumed that liberation is obtained by the knowledge and implementation of truth. The "rationality of good" made its fulfilment a rational necessity. Principles that stood in contradiction to it were considered coincidental and irrational. The Greek understanding of good was not linked to freedom.[13] This is well rendered in the words of Aristotle: "Everything is ordered together to one end; but the arrangement is like that in a household, where the free persons have the least liberty to act at random, and have all or most of their actions preordained for them, whereas the slaves and animals have little common responsibility and act for the most part at random; for the nature of each class is a principle such as we have described."[14] Hence in modern times we are dealing with a total reversal of the meaning of the word "freedom" in comparison to its ancient understanding. According to the contemporary take, free people, i.e., undetermined in their action, "could be considered as similar to ancient slaves, who know not what they do," remarks Pierre Aubenque, "while the actions of free people would, according to ancient criteria, appear more or less predetermined."[15] Additionally, their freedom is of a heteronomic nature, because although they establish some sort of order in the *polis* and grant themselves some rights, yet the order is inscribed in the order of the universe, which is independent of them.

Negative freedom is in practice a freedom not only in relation to good and evil, but also in relation to God, whom man can reject, which is reflected in the idea of the original fall (see Book of Genesis 3). God, according to the Bible, created human beings as free and

---

11. See N. Berdyaev, *The Meaning of History* (Transaction Publishers: 2006), 110.
12. See "The Metaphysical Problem of Freedom."
13. See *The Meaning of History*, 110.
14. Aristotle, *Metaphysics*, 1075a, http://www.perseus.tufts.edu/hopper/text?doc=Perseus%3Atext%3A1999.01.0052%3Abook%3D12%3Asection%3D1075a.
15. See P. Aubenque, *La Prudence chez Aristote* (Presses Universitaires de France, Paris 1963), 91.

The Theory of Religious Freedom

withdrew, leaving them to their own judgement (God "made them subject to their own free choice," Sirach 15:14). Christian freedom does not guarantee man's choice of God, or good, or even that man will abstain from destroying himself. Yet it is absolutely necessary, for Christianity professes that "good is the fruit of spiritual freedom, and only the good that is the fruit of the freedom of the spirit has genuine value and is authentic good."[16] Freedom carries the risk of choosing evil, but without freedom effectuating true good is impossible.[17]

If negative freedom were the only kind of freedom, man would ultimately end up subdued to the necessities of his lower nature, his urges, and the world would inevitably submerge in anarchy. Christianity—according to Berdyaev—found the secret of reconciling both types of freedom, by establishing their hierarchy. "In the correct understanding, when one does not reject the primary [negative] freedom and acknowledges its existence, the second type of freedom is the higher and final freedom, a genuine liberation of mankind and the world. True liberation is gained through learning and enacting truth that includes freedom."[18] Both types of freedom, positive and negative, exist jointly, or else each of them separately evolves into the reverse of freedom: anarchy or despotism. Freedom assumes the knowledge of truth. "A measure of truth," wrote Józef Tischner, "is how far we have tamed the world. We tame the world by knowing it. As a result of knowledge, the world ceases to scare us; we understand it, we know what it is that serves which purpose, what we can expect of the world and in it. With the knowledge of the world also comes the knowledge of the self. Knowledge uncovers the wisdom of the world as well as our own wisdom. Freedom reaches as far as wisdom."[19] Good appears on the horizon of human knowledge. The knowledge of truth and good does not enslave man; however, it does not impose itself with absolute necessity, but appears as a possible object of authentic choice. It also presupposes the possibility of its rejection. Freedom, therefore, may breed evil, yet there is no good without freedom. "Christianity proclaims the freedom of good," writes Berdyaev, "and that only such good can possess a true value

---

16. Berdyaev, *The Meaning of History*, 110.
17. See "The Metaphysical Problem of Freedom."
18. Ibid.
19. J. Tischner, *The Dispute over the Existence of Man*, 297.

and reality. It denies the compulsory and reasonable necessity of good."[20]

The freedom of the ancients is a freedom within a community. This is suggested by the etymology of both the word "freedom" and "community." Freedom (Greek *eleutheria*, Latin *libertas*) is perceived *as* a relation and *in* relation: exactly the reverse of individual autonomy and self-reliance.[21] The primary meaning of the idea of freedom is not negative in the least—it is nothing to do with the absence of an obstacle, the removal of obstacles, or freedom from oppression. "It is deeply positive—both in a political, biological and physical meaning—and conveys expansion, development, and common growth, or the growth that means sharing."[22] Roberto Esposito reminds also the Latin etymology of the word "community" (*communitas*), which is derived from the word *munus*: responsibility, service, unpayable debt, or a gift that one may not keep. Belonging to a community is linked with an unpayable debt, with committing oneself to the duty of a mutual gift, which further means one should go outside of oneself to turn to others. Belonging to *communitas* is inevitably tied to a loss, to "expropriation," hence it potentially threatens one's individual identity and one's freedom. Others gain the right to transgress one's boundaries and to impact one's decisions. The individual may seek protection from "being infected by others" through *immunization*, turning toward oneself and closing oneself up within "the shell of one's person." Immunization not only frees from the social debt, but also interrupts the duty of mutual giving, which is so crucial for the existence of a community.[23] Christianity reconciles the two aspects: individual and communal, thanks to the notion of a person, as a *separate* being. Man as a relational entity can find fulfilment by remaining in a relationship with other people, in the manner of a free and responsible being. Social life is not something external to the

20. N. Berdyaev, *The Meaning of History*, 110.
21. "Both the Indo-European core *leuth* or *leudh* from which originate the Greek term *eleutheria* and Latin *libertas*, and Sanskrit core *frya*, from which derive, in turn, English *freedom* and German *Freiheit*, they refer to something that has to do with the common growth.... Both no doubt confirm the original communitarian connotation of freedom." R. Esposito, *Termini della politica; Communità, immunità, biopolitica* (Mimesis Edizioni 2008, Polish edition: Kraków 2015), 87.
22. Ibid., 88.
23. See ibid., 84.

The Theory of Religious Freedom

human being, and at the same time man does not lose individuality by becoming a mere part of a collective.[24]

The republican concept of freedom also emphasizes the positive aspect of community. "In the republican tradition freedom is not simply negative freedom, perceived as the lack of interference from outside, but as independence from an alien power that enslaves, even though it does not interfere with the subject's domain of freedom."[25] Individual freedom may therefore be guaranteed only in a free, independent State. If the discussion about freedom were to be reduced to a dichotomy of negative and positive freedom, then republican freedom would appear as an anachronistic manifestation of collectivism.

Philip Pettit considers that the singled-out elements of a division do not refer to the same criterion. A possible solution to this inconsistency is defining negative freedom not so much as lack of interference, but rather as lack of both subjugation and domination (*absence of mastery*).[26] The source of this concept is a reflection on the master-slave/servant relationship. In the intellectual experiment proposed by Pettit, he invites us to image a slave whose master is kind enough not to interfere in his affairs. It may turn out that the slave is shrewd enough to handle his master in such a way that he can achieve his own plans without obstacles. Although in this sort of situation interference in the slave's/servant's freedom does not occur, nevertheless he is subjected to domination. The lack of interference results only from a coincidence which takes place in a given moment. It could happen that the master dies or the slave is sold to a less good-spirited master. Freedom as the lack of interference does not release the individual from a fear of possible change in the coincidental favorable circumstances. It only comes about when lack of domination is guar-

---

24. See Pontifical Council for Justice and Peace, *Compendium of the Social Doctrine of the Church*, 149, http://www.vatican.va/roman_curia/pontifical_councils/justpeace/documents/rc_pc_justpeace_doc_20060526_compendio-dott-soc_en.html#THE%20SOCIAL%20NATURE%20OF%20HUMAN%20BEINGS.

25. Z. Krasnodębski, *Demokracja peryferii* (Democracy of the peripheries) (Wydawnictwo słowo-obraz-terytoria, Gdańsk 2003), 281.

26. See R. Wierzchosławski, "Czy ingerencja wyklucza wolność? Wokó? republikańskiego ujęcia *libertas*" (Whether interference excludes freedom? Around the Republican approach to *libertas*), in: J. Miklaszewska (ed.), *Liberalizm u schyłku XX wieku* (Liberalism at the end of the twentieth century) (Wydawnictwo Meritum, Kraków 1999), 289.

anteed.²⁷ "Domination takes place not only at the time of the actual interference, but, more importantly, in a situation, when arbitrary intervention *could*—though it does not actually *have to*—occur, since no effective barriers to the potential interference in the scope of my potential choices exist."²⁸ Only the lack of domination (the impossibility to perform arbitrary interference into the scope of potential choices) allows freedom as the possibility to rule over oneself (*self-mastery*) to be resistant, secure. Republican freedom as the lack of domination does not signify, in the opinion of Pettit, the absence of interference of any kind, but rather the lack of arbitrary interference. Non-arbitrary interference, performed in the name of safeguarding our interests and convictions, and with at least our presumed consent, is treated by the author in the same way, as a limitation of our possibility to choose due to non-intentional barriers.

The republican concept tightly binds freedom (*libertas*) with the social status of citizenship (*civitas*). Since the opposite of freedom is not interference, but a state of subjugation, to be free (*liber*) is more than to live as a *servus sine domino*. *Liber* is necessarily *civis*—a citizen who enjoys all the privileges that provide some protection against arbitrary interference. "Freedom as the lack of domination represents the freedom of the city, while freedom as the lack of interference stands for the freedom of fields and heathland," states Pettit.²⁹ While liberals derive freedom from the laws of nature, republicans see it as a right, guaranteed by positive laws as a result of living in a free State with a mixed government (*regimen mixtum*).

To sum up: in the tradition of thinking about freedom the following categories can be identified: individual and community freedom; private and public freedom; positive and negative freedom; freedom

---

27. "[I]n contrast to the founders of the liberal doctrine of freedom, advocates of republican liberty believed that slavery is not just a specific violation of the rights and freedoms of citizens, but also the possibility of such a breach—dependence on the will of another, to put it in terms of Roman law: to remain *in potestate domini*" A. Grześkowiak-Krwawicz, *Regina libertas. Wolność w polskiej myśli politycznej XVIII wieku* (*Regina libertas.* Freedom in Polish political thought in the eighteenth century) (Wydawnictwo słowo-obraz-terytoria, Gdańsk 2006), 23.

28. R. Wierzchosławski, in Miklaszewska, 290–91.

29. P. Pettit, "Liberal/Communitarian: MacIntyre's Dichotomy," in J. Horton, S. Mendus (ed.), *After MacIntyre: Critical Perspectives on the Work of Alasdair MacIntyre* (Cambridge: Polity Press, 1994), 199.

The Theory of Religious Freedom

as the possibility to act freely, and freedom as an institutionally guaranteed status of the subject.

Religious Freedom

Religion is usually interpreted as man's relationship toward God, or more broadly speaking, to divinity (*sacrum*), to something that somehow goes outside of the world of phenomena, that is "beyond." People imagine God/divinity in different ways, which means no universal "model of religion" exists, only various historical traditions.[30] What they all share is a division of the world into that which is divine (sacred) and that which is human (secular). This is accompanied by

---

30. Studying the Latin etymology of the term *religion* one can note a certain duality. Cicero's word *religio* derives from *relegere*, which means: to make things together again, reconsider something, read something again, repeat, proceed the same way. Hence *religiosi* are people who devote themselves to matters that concerns god, and they repeat it again and again (See Cicero, *De natura deorum*, II, 66, http://www.thelatinlibrary.com/cicero/nd2.shtml#66). Religion this way understood is primarily a set of beliefs and practices relating to the gods specific to the people and transmitted by tradition. Re-reading involves the use of reason, hence the *religio* can also be seen as the opposite of *superstitio*—superstition. Early Christianity more often associated the word *religion* with *re-ligare*, reconnect, bearing in mind, at first, to connect man with God (and not with the tradition), from whom man had separated himself, and subsequently also believers among themselves. See Lactantius, *Institutiones divinae*, IV, 28, http://www.documentacatholicaomnia.eu/30_10_0240-0320-_Lactantius.html. Religion, therefore, is based on a personal relationship with God, which is realized in the community of the Church. The risen Christ is the only Mediator between the Father and men. At the same time, however, He has broken down the barrier which used to keep people apart, by destroying in his own person hostility, and making out of two kinds of people one man (See Letter to the Ephesians 2:14). There is no Jew nor Greek, no slave nor freeman, no male nor female. (See Letter to the Galatians 3:28). All these features lose their importance by the fact that adoption of man by God makes all of them His foster children. Since *religio* was associated primarily with the search for God in the way of reason and the traditional worship of many gods, the Christians relatively late (approx. 3rd–4th c. AD) began using the word to describe their faith. St. Augustine, speaking of Christianity as a "true religion," combines *religio* with *eligere*, which means: to choose, and *diligere*—to love (see St. Augustine, *The Confessions*, VIII, 12 and X, 6, iBooks, https://itun.es/pl/CS3Kx.l). Religion, therefore, has two dimensions: vertical and horizontal; is fulfilled through the implementation of the two commandments of love—for God and neighbor. (See J. Głodek, Nagie forum, *Religia w amerykańskiej przestrzeni publicznej według Richarda Neuhausa* (The Naked Public Square. Religion and Democracy in America, by Richard John Neuhaus) (W drodze, Poznan 2014), 108–11.

a conviction that God is the first to turn to Man, to talk to him, and man only responds. In this relation, man feels somehow determined in what he is by the one who is greater and more primordial.[31]

Man is not only a free and rational being, but he is also naturally open to Transcendence (*homo religiosus*). The reason behind this openness seems to be the experience of the fortuitousness of the human existence, the frailty and perishability of one's own existence, that of other people one is close to, and of the entire external world. Existential uncertainty felt particularly in extreme situations naturally triggers the need to turn to something or someone, who is the ultimate reason for the existence of the fortuitous.[32] The second subjective reason for the existence of religion is the potentiality of the human being. Man feels the need to constantly develop, to exceed his own limitations, to strive for the infinite. On the path to personal development he learns that finite goods cannot fully satisfy his desires. Seeking the absolute is inherent to human nature.[33] "*Thou awakest us to delight in Thy praise; for Thou madest us for Thyself,*" Saint Augustine will say, "*and our heart is restless, until it repose in Thee.*"[34] Man's interest in God does not simply result from curiosity. "The source of all preoccupation with metaphysics," writes Max Scheler, "is a bewilderment, that anything at all exists, rather than nothing.... As opposed to this the basis of religion can be found in the love of God and man's longing for ultimate salvation for himself and all things. Religion is first and foremost the path to salvation."[35]

Every religion includes a certain number of doctrinal assertions about God, man, and the path to salvation. Consequently, we are dealing also with some rules (ethical, ritual, etc.) concerning man's

---

31. See B. Welte, *Filozofia religii* (Philosophy of religion) (Wydawnictwo Znak, Kraków 1996), 38.

32. "I became a great riddle to myself," wrote St. Augustine after the death of his friend. St. Augustine, *The Confessions*, IV, 4; See Z. Zdybicka, *Człowiek i religia* (Man and Religion) (Lublin: Towarzystwo Naukowe Katolickiego Uniwersytetu Lubelskiego, 1993), 167.

33. See M. Piechowiak, *Wolność religijna—aspekty filozoficznoprawne* (Religious freedom—philosophical and legal aspects) (*Toruński Rocznik Praw Człowieka i Pokoju* 1994–1995, Toruń 1996), 14.

34. St. Augustine, *The Confessions*, I, 1.

35. M. Scheler, *Problem religii* (The Problems of Religion) (Wydawnictwo Znak, Kraków 1995), 60.

The Theory of Religious Freedom

proper behavior toward God, mankind, and the world.[36] When we speak of religion, however, what we have in mind are man's internal actions. "The exercise of religion, of its very nature, consists before all else in those internal, voluntary, and free acts whereby man sets the course of his life directly toward God."[37] Internal religious acts are inalterable and do not fall under the jurisdiction of any human authority. The external dimension of religion—though indispensable, because it is conditioned by man's social nature—is secondary to its internal dimension.[38] The human adventure with religion begins from a spontaneous search for truth, and above all the ultimate, religious truth.[39] The desire to learn the truth is man's natural aspiration. This activity need not be enforced by coercion or an external authority. The impulses flow from man's own interior, his "very nature."[40] On the path of searching for truth man must be free not only from external coercion, but also of psychological coercion.

The point is therefore not only for man to be free to act, but to be free himself, capable of making autonomous and responsible decisions. Freedom from coercion rules out contravening the relation between man's action/inaction, and his conscience, even if he chooses to change his religion.[41] Attempts at controlling his internal acts from the outside, for instance by intimidation, manipulation, or moral pressure, are inadmissible.[42] Truth imposes itself to man's conscience only by virtues of truth itself, by gently, but firmly engulfing the mind.[43] Coercion excluded by religious freedom is neverthe-

---

36. See J.A. Kłoczowski, "Religia" (Religion), in B. Szlachta (ed.), *Słownik społeczny* (Dictionary of Social Sciences) (Kraków: Wydawnictwo WAM, 2004), 1064.

37. Vatican Council II, *Dignitatis humanae*, 3, http://www.vatican.va/archive/hist_councils/ii_vatican_council/documents/vat-ii_decl_19651207_dignitatis-humanae_en.html#.

38. See P. Milcarek, "Glosa: Uwagi do doktryny Dignitatis humanae" (Gloss: Notes to the doctrine Dignitatis humanae), *Christianitas*, 48–49 (2012), 131 (hereinafter: *GDH*).

39. St. Augustine in these words expresses his most profound desire: *Deum et animam scire cupio. Nihilne plus. Nihil omnino.* (I desire to know God and the soul. And nothing more? Nothing whatever.) (St. Augustine, *Soliloquia*, II-7, http://oll.libertyfund.org/titles/augustine-the-soliloquies).

40. Vatican Council II, *Dignitatis humanae*, 2.

41. See *GDH*, 123.

42. See ibid.

43. See Vatican Council II, *Dignitatis humanae*, 1.

less something distinct from an internal pressure caused by the imposition to the mind of the truth learned, for example, in discussion with its followers.[44]

Religious freedom is strictly tied to the freedom of conscience. Man seeks the truth, but once he considers something to be the truth, he should embrace it by an act of will and subordinate his life to it. The reception of a discovered religious truth is a goal, served by religious freedom itself.[45] The honesty of conscience, especially in a situation of choices concerning the meaning of human existence or its meaninglessness is a matter of fundamental importance. Man has the moral obligation to act in accordance with the judgement of conscience, especially with regard to the essential matter of the relation to God, even if in the particular case the judgement of conscience is incorrect. "The conformity of decisions with the judgement of the conscience is of fundamental importance for personal growth both when one chooses a strictly speaking religious position, and when one adopts a non-religious position."[46] Yet even if one does not honestly search for truth, or ignores it after finding it, one does not lose the right to religious freedom, since—although one weakens one's moral dignity—one does not lose one's ontological dignity. Respect for human dignity requires recognition of man's religious dimension, and consequently of man's right to religious freedom.[47]

By emphasizing the importance of the freedom of conscience we underscore the personal dimension of religious freedom. After discovering the religious truth, man is bound in his conscience to organize his entire life according to its requirements.[48] Adhering to an identified religious truth fundamentally modifies the understanding of oneself and of the world. The individual's relation to God is not

---

44. See *GDH*, 117; "Truth can only be known and experienced in freedom; for this reason we cannot impose truth on others; truth is disclosed only in an encounter of love." Benedict XVI, *Ecclesia in Medio Oriente*, 27, http://w2.vatican.va/content/benedict-xvi/en/apost_exhortations/documents/hf_ben-xvi_exh_20120914_ecclesia-in-medio-oriente.html.

45. See *GDH*, 127.

46. M. Piechowiak, *Religious freedom—philosophical and legal aspects*, 11.

47. See John Paul II, *Christifideles laici*, 39, http://w2.vatican.va/content/john-paul-ii/en/apost_exhortations/documents/hf_jp-ii_exh_30121988_christifideles-laici.html.

48. See Vatican Council II, *Dignitatis humanae*, 2.

merely an "addition" to human life, but a constitutive element of the "being" and "existence" of an individual.[49] Hence in the life of an internally integrated individual there are no areas that can be exempt from the influence of the known religious truth. The whole of life receives a religious dimension, not only selected human activities such as private prayer, fasting, or almsgiving. Faith bears fruit in every aspect of activity and existence. A postulated or actual rift between faith and everyday life would point to incoherence in the life of a person.[50] The difference in the perception of the world between a believer and non-believer is so great, that—as worded by Saint John of the Cross—"the divinely wise and the worldly wise are fools in the estimation of each other."[51] Life "in different worlds" does not mean that there is nothing in common between the two worlds. All people, independently of their attitude toward faith, have the same nature, which in turn means community between them is made possible on the ground of natural law.[52]

Although the exercise of religion relies mainly on internal acts, "the social nature of man, requires that he should give external expression to his internal acts of religion: that he should share with others in matters religious; that he should profess his religion in

49. See John Paul II, *Christifideles laici*, 39.
50. See ibid., 59.
51. St. John of the Cross, *The Spiritual Canticle*, 26, 13 (Joseph Pich, 2012), iBooks. https://itunes.apple.com/pl/book/the-spiritual-canticle/id512376018?l=pl&mt=11.
52. "Unlike other great religions—reminds Benedict XVI in Bundestag—Christianity has never proposed a revealed law to the State and to society. . . . Instead, it has pointed to nature and reason as the true sources of law. . . . Christian theologians aligned themselves against the religious law associated with polytheism and on the side of philosophy, and that they acknowledged reason and nature in their interrelation as the universally valid source of law." Benedict XVI, "The Listening Heart Reflections on the Foundations of Law," Berlin, September 22, 2011, http://w2.vatican.va/content/benedict-xvi/en/speeches/2011/september/documents/hf_ben-xvi_spe_20110922_reichstag-berlin.html. This does not mean that between God's law and positive laws of there can be no ties, only that one should not make it through revelation, but through natural law, which—although it comes from God—can be recognized by natural reason. "According to this understanding," explains Benedict XVI, "the role of religion in political debate is not so much to supply these norms, as if they could not be known by non-believers—still less to propose concrete political solutions, which would lie altogether outside the competence of religion—but rather to help purify and shed light upon the application of reason to the discovery of objective moral principles." Benedict XVI, "Meeting with the Representatives of British

community."[53] The external dimension, even if secondary in relation to the internal dimension, is just as an indispensable element of the religious experience. "Faith and the search for sanctity is personal only in the sense, that no one can replace the individual in his/her encounter with God. God cannot be sought or found otherwise than in true internal freedom."[54] Yet once the individual makes his religious choice, his/her faith becomes a public matter. One cannot limit oneself to certain moments, or selected aspects of life; one is committed to profess one's faith and to act according to its principles in all circumstances. One does not admit the possibility of a divide into private life, in which one pursues religious practices, and public life in which one acts as if one where a non-believer. Such a dichotomy would resemble some sort of religious schizophrenia. Hence the reminder that in the case of believers, "There cannot be two parallel lives in their existence: on the one hand, the so-called spiritual life, with its values and demands; and on the other, the so-called secular life, that is, life in a family, at work, in social relationships, in the responsibilities of public life and in culture."[55] This holds true also for the choice of non-believers. It would be difficult to expect a non-believer to act as a believer in some situations.

Justice requires ensuring the right to religious freedom also in the

---

Society, Including the Diplomatic Corps, Politicians, Academics and Business Leaders," Westminster Hall, September 17, 2010, http://w2.vatican.va/content/benedict-xvi/en/speeches/2010/september/documents/hf_ben-xvi_spe_20100917_so cieta-civil e.html. Universal ethical principles are available to anyone using properly his natural reason, and religion itself adds nothing in this respect. *Novum* contributed by religion is its "corrective" role in relation to the natural reason. Religion is therefore to help man in being a fully rational being. It helps him, first, to free reason from superstition (*superstitio*). "Reason without Christian faith is always reason informed by some other faith, characteristically an unacknowledged faith, one that renders its adherents liable to error." (A. MacIntyre, *God, Philosophy, Universities: A Selective History of the Catholic Philosophical Tradition* (Rowman & Littlefield Publishers, Inc., 2011), 153. The second type of "correction" is to bring to light new questions by raising public awareness of such dimensions of existence through reason that man may not have noticed by himself.

53. Vatican Council II, *Dignitatis humanae*, 3.

54. John Paul II, Homily in Lubaczów, June 3, 1991, http://w2.vatican.va/content/john-paul-ii/it/homilies/1991/documents/hf_jp-ii_hom_19910603_messa-lubaczow.html.

55. John Paul II, *Christifideles laici*, 59.

The Theory of Religious Freedom

external dimension, namely the freedom to practice religion in social life. *Dignitatis humanae* reads as follows: "Injury therefore is done to the human person and to the very order established by God for human life, if the free exercise of religion is denied in society, provided just public order is observed."[56] As observed by Józef Krukowski:

> legal protection of religious freedom does not pertain to the content of religious beliefs, namely respect for the relation between the individual and God, but rather concerns the behavior of people towards each other because of the truth about God. The objects of religious freedom protection are therefore relations between people, as the subjects of judicial relations, as a result of their assignation to truth and good.[57]

The spiritual values of truth and good as such, are not protected by Law, only action leading to the achievement of those values.

The State is the main entity responsible for ensuring that citizens have the possibility to exercise the human rights they are entitled to, including the right to religious freedom. It should therefore recognize and support the religious life of the citizens. This allows us to speak about the limited competencies of the State in the area of religious freedom. Not only hostility, but also complete indifference (ignorance) of the State toward religion is abnormal.[58] "There is [therefore] a need to move beyond tolerance to religious freedom."[59]

The promotion of the right to religious freedom on the part of the State has two aspects: negative and positive. In the negative aspect, the authorities must not only abstain from attacking the citizens' religious freedom themselves but also adequately assure respect from all others. In the positive aspect, though the authorities may not direct the citizens' religious life, they should establish conditions that would encourage people to exercise their right to religious freedom.[60] By

---

56. Vatican Council II, *Dignitatis humanae*, 3.
57. J. Krukowski, *Kościół i państwo. Podstawy relacji prawnych* (Church and State. Fundamentals of legal relationships) (Redakcja Wydawnictw Katolickiego Uniwersytetu Lubelskiego, Lublin 2000), 91–92.
58. See *GDH*, 133.
59. Benedict XVI, *Ecclesia in Medio Oriente*, 27.
60. In this spirit spoke President Nicolas Sarkozy at the Lateran:

> C'est pourquoi j'appelle de mes vœux l'avènement d'une laïcité positive, c'est-à-dire une laïcité qui, tout en veillant à la liberté de penser, à celle de croire et de ne pas croire, ne considère pas que les religions sont un danger, mais plutôt un atout. Il ne s'agit pas de modifier

guaranteeing the freedom to make choices in accordance to what an individual recognizes as right, public authorities creates conditions conducive to the individual's fulfilment as a moral being.⁶¹ In a situation of conflict between a negative freedom of one person and a positive freedom of another, it seems that on the grounds of Catholic doctrine priority is granted to positive freedom. It is above all the right to manifest one's faith, instead of hiding it and being free from questioning on the part of private or public figures of authority.

An important role in this respect is played by culture. "At the heart of every culture lies the attitude man takes to the greatest mystery: 'the mystery of God,'" writes John Paul II. "Different cultures are basically different ways of facing the question of the meaning of personal existence. When this question is eliminated, the culture and moral life of nations are corrupted."⁶² A faith fully received, becomes culture.⁶³ Hence the protection of religious freedom, taking into account the cognitive component of religious acts, must include consideration of the function of culture in human cognition. The postulate of "religious neutrality of culture," seen as barring access to or "purging" certain areas of culture of religious content, is a postulate leading to the limitation of man's personal growth.⁶⁴ "That is why the postulate of denominational neutrality is justified mainly to the extent that the State should protect the freedom of conscience of all its citizens, regardless of their religion or worldview. Yet the postulate to eliminate the dimension of sanctity from social and public life is a call for the establishment of an atheist State and atheist social life,

---

les grands équilibres de la loi de 1905. Les Français ne le souhaitent pas et les religions ne le demandent pas. Il s'agit en revanche de rechercher le dialogue avec les grandes religions de France et d'avoir pour principe de faciliter la vie quotidienne des grands courants spirituels plutôt que de chercher à la leur compliquer.

"Discours de Nicolas Sarkozy au Palais du Latran," 20 Grudnia 2017, http://www.france-catholique.fr/Discours-de-Nicolas-Sarkozy-au.html; see *GDH*, 139–41.

61. See M. Piechowiak, *Religious freedom—philosophical and legal aspects*, 16.
62. John Paul II, *Centesimus annus*, 24, http://w2.vatican.va/content/john-paul-ii/en/encyclicals/documents/hf_jp-ii_enc_01051991_centesimus-annus.html.
63. See John Paul II, Letter to H. E. Cardinal Agostino Casaroli, Secretary of State, May 20, 1982, http://www.cultura.va/content/cultura/en/magistero/papa/JohnPaulII/fondazione.html.
64. See M. Piechowiak, *Religious freedom—philosophical and legal aspects*, 17–18.

The Theory of Religious Freedom

and has little to do with neutrality of worldview."[65] A thus-organized State of *negative confessionalism*[66] would treat believers as second-rate citizens and could force them to give up their right to be guided by their own conscience in the public domain.[67] We would then be dealing with "an unfair exclusion of religion from public life,"[68] or else the phenomenon of unjust secularization. This was pointed out by Rabbi Joseph Weiler in his speech in front of the European Court

---

65. John Paul II, Homily in Lubaczów, June 3, 1991.

> In 1905, the law of the separation of Church and State, which replaced the Concordat of 1804, was a painful and traumatizing event for the Church in France. The law regulated the way that the principle of secularity was to be lived in France. In this context the law provided for freedom of worship alone; at the same time it relegated the religious factor to the private sphere and failed to acknowledge the place of religious life and the Church institution in society. Thus, the religious journey of the human being was considered simply to be a personal sentiment, thereby overlooking the profound nature of the human being that is both personal and social in all its dimensions, including the spiritual. However, since 1920, we are grateful to the French Government itself for having recognized in a certain way the place of religion in social life, the personal and social religious dimension and the hierarchical composition of the Church that constitutes her unity.

John Paul II, Letter to the Bishops of France, Rome, February 11, 2005, http://w2.vatican.va/content/john-paul-ii/en/letters/2005/documents/hf_jp-ii_let_20050211_french-bishops.html.

66. Paul VI, To the Diplomatic Corps, January 14, 1978, in: G. Filibeck, *Human Rights in the Teaching of the Church from John XXIII to John Paul II* (Libreria Editrice Vaticana: Vatican City, 1994), 327.

67. John Paul II draws attention to this in the context of attempts to coerce civil servants and health professionals to behave in a non-religious way or even to fulfill the law contrary to their conscience: "Individual responsibility is thus turned over to the civil law, with a renouncing of personal conscience, at least in the public sphere." John Paul II, *Evangelium vitae*, 69, http://w2.vatican.va/content/john-paul-ii/en/encyclicals/documents/hf_jp-ii_enc_25031995_evangelium-vitae.html.

> Indeed, even the phenomenon of unbelief, a-religiousness and atheism, as a human phenomenon, is understood only in relation to the phenomenon of religion and faith. It is therefore difficult, even from a "purely human" point of view, to accept a position that gives only atheism the right of citizenship in public and social life, while believers are, as though by principle, barely tolerated or are treated as second-class citizens or are even—and this has already happened—entirely deprived of the rights of citizenship.

John Paul II, *Redemptor hominis*, 17, http://w2.vatican.va/content/john-paul-ii/en/encyclicals/documents/hf_jp-ii_enc_04031979_redemptor-hominis.html.

68. See J. Habermas, Faith and Knowledge: An Opening Speech by Jürgen Habermas accepting the Peace Price of the German Publishers and Booksellers Association, Paulskirche, Frankfurt, 14 October 2001, http://amsterdam.nettime.org/Lists-Archives/nettime-l-0111/msg00100.html.

of Human Rights in which he argued that secularity is not an empty category, equivalent to the absence of faith in the public domain. Forbidding religious access to the public sphere, removing religious symbols constitutes a choice in terms of outlook. A wall from which a crucifix was removed would not be a neutral wall, but an empty wall from which a crucifix had been deliberately removed.[69] Such a decision would be an instance of hostility toward the phenomenon of religion, treaded due to prejudice as the manifestation of human weakness and a source of alienation.[70] It would be an instance of a reductionist attitude to the human person, perceived as a being reduced to the horizontal dimension.[71]

A guarantee of religious freedom on the part of the State is tantamount to the absolute prohibition of imposing faith by force, including a ban of religious proselytism (dishonest or insufficiently justified incitement).[72] Faith may be offered, but not imposed.[73] Public authorities, however, are committed to recognize the religious dimension of the individual, and to create a social climate conducive to the full enjoyment of all the aspects of the right to religious freedom to which citizens are entitled.[74]

First and foremost, every individual is the subject of religious freedom, independently of his/her attitude to religion. "The human person has a right to religious freedom," we read in the Declaration on religious freedom: "This freedom means that all men are to be immune from coercion on the part of individuals or of social groups and of any human power, in such wise that no one is to be forced to act in a manner contrary to his own beliefs, whether privately or publicly, whether alone or in association with others, within due limits."[75]

---

69. See Oral submission by Professor JHH Weiler on behalf of Armenia, Bulgaria, Cyprus, Greece, Lithuania, Malta, The Russian Federation and San Marino—Third Party Intervening States in the Lautsi Case before the Grand Chamber of the European Court of Human Rights, June 30, 2010, http://eclj.org/pdf/weiler_lautsi_third_parties_submission_by_jhh_weiler.pdf.

70. See Paul VI, To the Diplomatic Corps, January 14, 1978.

71. See John Paul II, *Redemptoris missio*, 8, http://w2.vatican.va/content/john-paul-ii/en/encyclicals/documents/hf_jp-ii_enc_07121990_redemptoris-missio.html.

72. See Vatican Council II, *Dignitatis humanae*, 4 and 10.

73. See John Paul II, *Redemptoris missio*, 39.

74. See John Paul II, *Christifideles laici*, 39.

75. Vatican Council II, *Dignitatis humanae*, 2.

The Theory of Religious Freedom

Individual religious freedom has two aspects: positive and negative. In the positive aspect it includes:

1. Freedom to hold or not to hold a particular faith and to join the corresponding confessional community;

2. Freedom to perform acts of prayer and worship, individually and collectively, in private or in public, and to have churches or places of worship according to the needs of the believers;

3. Freedom for parents to educate their children in the religious convictions that inspire their own life, and to have them attend catechetical and religious instruction as provided by their faith community;

4. Freedom for families to choose the schools or other means which provide this sort of education for their children, without having to sustain directly or indirectly extra charges which would in fact deny them this freedom;

5. Freedom for individuals to receive religious assistance wherever they are, especially in public health institutions (clinics and hospitals), in military establishments, during compulsory public service, and in places of detention.[76]

In the negative aspect, the freedom to which every individual is entitled includes:

1. Freedom, at personal, civic or social levels, from any form of coercion to perform acts contrary to one's faith, or to receive an education or to join groups or associations with principles opposed to one's religious convictions;

2. Freedom not to be subjected, on religious grounds, to forms of restriction and discrimination, vis-a-vis one's fellow citizens, in all aspects of life (in all matters concerning one's career, including study, employment or profession; one's participation in civic and social responsibilities, etc.).[77]

The possibility of exercising these rights should be guaranteed by the State to every individual, without any discrimination based on faith.

---

76. John Paul II, Message on the value and content of freedom of conscience and of religion, November 14, 1980, http://w2.vatican.va/content/john-paul-ii/en/messages/pont_messages/1980/documents/hf_jp-ii_mes_19800901_helsinki-act.html.

77. Ibid.

Parents are a special subject of the right to religious freedom. This is a consequence of considering the family as a natural community, which as a result is also the subject of natural rights. This is expressed, in the "Charter of the Rights of the Family," where we read:

1. Parents have the right to educate their children in conformity with their moral and religious convictions, taking into account the cultural traditions of the family which favour the good and the dignity of the child; they should also receive from society the necessary aid and assistance to perform their educational role properly.

2. Parents have the right to freely choose schools or other means necessary to educate their children in keeping with their convictions. Public authorities must ensure that public subsidies are so allocated that parents are truly free to exercise this right without incurring unjust burdens. Parents should not have to sustain, directly or indirectly, extra charges which would deny or unjustly limit the exercise of this freedom.

3. Parents have the right to ensure that their children are not compelled to attend classes which are not in agreement with their own moral and religious convictions. In particular, sex education is a basic right of the parents and must always be carried out under their close supervision, whether at home or in educational centers chosen and controlled by them.

4. The rights of parents are violated when a compulsory system of education is imposed by the State from which all religious formation is excluded.[78]

These rights are vested in parents, since they are the first and principal educators of their children. Other entities: persons, groups, institutions, or the State play a solely auxiliary role.

Due to the social nature of Man and religion, the right to religious freedom is inherent not only to individuals (individual freedom), and communities (community freedom), but to religious institutions as well (institutional freedom).[79] It is exercised both in the pri-

---

78. Charter of the Rights of the Family, 5 a-d, http://www.vatican.va/roman_curia/pontifical_councils/family/documents/rc_pc_family_doc_19831022_family-rights_e n.html.

79. See Vatican Council II, *Dignitatis humanae*, 4.

vate and public dimension. Individuals as well as communities have the right to freely enter the public domain based on prerogatives that should be guaranteed constitutionally. Believers also have the right to establish religious institutions, which on account of being religious institutions, should be treated by the State as a partner in the social dialogue.[80] The proper subjects of this freedom remain individual people, who are nevertheless entitled to the right to act jointly and to institutionalize this activity, namely to establish an institution of a religious nature.

> Provided the just demands of public order are observed, religious communities rightfully claim freedom in order that they may govern themselves according to their own norms, honor the Supreme Being in public worship, assist their members in the practice of the religious life, strengthen them by instruction, and promote institutions in which they may join together for the purpose of ordering their own lives in accordance with their religious principles.[81]

The opportunity to be guided by one's own standards is what we call autonomy. In the ontological sense, this term means that a given entity has its own value and for this reason cannot be treated instrumentally by another autonomous entity, particularly not by the State. In the normative sense, autonomy signifies that a given entity may apply its own law in a given field of activity.[82] The respect for the autonomy of a religious community is linked with the non-interference of the State in the affairs of the community and the possibility for the community to acquire legal status.[83]

The rights of churches and religious communities include, *inter alia*:

---

80. "Expressly, it will be necessary to recognize and safeguard the dignity of the human person and the right to religious freedom in its threefold dimension: individual, collective and institutional." John Paul II, "To a Study Session: Towards a European Constitution," Vatican, June 20, 2002, https://www.ewtn.com/library/PAPALDOC/JP2EURCO.HTM.

81. Vatican Council II, *Dignitatis humanae*, 4.

82. See J. Krukowski, *Church and State. Fundamentals of legal relationships*, 105.

83. See EU Guidelines on the promotion and protection of freedom of religion or belief, http://www.consilium.europa.eu/uedocs/cms_data/docs/pressdata/EN/foraff/137585.pdf.

1. Freedom to have their own internal hierarchy or equivalent ministers freely chosen by the communities according to their constitutional norms;

2. Freedom for religious authorities (notably, in the Catholic Church, for bishops and other ecclesiastical superiors) to exercise their ministry freely, ordain priests or ministers, appoint to ecclesiastical offices, communicate and have contacts with those belonging to their religious denomination;

3. Freedom to have their own institutions for religious training and theological studies, where candidates for priesthood and religious consecration can be freely admitted;

4. Freedom to receive and publish religious books related to faith and worship, and to have free use of them;

5. Freedom to proclaim and communicate the teaching of the faith, whether by the spoken or the written word, inside as well as outside places of worship, and to make known their moral teaching on human activities and on the organization of society: this being in accordance with the commitment, ... to facilitate the spreading of information, of culture, of exchange of knowledge and experiences in the field of education; which corresponds, moreover, in the religious field to the Church's mission of evangelization;

6. Freedom to use the media of social communication (press, radio, television) for the same purpose;

7. Freedom to carry out educational, charitable and social activities so as to put into practice the religious precept of love for neighbor, particularly for those most in need.[84]

In the case of religious communities with international structures, it is possible to additionally identify the following freedom rights:

1. With regard to religious communities which, like the Catholic Church, have a supreme authority responsible at world level (in line with the directives of their faith) for the unity of communion that binds together all pastors and believers in the same confession (a responsibility exercised through Magisterium and jurisdiction):

---

84. John Paul II, Message on the value and content of freedom of conscience and of religion.

The Theory of Religious Freedom

freedom to maintain mutual relations of communication between that authority and the local pastors and religious communities; freedom to make known the documents and texts of the Magisterium (encyclicals, instructions, etc.);

2. At the international level: freedom of free exchange in the field of communication, cooperation, religious solidarity, and more particularly the possibility of holding multi-national or international meetings;

3. Also at the international level, freedom for religious communities to exchange information and other contributions of a theological or religious nature.[85]

In conformity with the principle of the equality of churches and religious communities, the above rights are vested in all of those entities. The State should also ensure that none of them be subjected to discrimination.

In the context of the presence of Christians in the Middle East and their relation with the Muslims, who constitute the vast majority of the societies living there, Pope Benedict XVI underlines the importance of citizenship, guaranteed by the State and non-differentiated.

The Catholics of the Middle East, the majority of whom are native citizens of their countries, have the duty and right to participate

---

85. Ibid., *Dignitatis humanae* describes these rights as follows:

Religious communities also have the right not to be hindered, either by legal measures or by administrative action on the part of government, in the selection, training, appointment, and transferral of their own ministers, in communicating with religious authorities and communities abroad, in erecting buildings for religious purposes, and in the acquisition and use of suitable funds or properties. Religious communities also have the right not to be hindered in their public teaching and witness to their faith, whether by the spoken or by the written word. However, in spreading religious faith and in introducing religious practices everyone ought at all times to refrain from any manner of action which might seem to carry a hint of coercion or of a kind of persuasion that would be dishonorable or unworthy, especially when dealing with poor or uneducated people. Such a manner of action would have to be considered an abuse of one's right and a violation of the right of others. In addition, it comes within the meaning of religious freedom that religious communities should not be prohibited from freely undertaking to show the special value of their doctrine in what concerns the organization of society and the inspiration of the whole of human activity. Finally, the social nature of man and the very nature of religion afford the foundation of the right of men freely to hold meetings and to establish educational, cultural, charitable and social organizations, under the impulse of their own religious sense.

Vatican Council II, *Dignitatis humanae*, 4.

fully in national life, working to build up their country. They should enjoy full citizenship and not be treated as second-class citizens or believers. As in the past when, as pioneers of the Arab Renaissance, they took full part in the cultural, economic and scientific life of the different cultures of the region, so too in our own day they wish to share with Muslims their experiences and to make their specific contribution.... It is wrong to claim that these rights are only Christian human rights. They are nothing less than the rights demanded by the dignity of each human person and each citizen, whatever his or her origins, religious convictions and political preferences.[86]

It is therefore not a question of the majority or minority religion, but of the inalienable right of every human person.[87] Every human person is capable of understanding this right, regardless of the professed religion.

Christians and Muslims agree that in religious matters there can be no coercion. We are committed to teaching attitudes of openness and respect towards the followers of other religions. But religion can be misused, and it is surely the duty of religious leaders to guard against this. Above all, whenever violence is done in the name of religion, we must make it clear to everyone that in such instances we are not dealing with true religion. For the Almighty cannot tolerate the destruction of his own image in his children.[88]

A limitation on the right to religious freedom is implicit in the definition of the notion itself.[89] "The right to religious freedom is exercised in human society: hence its exercise is subject to certain regulatory norms."[90] However, strictly speaking it is not the right to religious freedom that is subject to limitations, but its exercise.[91] One can say that the right to religious freedom is absolute in the internal dimension, but restricted in the external forms of expression.[92]

---

86. Benedict XVI, *Ecclesia in Medio Oriente*, 25.
87. See John Paul II, *Redemptoris missio*, 39.
88. John Paul II, "Meeting with Muslim Leaders," *Abuja*, March 22, 1998, http://w2.vatican.va/content/john-paul-ii/en/speeches/1998/march/documents/hf_jp-ii_spe_19980322_nigeria-muslim.html.
89. See *GDH*, 123.
90. Vatican Council II, *Dignitatis humanae*, 7.
91. See *GDH*, 145.
92. See footnote 102.

The Theory of Religious Freedom

Although the exercise of the right to freedom is subject to certain internal moral limitations (in man's conscience), nevertheless from a social point of view only those moral limitations are significant which have a bearing on regulatory norms.

The particular role of the State in the field of protecting religious freedom stems from the fact that only the State has the instruments of law enforcement. Interventions of civil authorities should not, however, be executed in an arbitrary fashion or in an unfair spirit of partisanship. Its action is to be controlled by juridical norms which are in conformity with the objective moral order. These norms arise out of the need for the effective safeguard of the rights of all citizens and for the peaceful settlement of conflicts of rights, also out of the need for an adequate care of genuine public peace, which comes about when men live together in good order and in true justice, and finally out of the need for a proper guardianship of public morality. These matters constitute the basic component of the common welfare: they are what is meant by "public order."[93] "Society defends itself not against the execution of the right to religious freedom, but against abuses, that try to justify themselves by this right."[94]

The principle of equality that is referred to here means that it is unacceptable to favor one of the parties at the expense of the other, but not to differentiate in a way that results from distributive justice.[95] The equal treatment of citizens is not equivalent to the identical treatment of whole religious communities, conditioned by, for

---

93. Vatican Council II, *Dignitatis humanae*, 7.
94. *GDH*, 147.
95. See *GDH*, 147; The principle of equality in positive aspect means that religious communities should be treated identically, where each of them equally has a specific trait, and only because of this characteristic, and in a different way, where among them there are significant differences. If there is a specific feature of all religious communities, the law should not make any differentiation among them. However, if only one or some have that characteristic variation is required. This applies to e.g., the possibility of regulating the legal situation of the Catholic Church by an international agreement. In negative aspect equality means giving no preference to any of the religious communities in a way that would mean discrimination against other religious groups. The State, therefore, cannot grant any special rights to one of the communities where all of them have the same attributes. See J. Krukowski, *Church and State. Fundamentals of legal relationships*, 278–80; See P. Mazurkiewicz, "Autonomy of the Church and Freedom of Religion in Poland," in: G. Robbers (ed.), *Church Autonomy* (Peter Lang, Frankfurt am Main 2001), 364–65.

example, their contribution to the common good. "If, in view of peculiar circumstances obtaining among peoples, special civil recognition is given to one religious community in the constitutional order of society, it is at the same time imperative that the right of all citizens and religious communities to religious freedom should be recognized and made effective in practice. Finally, government is to see to it that equality of citizens before the law [...] is never violated, whether openly or covertly, for religious reasons. Nor is there to be discrimination among citizens."[96] The judicial position of individual citizens cannot be differentiated based on their personal denomination or religious involvement.[97]

The criterion of limiting the execution of the right to freedom is juridical (good order) and moral (public morality), yet the latter only pertains to public activities, their public reception and social consequences. Public order, as the main component of common good, indispensable for the survival of society, is the reference point in assessing the need to apply judicial limitations and not the entire common good. Nor is it the reason of the State, as defined by governments. The protection of religious freedom cannot be suspended when an extraordinary danger threatens the survival of a nation.[98] The previous sentence includes a norm that limits the limitation norm: the goal of preserving integral freedom in society means that the right to religious freedom is not just one of many human rights, but the most fundamental right, which is inherent not because of man's subjective disposition, but based on his very nature. Religious freedom is the first of human liberties and the foundation of all remaining human rights. In a way, it forms the axis of human rights. "The civil and social right to religious freedom," writes John Paul II, "inasmuch as it touches the most intimate sphere of the spirit, is a

---

96. Vatican Council II, *Dignitatis humanae*, 6.
97. See *GDH*, 143.
98. According to the International Covenant on Civil and Political Rights, the right to religious freedom cannot be suspended even in the event of a state of emergency. However, "freedom to manifest one's religion or belief" may be subject to limitations as are prescribed by law and necessary to protect public safety, order, health or morals or the fundamental freedoms of others. See International Covenant on Civil and Political Rights, Art. 4.2 and 18.3, https://treaties.un.org/doc/Publication/UNTS/Volume%20999/volume-999-I-14668-English.pdf. See also M. Piechowiak, *Religious freedom—philosophical and legal aspects*, 9.

point of reference for the other fundamental rights and in some way becomes a measure of them."[99] "Actuation of this right is one of the fundamental tests of man's authentic progress in any regime, in any society, system or milieu."[100]

Conclusion

Every person has the right to religious freedom. In the internal aspect that freedom means the freedom of conscience, the capacity of a person to make a moral choice of the known truth according to the imperative of the conscience. This right also includes the right to change one's religion. Religious freedom in the external aspect covers the freedom to express religious beliefs, privately and publicly, individually and in a community, and the freedom from external coercion in the manifestation of religious conviction. In the negative aspect this means that no one should be forced to act against his/her conscience; neither should anyone encounter obstacles in acting according to one's conscience. This concerns freedom from coercion on the part of other people, groups, communities, or public authorities. In the positive aspect, it implies the freedom to manifest religious convictions and the protection of that freedom on the part of public authorities.[101] Every human being, family, community, and religious institution is the subject of religious freedom perceived in this way.[102] The right to religious freedom is absolute in the internal dimension, whereas benefiting from it in the external dimension falls under certain regulatory limitations in consideration of public order.

---

99. John Paul II, *Christifideles laici*, 39.
100. John Paul II, *Redemptor hominis*, 17.
101. See J. Krukowski, *Church and State. Fundamentals of legal relations*, 91–92.
102. E.W. Böckenförde proposes the following categorization: religious freedom is the right to have or not have faith (freedom of belief), to profess or not to profess (freedom of religion), to public exercise of religious practices or not to fulfill them (freedom of worship) and the right to belong to a religious community (freedom of religious associations). See E.W. Böckenförde, *Staat—Nation— Europa* (Studien zur Staatslehre, Verfassungstheorie und Rechtsphilosophie, Suhrkamp, 1999), 256–57.

Appendices

Appendix I

Message of John Paul II on the Value and Content of Freedom of Conscience and of Religion, 14 November 1980.

On the eve of the Madrid Conference on European Security and Cooperation, September 1, 1980, His Holiness Pope John Paul II sent a personal letter to the heads of state of the nations who signed the Helsinki Final Act (1975), enclosing the following document wherein he submits for their consideration and that of their respective governments an extensive reflection on the value and content of freedom of conscience and of religion with special reference to the implementation of the Final Act.

1. Because of her religious mission, which is universal in nature, the Catholic Church feels deeply committed to assisting today's men and women in advancing the great cause of justice and peace so as to make our world ever more hospitable and human. These are noble ideals to which people eagerly aspire and for which governments carry a special responsibility. At the same time, because of the changing historical and social situation, their coming into effect—in order to be ever more adequately adapted—needs the continued contribution of new reflections and initiatives, the value of which will depend on the extent to which they proceed from multilateral and constructive dialogue.

If one considers the many factors contributing to peace and justice in the world, one is struck by the ever increasing importance, under their particular aspect, of the wide-spread aspiration that all men and women be guaranteed equal dignity in sharing material goods, in effectively enjoying spiritual goods, and consequently in enjoying the corresponding inalienable rights.

During these last decades the Catholic Church has reflected deeply on the theme of human rights, especially on freedom of conscience and of religion; in so doing, she has been stimulated by the daily life experience of the Church herself and of the faithful of all areas and social groups. The Church would like to submit a few special considerations on this theme to the distinguished authorities of the Helsinki Final Act's signatory countries, with a view to encouraging a serious examination of the present situation of this liberty so as to ensure that it is effectively guaranteed everywhere. In doing so, the Church feels she is acting in full accord with the joint commitment contained in the Final Act, namely, "to promote and encourage the effective exercise of civil, political, economic, social, cultural, and other liberties and rights, all deriving from the dignity inherent in the human person, and essential for his free and integral development"; she thus intends to make use of the criterion acknowledging "the universal importance of human rights and fundamental liberties, the respect of which is an essential factor of peace, justice, and welfare necessary to the development of friendly relationships and cooperation among them and among all States."

2. *International Community's Interest*

It is noted with satisfaction that during the last decades the international community has shown interest in the safeguarding of human rights and fundamental liberties and has carefully concerned itself with respect for freedom of conscience and of religion in well-known documents such as:

a) the U.N. Universal Declaration on Human Rights of December 10, 1948 (article 18);

b) the International Covenant on Civil and Political Rights approved by the United Nations on December 16, 1966 (article 18);

c) the Final Act of the Conference on European Security and Cooperation, signed on August 1, 1975 ("Questions related to security in Europe, 1, a. Declaration on the principles governing mutual relationships among participating states: VIII. Respect for human rights and fundamental liberties, including freedom of thought, conscience, religion or conviction").

Furthermore, the Final Act's section on cooperation regarding "contacts among persons" has a paragraph wherein the participating states "confirm that religious cults, and religious institutions and organizations acting within the constitutional framework of a particular state, and their representatives, may, within the field of activity, have contacts among themselves, hold meetings and exchange information."

Moreover, these international documents reflect an ever-growing worldwide conviction resulting from a progressive evolution of the question of human rights in the legal doctrine and public opinion of various countries. Thus today most state constitutions recognize the principle of respect for freedom of conscience and religion in its fundamental formulation as well as the principle of equality among citizens.

On the basis of all the formulations found in the foregoing national and international legal instruments, it is possible to point out the elements providing a framework and dimension suitable for the full exercise of religious freedom.

First, it is clear that the starting point for acknowledging and respecting that freedom is the dignity of the human person, who experiences the inner and indestructible exigency of acting freely "according to the imperatives of his own conscience" (cf. text of the Final Act under (c) above). On the basis of his personal convictions, man is led to recognize and follow a religious or metaphysical concept involving his whole life with regard to fundamental choices and attitudes. This inner reflection, even if it does not result in an explicit and positive assertion of faith in God, cannot but be respected in the name of the dignity of each one's conscience, whose hidden searching may not be judged by others. Thus, on the one hand, each individual has the right and duty to seek the truth, and, on the other hand, other persons as well as civil society have the corresponding duty to respect the free spiritual development of each person.

This concrete liberty has its foundation in man's very nature, the characteristic of which is to be free, and it continues to exist—as stated in the Second Vatican Council's declaration—"even in those who do not live up to their obligation of seeking the truth and adhering to it; the exercise of this right is not to be impeded, provided that the just requirements of public order are observed" (*Dignitatis humanae*, No. 2).

A second and no less fundamental element is the fact that religious freedom is expressed not only by internal and exclusively individual acts, since human beings think, act and communicate in relationship with others; "professing" and "practicing" a religious faith is expressed through a series of visible acts, whether individual or collective, private or public, producing communion with persons of the same faith, and establishing a bond through which the believer belongs to an organic religious community; that bond may have different degrees or intensities according to the nature and the precepts of the faith or conviction one holds.

The Theory of Religious Freedom

3. *Church's Thinking on the Subject*

The Catholic Church has synthesized her thinking on this subject in the Second Vatican Council's Declaration, *Dignitatis humanae*, promulgated on December 7, 1965, a document which places the Apostolic See under a special obligation.

This declaration had been preceded by Pope John XXIII's Encyclical, *Pacem in terris*, dated April 11, 1963, which solemnly emphasized the fact that everyone has "the right to be able to worship God in accordance with the right dictates of his conscience."

The same declaration of the Second Vatican Council was then taken up again in various documents of Pope Paul VI, in the 1974 Synod of Bishops' message, and more recently in the message to the United Nations Organization during the papal visit on October 2, 1979, which repeats it essentially: "In accordance with their dignity, all human beings, because they are persons, that is, beings endowed with reason and free will and, therefore, bearing a personal responsibility, are both impelled by their nature and bound by a moral obligation to seek the truth, especially religious truth. They are also bound to adhere to the truth once they come to know it and to direct their whole lives in accordance with its demands" (*Dignitatis humanae*, No. 2). "The practice of religion by its very nature consists primarily of those voluntary and free internal acts by which a human being directly sets his course towards God. No merely human power can either command or prohibit acts of this kind. But man's social nature itself requires that he give external expression to his internal acts of religion, that he communicate with others in religious matters and that he profess his religion in community" (*Dignitatis humanae*, No. 3).

"These words," the U.N. address added, "touch the very substance of the question. They also show how even the confrontation between the religious view and the agnostic or even atheistic view of the world, which is one of the 'signs of the times' of the present age, could preserve honest and respectful human dimensions without violating the essential rights of conscience of any man or woman living on earth" (Address to the 34th General Assembly of the United Nations, No. 20).

On the same occasion, the conviction was expressed that "respect for the dignity of the human person would seem to demand that, when the exact tenor of the exercise of religious freedom is being discussed or determined with a view to national laws or international conventions, the institutions that are by their nature at the service of religion should also be brought in." This is because, when religious freedom is to be given substance, if the participation of those most concerned in it and who have special experience of it and responsibility for it is omitted, there is a danger of setting arbitrary norms of application and of "imposing, in so intimate a field of man's life, rules or restrictions that are opposed to his true religious needs" (Address to the U.N. 34th General Assembly, No. 20).

4. On the Personal and Community Levels

In the light of the foregoing premises and principles, the Holy See sees it as its right and duty to envisage an analysis of the specific elements corresponding to the concept of "religious freedom" and of which they are the application insofar as they follow from the requirements of individuals and communities, or insofar as they are necessary for enabling them to carry out their concrete activities. In fact, in the expression and practice of religious freedom, one notices the presence of closely interrelated individual and community aspects, private and public, so that enjoying religious freedom includes connected and complementary dimensions:

a) at the personal level, the following have to be taken into account:

—freedom to hold or not to hold a particular faith and to join the corresponding confessional community;

—freedom to perform acts of prayer and worship, individually and collectively, in private or in public, and to have churches or places of worship according to the needs of the believers;

—freedom for parents to educate their children in the religious convictions that inspire their own life, and to have them attend catechetical and religious instruction as provided by their faith community;

—freedom for families to choose the schools or other means which provide this sort of education for their children, without having to sustain directly or indirectly extra charges which would in fact deny them this freedom;

The Theory of Religious Freedom

—freedom for individuals to receive religious assistance wherever they are, especially in public health institutions (clinics and hospitals), in military establishments, during compulsory public service, and in places of detention;

—freedom, at personal, civic or social levels, from any form of coercion to perform acts contrary to one's faith, or to receive an education or to join groups or associations with principles opposed to one's religious convictions;

—freedom not to be subjected, on religious grounds, to forms of restriction and discrimination, vis-a-vis one's fellow citizens, in all aspects of life (in all matters concerning one's career, including study, employment or profession; one's participation in civic and social responsibilities, etc.).

b) at the community level, account has to be taken of the fact that religious denominations, in bringing together believers of a given faith, exist and act as social bodies organized according to their own doctrinal principles and institutional purposes.

The Church as such, and confessional communities in general, need to enjoy specific liberties in order to conduct their life and to pursue their purposes; among such liberties the following are to be mentioned especially:

—freedom to have their own internal hierarchy or equivalent ministers freely chosen by the communities according to their constitutional norms;

—freedom for religious authorities (notably, in the Catholic Church, for bishops and other ecclesiastical superiors) to exercise their ministry freely, ordain priests or ministers, appoint to ecclesiastical offices, communicate and have contacts with those belonging to their religious denomination;

—freedom to have their own institutions for religious training and theological studies, where candidates for priesthood and religious consecration can be freely admitted;

—freedom to receive and publish religious books related to faith and worship, and to have free use of them;

—freedom to proclaim and communicate the teaching of the faith, whether by the spoken or the written word, inside as well as outside places of worship, and to make known their moral teaching on human activities and on the organization of society: this being in accordance with the commitment, included in the Helsinki Final Act, to facilitate the spreading of information, of culture, of exchange of knowledge and experiences in the field of education; which corresponds, moreover, in the religious field to the Church's mission of evangelization;

—freedom to use the media of social communication (press, radio, television) for the same purpose;

—freedom to carry out educational, charitable and social activities so as to put into practice the religious precept of love for neighbor, particularly for those most in need.

Furthermore:

—With regard to religious communities which, like the Catholic Church, have a supreme authority responsible at world level (in line with the directives of their faith) for the unity of communion that binds together all pastors and believers in the same confession (a responsibility exercised through Magisterium and jurisdiction): freedom to maintain mutual relations of communication between that authority and the local pastors and religious communities; freedom to make known the documents and texts of the Magisterium (encyclicals, instructions, etc.);

—at the international level: freedom of free exchange in the field of communication, cooperation, religious solidarity, and more particularly the possibility of holding multi-national or international meetings;

—also at the international level, freedom for religious communities to exchange information and other contributions of a theological or religious nature.

5. Person's Primary Right

As was said earlier, freedom of conscience and of religion, including the aforementioned elements, is a primary and inalienable right of the human person; what is more, insofar as it touches the innermost sphere of the spirit, one can even say that it upholds the justification, deeply rooted in each individual, of all other liberties. Of course, such freedom can only be exercised in a responsible way, that is, in accordance with ethical principles and by respecting equality and justice, which in turn can be strengthened, as mentioned before, through dialogue with those institutions whose nature is to serve religion.

6. *No Geographical Borders*

The Catholic Church is not confined to a particular territory, and she has no geographical borders; her members are men and women of all regions of the world. She knows, from many centuries of experience, that suppression, violation, or restriction of religious freedom has caused suffering and bitterness, moral and material hardship, and that even today there are millions of people enduring these evils. By contrast, the recognition, guarantee, and respect of religious freedom bring serenity to individuals and peace to the social community; they also represent an important factor in strengthening a nation's moral cohesion, in improving people's common welfare, and in enriching the cooperation among nations in an atmosphere of mutual trust.

In addition, the wholesome implementation of the principle of religious freedom will contribute to the formation of citizens who, in full recognition of the moral order, "will be obedient to lawful authority and be lovers of true freedom; people, in other words, who will come to decisions on their own judgment, and, in the light of truth, govern their activities with a sense of responsibility, and strive after what is true and right, willing always to join with others in cooperative effort" (*Dignitatis humanae*, No. 8).

Moreover, if it is properly understood, religious freedom will help to ensure the order and common welfare of each nation, of each society, for, when individuals know that their fundamental rights are protected, they are better prepared to work for the common welfare.

Respect for this principle of religious freedom will also contribute to strengthening international peace which, on the contrary, is threatened by any violation of human rights, as pointed out in the aforementioned U.N. address, and especially by unjust distribution of material goods and violation of the objective rights of the spirit, of human conscience, and creativity, including man's relation to God. Only the effective protection of the fullness of rights for every individual without discrimination can guarantee peace down to its very foundations.

7. To Serve the Cause of Peace

In this perspective, through the above presentation the Holy See intends to serve the cause of peace, in the hope it may contribute to the improvement of such an important sector of human and social life, and thus of international life also.

It goes without saying that the Apostolic See has no thought or intention of failing to give due respect to the sovereign prerogatives of any state. On the contrary, the Church has a deep concern for the dignity and rights of every nation; she has the desire to contribute to the welfare of each one and she commits herself to do so.

Thus the Holy See wishes to stimulate reflection, so that the civil authorities of the various countries may see to what extent the above considerations deserve thorough examination. If such reflection can lead to recognizing the possibility of improving the present situation, the Holy See declares itself fully available to open a fruitful dialogue to that end, in a spirit of sincerity and openness.

L'Osservatore Romano (weekly edition in English, 1981) n.3, 12–14.

Appendix II

International Covenant on Civil and Political Rights

Article 18. 1. Everyone shall have the right to freedom of thought, conscience and religion. This right shall include freedom to have or to adopt a religion or belief of his choice, and freedom, either individually or in community with others and in public or private, to manifest his religion or belief in worship, observance, practice and teaching.

2. No one shall be subject to coercion which would impair his freedom to have or to adopt a religion or belief of his choice.

3. Freedom to manifest one's religion or beliefs may be subject only to such limitations as are prescribed by law and are necessary to protect public safety, order, health, or morals or the fundamental rights and freedoms of others.

4. The States Parties to the present Covenant undertake to have respect for the liberty of parents and, when applicable, legal guardians to ensure the religious and moral education of their children in conformity with their own convictions.

https://treaties.un.org/doc/Publication/UNTS/Volume%20999/volume-999-I-14668-English.pdf.

Bartella, Iraq. Remnants of St. George Syriac Catholic church (March, 2017).

Three children who were held hostage by ISIS.
They later escaped Mosul with their parents.

8

The Holy See's Diplomatic Response to the Crisis in Syria

John M. Czarnetzky

CATHOLICS BELIEVE that the Roman Catholic Church is "holy, catholic, and apostolic;" that the Church is instituted by God through its founder Jesus Christ,[1] and under the guidance of the Holy Spirit who works through the Church; that the Church is universal and so is the Church's mission; and that Jesus entrusted the Church to his Apostles, whose successors today continue the work of the Apostles through the Church.[2] Thus, the Roman Catholic Church is a human institution whose spiritual mission has played out in human affairs beginning with the Apostles, through two thousand years of history, down to the present. As a spiritual institution enmeshed in human affairs, the Church must act in the world.

In so acting, the Church lends its voice to the discussion at every level of human affairs on the common good of humanity and of the individual human person. At the local and national levels, the Church's voice primarily (though not exclusively)[3] emanates from its

---

1. For the sake of brevity, in this essay I will refer to the Roman Catholic Church as the "Church." This is not meant to exclude other Christians or faiths, but rather recognizes that this essay is exclusively about the diplomatic efforts of the Roman Catholic Church.

2. See *Catechism of the Catholic Church*, §§ 823–70.

3. It is essential to qualify statements about how the Church acts at any level of society with the adverb "primarily." The local bishops are understood always to be acting in unity with the pope and thus with the universal Church, and vice versa— the pope is understood to be acting in unity with the bishops of the Church throughout the world, and thus all the faithful.

local dioceses through the bishops who lead them and through the voices of the faithful. At the international level, the Church acts primarily through its leader, the pope, the successor to the Apostle Peter as the head of the Church. Unsurprisingly, popes throughout history have engaged in diplomacy to further the Church's participation in international affairs. Given its nature, history, and mission, the Church's diplomatic work is unique. In discussions over how to proceed concerning international questions, the Church "does not offer a purely political, commercial, or technical contribution. Instead, it approaches them from a moral and spiritual point of view, offering perspectives and insights that would otherwise not always be heard or taken into account, in the hope of overcoming inadequate or partial positions so as to promote the genuine good of all. In its contributions, the Holy See is guided, among other things, by the social teaching of the Church, which is based on four fundamental principles: the dignity of the human person, the common good, solidarity and subsidiarity.[4]

This chapter concerns the Church's application of this philosophy to an urgent international situation—the current crisis in Syria.

The Holy See and Diplomacy

The Church enjoys unique status in international diplomacy.[5] There is an internationally recognized entity, the Vatican City State, which

---

4. Cardinal Pietro Parolin Address on the Holy See and International Relations, University of Tartu, Estonia (May 11, 2016), https://holyseemission.org/contents//newsletters/574da9c5698914.13966720.php (citing Pope Francis, *Evangelii Gaudium: Apostolic Exhortation on the Proclamation of the Gospel in Today's World* [November 24, 2013], No. 241). See also Ronald J. Rychlak and John M. Czarnetzky, "The International Criminal Court and the Question of Subsidiarity," *Third World Legal Studies* 2000–2003 (questioning the new doctrine of complementary); Rome Statute, Art. 17(1)(a).

5. The material on the Holy See's status and history of diplomacy in international affairs largely is drawn from the work of Robert J. Araujo, SJ and John A. Lucal, SJ. See Robert John Araujo, SJ & John A. Lucal, SJ, *Papal Diplomacy and the Quest for Peace: The Vatican and International Organizations from the Early Years to the League of Nations* (Ann Arbor: Sapientia Press, 2004) [hereinafter "Araujo & Lucal"]; Robert J. Araujo, SJ, The "International Personality and Sovereignty of the Holy See," 50 *Cath. U. L. Rev.* 291 (2001) [hereinafter, "Araujo"]. For additional sources concerning

Holy See's Diplomatic Response to the Crisis in Syria

has the attributes of a "state" for purposes of international law—a territory, a population, and the capacity to engage in formal relations with other states and international actors. The Church, however, exercises its diplomacy primarily not as "Vatican City," but rather as the "Holy See." The Holy See is different from merely a sovereign nation. As the name implies, the Holy See is also the "seat" of the first pope, Peter, and his successors, and therefore is the true heart of the Church.[6]

The Church's Code of Canon Law clearly distinguishes between the Church in general and the Holy See, though it holds that both are ordained by divine law and are united in the person of the pope. Legally speaking, the Holy See refers to the pope, the Roman Curia, and the administrative apparatus that the pope uses to administer the affairs of the Church. This includes, of course, the Holy See's diplomats who are part of the Secretariat of State of the Holy See, which is administered by the Cardinal Secretary of State. The unique tripartite nature of the Church acting in the world—the Holy See, the Vatican City State, and the Roman Catholic church in its dioceses worldwide—means that the international legal position of the Holy See is more ambiguous than that of nation states.

It has not always been so. For many centuries, the question of the Church's international juridical status was not controversial. Until the late nineteenth century, the pope was the ruler of the Papal States, and thus a temporal monarch as well as a spiritual leader. When Italy annexed the Papal States in 1870, however, the pope lost

---

the longstanding debates regarding the juridical status of the Holy See in international affairs, see Joseph Bernhart, *The Vatican as a World Power* (George N. Shuster, trans.) (1939); Hyginus Eugene Cardinale, *The Holy See and the International Order* (1976); Carl Conrad Eckhardt, *The Papacy and World Affairs* (1937); Robert A. Graham, SJ, *Vatican Diplomacy: A Study of Church and State on the International Plane* (1959); Eric O. Hanson, *The Catholic Church in World Politics* (1987); J. Derek Holmes, *The Papacy in the Modern World* (1981); Jacques Maritain, *The Things That Are Not Caesar's* (J. F. Scanlan, trans., French ed.) (1930); Charles Pichon, *The Vatican and Its Role in World Affairs* (Jean Misrahi, trans.) (1950); Francis Rooney, *The Global Vatican: An Inside Look at the Catholic Church, World Politics, and the Extraordinary Relationship Between the United States and the Holy See* (2013).

6. The word "See" in this context is derived from the Latin word "*sedes*" meaning seat or chair.

most of his physical domain, but not his spiritual authority.[7] Even without territory, the pope continued to conduct foreign affairs from the Vatican, and the Italian government recognized the sovereignty of the Holy See in international affairs even before the establishment of the Vatican City State in the Lateran Treaty in 1929.[8]

With the reacquisition of territory in the form of the tiny Vatican City State, the Holy See's international juridical position strengthened, though it is evident that the Holy See is not a traditional nation state. What is also evident, however, is that other states recognize the Holy See as an actor in international affairs as if it were a nation state. Therefore, despite the peculiarities inherent in the relationship between the Holy See, Vatican City, and the Church, the Holy See is a separate "international person" due to the simple fact that most of the rest of the world treats the Holy See as such.[9] The practical effect of this recognition of the Holy See is crucially important to any discussion of the Church's response to international crises. As Araujo and Lucal summarize it:

> The Holy See is respected by the international community of sovereign States and treated as a subject of international law having the capacity to engage in diplomatic relations and to enter into binding agreements... that are largely geared to establishing and preserving peace in the world.... Its voice in this realm speaks not just for some, but for all of humanity in its quest for peace.[10]

To a great extent, the complexity of the Holy See's international status is due to its mission, which the Church understands to transcend legal niceties. From the very beginning, the Church's mission was universal and evangelical. Rather than remain together, the apostles left their native lands and spread the gospel throughout the world. From that time to the present, the Church has witnessed and participated in several distinct international orders—the chaos after

---

7. For discussions of the recent history of the Holy See's legal personality in international affairs, and an analysis of its current status, see Araujo & Lucal, 1–17; Roland Portman, *Legal Personality in International Law* (Cambridge: Cambridge Univ. Press 2010), 115–19.

8. Araujo & Lucal, 4–7.

9. See Portman, *Legal Personality*, 116–18.

10. Araujo & Lucal, 16.

Holy See's Diplomatic Response to the Crisis in Syria

the fall of the Roman Empire, medieval Christendom, the post-Westphalia rise of the nation state, the convulsions of the twentieth century, and now the post-Cold War era. The Church has survived as a human institution in large part by adapting the means by which it carries out its mission as human history unfolds over time.[11]

Today, stripped of most of its physical territory, the Church has been able to focus on its spiritual and religious mission. At its core, that mission is "to safeguard the principles of ethics and religion, but also to intervene authoritatively with Her children in the temporal sphere, when there is a question of judging the application of those principles to concrete cases."[12] Having no military or economic power, the Church pursues her mission by preaching the Gospel and imparting divine law, which contributes to strengthening peace and to placing brotherly relations between individuals and peoples on solid ground. Therefore, to encourage and stimulate cooperation among men, the Church must be thoroughly present in the midst of the community of nations. She must achieve such a presence both through her public institutions and sincere collaboration with all Christians.[13] In practice, the Church's "public institutions" whose presence is "in the midst" of world affairs include the Holy See's diplomatic apparatus.

The head of the Holy See—indeed, the occupant of the "See" of Peter—is the pope, whose dual role as a head of state and spiritual leader inevitably means that he commands a bully pulpit. The pope's power to pronounce Church doctrine and govern the Church ultimately rests upon apostolic succession.[14] As the successor to Peter, the pope also is the visible symbol of unity and the pastor of the entire Church, and he may govern the universal Church "unhindered."[15] The college of bishops also has full authority to govern the

---

11. For a brief history of the Church's role in international affairs from its founding through today, see Araujo, 293–319.

12. Pope John XXIII, *Pacem in Terris: Encyclical Letter on Establishing Universal Peace in Truth, Justice, Charity and Liberty* (1963).

13. Vatican Council II, *Pastoral Constitution on the Church in the Modern World* (*Gaudium et Spes*) (1962) at ¶ 89.

14. *Catechism of the Catholic Church* (rev. ed., United States Catholic Conference-Libreria Editrice Vaticana, 1997) [hereinafter CCC] § 553, 869.

15. CCC, at § 882.

Church, but that authority only may be exercised in unity with the pope. This history and structure ensures that pronouncements of the pope carry great weight, even in matters that are not strictly theological.

The pope's sphere of action in international affairs is not limited merely to rhetoric, however. The Holy See has a diplomatic corps, composed of priests, which is overseen by the Secretary for Relations with States, a component of the Secretariat of State of the Holy See. The Secretary for Relations with States is roughly equivalent to a foreign minister. The Cardinal Secretary of State, in turn, reports directly to the pope. The Holy See trains its diplomats at the Pontifical Ecclesiastical Academy in Rome, which was founded in 1701 and counts five popes among its alumni, most recently Paul VI.[16] Presently, the Holy See has diplomatic relations with 180 nations.

Papal representatives are called "nuncios," and the majority of nuncios are archbishops resident in the country to which they are accredited. Nuncios are not sent to interfere with local bishops; rather, they gather and pass on information to the Holy See, assist the local bishops in any appropriate manner, and suggest candidates for the office of bishop.[17] The nuncio must also "strive to promote matters which pertain to the peace, progress, and cooperative effort of peoples."[18]

The Holy See also has diplomatic relations with a number of international organizations. Importantly, the United Nations granted the Holy See permanent observer status in 1964. As a permanent observer, the Holy See may participate in virtually all the activities of the United Nations open to member states, and it maintains missions headed by Nuncios in both New York and Geneva. In an important moment for both the United Nations and the Church, Pope Paul VI traveled to New York the following year and spoke to the General Assembly. Consistent with the Holy See's modern role in interna-

---

16. The diplomats are priests who have been recommended for the diplomatic service by their local bishops. Because they are priests and therefore already have academic degrees, the Academy's curriculum focuses on practical skills and the academic study of diplomacy.
17. 1983 Code c.364.
18. Ibid.

Holy See's Diplomatic Response to the Crisis in Syria

tional affairs, Paul declared that the Church's role at the United Nations was to be an "expert in humanity" with long experience in the subject. He called the establishment of the Holy See's mission at the U.N. "the end of a laborious pilgrimage in search of a colloquy with the whole world, a pilgrimage which began when We were given the command: 'Go and bring the good news to all nations.' And it is you who represent all nations."

Given its unique history and status in international affairs, the Holy See's diplomatic priorities are different than most nation states. The former Secretary for Relations with States, Archbishop (now Cardinal) Dominique Mamberti, in a speech to the bishops of Australia, described the goals and bases of Holy See diplomacy.[19] The Holy See acts through "soft diplomacy," as "a voice of conscience, at the service of the common good, by drawing attention to the anthropological, ethical and religious aspects of the various questions affecting the lives of peoples, nations and the international community as a whole."[20]

In doing so, the Holy See is guided by the Church's philosophy that the human person is created in the image of God, endowed with reason and free will, and entitled to innate dignity. This philosophical anthropology is the basis for the Church's social teachings that have developed over the centuries and which "concern the organisation of society and various issues which affect the human person in his or her social dimension, such as the family, economics, culture, politics, justice, human rights, peace and the environment."[21] The Holy See's diplomatic positions, therefore, are formed with reference to its social doctrine, and mainly are concerned with the promotion of an ethical vision in the various questions which affect human life, society, and development, the defense of human dignity and human rights, the promotion of reconciliation and peace, the promotion of

---

19. Archbishop Dominique Mamberti, "The Diplomatic Activity of the Holy See, Address to the Bishops of Australia" (November 25, 2014) (transcript available at The Diplomatic Activity of the Holy See: Archbishop Mamberti to the Bishops of Australia, News.va, November 25, 2014, http://www.news.va/en/news/the-diplomatic-activity-of-the-holy-see-archbishop [hereinafter "Mamberti, Diplomatic Activity"]).
20. Ibid.
21. Ibid.

integral human development and humanitarian interests, the protection of the environment and, when requested, the mediation of disputes.²²

The Syrian Conflict

The present crisis in Syria is one of the many diplomatic challenges the Holy See has faced over the centuries. Syria descended into civil war and violence after an incident in March 2011 when security forces killed several democracy protestors.²³ What began as a movement to unseat the Assad government quickly became a sectarian conflict, initially pitting armed forces of the Sunni majority against President Assad's Alawite sect. Regional and international actors, including the Kurdish minority in northern Syria, Hezbollah militias, the jihadist Islamic State group, Russia, and a coalition led by the United States quickly joined the conflict to one degree or another. In particular, the Islamic State group captured and now exercises control over a great deal of territory in Syria and Iraq, and in June 2014 it declared a "caliphate" in that area.

Complicating matters further, the conflict has become a proxy war reflecting larger tensions in the region. The Assad government is backed by Shia Iran and its ally Russia, as well as the Shia group, Hezbollah. The rebels are backed by Sunni countries Turkey, Jordan, and Saudi Arabia, as well as the United States, France, and the United Kingdom, among others.

The situation in Syria is a humanitarian disaster. Estimates vary, but at least 250,000 people have died, and 11 million have been displaced from their homes. The United Nations has accused all parties to the conflict of committing atrocities, which include indiscriminate

---

22. Id; see also Archbishop Jean-Louis Tauran, "Lecture on the Presence of the Holy See in International Organizations," Catholic University of Milan, Italy (April 22, 2002), http://www.vatican.va/roman_curia/secretariat_state/documents/rc_seg-st_doc_20020422_tauran_en.html.

23. The Syrian conflict is complex and nuanced, and a full treatment of it is beyond the scope of this essay. The following brief discussion of the facts, including estimates of casualties and refugees, is, unless otherwise noted, drawn from the BBC News summary of the conflict. See http://www.bbc.com/news/world-middle-east-26116868.

Holy See's Diplomatic Response to the Crisis in Syria

use of weapons against civilians, murder, torture, rape, and forced disappearances. The Islamic State is accused of mass killings of rivals and religious minorities, including Christians, and of murdering hostages, including by beheading. Though it is not clear who was to blame—the Syrian government and the rebels each blame the other—both nerve gas and chlorine reportedly have been employed in deadly attacks, and the Islamic State is accused of using blister agents as well.

This grave humanitarian crisis has had enormous international repercussions. Of the eleven million displaced Syrians, approximately four and a half million have left the country. Neighboring countries such as Lebanon, Turkey, and Jordan have taken in the majority, but approximately ten percent of the refugees have sought asylum in Europe. Not surprisingly, such a large influx of refugees has led to political controversy and practical difficulties. Moreover, the United Nations has estimated that it will cost billions of dollars to provide humanitarian assistance, including basic necessities such as clean drinking water and food, to the six and a half million Syrians who remain homeless as a result of the conflict within the country.

Since 2013, the international community, including Europe and the United States, seems committed to a nonmilitary, political solution, although Russia continues to conduct airstrikes. Several rounds of negotiations in Geneva involving regional and international actors, including the United Nations, over possible frameworks for a peaceful settlement to the conflict have not been successful, though there has been some fitful progress. The United States and Russia brokered a partial cease-fire between the government and the rebels, but not including the Islamic State, which began on February 27, 2016. Meanwhile, negotiations continued to focus on a United Nations proposal which would entail a transitional, nonsectarian government, followed by a new constitution and elections. The Assad regime unsurprisingly rejected any such "roadmap." By July 2016, the partial ceasefire appeared in danger of collapse.[24]

---

24. See "Syrian Army, Rebels, Agree to 72-hour Eid Truce, but Fighting Continues," *Reuters*, July 6, 2016, http://www.reuters.com/article/us-mideast-crisis-syria-truce-idUSKCN0ZM0PZ.

The Holy See's Diplomatic Response to the Syrian Conflict

Within the limits of its mission and resources, the Church has responded forcefully to the crisis in Syria on a number of fronts. For example, on a purely humanitarian level, in 2015 Church dioceses worldwide, Catholic Church aid agencies, and Catholic NGOs donated $150 million to aid directly four million people in Syria or Syrian refugees in neighboring countries.[25] The Vatican took in twelve Syrian refugees in a visible sign of solidarity with displaced Syrians, and as an example for other nations.[26] As important as these and many other efforts have been, the Holy See's diplomatic efforts have had an important and ongoing impact on the unfolding crisis.

From the beginning, Popes Benedict and Francis have given the situation personal attention involving the highest levels of the Holy See.[27] The Holy See's former foreign minister outlined the Holy See's diplomatic approach to the crisis, which begins with the Church's insistence on the primacy of peace and the avoidance of war if at all possible.[28] Catholic social doctrine *does* provide that military force is sometimes justified, which Pope Francis has affirmed, to stop an unjust aggressor or to prevent genocide or other crimes against humanity provided this is done in a proportionate way and in accordance with international law, not in a unilateral fashion. For this reason, the United Nations and the entire international community, in

---

25. "Vatican Foreign Minister Urges Increased Support for Syrian Refugees," *Vatican Radio*, April 2, 2016, http://en.radiovaticana.va/news/2016/02/04/vatican_foreign_minister_urges_increased_support_for_syria/1205953.

26. Jim Yardley, "12 Syrians Get Gift of Refuge From the Pope," *New York Times*, April 17, 2016, A1.

27. Pope Benedict XVI was pope when the conflict began, and he persistently called for peace and negotiations to settle the conflict. See, e.g., Edward Pentin, "Pope and Nuncio Issue Urgent Appeals for Peace in Syria," *Terrasanta.net*, July 31, 2012, http://www.terrasanta.net/tsx/articolo.jsp?wi_number=4130&wi_codseq=%20%20%20%20%20&language=en. When Pope Francis succeeded Pope Benedict in 2013, the conflict had intensified and become an international crisis. As a consequence, Pope Francis seems to have intensified the Holy See's diplomatic efforts as well. Unless otherwise specifically noted, references to the "pope" in the remainder of this chapter refer to Pope Francis.

28. Mamberti, Diplomatic Activity.

Holy See's Diplomatic Response to the Crisis in Syria

particular the various States of the Middle East region, must be involved. This is the best way to guarantee that the actions of the international community have an adequate objective legal base and to ensure that the common good prevails over one-sided interests.[29]

Thus, any use of military force must be limited in this fashion to avoid the appearance of unilateralism or western imperialist or religious motivations. Other than its stance on military intervention, the Holy See in general "does not propose technical solutions but it is tirelessly involved in raising international awareness and in appealing to the international community to intervene as a matter of urgency in order to stop the aggressor, provide humanitarian aid and address the root causes of the present crisis."[30]

Pope Francis successfully deployed these bedrock principles in a robust diplomatic effort to avert an international military response after the Syrian government used chemical weapons on several occasions in 2013, resulting in the death of hundreds of civilians.[31] These attacks were so egregious that military intervention led by the United States was imminent. The pope sprang into action.

First, he called upon the Catholic faithful to pray and fast for Syria on September 7, 2013, the day the Church commemorates Mary, Queen of Peace. The pope stated that he was "deeply wounded in particular by what is happening in Syria and anguished by the dramatic developments which are looming," and that "[h]umanity needs to see these gestures of peace and to hear words of hope and peace!"[32] He invited all of humanity to join him and the Church in this effort. The Vatican then sent information to the episcopal conferences worldwide, encouraging the local dioceses to join with the

---

29. Ibid.
30. Ibid.
31. See "United Nations Mission to Investigate Allegations of the Use of Chemical Weapons in the Syrian Arab Republic," Final Report, December 13, 2013, https://unoda-web.s3.amazonaws.com/wp-content/uploads/2013/12/report.pdf.
32. Pope Francis, Angelus, Vatican, September 1, 2013, https://w2.vatican.va/content/francesco/en/angelus/2013/documents/papa-francesco_angelus_20130901.html. For a summary of the events leading up to the day of prayer and fasting, see Edward Pentin, "Diplomatic Source: Pope's Appeal for Peace in Syria Hard to Ignore," *Terra Santa.net*, September 4, 2013, http://www.terrasanta.net/tsx/showPage.jsp?wi_number=5485 [hereinafter "Pentin, Pope's Appeal"].

pope in the day of prayer and fasting. The Vatican gathered diplomats accredited to the Holy See in Rome to brief them in advance and to present them with a six-point peace plan for Syria which called for, among other points, maintaining the territorial integrity of Syria, establishment of a ministry dedicated to minorities, establishment of the concept of citizenship with equal dignity for all, and respect for human rights and religious freedom.[33]

The pope also wrote to the Russian President Vladimir Putin, the Assad regime's primary foreign backer, who was hosting the G20 summit of the leaders of the world's largest economies in St. Petersburg in the days leading up to the day of prayer. The Vatican released the letter to the public, and Putin read the letter to the gathered diplomats.[34] On the day itself, an estimated crowd of 100,000 people joined the pope in St. Peter's Square for the five-hour ceremony.[35] The result of this combination of spiritual and diplomatic action was that no military intervention took place, and the parties resorted to negotiations instead.

After this stunning diplomatic success, the pope redoubled his efforts to pressure the international community to find peaceful solutions to the crisis. For example, in August 2014, the pope wrote to the United Nations General Secretary, Ban Ki-moon, in response to events in Northern Iraq, and succinctly expressed the Holy See's roadmap for settling the crisis in the Middle East: "[t]he tragic experiences of the Twentieth Century, and the most basic understanding of human dignity, compels the international community, particularly through the norms and mechanisms of international law, to do

---

33. Edward Pentin, "Holy See Proposes Six-Point Plan for Peace in Syria," *Terrasanta.net*, September 10, 2013, http://www.terrasanta.net/tsx/articolo.jsp?wi_number =5489&wi_codseq=%20%20%20%20%20%20&language=en. See also Sheila Gribbens Liaguminas, "Pope Francis and the Syrian Intervention," *Mercatornet*, September 10, 2013, http://www.mercatornet.com/sheila_liaugminas/view/pope_francis_and_syrian_intervention/12733.

34. Letter of Pope Francis to H.E. Vladimir Putin, September 4, 2013, https://w2.vatican.va/content/francesco/en/letters/2013/documents/papa-francesco_20130904_putin-g20.html.

35. Edward M. Pentin, "Pope Francis' Solemn Plea for Peace," *National Catholic Register*, September 9, 2013, http://www.ncregister.com/daily-news/pope-francis-solemn-plea-for-peace/.

Holy See's Diplomatic Response to the Crisis in Syria

all that it can to stop and to prevent further systematic violence against ethnic and religious minorities."[36]

Shortly after that plea, on October 2–4, 2014, the pope called a meeting in the Vatican of his diplomatic representatives to Jordan-Iraq, Iran, Lebanon, Egypt, Israel-Jerusalem-Palestine, Syria, Turkey, the United Nations Organizations in New York and Geneva, and to the European Union. In addition, a number of the most senior members of the Roman Curia also took part, including the Secretary of State, Cardinal Pietro Parolin, the Secretary and Under-Secretary for Relations with States, and the heads of several important departments within the Church bureaucracy. Thus, the Holy See's representatives on the ground in the Middle East were able to brief high-ranking members of the Roman Curia and diplomats in person. On October 20, 2014, the pope then called a meeting of the College of Cardinals, to exchange information about the situation, and to discuss the Holy See's response to it.

Not long after these meetings, and presumably as a result of what was learned through them, the pope in his 2014 Christmas letter to Christians in the Middle East stated that the international community must act, "above all by promoting peace through negotiation and diplomacy, for the sake of stemming and stopping as soon as possible the violence which has already caused so much harm."[37] Since that time, the pope consistently has supported a ceasefire, a goal which was partially achieved in 2016.

Parallel to these diplomatic efforts, the Holy See has suggested that international law must develop to meet the novel circumstances of Syria today. The centerpiece of this legal strategy seems to be the Holy See's support for the development of a legal duty to protect vulnerable persons and populations in modern conflicts. For example, Secretary of State Cardinal Parolin, in a speech to the United Nations General Assembly, began by stressing the importance of peace and

---

36. Letter of Pope Francis to Secretary-General Ban Ki-moon, August 9, 2014, https://w2.vatican.va/content/francesco/en/letters/2014/documents/papa-francesco_20140809_lettera-ban-ki-moon-iraq.html [hereinafter "Pope Francis, Letter to Ban Ki-moon"].

37. Letter of Pope Francis to the Christians in the Middle East, December 24, 2014, https://w2.vatican.va/content/francesco/en/letters/2014/documents/papa-francesco_20141221_lettera-cristiani-medio-oriente.html.

dialogue among cultures, religions, and peoples, and by positing the political thesis that peace is not the result of balance-of-power politics, but rather "the result of justice at every level, and most importantly, the shared responsibility of individuals, civil institutions and governments."[38]

Dovetailing with that emphasis on justice, and clearly referring in part to the problem of ISIS in Syria, Cardinal Parolin then asserted that norms establishing a legal "responsibility to protect" in international law must be developed. Because there is no legal basis for unilateral policing of transnational terrorism beyond one's borders, the development of such norms is the responsibility of the Security Council through multilateral action. The founding documents of the United Nations do not contain any such legal duty, but the spirit of those documents and of the United Nations is that it is the "responsibility of the entire international community, in a spirit of solidarity, to confront heinous crimes such as genocide, ethnic cleansing and religiously motivated persecution."[39]

The Vatican's foreign secretary was even more direct in remarks to the General Assembly. After noting the dispiriting frustration at what the Secretary-General had labeled the "collective defeat" of the international community to solve the humanitarian crisis in Syria, Archbishop Mamberti urged the adoption of political and legal concept of "responsibility, nationally and internationally, to protect populations from genocide crimes and ethnic cleansing and crimes against humanity."[40] The justification for a legal "responsibility to protect" can be found in the United Nations Charter, though only implicitly. Such a duty must be properly understood; it is not a justification for unilateral resort to arms, but rather is a requirement of solidarity of the international community to use all measures—diplomatic, eco-

---

38. Cardinal Piero Parolin, Address to the 69th General Assembly of the United Nations, New York, September 29, 2014, http://www.vatican.va/roman_curia/secretariat_state/parolin/2014/documents/rc_seg-st_20140929_69th-un-general-assembly_en.html.

39. Ibid.

40. Archbishop Dominique Mamberti, Address to the 69th Meeting of the United Nations General Assembly, New York, October 1, 2013, http://www.vatican.va/roman_curia/secretariat_state/2013/documents/rc_seg-st-20131001_mamberti-pace-svilluppo_fr.html (original in French, all translations by the author).

Holy See's Diplomatic Response to the Crisis in Syria

nomic, and, in appropriate cases, military—to provide solutions to humanitarian crises. Syria provides both a challenge and an opportunity to develop proper mechanisms for enforcing this requirement of solidarity. To date, the Holy See consistently has supported the efforts of the Security Council to develop the contours of the responsibility to protect, though those efforts have not yielded tangible results.

The Holy See's observer status at the United Nations ensures that its diplomatic and moral suasion as an "expert in humanity" at least will reach the ears of the parties with the power to solve international crises. In multiple statements at the U.N. in both New York and Geneva, the Holy See's representatives repeatedly have reminded the world of all aspects of the humanitarian disaster in Syria, and have offered the Holy See's advice on how to proceed, always grounding such suggestions firmly in the Church's social philosophy and anthropology.

In particular, the Holy See has raised concerns in the United Nations about violence against religious and ethnic minorities, including Christians, in Syria and elsewhere in the Middle East. The Holy See on many occasions has reminded the Security Council and other organs of the United Nations that "[t]he most basic understanding of human dignity compels the international community, particularly through the norms and mechanisms of international law, to do all that it can to stop and prevent further systematic violence against ethnic and religious minorities and to protect innocent peoples."[41]

Along those same lines, the Holy See, along with Russia and Lebanon, helped draft a statement to the United Nations Human Rights Council in Geneva, which was joined by several dozen other countries, that called "upon the international community to support the deeply rooted historical presence of all ethnic and religious communities in the Middle East.... [W]e ask all States to reaffirm their commitment to respect the rights of everyone, in particular the right to freedom of religion, which is enshrined in the fundamental inter-

---

41. Archbishop Bernardito Auza, Statement to the United Nations Security Council, New York, October 22, 2015, https://holyseemission.org/contents//statements/562fefb0f05169.94168102.php (quoting Pope Francis, Letter to Ban Ki-moon).

national human rights instruments."[42] This statement was particularly significant because it apparently was the first time there had been explicit mention of the category of Christians before the United Nations Human Rights Council.

Archbishop Bernardito Auza, the Papal Nuncio to the United Nations in New York, convened a conference in July 2016 concerning the genocide against Christians in Syria and elsewhere in the Middle East. The Nuncio neatly summarized the goals of the conference and of the Holy See's ongoing efforts at the United Nations in his opening remarks:

> [W]hat we hope to accomplish is... not only to raise awareness about similar suffering anywhere and everywhere it is occurring, but also to raise up... the effective, practical and constant will necessary to stop these outrages against human dignity and persons, bring to justice those who treat such barbarous violence almost as a sport or game, and address the causes of extremist violence at their roots.
>
> ...
>
> [T]he magnitude and downright savage nature of what is going on requires the whole world to wake up to the need to get involved.
>
> For when human dignity is being treated with as much contempt as it is now in these broad theaters, the world must become a global neighborhood in which we all rise up in solidarity and sacrifice to defend, assist and concretely love our neighbor, because the contempt they are being shown is likewise intended for all of us.[43]

The Holy See at the United Nations has not hesitated to highlight the "contempt" of their fellow human beings shown by some parties to the Syrian crisis, and to provide "practical" suggestions by which the world might "wake up" and "get involved." These suggestions have

---

42. Press Statement, Archbishop Silvano M. Tomasi, Supporting the Human Rights of Christians and other Communities, Particularly in the Middle East, (March 13, 2015), https://press.vatican.va/content/salastampa/it/bollettino/pubblico/2015/03/13/0186.pdf.

43. Archbishop Bernardito Auza, Opening Remarks at the Event on Defending Religious Freedom and Other Human Rights: Stopping Mass Atrocities Against Christians and Other Believers Organized by the Permanent Mission of the Holy See to the United Nations, New York, April 28, 2016, https://holyseemission.org/contents//events/5723c02f906792.97161562.php (internal quotations omitted).

Holy See's Diplomatic Response to the Crisis in Syria

not been limited to mere rhetoric, however. The Holy See has made several practical, political, and legal suggestions. For example, Archbishop Auza in the Security Council decried the use of weapons that permit remote-controlled killing, which "bring to the fore ethical and legal questions that merit careful review and perhaps even a challenge on the basis of international humanitarian law."[44] Given the use of drones by countries such as the United States, any suggestion to make their use illegal is sure to meet significant resistance.

Even more intriguing is the Holy See's support for the proposal that members of the Security Council not exercise their veto when a credible resolution is before the Council to prevent or end genocide, crimes against humanity, or war crimes. The obligation not to exercise the veto stems from the "duty to protect" against such crimes, which, its supporters contend, obviates any concern that such an obligation violates the sovereignty of the Council member.[45] If adopted, which seems unlikely at present, this suggestion would remove a frustrating impediment to Security Council action in such dire international crises.

Finally, the Holy See's position is that the best vehicle for such a political settlement is the Geneva multilateral peace talks, in which the Holy See has participated. The Holy See's goals for the Geneva talks are also a roadmap to a workable political settlement in Syria—a permanent ceasefire with no delay for any reason, immediate humanitarian aid and rebuilding, and international peacekeeping under the auspices of the United Nations.[46]

Conclusion

The Holy See lacks military and economic power, but, given its history and its mission, it has the moral standing to influence and change the course of human affairs through diplomacy. It has done just that in the Syrian crisis. Through the personal efforts of the

---

44. Archbishop Bernardito Auza, Statement to the United Nations Security Council, New York, July 13, 2016, https://holyseemission.org/contents//statements/5787af00432a4.php.

45. Ibid.

46. Archbishop Francis Chullikat, Statement to the United Nations Security Council, New York, January 20, 2014, https://holyseemission.org/contents//statements/55e34d3727eaa1.75285605.php.

pope, the Curia, and its diplomats, the Holy See has been a consistent voice for peace and an end to violence. The Church in its role of an "expert on humanity" has appealed to the consciences of all parties involved. Not satisfied with relying on rhetoric, the Holy See has acted tirelessly, using the means available to it, to bring all parties together through diplomacy, to formulate and support peace plans, to urge changes to international law and its mechanisms, and to keep the attention of the world focused on the human toll of the crisis. Whether the Syrian situation can be peacefully resolved remains to be seen, but the Holy See's contributions demonstrate the crucial role it plays in international affairs. To date, the Holy See's efforts have been resolutely true to its mission to serve mankind, and, hopefully, will continue to be.

Erbil, Iraq. Child at Christian IDP camp awaiting move to new camp, 2016.

Erbil, Iraq. Child in Christian IDP camp, 2016.

9

Using the Torture Act Against the Persecution of Christians

Mark Healy Bonner

WHERE RELIGIOUS PERSECUTION includes torture, United States law can send the offenders to prison, even when the torture occurs abroad.[1] There are various means to combat the persecution of Christians: diplomatic, economic, moral condemnation, international legal action, and military action.[2] An additional means considered in this chapter is domestic criminal prosecution; more par-

---

1. The scope of this chapter is limited to the crime of torture abroad because U.S. law currently allows for such prosecution but does not as yet criminally cover religious persecution abroad that does not involve torture.

2. The U.S. Commission on International Religious Freedom (USCIRF), an independent, bipartisan U.S. government advisory body, separate from the State Department, was created by the International Religious Freedom Act of 1998 (IRFA). The Commission's 2015 Annual Report calls on the United States government to "Call for or support a referral by the U.N. Security Council to the International Criminal Court to investigate ISIL violations in Iraq and Syria against religious and ethnic minorities, and *continue to call for an International Criminal Court investigation into crimes committed by the al-Assad regime.*" 2015 Annual Report at 118 (emphasis added), http://www.uscirf.gov/sites/default/files/USCIRF%20Annual%20Report%202015%20%282%29.pdf. The 2016 Annual Report similarly calls for "taking steps to end violence and policies of discrimination against religious and ethnic minorities, *including the investigation and prosecution of those perpetrating or inciting violence,*" 30 (emphasis added), http://www.uscirf.gov/sites/default/files/USCIRF%202016%20Annual%20Report.pdf.

ticularly, criminal prosecution of persecutors of Christians where the persecution includes torture.³ Such prosecutions, done in the United States, are available even where the torturer, victim, and act of torture all occur abroad. The legal vehicle for such prosecution is the Torture Act.⁴ Prosecution under the Torture Act does not require the acquiescence of any foreign government; the prosecution can be entirely unilateral by the United States. Recently the Torture Act has been successfully used to convict and imprison a defendant in the United States for torturing people in Liberia.⁵

Persecution has many forms, one of which is actual torture, e.g., crucifixion, serial rape, ritual beheading, persistent death threats.⁶ The United States law against foreign torture is quite concise, and a reading of it goes a long way to demonstrating its suitability as a prosecution vehicle against those who torture, including Islamic State jihadists bent on religious cleansing by means of torture.⁷

---

3. See The ISIS Genocide Declaration: What Next?, Opening Statement of Carl Anderson before the subcommittee on Global Human Rights of the Committee on Foreign Affairs, U.S. Senate, May 26, 2016, http://kofc.org/en/news/releases/isis-genocide-declaration.html (listing six policy principles to combat the humanitarian crisis in the Middle East).

4. Title 18, United States Code, Sections 2340–340A. There is also a civil counterpart to this criminal statute: the Torture Victim Protection Act of 1991, 28 U.S.C. 1350 (TVPA), which provides a cause of action against individuals for certain acts of torture or extrajudicial killing committed under authority or color of any foreign law. See Mohamad v. Palestinian Authority, 132 S. Ct. 1702 (2012).

5. United States v. Belfast, 611 F. 3d 783 (11th Cir. 2010), cert. denied, 562 U.S. 1551 (2011).

6. See Podgor and Clark, *Understanding International Criminal Law* (LexisNexis, 3d Ed. 2013), 221. "Sexual violence has been recognized in both international documents and courts as an international crime. In some instances, rape has been identified as 'a form of torture or inhuman treatment.' For example, '[s]ince 1986, reports of the Special Rapporteur on Torture of the U.N. . . . have defined the rape of female prisoners while in detention or under interrogation as an act of torture.'" Ibid. (internal citations omitted). See also Charlotte Alter, "Girls Who Escaped ISIS Describe Systematic Rape," *Time*, April 16, 2015, http://time.com/3825066/girls-who-escaped-isis-describe-systematic-rape/.

7. See Final Report of Committee of Experts established pursuant to U.N. Security Council Resolution 780 ("'ethnic cleansing' is a purposeful policy designed by one ethnic or religious group to remove by violent and terror-inspiring means the civilian population of another ethnic or religious group from certain geographic

Using the Torture Act Against the Persecution of Christians

Regardless of where the offense occurs, United States criminal law is violated, and the torturer is liable to prosecution and conviction in U.S. courts and subsequent incarceration. The death penalty is even available.

Photographs of and articles concerning the crucifixion of Christians in the Middle East by Islamic jihadists are legion.[8] Several examples are noted below.[9] As related by a U.S. Ambassador and reported in the *New York Times Magazine*: "Everyone has seen the forced conversions, crucifixions and beheadings." David Saperstein, the United States Ambassador at large for religious freedom said, "To see these communities, primarily Christians, but also the Yazidis and others, persecuted in such large numbers is deeply alarming."[10]

The Convention Against Torture ("CAT") was adopted by the United Nations General Assembly in December, 1984, and it was ratified by the United States in 1994. The Torture Act was enacted by

---

areas"), 33, http://www.icty.org/x/file/About/OTP/un_commission_of_experts_report1994_en.pdf. See also "Church Fears 'ethnic cleansing' of Christians in Homs, Syria," *Los Angeles Times*, March 23, 2012, http://latimesblogs.latimes.com/world_now/2012/03/church-fears-ethnic-cleansing-of-christians-in-homs-syria.html. New York-based Human Rights Watch reports: "The extremist group Islamic State (also known as ISIS), and Al-Qaeda's affiliate in Syria, Jabhat al-Nusra, were responsible targeting civilians, kidnappings, and executions." See Human Rights Watch, https://www.hrw.org/middle-east/n-africa/syria.

8. Perhaps the best source of detailed information on Islamic persecution of Christians in the Middle East is "Genocide against Christians in the Middle East," a 278-page report submitted to Secretary of State John Kerry by the Knights of Columbus and In Defense of Christians, March 9, 2016, http://www.stopthechristiangenocide.org/en/resources/Genocide-report.pdf.

9. "Isis Begins Killing Christians in Mosul," *Catholic Online*, August 8, 2014, http://www.catholic.org/news/international/middle_east/story.php?id=56481; "ISIS Crucifies 11 Christian Missionaries," *CP World*, October 10, 2015, http://www.christianpost.com/news/isis-crucifies-11-christian-missionaries-147317/; Edwin Mora, "Report: ISIS Has Crucified, Tortured Thousands of Christians in Iraq, Syria," *Breitbart*, September 29, 2015, http://www.breitbart.com/national-security/2015/09/29/report-isis-crucified-tortured-thousands-christians-iraq-syria/.

10. Eliza Griswold, "Is This the End of Christianity in the Middle East? ISIS and other extremist movements across the region are enslaving, killing and uprooting Christians, with no end in sight," *New York Times Magazine*, July 22, 2015, http://www.nytimes.com/2015/07/26/magazine/is-this-the-end-of-christianity-in-the-middle-east.html?_r=0.

Congress and signed by President Clinton in order to fulfill CAT's provision that signatory states enact legislation to implement CAT.[11]

Roy M. Belfast, Jr., a/k/a Charles McArthur Emmanuel, a/k/a Charles Taylor, Jr., a/k/a Chuckie Taylor II (Chuckie) was formerly engaged in the practice of torturing people in Liberia. He is now behind bars in federal prison. During Liberia's bloody civil war, Chuckie's father, Charles Taylor (Charles), was the leader of an armed insurgent group known as the National Patriotic Front.[12] By 1997 Charles had been elected President of Liberia and had appointed his son, Chuckie, to oversee an Anti-Terrorism Unit, appropriately known in Liberia as the "Demon Forces," with the responsibility of protecting Charles and his family.[13] Chuckie got to work, and between 1999 and 2003 he inflicted "branding, scalding, severe beating, decapitation, the administration of electrical shocks, and the extended confinement of individuals with infected wounds in rancid water-filled pits."[14] He also put people "in water- and corpse-filled pits with little or no clothing, and with festering wounds and burns."[15] All of the victims, and all conduct constituting torture occurred in Liberia; none of the victims were U.S. citizens.[16]

Chuckie was convicted in the U.S. District Court for the Southern District of Florida of "numerous acts of torture and other atrocities," acts of "extraordinary cruelty and evil," and he was sentenced on January 8, 2009.[17] His conviction was affirmed by the U.S. Court of

---

11. United States v. Belfast. See also Convention Against Torture and Other Cruel, Inhuman or Degrading Treatment or Punishment, Art. 1, Dec. 10, 1984, S. Treaty doc. No. 100-20 (1988), 1465 U.N.T.S. 85, http://www.ohchr.org/EN/ProfessionalInterest/Pages/CAT.aspx [hereinafter CAT] CAT, Art. 4(1) ("Each State Party shall ensure that all acts of torture are offences under its criminal law. The same shall apply to an attempt to commit torture.").

12. United States v. Belfast, 611 F. 3d at 793.

13. Ibid.

14. Ibid., 823

15. Ibid., 828. Details of these atrocities are reported at ibid., 794–801.

16. Ibid., 794–801. Chuckie was a U.S. citizen, but the Court stated that it did not matter under the Torture Act. "Plainly, even if subsection (b)(2) [offender 'present in the United States'] had provided the exclusive basis for jurisdiction in this case . . . that fact would not have rendered Emmanuel's [Chuckie's] convictions infirm in any way." Ibid., 810.

17. Ibid., 793.

Using the Torture Act Against the Persecution of Christians

Appeals for the Eleventh Circuit on July 15, 2010, and the Supreme Court denied review.[18]

Chuckie Taylor, formerly head of the Demon Forces, is now serving a 1,164-month federal sentence (ninety-seven years) for violation of the Torture Act. As of this writing he is in the High Security U.S. Penitentiary in Lee County, Virginia.[19] He is being punished for his terrible atrocities, and he is no longer in a position to continue them. Some justice has been afforded to his victims, and a message has been sent to those who might want to emulate him. This process should be repeated for torturers of Christians.[20]

Title 18, United States Code, Section 2340 provides:

§ 2340. Definitions
As used in this Chapter [Chapter 113—Torture]—

(1) "torture" means an act committed by a person acting under the color of law specifically intended to inflict severe physical or mental pain or suffering (other than pain or suffering incidental to lawful sanctions) upon another person within his custody or physical control;

(2) "severe mental pain or suffering" means the prolonged mental harm caused by or resulting from—

(A) the intentional infliction or threatened infliction of severe physical pain or suffering;

(B) the administration or application, or threatened administration or application, of mind-altering substances or other procedures calculated to disrupt profoundly the senses or the personality;

(C) the threat of imminent death;

---

18. The judicial opinion affirming his conviction and the constitutionality of the Torture Act is particularly well written and comprehensive. It is published as United States v. Belfast, 611 F. 3d 783 (11th Cir. 2010), cert. denied, 562 U.S. 1551 (2011).

19. Chuckie's Bureau of Prisons Register Number is 76556-004 under the name Roy Belfast, Jr.

20. Chuckie's father, President Charles Taylor, was extradited to The Hague, convicted by a special U.N. court of crimes against humanity, and on May 30, 2012, was sentenced to 50 years in prison. See site for Special Court for Sierra Leone, available at http://www.rscsl.org/Taylor.html.

(D) the threat that another person will imminently be subjected to death, severe physical pain or suffering, or the administration or application of mind-altering substances or other procedures calculated to disrupt profoundly the senses or personality; and

(3) "United States" means the several States of the United States, the District of Columbia, and the commonwealths, territories, and possessions of the United States.

§2340A. Torture

(a) **Offense**—Whoever outside the United States commits or attempts to commit torture shall be fined under this title or imprisoned not more than 20 years, or both, and if death results to any person from conduct prohibited by this subsection, shall be punished by death or imprisoned for any term of years or for life.

(b) **Jurisdiction**—There is jurisdiction over the activity prohibited in subsection (a) if—

(1) the alleged offender is a national of the United States; or

(2) the alleged offender is present in the United States, irrespective of the nationality of the victim or alleged offender.

(c) **Conspiracy**—A person who conspires to commit an offense under this section shall be subject to the same penalties (other than the penalty of death) as the penalties prescribed for the offense, the commission of which was the object of the conspiracy.

The U.S. Department of Justice has analyzed the elements of the offense of torture under §2340A:

Thus, to establish the offense of torture, the prosecution must show that: (1) the torture occurred outside the United States; (2) the defendant acted under the color of law; (3) the victim was within the defendant's custody or physical control; (4) the defendant specifically intended to cause severe physical or mental pain or suffering; and (5) that the act inflicted severe physical or mental pain or suffering.[21]

---

21. John C. Yoo, Deputy Assistant Attorney General, U.S. Department of Justice Office of Legal Counsel, Memorandum for William J. Haynes II, general Counsel of the Department of Defense (March 14, 2003), 36, http://nsarchive.gwu.edu/torturingdemocracy/documents/20030314.pdf. See also S. Exec. Rep. No. 101-30, at 6 (1990)

Using the Torture Act Against the Persecution of Christians

The statute's culpable mental state requirement, "the intentional infliction or threatened infliction" is classic specific intent, that is, the *mens rea*, the guilty mind that a criminal must possess at the time he commits the *actus reus*, the guilty act, in order for a criminal offense to occur. What is explicitly prohibited is the "intentional infliction ... of severe physical pain or suffering."

The *mens rea* of the torture offense has been muddied in the global war on terrorism context both by the Department of Justice's attempt concerning waterboarding to recast the *mens rea* of "torture" in terms of motive (i.e., that if the motive was to obtain information and the pain and suffering inflicted was just a means to this end, that torture did not occur,[22] a position long-since repudiated).[23] Confusion was compounded by scholarly argument buying into the motive argument, but arguing that the pain-inflicting acts must be "for a purpose prohibited by the Convention Against Torture."[24] Chuckie raised this issue himself on appeal;[25] it was rejected by the Court of Appeals.[26] The U.S. Court of Appeals for the 11th Circuit has made it clear that the Torture Act means what it says, "that the acts must have been 'specifically intended' to result in torture'"[27] and that motives,

---

("For an act to be 'torture' it must ... cause severe pain and suffering and be intended to cause severe pain and suffering.") The U.S. Court of Appeals for the 11th Circuit approved a jury instruction consonant with this formulation. United States v. Belfast, 611 F. 3d at 822–23.

22. Memorandum from Jay S. Barbee, Assistant Attorney General, to Alberto R. Gonzales, Counsel to the President, on Standards of Conduct for Interrogation under 18 U.S.C. §§ 2340–2340A, 1, 6 (August 1, 2002).

23. Memorandum from Daniel Levin, Acting Assistant Attorney General, to James B. Comey, Deputy Attorney General, on Legal Standards Applicable under 18 U.S.C. §§ 2340–2340A, 2 (Dec. 30, 2003).

24. Oona Hathaway, Aileen Nowlan, and Julia Spiegel, "Tortured Reasoning: The Intent to Torture Under International and Domestic Law," 59 *Virginia Journal of International Law* 794, 799 (2012) (noting Obama Administration's repudiation of DOJ's motive argument, and arguing that violation of 18 U.S.C. § 2340 requires proof of pain-infliction "for a purpose prohibited by the Convention.")

25. Belfast, 611 F.3d at 803 ("the Torture Act does not require the government to prove the defendant's motive.")

26. Ibid., 806 (court rejects argument that motive must be proved, observing "the CAT declares broadly that its provisions are 'without prejudice to any international instrument or national legislation which does or may contain provisions of wider application.'")

27. Ibid., 807.

while they may shed light on intent, are not part of the elements of the offense.[28] In the context of Islamic Jihadist crucifixion of Christians the spurious "intent/motive" debate is of no consequence because the Convention prohibits the intentional infliction of pain or suffering for purposes which include: "[I]ntimidating or coercing him or a third person, *or for any reason based on discrimination of any kind.*"[29] Thus, even a restricted reading of the Torture Act would suffice for criminal liability in the context of torturing Christians for being Christians and for not converting to Islam.

The utility of the phrase "under the color of law" is to exclude ordinary, private crime from coverage under the statute. The prohibited action must be cloaked with at least the pretense of some public authority. Chuckie Taylor, head of Liberia's Demon Forces, committed his torturing under the color of law by virtue of his official position. By contrast, the torturing of a DEA Special Agent by ordinary drug criminals in Mexico would not constitute action under the color of law. Since "misuse of power possessed by virtue of any state law and made possible only because the wrongdoer is clothed with the authority of state law, is action taken 'under color of state law,'"[30] torture of Christians by Islamic State soldiers in furtherance of Islamic State's program of religious cleansing should constitute an action taken under the color of law.

In enacting the Torture Act, "Congress's concern was not to prevent official torture within the borders of the United States,[31] but in nations where the rule of law has broken down and the ruling gov-

---

28. Ibid., 793, 807. The court held that the United States validly adopted CAT pursuant to the President's treaty-making authority under Article II of the Constitution, and that it was well within Congress' power under the Necessary and Proper Clause, Article I, Section 8, Clause 18 to criminalize both torture and conspiracy to commit torture. Belfast at 804–06, 813.
29. CAT art. 1 (emphasis added).
30. United States v. Classic, 313 U.S. 299, 326 (1941).
31. See Podgar and Clark, *Understanding International Criminal Law* (3d ed. LexisNexis 2013).

> The Committee Against Torture has faulted the United States for not legislating to criminalize torture as defined in the Convention when it is committed in the United States itself. [Citing Conclusions and Recommendations of the Committee against Torture, May 15, 2000, U.N. Doc. A/55/44,¶179(a) (2000) (commenting on first report submitted by the U.S.

ernment has become the enemy, rather than the protector, of its citizens."[32] While it is obvious that a country can pass laws criminalizing activity on its own territory (e.g., the U.S. or the State of Illinois making it a crime to torture someone to death in Chicago), it is not so obvious that a nation would have the authority to criminalize actions done entirely abroad. Indeed, there is a medieval maxim *Statuta suo clauduntur territorio, nec ultra territorium disponunt* ("Statutes are confined to their own territory and have no extraterritorial effect").[33] This maxim has evolved into a presumption of non-extraterritoriality unless Congressional intent is clearly to the contrary: "[T]he Supreme Court has reaffirmed that the presumption against extraterritoriality applies 'unless there is the affirmative intention of the Congress clearly expressed' to give a statute extraterritorial effect."[34]

CAT calls for the U.S. to exercise such jurisdiction. The Constitution, article I, section 8, clause 10 authorizes Congress "[t]o define and punish Piracies and Felonies committed on the high Seas and Offences against the Law of Nations." There is a two-part inquiry in analyzing the territorial application of a criminal law:[35] determining whether Congress intended the law to be applied extraterritorially,[36] and determining whether such application is consistent with princi-

---

under the Convention); Conclusions and Recommendations of the Committee against Torture, May 17 and 18, 2006, U.N. Doc. CAT/C/CO/2 ¶13 (commenting on second report submitted by the U.S. under the Convention)]. The United States takes the position that the offense is already adequately punished under existing federal and state law on offenses against the person.

Ibid. 221.

32. Belfast, 811.

33. *Black's Law Dictionary* 1874 (9th ed. 2009) quoted in Antonin Scalia and Bryan A. Garner, *Reading Law: The Interpretation of Legal Texts* (Thompson/West, 2012), 268.

34. Scalia and Garner, *Reading Law*, 272, quoting Morrison v. National Australia Bank Ltd., 130 S. Ct. 2869, 2877 (2010).

35. See generally Jimmy Gurulé, *Complex Criminal Litigation* (Juris Publishing; 3rd ed. 2013), 592 *et seq.*

36. See United States v. Bowman, 260 U.S. 94, 98 (1922); see also United States v. Vasquez-Velasco, 15 F.3d 833, 899 (9th Cir. 1994) ("Generally there is no constitutional bar to the extraterritorial application of United States penal laws.")

ples of international law.[37] Congress could not have been more clear about intending that the Torture Act have extraterritorial effect, providing explicitly in Section 2340A "Whoever outside the United States commits ... torture ... [t]here is jurisdiction ... if ... the alleged offender is present in the United States, irrespective of the nationality of the victim or alleged offender." As to consonance with principles of international law, the Restatement (Third) of Foreign Relations Law recognizes four principles of extraterritorial jurisdiction, among which is the "universal principle": jurisdiction over crimes so heinous that they are universally condemned by all nations.[38] According to this principle, "any state if it captures the offender may prosecute and punish that person on behalf of the world community regardless of the nationality of the offender or victim or where the crime was committed."[39] "Such crimes are often a matter of international conventions or treaties."[40] Torture is, of course, what CAT is all about.

The presence of the torturer in the United States is a statutory requirement for his prosecution. Importantly, this does not mean present when the defendant did the torturing, nor that the offender nor victim be United States citizens, nor that the torture happen in the United States.[41] The Torture Act provides jurisdiction where the defendant is either "a national of the United States" or "is present in the United States." How can this presence in the United States be had? Options run between arresting a defendant already in the United States, having him expelled by a foreign country, using the

---

37. The Supreme Court has interpreted clause 10 to grant Congress the power to define and punish three categories of crimes: piracies, felonies, and violations of the law of nations. See United States v. Smith, 18 U.S. [5 Wheat.] 184, 198 (1820).

38. Restatement (Third) of Foreign Relations Law §404.

39. United States v. Yunis, 681 F. Supp. 896, 900 (D.D.C. 1988); quoting M. Bassiouni, *II International Criminal Law*, 298 (1986).

40. Ibid., 900.

41. Ibid., at 814 ("As with Congress's ability to regulate the conduct of United States citizens abroad, it is well established that Congress can regulate conduct outside of the territorial bounds of the United States (not just that of its own citizens); EEOC v. Arabian Am. Oil Co., 499 U.S. 244, 248, 111 S. Ct. 1227, 113 L. Ed. 2d 274 (1991), *superseded on other grounds by statute*, Civil Rights Act of 1991, Pub. L. No. 1102-166, 105 Stat. 1074").

Using the Torture Act Against the Persecution of Christians

"normal" procedure of extradition when there's a treaty and the rule of law is functioning, or unilaterally arresting him outside the United States and bringing him here:

1) Arrest while in the United States. Chuckie Taylor, for example, was arrested at Miami International Airport on March 30, 2006 upon his arrival on a flight from Trinidad, for attempting to enter the U.S. using a false passport, and subsequently indicted for violation of the Torture Act.[42]

2) Deportation. Removal from the foreign country to the United States, or vice-versa, removal (deportation) from the U.S. to a foreign state. Sobibor Nazi extermination camp guard John Demjanjuk was recipient of both extradition (to Israel),[43] and after his voluntary return to the U.S., deportation to Germany after having been stripped of his U.S. citizenship.[44] The converse is for the foreign government to expel (deport) the criminal to the United States, often as an accommodation between the countries' law enforcement authorities or Executives.[45]

3) Formal extradition: Yet another way, among civilized countries, is for the United States to request the defendant's extradition from whatever country he's presently in. A formal request is made by the requesting country to the requested country for 1) provisional arrest, and 2) extradition after judicial proceedings thereon. This process is governed by bilateral extradition treaties. The United

---

42. Belfast, 611 F. 3d at 799.
43. See In re Extradition of Demjanjuk, 612 F. Supp. 544 (N.D. Ohio 1985), aff'd sub nom Demjanjuk v. Petrovsky, 776 F. 2d 571 (6th Cir. 1985).
44. See Demjanjuk v. Mukasey, 514 F. 3d 616 (6th Cir. 2008); See also "John Demjanjuk: Prosecution of A Nazi Collaborator," United States Holocaust Memorial Museum, "Introduction to the Holocaust," *Holocaust Encyclopedia*, www.ushmm.org /wlc/en/article.php?ModuleId=10005143. For a different take on Demjanjuk, see Patrick J. Buchanan, "The Persecution of John Demjanjuk" (May 13, 2011), http:// buchanan.org/blog/the-persecution-of-john-demjanjuk-4743.
45. See Ntakirutimana v. Reno, 184 F. 3d 419 (5th Cir. 1999) (extradition based on Executive Agreement between the U.S. and the *Ad Hoc* Criminal Tribunal for the Prosecution of Persons Responsible for Genocide and Other Serious Violations of Humanitarian Law Committed in the Territory of Rwanda did not violate the U.S. Constitution).

States has extradition treaties with over one hundred countries.[46] The process between States, such as, e.g., New York and Florida, is called interstate rendition, and is governed by the U.S. Constitution.[47] Where a defendant is arrested in one federal district, but charged in another, an Identity and Removal hearing is required to transfer the defendant to the charging district for trial.[48]

4) Military capture and removal: Manuel Antonio Noriega was the soi-disant "Maximum Leader of National Liberation" of Panama. He was also in the cocaine business. In 1989, U.S. President George H.W. Bush "directed United States armed forces into combat in Panama for the stated purposes of . . . seizing Noriega to face federal drug charges in the United States [citation omitted]. The ensuing military conflagration resulted in significant casualties."[49] He was captured by the United States military and brought to Miami, where he was convicted and sentenced to 20 years in prison.[50] Noriega complained of the manner in which he was brought to the United States; the Court rejected his argument, basing its decision on a doctrine of law that provides that a defendant cannot defeat personal jurisdiction by asserting the illegality of the procurement of his presence.[51] This doctrine is discussed immediately below.

5) Forcible abduction and extraordinary rendition: Extraordinary rendition by means of forcible abduction has been used in several different contexts, including the taking into custody for purposes of prosecution in the United States of terrorists (e.g., Fawaz Yunis, discussed below) and criminals (e.g., Alvarez-Machain, also discussed below). Obtaining custody of the offender and what is done with the offender after custody is secured are separate concepts. This section deals with gaining custody for purposes of criminal prosecu-

---

46. A list of United States extradition treaties is found in 18 U.S.C. §3181.

47. "A Person charged in any State with Treason, Felony, or other Crime, who shall flee from Justice, and be found in another State, shall on Demand of the executive Authority of the State from which he fled, be delivered up, to be removed to the State having Jurisdiction of the Crime." U.S. Constitution, Article IV, Section 2, Clause 2.

48. Rule 5(c)(3)(D), Federal Rules of Criminal Procedure.

49. United States v. Noriega, 117 F. 3d 1206, 1210 (11th Cir. 1997).

50. Ibid.

51. Noriega, 117 F. 3d at 1214 ("Noriega's due process claim 'falls squarely within the [Supreme Court's] Ker-Frisbie doctrine.'")

Using the Torture Act Against the Persecution of Christians

tion of those charged with committing heinous crimes universally condemned (or at least condemned by civilized countries).[52]

Extraordinary rendition as used here is the process of having United States officers unilaterally arrest the defendant abroad and return him to the United States. In dealing with a civilized country such as the United Kingdom,[53] this process would be both unnecessary and ill-advised for many obvious reasons. In dealing with uncivilized rogue entities such as Islamic State, the necessity of the process is likewise obvious. The United States Supreme Court jurisprudence on this issue is both long-settled and clear: the Court will not inquire as to how a defendant came before it, at least as far as bringing the defendant to trial and punishing him if convicted is concerned. In *Ker v. Illinois*, 119 U.S. 436, 444 (1886) and *Frisbie v. Collins*, 342 U.S. 519 (1952) the Supreme Court held that the power of a court to try a person for a criminal offense is not impaired by the fact that the defendant appears before the court as the result of a "forcible abduction." In the former case, the defendant was kidnapped in Peru and brought to the United States; in the latter he was kidnapped in Illinois and transported to Michigan. Together, these cases comprise the Ker-Frisbie Doctrine. In *United States v. Alvarez-Machain*, the defendant, a medical doctor, was charged with medicating and reviving a captured DEA agent in Mexico so that narcotics thugs could continue to torture and interrogate the DEA agent, whom they finally murdered. Alvarez-Machain was abducted from Mexico at the instigation of U.S. law enforcement and brought to the United States. The Supreme Court held that the forcible abduction did not deprive the U.S. of jurisdiction to try the defendant for violations of federal criminal law and reaffirmed the continuing viability of the Ker-Frisbie doctrine.[54]

---

52. It has also been used for the purpose of taking foreign terrorists into custody, not for purposes of criminal prosecution in the United States, but for purposes of interrogation outside the United States. In popular media, the term "rendition" has conflated the concept of using the process for ordinary criminal prosecution in the United States with the concept of using the process for illegal interrogation abroad.

53. It is worthy of note that the British practice of forcibly pressing seamen from U.S. ships was a major contributing factor in the War of 1812.

54. United States v. Alvarez-Machain, 504 U.S. 655, 662 (1992) ("the rule in *Ker* applies and the court need not inquire as to how respondent came before it.")

The doctrine applies not only as between the United States and a foreign country, but also as between States of the United States. In *Alvarez-Machain*, the Supreme Court noted "We have applied *Ker* to numerous cases where the presence of the defendant was obtained by an interstate abduction."[55]

Mahon v. Justice is a colorful case involving the famous feud between the Hatfields and McCoys in West Virginia and Kentucky.[56] A posse from Kentucky illegally entered West Virginia, captured and abducted one Plyant Mahon, a Hatfield family member, to Kentucky. West Virginia sought a writ of habeas corpus for Mahon to be returned to West Virginia. The Supreme Court upheld the denial of the writ, on the basis that "The jurisdiction of the court in which the indictment is found is not impaired by the manner in which the accused is brought before it."[57] Mahon was convicted of murder in Kentucky and hanged.

Examples of extraordinary rendition for purposes of prosecution include the arrest of Palestine Liberation Front aircraft hijacker Fawaz Younis. The FBI lured him onto a yacht in the Mediterranean with promises of a big drug deal, and arrested him. During his arrest his wrists were accidentally broken. In affirming his conviction, the Court of Appeals followed the Ker-Frisbie doctrine.[58] The court also observed that the Hostage Taking Act was enacted to execute the International Convention Against the Taking of Hostages and viewed the "universal principle" with favor as justification for extraterritorial jurisdiction. Ultimately, though, the intent of Congress, and not customary international law controls. The Court held:

> Yunis seeks to portray international law as a self-executing code that trumps domestic law whenever the two conflict. That effort misconceives the role of judges as appliers of international law and as participants in the federal system. Our duty is to enforce the Constitution, laws, and treaties of the United States, not to conform the law of the land to norms of customary international law. *See*

---

55. Alvarez-Machain, 504 U.S. at 662 n8, citing Mahon v. Justice, 127 U.S. 700, 32 L. Ed. 283, 8 S. Ct. 1204 (1888); Cook v. Hart, 146 U.S. 183, 36 L. Ed. 934, 13 S. Ct. 40 (1892); Pettibone v. Nichols, 203 U.S. 192, 215–16, 51 L. Ed. 148, 27 S. Ct. 111 (1906).
56. Mahon v. Justice, 127 U.S. 700, 32 L. Ed. 283, 8 S. Ct. 1204 (1888).
57. 127 U.S., 707.
58. United States v. Yunis, 924 F. 2d 1086, 1092–093 (D. C. Cir. 1991).

Using the Torture Act Against the Persecution of Christians

U.S. Const. art. VI. As we said in *Committee of U.S. Citizens Living in Nicaragua v. Reagan*, 859 F.2d 929 (D.C. Cir. 1988): "Statutes inconsistent with principles of customary international law may well lead to international law violations. But within the domestic legal realm, that inconsistent statute simply modifies or supersedes customary international law to the extent of the inconsistency." Ibid, 938.[59]

The United States is not alone. The nation of Israel deployed the practice of extraordinary rendition in the well-known case of Nazi Adolph Eichmann, kidnapped by the Israeli government from Argentina and brought to Israel.

Eichmann played [a] central role in the deportation of over 1.5 million Jews from all over Europe to killing centers and killing sites in occupied Poland and in parts of the occupied Soviet Union. . . . In 1960, agents of the Israeli Security Service (Mossad) abducted Eichmann and brought him to Israel to stand trial. . . . On December 15, 1961, Eichmann was found guilty of crimes against the Jewish people. He was hanged at midnight between May 31 and June 1, 1962.[60]

The Torture Act contains a specific section criminalizing conspiracy to commit torture, 18 U.S.C. §2340A(c), which provides: "**(c) Conspiracy.** A person who conspires to commit an offense under this section shall be subject to the same penalties (other than the penalty of death) as the penalties prescribed for the offense, the commission of which was the object of the conspiracy." In finding this section constitutional, the Court of Appeals in *Belfast* observed that the Torture Act's inclusion of conspiracy as a criminal offense was in accord with the Convention Against Torture:

Article 4(1) of the CAT explicitly requires that "[e]ach State Party . . . ensure that all acts of torture are offenses under its criminal law" and it provides that "[t]he same shall apply . . . to an act by

---

59. *Yunis*, 924 F.2d, at 1091. See also Federal Trade Comm'n. v. Compagnie de Saint-Gobain-Pont-a-Mousson, 205 U.S. App. D.C. 172, 636 F.2d 1300, 1323 (D.C. Cir. 1980) (U.S. courts "obligated to give effect to an unambiguous exercise by Congress of its jurisdiction to prescribe even if such an exercise would exceed the limitations imposed by international law.")

60. United States Holocaust Memorial Museum, "Introduction to the Holocaust," *Holocaust Encyclopedia*, www.ushmm.org/wlc/en/article.php?ModuleId=10005143.

any person which constitutes *complicity* or *participation* in torture." CAT, Art. 4(1) (emphasis added). In other words, the CAT specifically instructs its signatories to criminalize not only the act of torture itself, but also conduct that encourages and furthers the commission of torture by others. Conspiracy plainly amounts to such conduct.[61]

The utility of criminal prosecution of torturers of Christians can be discerned by considering the factors appropriate in federal criminal sentencing, which include elements of retribution, deterrence, incapacitation, denunciation, and rehabilitation. 18 U.S.C. §3553 provides the factors to be considered in imposing a sentence on a criminal, and provides in pertinent part:

(a) The court, in determining the particular sentence to be imposed, shall consider—

(1) the nature and circumstances of the offense and the history and characteristics of the defendant;

(2) the need for the sentence imposed—

(A) to reflect the seriousness of the offense, to promote respect for the law, and to provide just punishment for the offense;

(B) to afford adequate deterrence to criminal conduct;

(C) to protect the public from further crimes of the defendant;

(D) to provide the defendant with needed educational or vocational training, medical care, or other correctional treatment in the most effective manner.

---

61. Belfast, 611 F. 3d, 811. Chuckie was charged, *inter alia*, with such conspiracy. The object of the conspiracy was to "maintain, preserve, protect and strengthen the power and authority of Charles McArthur Taylor's presidency, and to intimidate, neutralize, punish, weaken and eliminate actual and perceived opponents of and threats to his administration by means of torture in violation of Title 18, Unites States Code, Sections 2340A and 2340(1)." *Belfast*, 611 F. 3d, 812. An indictment for conspiring to torture Christians could easily substitute the religious cleansing object for the political object. The Torture Act also requires that the torture be done "under color of law." See Ulrike Putz, "Christians Flee from Radical Rebels in Syria," Spiegel Online (July 25, 2012), http://www.spiegel.de/international/world/christians-flee-from-radical-rebels-in-syria-a-846180.html (Civilians "killed by rebel fighters... murdered because they were Christians, people who in the eyes of radical Islamist freedom fighters have no place in the new Syria.")

Using the Torture Act Against the Persecution of Christians

Putting torturers behind bars in prison is an effective way to put an end to the torturer's career and to give some justice to his victims. Chuckie Taylor is presently out of the torture business, and will remain so for the rest of his life. Deployed often and severely enough, such incarceration should have all the salutary effects of domestic criminal punishment on this universally-detested crime of torture: reflecting the seriousness of the crime, promoting respect for the rule of law, providing just punishment for the criminal, deterring others from similar conduct, protecting the public from further crimes of the defendant, and providing some measure of justice for the victims.

Al-Qaryatayn, Syria. A Syriac Catholic deacon in the demolished church of the monastery of St. Elian (April, 2016).

10

International Criminal Law

Kevin Cieply

AT THE END OF World War II, the Allies faced the dilemma of how to grapple with the leaders of the Nazi regime who had conceived, orchestrated, and carried out the Holocaust. The laws of war in place, Hague and Geneva, appeared inadequate to fully capture what had occurred and seemed ill equipped to mete out the proper just deserts. Specifically, individual criminal responsibility under international law was not an established concept. Numerous options, therefore, were floated between the Allies, including summary execution and show trials. In the end, the London Charter was created and signed, the Nuremberg Trials commenced and concluded, and the most culpable of the surviving leaders were held accountable.[1]

In the Far East, a similar reckoning took place—a U.S. military commission convicted General Yamashita under a theory of Command Responsibility for massive crimes committed by his subordinates in the Philippines. General Yamashita was hanged for his role in the atrocities. In Tokyo, a Charter was patterned off Nuremberg. Twenty-eight defendants were tried, with no acquittals.[2] Seven defendants were sentenced to death, including Prime Minister Tojo,

---

1. In addition to the International Military Tribunal at Nuremberg, the Allies held subsequent Nazi Trials under a statute they enacted together: Allied Control Council Law No. 10, http://avalon.law.yale.edu/imt/imt10.asp. While the IMT focused on the German leadership, the second round of trials under CCL 10 focused on professional categories of the defendants: doctors, industrialists, lawyers, etc. Thousands of German defendants were tried by the Allies under CCL 10. Luban, O'Sullivan, and Stewart, *International and Transnational Criminal Law* (2010), 87–91.

2. See Luban, O'Sullivan & Stewart, *International*, 92.

who was convicted of waging aggressive war as well as ordering, authorizing, and permitting inhumane treatment of prisoners of war, among other things. Prime Minister Tojo was hanged for his crimes; he was 63 years old.

Post-World War II was a watershed period for international criminal law. The trials of the major war criminals established individual responsibility for military commanders and soldiers, as well as civilian leaders. Up to that point, military and civilian leaders, as well as those under their authority, could generally carry out criminal action during times of armed conflict with impunity, hiding behind a shield of state sovereignty. Not only did the trials establish individual responsibility, but they also developed concepts in international criminal law, such as crimes against humanity and the recognition of genocide as a separate international criminal offense.

The events of World War II also precipitated the creation of the United Nations (U.N.). The Charter for the U.N. was signed on June 26, 1945, and ratified on October 24, 1945. The U.N. Charter established the General Assembly in which all of its Member States participate (currently 193 countries), and a Security Council which is comprised of fifteen members. Five members of the Security Council are permanent members (P5)—United States, United Kingdom, France, China, and Russia. The other ten members are elected from the General Assembly; they serve two-year terms.

Under Chapter VII of the U.N. Charter, the Security Council is charged with the power to determine what potential threats should be considered actual threats to international peace and security. When the Security Council deems a situation to be an international threat, it possesses the exclusive authority to decide what measures, if any, need to be taken to maintain international peace and security.

The P5 each have veto authority, meaning that any one of the P5 can paralyze Security Council action in reference to a given situation. That is precisely what occurred concerning the Korean and Vietnam wars, as P5 members found themselves on opposing sides of those conflicts. The intractable positions left any prosecution for criminal violations to the national courts, essentially eschewing justice.

It took almost fifty years after the inception of the United Nations and Security Council for the international community to once again face threats to international peace that met the requirements of the P5. One was the horrific genocide of 1994 in Rwanda, where many

International Criminal Law

Hutu people committed genocide against Tutsi people. The other was the Balkans conflict, concerning the break-up of the former Yugoslavia. In both situations, the Security Council was able to find consensus, and using its Chapter VII authority, created *ad hoc* tribunals—the International Criminal Tribunal of Rwanda (ICTR) and the International Criminal Tribunal of Yugoslavia (ICTY).

The *ad hoc* tribunals proved to be effective instruments of justice, ensuring those who were the most culpable for the atrocities did not escape justice. Combined, the tribunals indicted over 250 persons and convicted approximately 150. The ICTR closed on December 31, 2015. At the time of this writing, the ICTY continues its operation but is also near its end, with only has six cases left on appeal, and one at trial—that of Ratko Mladić, the former Commander of the Main Staff of the Serb Army in Bosnia and Herzegovina.[3]

While the ICTY was created to address specific situations, their contributions to this area of the law—known as "International Criminal Law" or "International Humanitarian Law"—cannot be overstated. The tribunals essentially picked-up where post World War II trials of major war criminals left off, fleshing out the elements of genocide, crimes against humanity, and war crimes, and in particular expanding the number of crimes recognized under crimes against humanity. Moreover, they further developed modes of individual responsibility such as Joint Criminal Enterprises, defined when an "armed attack" occurs, and laid bare what worked and did not work in the courtroom when trying cases of mass atrocities. All of those aspects, and many more, made the tribunals extremely influential in the creation and development of the Statute and Elements of Crimes for today's International Criminal Court (ICC).[4]

The ICC is the first permanent international criminal court. It was developed in the summer of 1998, when 120 nations negotiated the Rome Statute, which is the treaty creating the court. The Rome Statute became effective on July 2, 2002, when the 60th nation ratified it. The ICC is based in The Hague, Netherlands, and exclusively addresses the crimes of genocide, crimes against humanity, war

---

3. Mladić is charged with genocide, crimes against humanity, and violations of the laws of war. *See* Mladić (IT-09-92) available at: http://www.icty.org/en/action/cases/4.

4. *The International Criminal Court, Elements of Crimes and Rules of Procedure and Evidence* (Roy S. Lee, ed. 2001), xi–xiii. See chapter eleven in this book.

crimes, and the crime of aggression. Article 5 of the ICC explains that its jurisdiction is limited to those "most serious crimes of concern to the international community as a whole."

The ICC represents the most current, complete, and accessible body of international criminal law today.[5] The Rome Statute provides definitions and elements for the crimes of genocide, crimes against humanity, war crimes, and the crime of aggression. It also provides for jurisdiction, rules of procedure, including rules of evidence, defenses, and sentencing. The ICC is still a relatively new court with only a few completed cases. This chapter, therefore, relies on not only the Rome Statute, but also the ICTR and ICTY statutes, as well as case law from those tribunals.

Before moving forward, it may be useful to quickly discuss the difference between International Criminal Law/International Humanitarian Law (IHL) and Human Rights Law (HRL).[6] Historically, in the most general of terms, it was the difference between laws that apply during times of war (IHL) and times of peace (HRL). Human Rights Law addresses a broad array of rights and addresses how states should treat their own citizens in times of peace. HRL includes civil, political, cultural, and economic rights. International Criminal Law/Humanitarian Law, on the other hand, has been concerned exclusively with the law between nations during war or between factions in times of conflict. Over the years, International Criminal Law/IHL has expanded, no longer being completely tethered to war/armed conflict, but rather it also includes situations of genocide and crimes against humanity, neither requiring a war nexus. Perhaps now, when speaking as to where the line is drawn between IHL and HRL, instead

---

5. This is not a comment on the effectiveness of how the court is administered, only that the Rome Statute itself is the most complete reflection of contemporary international criminal law.

6. Human Rights Law (HRL) also experienced its most significant growth immediately following WWII. In 1948, the U.N. produced the Universal Declaration of Human Rights (UDHR). The UDHR inspired a number of HRL conventions, such as the International Covenant on Civil and Political Rights (ICCPR), and the International Covenant on Economic, Social, Cultural Rights (ICESCR). The UDHR, ICCPR, and ICESCR, together, are considered the "Bill of Rights" for International Law. See Henry J. Steiner and Philip Alston, *International Human Rights in Context, Law, Politics, Morals* (2nd Ed. 2000), 136–53.

of stating that the line falls between war and peace, it is more accurate to say that the line is drawn at the point where the international community is willing to pierce the veil of sovereignty, and take on the task of criminally prosecuting one or more individuals in an international court of law. As of now, that includes only four crimes: genocide, crimes against humanity, war crimes, and the crime of aggression.

Because the focus here, of course, is the persecution of Christians, this chapter will concentrate on International Criminal Law/IHL, and not HRL. While potentially there is much that could be discussed as to what countries could or should do in the area of HRL, the emphasis here is on the current situations found in places such as Syria, Iraq, and Darfur, where there is armed conflict, as well as to focus on specific organizations such as al Qaeda and the Islamic State of Iraq and Syria (ISIS), which have made their intentions clear—to continue committing the crimes of genocide, crimes against humanity, war crimes, and crimes of aggression.

Genocide

The Nazis used the phrase "Final Solution to the Jewish Problem" to describe their strategy for eliminating the Jewish People. Now, this is known as "genocide," and it holds the status of being considered the "crime of crimes." The word genocide comes from the Greek word for tribe—*genos*, and the Latin word for the act of killing—*cidium*.[7] It is a word created in 1944 by a Polish-Jewish lawyer who fled the Nazi invasion of Poland during World War II and came to the United States.[8]

Genocide officially became recognized as a distinct and separate international crime in 1948 when the United Nations approved the text of the "Convention on the Prevention and Punishment of the

---

7. See Luban, O'Sullivan & Stewart, *International*, 985.
8. Ibid. The Polish-Jewish lawyer was Raphael Lemkin. In its indictment against the Nazis after World War II, the International Military Tribunal (IMT) at Nuremberg did in fact use the term "genocide" to describe acts committed by the defendants that constituted War Crimes. Genocide was not charged as a separate crime, nor was it used in the judgment. John Q. Barrett, "Raphael Lemkin and genocide at Nuremberg," 1945–1946, 51–52, in *The Genocide Convention Sixty Years After Its Adoption* (Christoph Safferling & Eckart Conze, eds., Asser Press, 2010).

Crime of Genocide" (Genocide Convention). The definition of genocide established in 1948 by the Genocide Convention, remains good law. Indeed, the Rome Statute adopted the Genocide Convention's language, readily accepting it as representing customary international law.[9] Genocide is an international crime whether committed in time of war or in time of peace.[10]

Basically, there are three elements to genocide. First, the perpetrator has a specific intent to "destroy, in whole or in part, a national, ethnic, racial or religious group as such." Second, the perpetrator has committed one of the following underlying crimes against the target group: murder, causing serious bodily or mental harm, inflicting conditions of life calculated to bring about physical destruction, imposing measures to prevent births, or forcibly transferring children. Third, the perpetrator's role in the crime is recognized as criminally culpable.

The first element, that the perpetrator had the intent to destroy, in whole or in part, a national ethnic, racial, or religious group as such, is what is referred to in international criminal law as the "chapeau" element.[11] The chapeau element is best understood when it is broken-down into following five sub-elements: 1) an intent; 2) to destroy; 3) in whole or in part; 4) a national, ethical, racial, or religious group; 5) as such.

The requisite intent for genocide is no ordinary criminal intent—it is the highest form of intent known in criminal law, and thus the most difficult to prove. The perpetrator must act with *purpose*. In the legal scheme of criminal intent, negligence is the lowest form and purpose the highest. In addition, the purpose must specifically be to "destroy" the group, meaning the actual physical or biological destruction of the group. Making the group suffer or discriminating

---

9. *The International Criminal Court, The Making of the Rome Statute, Issues, Negotiations, Results* (Roy S. Lee ed., Kluwer Law International, 1999, 2002), 89.

10. U.N. General Assembly, Convention on the Prevention and Punishment of the Crime of Genocide, December 9, 1948, United Nations, Treaty Series, Art. I [hereinafter Genocide Convention].

11. Chapeau in French means "hat." Imagine the chapeau element sitting on top of the other elements, identifying its character as an international crime, much like the white or black hat in Western movies served as an identifier as to who was the lawman and who was the outlaw.

against the group does not suffice for genocide. The intended effect must be to actually eliminate the group, physically.

The intent to destroy must also go toward the "whole" or at least "part" of the group, meaning intent directed toward just one person or a limited portion of the group, is not good enough. Moreover, the targeted group must be the right "type" of group. That is to say that the group must be recognized under international law as a protected group. Currently, there are only four types of groups recognized under international genocide law as protected: national, ethnic, racial, or religious groups. Political groups and social groups are not protected.

The last chapeau sub-element involves the following language: "as such." This language is meant to highlight a particular characteristic of genocide. That is, when the perpetrator commits a crime against a particular victim, in order for the crime to qualify as genocide, it is not good enough that the victim is a member of a protected group. The prosecutor must establish that the perpetrator committed the crime against the victim *precisely because* the victim is a member of the protected group.

The key turns on how the particular court defines who constitutes the relevant victim group. That is, how broad or narrow does the court circumscribe the targeted group? In addressing that question, courts have been willing to define groups based on regional or even smaller defined geographical areas.[12] Once the group is fixed, courts require a showing that the perpetrator intended to destroy a "substantial" or "considerable" portion of the group to qualify as genocide.[13]

When the numbers are not "substantial" or "considerable," courts have even been willing to analyze the issue qualitatively, that is to say courts have been willing to decide whether the intent to destroy may be established based on the significance of those targeted—for instance, targeting the leadership, or a segment of the group that makes up an essential element of a group's ability to survive, has

---

12. Prosecutor v. Krstić, ICTY Case No. IT-98-33-T, ¶ 589 (2 August 2001).

13. Ibid., ¶ 586. As far as how much of a group a perpetrator must intend to destroy for it to qualify as genocide, there is no easy answer. Even Hitler did not set out to destroy all the Jewish people—Hitler's intention was to destroy the Jews in Europe, not every Jewish person on earth.

qualified. The key seems to come down to whether the intent to destroy would qualify as an existential threat to the targeted group.

As an example, the International Criminal Tribunal of Yugoslavia (ICTY) convicted Serbs of genocide for killing 7,000 to 8,000 Bosnian Muslim men from the city of Serbrencia and its surrounding area. The defendants did not intend to kill all Muslims worldwide, and they did not intend to kill all European Muslims, or even all of the Muslims in Bosnia, only those from Serbrencia and surrounding areas, and only Muslim men, not women and children. Yet, the ICTY deemed that the intent to kill the Muslim men of military age in Serbrencia was indeed an adequate part of the population to qualify as genocide.[14] Specifically, the ICTY explained it in this manner:

> The killing of all members of the part of a group located within a small geographical area, although resulting in a lesser number of victims, would qualify as genocide if carried out with the intent to destroy the part of the group as such located in this small geographical area. Indeed, the physical destruction may target only a part of the geographically limited part of the larger group because the perpetrators of the genocide regard the intended destruction as sufficient to annihilate the group as a distinct entity in the geographic area at issue. In this regard, it is important to bear in mind the total context in which the physical destruction is carried out.[15]

There are five enumerated actions that if committed by a perpetrator with the chapeau intent, qualify as genocide. They are as follows: 1) killing; 2) causing serious bodily or mental harm; 3) inflicting conditions of life calculated to bring about physical destruction; 4) imposing measures to prevent births; and 5) forcibly transferring children.

The first action listed, killing, is fairly straightforward. Perhaps the only issue that may cause confusion would be that the killing must be intentional. Killings as a result of negligence or recklessness do not suffice. Causing serious bodily or mental harm is also fairly straightforward. As far as serious bodily harm, it means "serious acts of physical violence falling short of killing that seriously injure the health, cause disfigurement, or cause serious injury to external or

---

14. Ibid., ¶598.
15. Ibid., ¶590.

International Criminal Law

internal organs or senses. Serious mental harm refers to more than minor or temporary impairment of mental faculties. The serious bodily or mental harm, however, need not be an injury that is permanent or irremediable."[16] Perhaps the best way of thinking about serious bodily or mental harm is that it must be the type of harm that has a legitimate potential to destroy the group, even if that potential was not realized.[17]

Inflicting conditions of life calculated to bring about physical destruction is distinguished from the act of killing, in that it refers to situations where death, while reasonably likely, is a more attenuated outcome and likely to occur over an extended period of time. Starvation, intentionally exposing a group to deadly disease, death marches, concentration camps, and denying the availability of basic health care, are all poignant examples.

Actions intended to prevent births include but are not limited to: sexual mutilation, forced sterilization, forced birth control, prohibiting marriage within the targeted group or with others and the targeted group, and rape with the intent to deliberately impregnate or to cause such severe mental trauma that the victim will not desire to procreate.[18]

Lastly, forcibly transferring children of one group to another includes not only carrying out the actual transfer but also the threat to do so.[19]

The list of the five actions stated above appears to be exhaustive, meaning that any other actions or crimes that cannot fold into one of those five categories do not suffice for genocide. There are some crimes, however, that seemingly will always fit within one of those five categories. For instance, torture and rape are likely to always qualify as "causing serious bodily or mental harm." In some cases, they may also qualify as inflicting conditions of life calculated to bring about physical destruction or imposing measures to prevent births.

---

16. Prosecutor v. Ntagerura et al., Case No. ICTR-99-46-T, ¶ 664 (25 Feb. 2004).
17. Guénaël Mettraux, *International Crimes and the Ad Hoc Tribunals* (Oxford, 2005), 238.
18. Prosecutor v. Akayesu et al., Case No. ICTR-96-4-T, ¶ 507–08 (Sept. 2, 1998).
19. Ibid., ¶ 509.

Crimes Against Humanity

Crimes against Humanity was first prosecuted as a specific crime against the Nazis at Nuremberg. U.S. Supreme Court Justice Robert H. Jackson, who served as one of the drafters of the Nuremberg Charter and as the Chief Prosecutor for the United States at Nuremberg, came up with the verbiage. Initially, "genocide" was explicitly listed in the draft Charter. But "genocide" was a new term, unfamiliar at the time to most, and thus for many would have required further explanation. After consulting with renowned international lawyer and scholar Sir Hersch Lauterpacht, Justice Jackson settled on using language that seemed more self-evident: "crimes against humanity."[20]

The *ad hoc* tribunals and the ICC have done much to develop crimes against humanity into a distinct body of international criminal law. Professor Luban describes the impact the phrase has garnered over the years, as follows:

> The phrase "crimes against humanity" has acquired enormous resonance in the legal and moral imaginations of the post-World War II world. It suggests, in at least two distinct ways, the enormity of these offenses. First, the phrase "crimes against humanity" suggests offenses that aggrieve not only the victims and their own communities, but all human beings, regardless of their community. Second, the phrase suggests these offenses cut deep, violating the core humanity that we all share and that distinguishes us from other natural beings.

The inspiration for the phrase likely came from the "Martens Clause," found in the Preamble of both the 1899 and 1907 Hague Conventions. Specifically, the Martens Clause makes a somewhat fleeting mention of the "laws of humanity," in that they are always in place to protect civilians and belligerents alike. While the Martens Clause did not specifically address what the "laws of humanity" entailed, and while it did not create an international crime or allot individual criminal liability, the Martens Clause language did, apparently, germinate an idea that has spawned into what is today an ever-growing and ever-increasing influential body of international law.

---

20. Luban, O'Sullivan & Stewart, *International*, 955.

International Criminal Law

There are two layers to this crime. The first, as in genocide, is the chapeau element. Like the chapeau element of genocide, it is an element that gives the crime its international character. The chapeau element also distinguishes crimes against humanity from other international crimes, such as the crime of genocide and from war crimes.[21]

For crimes against humanity, the chapeau element specifically requires a "widespread or systematic attack directed against any civilian population."[22] It is best understood when separated into five separate sub-elements: (a) An attack; (b) directed against any civilian population; (c) that is widespread or systematic; and, (d) the defendant must have knowledge of the attack.

The ICTR and ICTY statutes did not define exactly what was required to qualify as "an attack." The ICTY Trial Chamber did, however, define it as "a course of conduct involving the commission of acts of violence."[23] More helpful is the Rome Statute, which defines it as "a course of conduct involving the multiple commissions of acts referred to in paragraph 1 against any civilian population, pursuant to or in furtherance of a State or organizational policy to commit such attack."[24] The reference to paragraph 1 refers to the list of inhumane acts that serve as the underlying offenses, including murder, extermination, persecution, torture, and rape, to name a few, as well as the catch-all category of other inhumane acts of similar character.[25]

The obvious aspect here is that the targeted group must be "civilian," as opposed to combatants. Every person targeted need not be civilian; a small number of soldiers in the targeted population would not necessarily mean this element would fail, but the group must be decisively civilian.

A subtler aspect to this element, but just as important, is the scale it requires. Population connotes a minimal degree of scale, certainly

---

21. G. Mettrauex, 155, supra note 17.
22. The ICC abandoned requiring a war nexus, which the ICTY had required.
23. Prosecutor v. Kunarac et al., ICTY Case No. IT-96-23-T, ¶ 415 (Feb. 22, 2001).
24. U.N. Diplomatic Conference on Plenipotentiaries on the Establishment of an International Criminal Court, U.N. Doc. A/Conf. 183/9th (2002) [hereinafter Rome Statute or ICC Statute], Art. 7(2)(a).
25. Ibid., Art. 7(1).

not to the level of the sub-element—widespread or systematic—but nonetheless it implies that the attack must be directed at a certain size group, not simply an individual or a few individuals. The group, moreover, cannot be any random group, it must be one that is sizeable enough and possesses distinctive common characteristics to the extent that it constitutes a "population."

The type of "population" is of little significance, however. Crimes against humanity are different in this regard from genocide. For crimes against humanity, the group need not be designated by their nationality, race, religion, or ethnicity, as it must with genocide. On the other hand, the kind of group is not without boundaries—a gathering of individuals, such as for a soccer match, would not qualify as a "population." As with genocide, the court's decision as to what qualifies or fails to qualify as a sufficient group, can be a critical factor.

Perhaps even more subtle is the requirement that the attack must be "directed" against the population. That brings into play the fact that the population must be the primary target of the attack, not simply the product of collateral damage.

Notice also that the requirement for the attack to be "widespread or systematic" is in the disjunctive. Either will suffice. But the significance of the disjunctive, in practice, may be slight. When this element is considered in light of the requirement that the attack must be done "pursuant to or in furtherance of a State or organizational policy," there are likely to be few instances where the gravity of the situation does not produce both widespread and systematic violence. The policy requirement highlights that these attacks are committed by organized groups, if not state entities. It is meant to address group against group violence, which tends to require a widespread and systematic approach. In any case, the chapeau element is intended to require a grave situation, a situation that shocks the conscience, violence at the level of organized violence, violence at a level significant enough to create international concern.

The last chapeau sub-element concerns the perpetrator's state-of-mind, or what is often referred to by its Latin name—*mens rea*. The defendant must have acted, meaning committed an underlying offense, with knowledge of the attack. It is important to understand that with crimes against humanity, there are two layers of *mens rea*. The first layer, concerns the chapeau *mens rea* addressed here—

knowledge of the attack. A second *mens rea*, for the underlying inhumane act, is addressed below.

The chapeau element sets the context for the underlying offense. The underlying offense may include persecution, extermination, murder, rape, or any other similar inhumane act. The ICTR, ICTY, and the ICC all explicitly set forth a list of underlying inhumane acts that serve, as in genocide, as the underlying offense.[26] The list of underlying offenses for crimes against humanity is much longer than genocide. In addition, the ICTR, ICTY, and the ICC each have a catch-all category that sweeps in any other inhumane act not explicitly listed, so long as they are similar in character, which essentially means they must cause great suffering. Three of the most relevant underlying acts for the purposes of this book are persecution, extermination, and murder.

The ICC defines persecution in the following manner: when targeting a group based on its political, racial, national, ethnic, cultural, religious, or gender characteristics,[27] an "intentional and severe deprivation of fundamental rights contrary to international law by reason of the identity of the group or collectivity."[28]

The elements for persecution are as follows: (1) discriminatory act; (2) based on one of the listed characteristics; and (3) intent to deprive a fundamental right. There is no comprehensive list of all potential discriminatory acts that could qualify as an act of persecution. Some of the persecutory acts recognized by the *ad hoc* tribunals have included:

> Indiscriminate attacks on cities, towns and villages, as well as the seizure, collection, segregation, and forced transfer of civilians to camps, calling-out of civilians, beatings, and killings; acts of torture or rape and other forms of sexual assault; murder, imprisonment, and such attacks on property as would constitute a destruction of the livelihood of a certain population; destruction or willful damage to religious and cultural buildings; or the destruction and plunder of property where serious enough, either by reason of its magnitude or because of the value of the stolen property or the

---

26. ICTR and ICTY both have 8 listed acts plus the catch-all category of other inhumane acts. The ICC has 10, plus the other inhumane acts category.
27. ICC Statute, Art. 7(2)(g).
28. Ibid.

nature and extent of the destruction; unlawful detention of civilians, deportation or forcible transfer of civilians, and serious bodily and mental harm or other serious inhumane treatment of civilians.[29]

The list is relatively long, but customary international law supports an expansive approach to protecting against discriminatory acts and defining persecution in a broad fashion. The intent for persecution is that the defendant had a purpose to discriminate on one of the stated grounds. It is, in other words, a specific intent crime.

Extermination is the purposeful killing of a large number of individuals. A large quantity is required, although there is no set amount. It is the scale of the killings that differentiates it from murder. There is no discriminatory requirement, however, which distinguishes it from persecution. There is no requirement of an intent to destroy an entire group, separating it from genocide.

Murder is the purposeful killing of an individual. One victim suffices; and there is no need to prove discriminatory intent or an intent to destroy an entire group. If the defendant intended to commit grievous bodily harm or inflict serious injury with knowledge that death was likely to occur, that would also suffice for murder.[30]

It is important to understand that there are two *mens rea* at play with crimes against humanity. The first concerns the chapeau, where the defendant must have knowledge of the overall widespread or systematic attack. The second is the *mens rea* that is required for the underlying inhumane act—the individual crime. For persecution, extermination, and murder, that *mens rea* is intent. But the defendant need not intend to perpetrate a widespread or systematic attack, the defendant only needs to be aware of it. In other words, the widespread or systematic attack provides the context; the defendant only needs to be aware of that context as the defendant commits the particular inhumane act. For the individual crime, the defendant must meet the *mens rea* required for that individual crime, for example, murder—the defendant must "intend" to kill.

---

29. Ibid., 184.
30. Ibid., 106.

International Criminal Law

Crime of Aggression and War Crimes

Traditionally, the intersection of law and war has involved two broad categories: just war theory and the laws of war. The first category—just war—in Latin is referred to as *jus ad bellum*. The second category—laws of war—in Latin is *jus in bello*, it concerns the conduct of warriors in battle, regardless of the illegality or righteousness of the war.[31]

A violation of *jus ad bellum*, in contemporary vernacular, is a "Crime of Aggression." In the most basic terms, it means starting an unjust war. The Nuremberg Charter referred to it as "crimes against peace" and defined it as "namely, planning, preparation, initiation or waging of a war of aggression, or a war in violation of international treaties, agreements or assurances, or participation in a common plan or conspiracy for the accomplishment of any of the foregoing."[32]

When the nations adopted the Rome Statute, it included the crime of aggression as a placeholder. There was no consensus as to the definition of the crime, and there was considerable concern over how the ICC would adjudicate that crime given that the Security Council operates as the final arbiter as to what is and what is not appropriate use of force.

After much work, debate, and compromise, consensus over the definition of the crime of aggression was reached and adopted at a conference in Kampala, Uganda, on June 11, 2010 (Kampala Amend-

---

31. Nineteen of the original twenty-four defendants at Nuremberg were indicted with crimes against peace. In the end, twelve were convicted. Bormann, Frank, Schirach, Streicher, and Kaltenbrunner were not indicted for Crimes Against Peace. Halbach was deemed unfit to stand trial, and Ley committed suicide before trial. Fritzsche, Papen, and Schacht were acquitted. Jewish Virtual Library, "Nuremberg Trial Judgements: Ernst Kaltenbrunner," http://www.jewishvirtuallibrary.org/jsource/Holocaust/JudgeKaltenbrunner.html. Of the indicted twelve, seven were sentenced to death; Jodl, Keitel, Ribbentrop, Rosenberg, Sauckel, and Seyss-Inquart all were hanged. Goering committed suicide the night before he was to hang. Corn et al., *The Law of Armed Conflict, An Operational Approach* (Wolters Kluwer 2012), 483.

32. Charter of the International Military Tribunal at Nuremberg, 82 U.N.T.S. 279, Art. 6(a) (Aug. 8, 1945) [hereinafter the Nuremberg Charter].

ments).[33] The definition is now found at Article 8*bis*[34] of the Rome Statute. It reads as follows:

> (1) [T]he planning, preparation, initiation or execution by a person in a leadership position of an act of aggression. Importantly, it contains the threshold requirement that the act of aggression must constitute a manifest violation of the Charter of the United Nations.
>
> (2) An act of aggression is defined as the use of armed force by one State against another State without the justification of self-defense or authorization by the Security Council. The definition of the act of aggression, as well as the actions qualifying as acts of aggression contained in the amendments (for example invasion by armed forces, bombardment and blockade), are influenced by the U.N. General Assembly Resolution 3314 (XXIX) of 14 December 1974.[35]

Article 8*bis* (2), goes on to list seven acts that qualify as aggression under U.N. General Assembly Resolution 3314: invasion or attack by armed forces of territory of another; bombardment; blockade; attack on the armed forces of another State; use of armed forces in another State under agreement, in contravention of agreement; allowing another State's armed force to launch an attack into a third State's territory; or, sending armed bands into another State to carry out acts of armed force.[36]

One of the elements for the crime of aggression is that the "perpetrator was a person in a position effectively to exercise control over or to direct the political or military action of the State which committed the act of aggression."[37] The perpetrator must control action of a

---

33. Coalition for the International Criminal Court, "Delivering on the promise of a fair, effective and independent Court, The Crime of Aggression," http://www.iccnow.org/?mod=aggression.

34. International Criminal Court (ICC), *Elements of Crimes* (2011), https://www.icc-cpi.int/NR/rdonlyres/336923D8-A6AD-40EC-AD7B-45BF9DE73D56/0/ElementsOfCrimesEng.pdf, [hereinafter ICC Elements of Crimes], Art. 8*bis*. Article 8 was amended by resolution RC/Res.6; see Official Records of the Review Conference of the Rome Statute of the International Criminal Court, Kampala, May 31–June 11, 2010 (International Criminal Court publication, RC/11), part II.

35. ICC Statute, Art. 8*bis*, Inserted by resolution RC/Res.6 of June 11, 2010.

36. Ibid.

37. ICC, Elements of Crimes, Art. 8*bis*, Element 2.

"State," that is, there must be State armed aggression against another State.[38]

The *sine qua non* of *jus in bello* is that war is not unlimited. There are rules, boundaries that if breeched, should be—must be—punished as crime. A violation of *jus in bello* is considered a "war crime." The boundaries, in rough form, are marked by four principles: military necessity, distinction, avoiding unnecessary suffering, and proportionality.

The first principle—military necessity—is not so much an authorization of force as it is a limit: there can be no use of force without military necessity. It is a threshold requirement that must be met prior to using combat power.

The second principle is distinction. At its core, and certainly for purposes here, the principle means that civilians cannot be targeted, ever. Civilians may become, and inevitably do become, casualties of war, but they cannot be intentionally targeted. Combatants must distinguish between enemy combatants and civilians. Enemy combatants who become *hors de combat*, also cannot be targeted.

The third general principle under the laws of war is the prevention of unnecessary suffering.[39] It is an important concept that can be easily misunderstood. It has little to do with the magnitude or lethality of force used to destroy or kill; it has everything to do with prohibiting extended, or particularly heinous, suffering. This principle focuses on the types of weapons that cause widespread and egregious suffering (i.e., poisonous gas, biological agents, projectiles shaped with the intent to cause heightened suffering or to go undetected by X-rays, etc.).

Lastly, the fourth principle is the concept of proportionality. Pro-

---

38. Prior to the ICC exercising jurisdiction over the Crime of Aggression, the State-Parties must vote to activate jurisdiction by a two-thirds majority after January 1, 2017, and the ICC must wait one year after the last required State-Party ratified the amendments, which is June 29, 2017. Amendments to the Rome Statute of the International Criminal Court, Kampala, June 11, 2010, https://asp.icc-cpi.int/iccdocs/asp_docs/RC2010/AMENDMENTS/CN.651.2010-ENG-CoA.pdf; see also ICC Statute, Art. 121. See also The Global Campaign and Ratification of the Kampala Amendments on the Crime of Aggression, http://crimeofaggression.info/role-of-the-icc/conditions-for-action-by-the-icc/.

39. Unnecessary suffering primarily applies to illegal weapons, such as poison gas, booby traps using excrement to cause infections, etc. See Corn, et al., 204–5.

portionality is a term of art under the laws of war. Barring unnecessary suffering, proportionality has little relevance *vis-à-vis* the targeted individual (the combatant); its primary relevance is to balance the military necessity against the possibility of collateral damage (protected persons such as civilians, combatants who are *hors de combat*, and prohibited structures). The amount of collateral damage cannot be out of proportion to the military necessity of the target.

All war crimes, in one shape or form, are a violation of one or more of those four general principles. As time has marched on, those four principals have been fleshed-out to a great degree through codes and tribunals such as the Lieber Code,[40] International Military Tribunal at Nuremberg, the Tokyo Trials, and the *ad hoc* tribunals of the ICTY and ICTR, in particular. Moreover, they have been developed and articulated in treaties such as the Hague Convention of 1899[41] and 1907,[42] the Four Geneva Conventions of 1949,[43] the Additional Protocols of 1977,[44] and the Rome Statute for the ICC.[45]

---

40. Frances Lieber, General Order No. 100, Instructions for the Government of Armies of the United States in the Field (Apr. 24, 1863).

41. Hague Convention (II) with Certain Powers Respecting the Laws and Customs of War on Land (July 29, 1899), 32 Stat. 1803, T.S. No. 403 [hereinafter 1899 Hague], https://ihl-databases.icrc.org/ihl/INTRO/150?OpenDocument.

42. Hague Convention (IV) Respecting the Laws and Customs of War on Land and Its Annex: Regulations Concerning the Laws and Customs of War on Land, 18 October 1907, 36 Stat. 227, 205 Consol. T.S. 277 [hereinafter 1907 Hague], https://ihl-databases.icrc.org/applic/ihl/ihl.nsf/385ec082b509e76c41256739003e636d/1d1726425f6955aec125641e0038bfd6.

43. Geneva Convention for the Amelioration of the Condition of Wounded and Sick in Armed Forces in the Field [GWS I] (Aug. 12, 1949); Geneva Convention for the Amelioration of the Condition of Wounded, Sick, and Shipwrecked Members of the Armed Forces at Sea, [GWS Sea II] (Aug. 12, 1949); Geneva Convention Relative to the Treatment of Prisoners of War [GPW III] (Aug. 12, 1949); and, Geneva Convention Relative to the Protection of Civilian Persons in Time of War [GC IV] (Aug. 12, 1949) [hereinafter all four referred to as 1949 Geneva Conventions].

44. Protocol Additional to the Geneva Conventions of August 12, 1949, and relating to the protection of Victims of International Armed Conflicts [hereinafter Protocol I], June 8, 1977, 1125 U.N.T.S. 4; and Protocol Additional to the Geneva Conventions of August 12, 1949, and relating to the protection of Victims of non-International Armed Conflicts [hereinafter Protocol II], June 8, 1977, 1125 U.N.T.S. 610. Much of the Protocols are considered Customary International Law concerning the Laws of War, even though the United States has not ratified them.

45. ICC Statute.

International Criminal Law

Unlike genocide and crimes against humanity, war crimes require a nexus with armed conflict, and generally, there are two types of armed conflict: 1) international armed conflict; and, 2) non-international armed conflict.

The easier situation to identify is international armed conflict. When two or more States use military forces against one another, international armed conflict exists.[46] International armed conflict falls under Common Article 2 of the 1949 Geneva Conventions, which invokes the "full corpus" of IHL.[47]

Identifying when non-international armed conflict exists can be much harder. The frequent issue is whether the situation rises to the level of actually being an armed conflict, or simply an internal disturbance. The ICTY boiled its focus down to whether there are organized armed groups involved in protracted and intense fighting, "referring more to the intensity of the armed violence than its duration."[48] When assessing the intensity, the ICTY considered the type of weapons, munitions, number of fighters, casualties, destruction, degree of civilians fleeing the area, etc.[49]

For international armed conflict, the ICC identifies grave breaches—those crimes found in the four 1949 Geneva Conventions, which are particularly heinous—crimes such as "willful killing, torture or inhumane treatment, including biological experiments" on humans.[50] Crimes designated as "grave breaches" must be prosecuted—that is, States have a heightened duty to search for and bring

---

46. Questions may arise, however, when one State exercises control over forces located in another State. That is precisely what happened in the ICTY *Tadić* case, where the ICTY found that the Yugoslavian government exercised "overall control" over the Serbs located in Bosnia, making what may have appeared on the surface to be an internal conflict, into an international conflict involving two separate States: Yugoslavia and Bosnia. Prosecutor v. Tadić, Case No.: IT-94-1-A (July 15, 1999), 145.

47. Corn, et al., 71–4.

48. Prosecutor v. Haradinaj, ICTY Case No.: IT-04-84-T (April 3, 2008), 49.

49. Ibid.

50. 1949 Geneva Conventions, GC IV, Art. 147. Article 8 of the ICC Statute identifies eight grave breaches: (i) Willful killing; (ii) Torture; (iii) Willfully causing great suffering; (iv) Extensive and unjustified destruction or appropriation of property; (v) Compelling PoW to serve for the enemy's armed forces; (vi) Depriving PoW of a fair and regular trial; (vii) Unlawful deportation, transfer, or confinement; and (viii) Taking of hostages. ICC Statute, Art. 8(2)(a).

to justice those alleged to have committed a grave breach, and if convicted, to punish the guilty.[51]

The ICC also identifies another twenty-six other war crimes, such as "intentionally directing attacks against the civilian population ...,"[52] launching an attack in the knowledge that such attack will cause incidental loss of life or injury to civilians...,[53] committing rape, sexual slavery,[54] ... and intentionally directing attacks against buildings dedicated to religion...,"[55] to name a few applicable for the purposes here.

Concerning non-international armed conflict, there are no "grave breaches," but war crimes are nonetheless applicable. Non-international armed conflict ("NIAC") falls under Common Article 3 of the 1949 Geneva Conventions. Common Article 3 prohibits murder, mutilation, cruel treatment and torture, taking hostages, humiliating and degrading treatment against persons not taking part in the hostilities.[56]

The ICC identifies fourteen war crimes applicable during NIAC,[57] including, but not limited to: murder and torture,[58] intentionally attacking civilians,[59] destruction of religious buildings,[60] rape and sexual slavery,[61] as well as physical mutilation.[62] The ICC explicitly claims jurisdiction over war crimes, "in particular,"[63] when they are

---

51. Gary D. Solis, *The Law of Armed Conflict* (Cambridge, 2016), 92. Referring to common articles found in the 1949 Geneva Conventions, Professor Solis writes: "The first of the four 1949 innovations, enactment of domestic legislation to punish grave breaches, is required by common Article 49/50/120/146." Ibid., Article 146 of C.G. IV, states: "Each High Contracting Party shall be under the obligation to search for personals alleged to have committed ... such grave breaches, and shall bring such persons, regardless of their nationality, before its own courts." 1949 Geneva Conventions, GC IV, Art. 146.
52. ICC Statute, Art. 8(2)(b)(i).
53. Ibid., Art. 8(2)(b)(iv).
54. Ibid.
55. Ibid., Art. 8(2)(b)(ix).
56. 1949 Geneva Conventions, Common Art. 3.
57. ICC Statute, Art. 8(2)(c) and (e).
58. Ibid., Art. 8(2)(c)(i).
59. Ibid., Art. 8(2)(e)(i).
60. Ibid., Art. 8(2)(e)(iv).
61. Ibid., Art. 8(2)(e)(vi).
62. Ibid., Art. 8(2)(e)(xi).
63. Ibid., Art. 8(1).

committed "as part of a plan or policy or as part of a large-scale commission of such crimes."[64]

Modes of Participating in Crime

Charging those who physically carry out genocide, crimes against humanity, crimes of aggression, or war crimes, is a given. Often, however, it is not clear exactly who the individuals are. Time and time again, the grounds of mass atrocities have proven to be cauldrons of confusion, where thousands, tens-of-thousands, if not hundreds-of-thousands, or even millions of people fall as victims.[65] In that type of environment, crimes are not the result of one or even two individuals, but rather typically involve groups of individuals acting toward a common criminal design. Even when witnesses or forensics can accurately identify particular individuals as one of the perpetrators, accurately attributing the precise criminal actions to a particular person can be difficult. Further identifying the precise role the individual carried out in committing the crime is almost always a very challenging task, and yet it is a critical one.

Generally, there are two ways to describe the roles individuals play when committing a crime: either as a principal or as an accomplice. The differences between the two are not inconsequential. In most simple terms: the principal commits the crime and the accomplice helps or encourages the principal. The accomplice's culpability is derivative. The principal must actually commit the crime for the accomplice to have culpability, and the accomplice's culpability is tethered to the crime committed by the principal. The difference between the two also provides a way to allocate culpability—the principal is more culpable than the accomplice.

Properly labeling who is the principle and who is the accomplice, therefore, is significant. That is not to say that the task is easy—it is not. The principal is not always limited to the individual committing the ultimate criminal act. Throughout history, some of the most culpable individuals have been those who kept their distance from the

---

64. Ibid.
65. For instance, the Nazis murdered up to 6,000,000 Jews. See United States Holocaust Memorial Museum. https://www.ushmm.org/wlc/en/article.php?ModuleId=10008193.

scene, sending others to blow themselves up, to release the cyanide-laced gas, pull the trigger, or swing the machetes. More often than not, those who hatch the plans, issue the orders, organize the killings, fund the effort, or incite others to violence are the most dangerous and most deserving of punishment. Categorizing those individuals as principals, as opposed to accomplices, is crucial. To accommodate that need, the law allows there to be more than one principal—the law permits co-principals.

Allowing for the concept of co-principals is sound policy, but it complicates matters. Should the person who contributed to the crime, but did not actually pull the trigger, be a co-principal or an accomplice? That can be quite hard to decide.

At Nuremberg, the Allies' answer to that type of question was to charge the crime of conspiracy. Conspiracy allows the prosecutor to cast a large net, and it allows for everyone in the conspiracy to be held liable for all the crimes committed in furtherance of the conspiracy. While conspiracy was charged at Nuremberg, it was mentioned sparingly in the judgment. The reason it exerted limited influence was because conspiracy is a common law crime, not used in civil law systems. The concept proved difficult for the civil law countries involved in the Nuremberg trials, to fully grasp. Even after Nuremberg, the civil law countries seemed uncomfortable with the theory. As a result, the statutes for the *ad hoc* tribunals did not include the crime of conspiracy. The need in the tribunals for a theory of liability similar to conspiracy, however, proved to be great.

The sheer quantity of the killings in Rwanda and Yugoslavia made parsing defendants and assessing precise acts to particular individuals formidable. In Rwanda, for instance, over 800,000 Tutsis were massacred by Hutus between the months of April and July, 1994.[66] As mentioned above, in the former Yugoslavia, in and around Srebrenica, between 7,000 and 8,000 unarmed able-bodied Muslim men were slaughtered by Serbs in the matter of seven days.[67] The ICTY Trial Chamber, in a case concerning Srebrenica, addressed some of the difficulties that mass atrocities present: "most witnesses were unable to specify which units were responsible for the crimes com-

---

66. Romeo Dallaire, *Shake Hands with the Devil* (Da Capo Press, 2005), 375.
67. Prosecutor v. Krstić, ICTY Case No. IT-98-33, Amended Indictment (Oct. 27, 1999) para. 11; and Prosecutor v. Krstić, ¶ 2.

mitted during those days. Many witnesses heard screams, gunshots and stories of murder, without directly observing the crimes themselves."[68]

As a response to some of those difficulties, the ICTY created a mode of liability referred to as Joint Criminal Enterprises (JCE). The concept of JCE liability provides many of the same utilities as the charge of conspiracy.[69] The JCE concept was not explicitly found in the ICTY or ICTR statutes. It was a judge-made creation of the *ad hoc* tribunals based on customary international law.[70] It is important to understand that unlike conspiracy, which is a separate and inchoate crime, a JCE is not a separate crime at all: it is a mode of criminal responsibility. That is to say, a JCE simply represents a theory describing how an individual actor may be held criminally responsible for committing a particular crime.

A boiled-down definition of a JCE is that two or more individuals have an understanding to commit a crime, such as genocide, and then they commit the crime in a collective manner. Because they share a common intent to commit the crime, and share in actions to complete the crime, they share in responsibility for the crime, as co-principals. The level of participation, and the particular role that each participant engages in, may vary quite significantly. The *mens rea* can also vary slightly, depending on the type of JCE.

There are three types of JCEs. The first type is referred to as the "basic" type. It describes a situation where the actors share an intent to commit a crime, and then act together to bring about the crime. As stated above, each actor may have a separate role, and only one actor may commit the ultimate act, but because they all act in concert, unified to accomplish the criminal objective, they are equally guilty of the ultimate crime as principals.

Consider the following hypothetical bank robbery as an example: one person is the mastermind who selects the bank, maps out the route to and from the bank, sets the time of the robbery and how it will go down. Another drives everyone to and from the bank. The mastermind and driver stay in the vehicle and a third individual

---

68. Prosecutor v. Krstić, ¶ 152.

69. See Prosecutor v. Tadic, ICTY Case No. IT-94-1-A (July 15, 1999) [hereinafter *Tadic* Appeals Judgment], ¶¶ 188–192.

70. Ibid., ¶ 194.

actually goes inside the bank, points a gun at a teller, and takes the cash. Each actor had a substantial physical role in the robbery and each one shared in their intent to accomplish the robbery. Under the "basic" JCE theory, the mastermind and the driver are just as guilty as the actor who entered the bank, pointed the gun, and demanded the cash.

The second type of JCE is one that seems much more reflective of what most would consider an "enterprise." That is, there is an organized system in place that engages in accomplishing crime, over a period of time. It is coordinated and structured. Individuals fulfill a particular role and the operation is intended to efficiently and effectively produce or accomplish the criminal objective. The examples cited by the ICTY are the Nazi concentration camps.[71] At those camps, there was a commander, security guards, individuals that ran the gas chambers, those who brought the detainees to the camps, ran the logistics of the camp, buried the dead, as well as many other roles and tasks. Each person accomplished something that contributed to the ultimate detention, mistreatment, and killing of the detainees. The *mens rea* required for this type of JCE is that the defendant must be aware of the objective and intend to further that objective. The *mens rea* can be inferred from the particular facts—position of the accused, duties, surrounding environment, to name a few examples.[72]

The third and final type of JCE describes a situation that starts off as a basic JCE, where the actors all intend to accomplish a common purpose, but then one of the perpetrators commits a criminal act that, while foreseeable, falls outside of the original objective. Go back to the hypothetical bank robbery: if the individual who goes into the bank with a weapon actually shoots a bank teller, and the teller dies, then all the actors are guilty of murder, even if they had agreed that no one was to actually use force because they did not intend for anyone to be harmed. The act of murder, in this bank robbery hypothetical, was a natural and foreseeable consequence, and therefore each of the actors is treated similarly, as if they each had pulled the trigger and are each held culpable for the foreseeable killing.

The ICTY established the theory of JCE in the first case it

---

71. Ibid., ¶ 202.
72. Ibid., ¶ 203.

decided—*Prosecutor v. Tadic*.[73] In that case, the ICTY concluded that the facts fell within the third category of a JCE.[74] Specifically, Dusko Tadic participated with Serb forces in the town of Jaskići to forcibly remove all Muslims from the town ("ethnic cleansing"). In the course of doing so, the defendant and Serb forces separated the men from the women and children. The men were beaten and forced to march to an unknown location. Witnesses knew and recognized Tadic, and observed him participate in the beatings, the forced march, and they heard shots. At some point, five Muslim men were found dead (four were shot in the head).[75] Witnesses did not actually see the killings, but they observed Tadic and others commit the acts mentioned above, leading up to the killings. The Trial Chamber actually decided there was not enough evidence to find Tadic guilty of Crimes against Humanity for the murders. But the Appeals Chamber reversed the decision, deciding that even though there was no evidence that Tadic had personally fired the shots that killed the men, he was criminally responsible as a principal, nonetheless. The Appeals Chamber explained as part of their reasoning that "to hold criminally liable as a perpetrator only the person who materially performs the criminal act would disregard the role as co-perpetrators of all those who in some way made it possible for the perpetrator physically to carry out that criminal act. At the same time, depending upon the circumstances, to hold the latter liable only as aiders and abettors might understate the degree of their criminal responsibility."[76]

The Appeals Chamber went on to explain its reasoning behind the third type of JCE. In particular, the Appeals Chambers explained the following:

---

73. Prosecutor v. Tadic, ICTY Case No. IT-94-1.
74. The trial chamber actually found Tadic not guilty of this charge for lack of evidence. On appeal, the Appeals Chamber overturned that ruling (in the ICTY the Appeals Chamber has that authority). In the course of doing so, the Appeals Chamber established the JCE theory and concluded the evidence supported criminal responsibility under the third type of JCE. Tadic, Appeals Judgment, paras. 228 & 232.
75. Prosecutor v. Tadic, ICTY Case No. IT-94-1-T, Trial Judgment (May 7, 1997), para. 370.
76. Tadic Appeals Judgment, ¶ 192.

An example of this would be a common, shared intention on the part of a group to forcibly remove members of one ethnicity from their town, village or region (to effect "ethnic cleansing") with the consequence that, in the course of doing so, one or more of the victims is shot and killed. While murder may not have been explicitly acknowledged to be part of the common design, it was nevertheless foreseeable that the forcible removal of civilians at gunpoint might well result in the deaths of one or more of those civilians. Criminal responsibility may be imputed to all participants within the common enterprise where the risk of death occurring was both a predictable consequence of the execution of the common design and the accused was either reckless or indifferent to that risk.[77]

Using that analysis, the Appeals Chambers found that Tadic had indeed committed murder as part of a widespread and systematic attack, and thus found him guilty as a principal for committing crimes against humanity, among other things, and eventually sentenced Tadic to twenty years.[78]

Although the ICTY, and to a lesser extent the ICTR, relied substantially on the JCE as a theory of criminal responsibility, it is not a theory free from concern. Consider the second type of JCE, for instance. It is difficult to know exactly where to draw the line. Should everyone who works at a concentration camp be charged, no matter how insignificant or minimal their participation? The commander, for sure; the producer of the cyanide gas, yes; but what about the guard, the cook, the janitor, or the boy who shines the officers' boots at the gate? Where are the proper boundaries to liability? Concerning the third type of JCE, the potential breadth of the concept is sweeping. Indeed, the latitude the JCE provided prosecutors and judges in the ICTY has given it a bad name in some circles. For some, JCE is short for "Just Convict Everyone."[79]

Partly because of those concerns and the uneasiness civil law countries have with the crime of conspiracy, the drafters of the Rome

---

77. Ibid., ¶ 204.

78. See Prosecutor v. Tadic, ICTY Case No. IT-94-1, Summary of Appeals Chamber Sentencing Judgment, http://www.icty.org/x/cases/tadic/acjug/en/000126_summary_en.pdf.

79. Geraldine Coughlan, "JCE: Just Convict Everyone?" *International Justice Tribune* (2 March 2011), https://www.justicetribune.com/articles/jce-just-convict-everyone.

International Criminal Law

Statute decided to take a different, more exacting approach. Specifically, Article 25 of the Rome Statute for the International Criminal Court breaks out the two general categories of defendants into five specific areas of individual criminal responsibility: 1) commits the crime; 2) orders, solicits, or induces; 3) aids, abets, or assists; 4) contributes in "any other way"; and 5) incites others to commit genocide. The principals are those who fall within the first category—commits the crime. The ICC considers the remaining four categories as accomplices.

As far as who qualifies as committing the crime, and is thus considered to be a principal, the ICC uses a control test. Specifically, the ICC considers those who actually physically carry out the ultimate criminal act, or control the will of those who physically carry out the criminal act, or carry out an essential task, as principals ("commits the crime"). Essential tasks are those that if not done, would cause the criminal act to fail.[80] For defendants to qualify as a principal, they must be aware that they are exerting control over the crime.[81] Others who do not physically carry out the criminal act or exert a requisite degree of control, yet fall within one of the other four categories, are accomplices.

In their International and Transnational Criminal Law textbook, authors Luban, O'Sullivan, and Stewart point out that Article 25 appears to be organized in a hierarchical fashion.[82] They also discuss that while "Article 25 obviously does not explicitly differentiate between the various subsections in terms of sentencing ... it is likely that the ICC will use these distinctions in formulating appropriate sentences, given the effort made by the ICC Statute's drafters to more carefully distinguish between various modes of participating and to reflect these distinctions in the hierarchical structure of Article 25(3)."[83]

---

80. Prosecutor v. Lubanga, ICC Case No. ICC-01/04-01/06, Pre-Trial Chamber I (Jan. 29, 2007), ¶¶ 330–32.

81. Ibid., ¶ 332.

82. I have taught International Criminal Law from this textbook multiple times. It is an excellent textbook.

83. Luban, O'Sullivan, Stewart, *International*, 861–62. Article 78(1) of the Rome Statute, directs the ICC to "take into account such factors as the gravity of the crime and the individual circumstances of the convicted person," when determining the appropriate sentence. Ibid.

With Article 25, the ICC brings more granularity to the analysis of categorizing offenders in their proper role. Like the *ad hoc* tribunals, the ICC did not adopt the crime of conspiracy, but unlike the *ad hoc* tribunals, the ICC did not embrace the concept of JCEs. As far as principals, the ICC clearly narrowed the category. It circumscribed the definition of principals to only those who exert enough control over the situation to be in a position to determine whether the crime will or will not be completed.

On the other hand, the ICC may have expanded the universe of potential accomplices with its language that makes an accomplice of anyone who contributes in "any other way." For an accomplice to be liable under the ICC, he or she must act with "knowledge and intent."[84] That means that the accomplice must have actually meant to engage in the conduct and cause the consequence, or at least knew that it would occur in the ordinary course of events. Note also from Article 25 above that the ICC allows defendants to be held responsible for the crime of genocide if they "incite."[85]

In the end, only time will tell whether the ICC system turns out to be an improvement over the *ad hoc* tribunals. It certainly appears to be a narrower approach, requiring more involvement to be categorized as a principal, and a much more specific *mens rea* to be held liable as an accomplice.

Superior Responsibility

There is another important mode of responsibility—Command/Superior Responsibility. It is a concept that goes back at least to the fifteenth century, when King Charles VII of France issued the Ordinance of Orleans.[86] While the concept may go back to the Middle

---

84. ICC Statute, Art. 30(1) and (2).

85. By implication, this would not apply to crimes against humanity or war crimes.

86. Corn, et al., 531, citing to Theodor Meron, "Reflections on the Prosecution of War Crimes by International Tribunals," 100 *Am. J. Int'l L.* 551 (2006), 149 n.40. This provision held Captains and Lieutenants responsible for promptly bringing to justice any soldier who committed "abuses, ills and offenses." If the officer failed to bring his troops to justice, the officer was to be "deemed responsible for the offense as if he had committed it himself and shall be punished in the same way as the offender would have been." Ibid.

International Criminal Law

Ages, or beyond, it was not well-developed or well-known at the end of World War II when the United States tried Japanese General Tomoyuki Yamashita by military commission. Indeed, most today would associate the beginning of the concept of Command Responsibility with General Yamashita.

Yamashita had arrived in the Philippines on October 7, 1944, as the commander of all Japanese land forces. His mission was defense of the Philippines, but just eleven days later General MacArthur landed the largest combined arms force ever assembled to date in the Pacific, on the island of Leyte, and uttered his famous line: "I have returned."[87]

The American forces overwhelmed the Japanese forces on Leyte, killing 50,000 of the 60,000 Japanese soldiers defending that island.[88] As the American forces moved closer to the capital city of Manila, on the Island of Luzon, Yamashita divided his forces into three groups. He took the largest force with him to Baguio, north of Manila, in the mountains. The second group he placed northeast of Manila, to delay the American approach to the city, and the third he left to defend Clark Air Base as long as possible, and then to fall back into the mountains, to conduct a delay action.[89]

In his recent book, Professor Allan A. Ryan described the battle of Manila with the following words:

> The battle of Manila, the only urban combat in the Pacific theater at any point in the war and the largest urban battle fought by U.S. troops anywhere was a horror, not only for the citizens caught in its cross fire and victimized by the cruelties of [the Japanese] forces—to which the trial of Yamashita would devote weeks—but also for the American soldiers fighting it. What began with plans for a parade, with Filipinos cheering as American soldiers marched by, soon became one of the most vicious, destructive, and deadly battles of World War II.[90]

Indeed, the destruction that the Japanese inflicted on Manila "was one of the great tragedies of World War II. Of all Allied cities in those

---

87. Allan A. Ryan, *Yamashita's Ghost, War Crimes, MacArthur's Justice, and Command Accountability* (Univ. of Kansas Press 2012), 36.
88. Ibid., 40.
89. Ibid., 42–43.
90. Ibid., 48.

war years, only Warsaw suffered more."[91] Tens of thousands of Filipino men, women, and children suffered from the Japanese forces while General Yamashita was the "Supreme Commander."[92] He was put on trial before a military commission for the atrocities.

Yamashita's defense team argued it was not fair to hold him responsible for what took place in Manila after his retreat into the mountains. His defense team introduced substantial proof that he was isolated, unable to communicate with the troops that were left in Manila, and he was unable to exert control over the Japanese Naval forces operating in Manila. Yamashita's lawyers argued, therefore, he should not be responsible for the rapes and other atrocities that occurred.[93] The military commission rejected this argument. It convicted and sentenced him to death for failing to "discharge his duty as commander to control the operations of the members of his command, permitting them to commit brutal atrocities and other high crimes."[94]

The military commission never made clear whether General Yamashita was guilty of a separate crime of omission, whether he was being held vicariously liable for the crimes of his subordinates, or whether his lack of action or subsequent punishment was a form of complicity as a principal or accomplice.[95] Moreover, the state-of-

---

91. Ibid., quoting William Manchester, biographer of MacArthur.

92. Ibid., 41. Imperial General Headquarters sent word after the defeat of Leyte that the strategy in the Philippines would be left to General Yamashita.

93. Ibid., 231–36.

94. In re Yamashita, 327 U.S. 1 (1946), 13–14. The defense filed a writ of habeas corpus to the U.S. Supreme Court. The Court denied the writ. Two Supreme Court Justices, however, latched on to the defense's theme of "insurmountable difficulties," lack of personal involvement and lack of knowledge, and wrote passionate and seething dissents. Specifically, Justice Murphy cited the difficulties with General Yamashita's communication, a sudden assignment of the naval forces that were left in Manila, along with the alleged failure of the Japanese troops to obey General Yamashita's orders to withdraw from Manila. Justice Murphy took particular issue with the fact that General Yamashita was not on the scene and was not "personally participating in the acts of atrocity or with ordering or condoning their commission." Likewise, Justice Rutledge took great exception with Yamashita's conviction given that there was no finding that General Yamashita had "personally participated in, was present at the occurrence of, or ordered" any of the atrocities. Ibid., 50.

95. Ryan, *Yamashita's Ghost*, 251.

mind—*mens rea*—element for the crime was opaque, to say the least. It was not clear whether he was held strictly liable for the crimes of his subordinates, whether he was liable because he knew of the crimes and failed to act, whether he was reckless in not investigating, or whether he was simply criminally negligent?[96] It appeared to be enough that he was in command and he failed to control his troops.[97] Similarly, the International Military Tribunal of the Far East (Tokyo Tribunal) and the *German High Command Trial* both treated command responsibility as a distinct and separate criminal violation of omission under the laws and customs of war.[98]

After the flurry of activity following World War II, very little happened in the development of humanitarian law overall, including in the area of command responsibility until 1977, when Additional Protocol I and Additional Protocol II were adopted. The protocols not only provided an expansion of the protections initially established by the Geneva Conventions of 1949,[99] but in particular, for the first time in history, explicitly placed a duty upon commanders to "prevent or

---

96. In re Yamashita, 327 U.S. 1, 53 (dissent by Justice Rutledge).

97. See Guénaël Mettraux, *The Law of Command Responsibility* (Oxford, 2009), 7. See also Ryan, *Yamashita's Ghost*, 243 (Chief Prosecutor Major Robert M. Kerr argued that the commission needed to answer two questions: whether General Yamashita had failed to control his troops, and whether that failure constituted a war crime).

98. See G. Mettraux, *The Law of Command Responsibility*, 37, n.1. After the IMT, the United States conducted twelve military tribunals, including the High Command case, in which the tribunal unequivocally required individual culpability on behalf of the commander, with a *mens rea* no less than criminal negligence. Specifically, the U.S. military tribunal in the High Command case stated:

> There must be a personal dereliction. That can occur only where the act is directly traceable to him or where his failure to properly supervise his subordinates constitutes criminal negligence on his part. In the latter case it must be personal neglect amounting to a wanton, immoral disregard of the action of his subordinates amounting to acquiescence. Any other interpretation of International Law would go far beyond the basic principles of criminal law as known to civilized nations.

12 U.N. War Crimes Commission, Law Reports of Trials of War Criminals, The German High Command Trial (1949), 76. It appeared that the dissents of Justice Murphy and Justice Rutledge, as demonstrated by the *High Command Case*, swayed the international community more so than the majority opinion, and took quick effect, begging for a more exacting standard.

99. International Committee of the Red Cross, https://www.icrc.org/eng/resources/documents/misc/additional-protocols-1977.htm.

repress" violations,[100] or "to initiate disciplinary or penal action against violators."[101] In addition, Article 87(2) requires commanders to make their forces "aware of their obligations under the Conventions and this Protocol."[102]

The statutes for both the ICTY and ICTR included command responsibility, using essentially the same language.[103] Both *ad hoc* tribunals used the term "superior," as opposed to "commander," extending the concept to civilian leaders. Moreover, case law in the tribunals fleshed out that only *de facto*, as opposed to *de jure*, control over subordinates was required. As far as the requisite *mens rea*—the superior must know or have reason to know. Case law established that the *mens rea* required the superior to have specific information, information that would put him/her on notice that the subordinates were about to commit violations, or in the case of failure to prosecute, that they did commit violations.[104]

With the Rome Statute and creation of the ICC, the concept of Command/Superior Responsibility may now be set forth in a detailed, bifurcated approach with separate elements for military and civilian superiors. Article 28 of the Rome Statute is clearly concerned about culpability of the superior. Specifically, Article 28 states that the supervisor "shall be criminally responsible for crimes ... as a result of his or her failure to exercise control properly over such subordinates...."[105]

The *mens rea* required in the ICC differs, depending on whether the defendant is a civilian supervisor or military commander. For civilian supervisors, the *mens rea* is knowledge or conscious disregard, which is essentially the same standard from Additional Protocol I and the *ad hoc* tribunals. For military commanders, however, the standard appears to be criminal negligence—"should have known." This is a much more relaxed standard, making it easier for

---

100. Protocol Additional to the Geneva Conventions of August 12, 1949, and Relating to the Protection of Victims of International Armed Conflicts, June 8, 1977 [hereinafter AP I], Art. 86(2).

101. AP I, Art. 87(3).

102. AP I, Art. 87(2).

103. For the ICTR it is Art. 6(3) and for the ICTY it is Art. 7(3).

104. Prosecutor v. Mucic et al., ICTY Case No. IT-96-21-A, ¶ 233 (Feb. 20, 2001) [hereinafter "Čelebići Case"].

105. ICC Statute, Art. 28(1) and (2).

International Criminal Law

prosecutors to hold military commanders responsible. The rationale behind holding military commanders to a higher standard of conduct makes sense. With the authority of military command should also come the responsibility to adequately supervise subordinates.

As the Rome Statute was being drafted, one of the most contentious issues was whether to include conspiracy in the statute.[106] While conspiracy is a separate crime and not a mode of responsibility, it resolves many of the concerns and challenges that arise when attempting to properly assess culpability in situations involving mass atrocity. The drafters did not, however, include it in the Rome Statute. Instead, they used language from the 1997 Convention for the Suppression of Terrorist Bombing, which comprises paragraph 3(d) of the Article 25 of the Rome Statute.[107] Nevertheless, there are several theories available to a prosecutor in charging a commander/supervisor, and the prosecutor has great discretion.[108]

Conspiracy and JCE are not available in the ICC; however, it is possible for a prosecutor to charge a commander/supervisor under Article 25(3)(b) as an accomplice for "ordering" and at the same time, in the alternative, under Article 28 Responsibility of Commanders and other Supervisors. Yet, as Professor Mettraux has stated: "It would in fact seem wrong to punish an accused for taking part in the commission of a crime whilst at the same time holding him liable for failing to prevent or punish that crime."[109] Prosecutors understand this concept, and generally take great lengths to charge in a way that is supported by the evidence.

Jurisdiction for Prosecution

Normally, the most appropriate authority is the State where the crime occurred. Under the international system, States hold sovereignty over their own territory. The international system is based on States treating each other as equals, including the concept that each

---

106. Per Saland, "International Criminal Law Principles," in *The International Criminal Court: the Making of the Rome Statute, Issues, Negotiations, Results*, ed. Roy S. Lee (The Hague; Boston: Kluwer Law International 1999, 2002), 198–200.

107. Ibid.

108. G. Mettraux, *The Law of Command Responsibility*, 94 (citing to the Krajisnik case and the Krnojelac cases before the ICTY).

109. Ibid., 95.

State has primacy over its own territory and over any acts taking place within its territory.[110] Generally, when a crime occurs within the territory of a State, therefore, it is that State that possesses the greatest interest and right to address the situation.[111]

This territorial concept weighed heavily as countries embarked on forming the ICC and drafting the Rome Statute. One of the foundational concepts was to respect State sovereignty by maintaining the primacy of national jurisdictions. As a result, the ICC was specifically created to exercise its jurisdiction in a manner complementary to the national courts of each State. Indeed, in the Preamble of the Rome Statute, it explains that the "International Criminal Court established under this Statute shall be complementary to national criminal jurisdictions."[112] The concept is referred to as the principle of "complementarity."[113] It is further expressed in Article 17 of the Rome Statute, which provides that the ICC will not exercise its jurisdiction in cases where the State is investigating or prosecuting the crime. If the State is unwilling or unable to investigate or prosecute, the ICC may then exercise its jurisdiction.[114]

There are a variety of concepts under customary international law for States to exert authority to investigate and prosecute crime. One is the Territoriality Principle, mentioned above, when a crime occurs within a State's territory. The crime may occur within a State in a number of ways: the acts may be carried out in the State's territory, it may be carried out beyond the State's borders but the crime adversely effects the State, such as a submarine in international waters firing a missile and hitting a city of another State, or a crime may be intended to affect a State, such as a drug-smuggling ship from South

---

110. There are exceptions to this, such as Diplomatic Immunity for members of one state, located in another.

111. The ICTY and ICTR established the Security Council as an exception to this, as the Security Council gave those tribunals primacy over the national courts. See ICTY Statute, Art. 9(2), and ICTR Statute, Art. 8(2).

112. Rome Statute, Preamble ¶ 10.

113. John T. Holmes, "The Principle of Complementarity," in *The International Criminal Court: the Making of the Rome Statute, Issues, Negotiations, Results,* ed. by Roy S. Lee (The Hague; Boston: Kluwer Law International 1999, 2002), 41. See also Ronald J. Rychlak and John M. Czarnetzky, "The International Criminal Court and the Question of Subsidiarity," *Third World Legal Studies* 2000–2003, 115.

114. Rome Statute, Art. 17(1)(a).

America intercepted in international waters, headed for the Florida Keys.

A State may also exert jurisdiction over its nationals, even when they are abroad. A State may exert jurisdiction over the perpetrator because the perpetrator is a national (active personality jurisdiction) or may exercise jurisdiction over the perpetrator because the victim is a national (passive personality jurisdiction). States may exercise "protective jurisdiction," over any act that poses an existential threat to the State, regardless as to where it occurred or as to who the perpetrator may be.

Lastly, states may claim "universal jurisdiction" as the basis allowing for the investigation and prosecution, although it is relatively controversial. Universal jurisdiction is the concept of a State exercising jurisdiction where there is no other basis for jurisdiction; that is, the State has no basis to claim jurisdiction based on territory, nationality, or protective jurisdiction. The concept is based on the proposition that there are some crimes that are *Hostis Humani Generis*—the Enemies of Mankind. Piracy is the best historical example. The concept is beginning to gain support, and the crimes that potentially come under its jurisdiction are those of concern here: genocide, crimes against humanity, war crimes (especially grave breaches), and the crime of aggression.

There are times when national jurisdiction is not practical in the wake of war's destruction of infrastructure and support systems, or not preferable for want of security or risk of corruption. There may also be times when national jurisdiction is not even possible, when States do not cooperate and are likely to shield or exonerate those most responsible for mass crime.

In such cases, the international community has potential options in the form of *ad hoc* tribunals, the ICC, and hybrid courts. It is important to note that States have a duty to prosecute individuals who have committed a "grave breach," and parties to the Genocide Convention have a duty to prosecute those who commit genocide. If a State decides not to prosecute, it must extradite the perpetrators when they receive a request.

When war broke out in the former Yugoslavia and genocide was committed in Rwanda, the Security Council created the ICTR and the ICTY under Chapter VII of the United Nations Charter. Although Chapter VII does not explicitly mention the authority to create criminal tribunals, it explicitly makes the Security Council the final arbiter of deciding when a threat to international peace exists, and gives the Security Council the authority to "decide what measures shall be taken,"[115] including "measures not involving the use of armed force."[116]

In the *Tadic* case,[117] the ICTY directly addressed whether the Security Council possessed the authority to create tribunals. While acknowledging that the Security Council was not *"legibus solutus* (unbound by law),"[118] it found that "the establishment of the tribunal falls squarely within the powers of the Security Council under Article 41" of the U.N. Charter.[119]

The ICC was created by treaty. Generally speaking, it has authority only over crimes committed in the territory of a State that is a party to the ICC or which were committed by a national of a Party State.[120] There are two exceptions to this: the Security Council may refer a case to the court;[121] and a non-Party State may grant permission on an *ad hoc* basis for the ICC to have jurisdiction over one of its nationals or for a crime that occurred on its territory.[122]

To effectuate jurisdiction, a case must be referred to the ICC by a State-Party or by the Security Council.[123] In addition, the ICC prosecutor also may initiate investigations *proprio motu* (one's own motion) by first submitting a request to investigate to the Pre-Trial chamber. The prosecutor can only do this, however, for crimes occurring in the territory of State-Parties, or crimes committed by nationals of a State-Party.

Tribunals that possess both national and international aspects have been created post-conflict to address situations involving mass atrocities. For example, in January 2002, the United Nations and the government of Sierra Leone entered into a treaty creating the Special Court for Sierra Leone ("SCSL") "to prosecute persons who bear the

---

115. U.N. Charter, Ch. VII, Art. 39.
116. U.N. Charter, Ch. VII, Art. 41.
117. Tadic, Case No. IT-94-1.
118. Ibid., ¶ 29.
119. Ibid., ¶ 36.
120. Rome Statute, Art. 12.
121. Ibid., Art. 13(b).
122. Ibid., Art. 12(3).
123. Ibid., Art. 13(b).

International Criminal Law

greatest responsibility for serious violations of international humanitarian law and Sierra Leonean law committed in the territory of Sierra Leone since 30 November 1996."[124]

The seat of the court was in Sierra Leone. Judges for the SCSL were appointed by the government of Sierra Leone and the Secretary-General of the U.N. In addition, Secretary-General appointed the prosecutor. Nine individuals were convicted and sentenced, including former Liberian President Charles Taylor who was convicted of war crimes, crimes against humanity, and recruiting child soldiers. Charles Taylor was sentenced to fifty years in prison.

Other hybrid tribunals include the East Timor Tribunal and the Extraordinary Chambers in the Courts of Cambodia (ECCC). The advantages of hybrid tribunals can be numerous: they can be tailored to the particular situation, they are able to combine both international expertise along with extensive direct involvement from the State and local governments, they are able to incorporate State as well as international law, and they provide the advantage of placing the court near witnesses, experts, and the effected populace. Hybrid tribunals also help avoid the appearance that outsiders will dictate what justice means, and at the same time they permit enough outside assistance to provide needed expertise, support, and defenses against bias and corruption.

Isis and Al Qaeda

The situations in Iraq and Syria appear to satisfy the chapeau of genocide. Actions by ISIS and al Qaeda have occurred over an extended period of time, over a wide geographical area, using relatively similar and distinctive methods, such as beheading, and have been preceded by and followed by words that particularly manifest purpose. The purpose clearly appears to be the complete destruction of Christians, and other non-Muslims, in Syria and Iraq. The scale of that destruction has not been limited to a small group, but rather essentially all Christians in any area controlled by ISIS or al Qaeda, satisfying the requirement to have a purpose to destroy "in whole or

---

124. Agreement Between the United Nations and the Government of Sierra Leone on the Establishment of a Special Court for Sierra Leone, Art. 1, http://www.rscsl.org/Documents/scsl-agreement.pdf (accessed Nov. 17, 2016).

in part." The fact that the destruction may be geographically limited to Syria and Iraq, or even localized areas within those States, is not reason to think the element cannot be fulfilled. Their intent to destroy all Christians in any town, or a region they control, suffices. ISIS and al Qaeda have expressed the intent to reach far beyond that—seemingly their intent is to literally destroy all Christians, indeed all non-Muslims, everywhere. The fact that Christians and non-Muslims are being targeted specifically because of their religion fulfills the chapeau sub-elements that the destruction must target groups based on their nationality, ethnicity, race, or religion, as such.

The specific actions that ISIS and al Qaeda have engaged in include each of the listed enumerated actions for genocide: killings, serious bodily harm, inflicting life-threatening conditions, measures to prevent birth, and forcibly transferring children. Of course, any one of those listed actions suffices for the crime of genocide. The overall strategy of both ISIS and al Qaeda, with public beheadings, kidnappings, required conversions and jizya payments, sex slave markets for fighters, etc., all provide evidence of an intent to create conditions of life calculated to bring about physical destruction. The result of reducing the Christian population from 1.4 million to 250,000 in Iraq, corroborates that intent.

Until there is military defeat of ISIS, and to a lesser degree al Qaeda, there is little hope for any legal strategy to have a true and lasting effect. Threat of prosecution, warrants for arrest, even capture, investigation, conviction, and sentencing of ISIS leaders or foot soldiers, will not deter them if they continue to be militarily viable. This enemy must first be brought to unconditional military capitulation; then a legal response has a chance to be effective.

In a perfect world, the best legal response would be for the ICC to start investigations, followed by prosecutions. The ICC was created precisely to address situations such as what now exists concerning the treatment of Christians by ISIS and al Qaeda in Syria and Iraq. Unfortunately, neither Iraq nor Syria are parties to the Rome Statute. Because of that, the prosecutor does not have territorial jurisdiction to initiate an investigation *proprio motu*, only authority to do so over individuals who are nationals of a State-Party. Abu Bakr al-Baghdadi, the leader of ISIS, is Iraqi, and thus unreachable to the ICC prosecutor under *proprio motu* powers.

A referral from the Security Council ("ICC referral") is conceivable but highly unlikely. The Security Council has only referred two situations to the ICC, Darfur in 2005 and Libya in 2011. Plus, Russia can veto any ICC referral attempt, and almost certainly would concerning Syria. For similar reasons, creation of an *ad hoc* tribunal by the Security Council is also unlikely.[125]

Conclusion

The situation is critical. Christians and other non-Muslims civilians in Syria and Iraq are being slaughtered, sexually violated, displaced, and tortured. The international community should continue to pursue justice and ensure that the leaders of ISIS and al-Qaeda are captured and duly punished. If that proves impossible, at the very least, serious efforts must be directed toward stopping the outrages.

---

125. A hybrid tribunal would need only to involve the Secretary-General, as opposed to the Security Council, and the individual countries working together. But neither Iraq nor Syria have given any indications their countries are open to that possibility.

East Aleppo, Syria. A man sitting on a defused barrel bomb in the Christian quarter of Al-Midan (January, 2016).

11

Persecution of Christians in the Middle East: The Failed Promise of the International Criminal Court

Ronald J. Rychlak

FOR SOME TIME NOW, in areas controlled by the Islamic State of Iraq and al-Sham/Greater Syria (ISIS, *aka* ISIL, Daesh, or IS), members of that group have brutally murdered Christians and other religious minorities who refuse to convert to Islam. This persecution has horrified the civilized world. In an effort to find an answer, some have turned a hopeful eye to the International Criminal Court (ICC) or other international tribunals.[1] On the surface, this would seem to be a reasonable approach. Unfortunately, shortcomings inherent in the structure of the ICC render it largely ineffective in countering the horror. While the ICC might eventually play a role in meting out punishment to the leaders of ISIS, the more immediate relief will have to come from other entities.

---

1. Advocates for the Yazidi people of northern Iraq, who have been targeted by Islamic State because they are not Muslims, met with ICC Prosecutor Fatou Bensouda, urging her to investigate their persecution as a potential case of genocide. See Toby Sterling, "Persecuted by Islamic State, Yazidis turn to ICC for justice," *Reuters*, Sept. 24, 2015 (http://www.reuters.com/article/us-mideast-crisis-icc-yazidis-idUSKC N0RO14G20150924). The ICC, in fact, has been investigating the militant Islamist sect Boko Haram for crimes against humanity. Christian Persecution Update, "The International Criminal Court (ICC) is investigating Boko Haram, Islamic Militants in Nigeria" (August 8, 2013), http://www.persecution.in/category/topic/-internatio nal-criminal-court-icc.

The ICC came into being in April 2002, when the 60th ratification of the Rome Statute of the International Criminal Court was submitted at the preparatory meeting held at the United Nations building in New York City. Unlike the International Court of Justice, which was established as the judicial arm of the United Nations to resolve disputes between nations, the ICC has jurisdiction over individuals who have committed horrific crimes of an international magnitude.

The Rome Statute was developed at the Diplomatic Conference of Plenipotentiaries for the Establishment of an International Criminal Court in the summer of 1998 in Rome (the Rome Conference). One hundred sixty nations, including the Holy See, took part in these negotiations. The treaty adopted during that conference—the Rome Statute—defined the crimes falling under jurisdiction of the ICC and the rules of procedure and the mechanisms for nations to cooperate with the ICC. The countries which accepted these rules are known as States Parties to the ICC.[2]

The specific crimes that fall under the jurisdiction of the ICC are: crimes against humanity, genocide, war crimes, and crimes of aggression. Each ICC crime is further broken down so that in certain cases the ICC has jurisdiction over matters such as serious injury to mental health and outrages upon personal dignity. For instance, the Rome Statute defines "crimes against humanity" so that it may include things like murder, enslavement, and torture when they are "committed as part of a widespread or systematic attack directed against any civilian population, with knowledge of the attack." The term may also include: "Rape, sexual slavery, enforced prostitution, forced pregnancy and enforced sterilization or any other form of sexual violence of comparable gravity."[3] A "war crime" is defined as any of several "grave breaches" of the Geneva Conventions of 1949, "[o]ther serious violations of the laws and customs applicable in international armed conflict, within the established framework of international law," and similar offenses when the conflict is not of an international nature. Article Six of the Rome Statute defines "geno-

---

2. See Rome Statute of the International Criminal Court, July 17, 1998, U.N. Doc. A/Conf.183/9 (1998), 37 I.L.M. 999, http://legal.un.org/icc/statute/99_corr/cstatute.htm [hereinafter Rome Statute].

3. Rome Statute, Art. 7(2)(f), July 17, 1998, 2187 U.N.T.S., 90.

The Failed Promise of the International Criminal Court

cide" as actions taken with the "intent to destroy, in whole or in part, a national, ethnical, racial or religious group."[4] This can include killing members of the group, causing serious physical or mental harm, or forcibly transferring children of the targeted group to another group.[5] Destruction of historical culture can also be prosecuted in the ICC.[6]

The ICC's jurisdiction is said to be "complementary to national criminal jurisdictions." As such, the Court is designed to take jurisdiction only when a nation is "unwilling or unable" to act. This language appears to protect national sovereignty, and to assure that it does not intrude upon questions such as culture and religious practices that, according to the U.N. charter, are "within the domestic jurisdiction" of a nation-state.[7]

There is little doubt that ISIS has repeatedly committed actions that are criminal under the Rome Statute. It has been systematically murdering, exterminating, enslaving, forcibly transporting, raping, committing other sexually violent acts, persecuting groups based on their religion and ethnicity, and committing "inhumane acts of a similar character intentionally causing great suffering, or serious injury to body or to mental or physical health." The U.N. Assistance Mission for Iraq and the Office of the U.N. High Commissioner for Human Rights released a report on ISIS's actions against civilians, specifically actions against women and children from July 6, 2014, to September 10, 2014. The report described how ISIS forced children as young as twelve or thirteen years old into service by donating their blood to treat wounded ISIS soldiers, patrolling ISIS controlled

---

4. Rome Statute, Art. 6, 2187 U.N.T.S. 90, 37 I.L.M. 999.

5. Article 31 of the Rome Statute codifies grounds for excluding criminal responsibility, including: mental disease, intoxication, defensive force (self-defense), and duress or necessity. Article 32 also codifies the defenses of mistake of fact and mistake of law, and Article 33 codifies a limited defense of superior orders.

6. See Owen Bowcott, "ICC's first cultural destruction trial to open in The Hague," *The Guardian*, February 28, 2016. ISIS has certainly committed such crimes. See James Harkin, "Murdering History," *Smithsonian Magazine*, March 2016.

7. The decision as to whether an affected nation is "unwilling or unable" to prosecute is determined by judges from the ICC, meaning that the nation's sovereignty may well be compromised. See Ronald J. Rychlak and John M. Czarnetzky, "The International Criminal Court and the Question of Subsidiarity," *Third World Legal Studies*, vol. 1 (2000–2003), 115.

towns, and manning ISIS checkpoints.[8] ISIS has also used children as shields in skirmishes with Iraqi and other resistance forces. The report called on the International Criminal Court to launch an investigation into these crimes.

Ever since ISIS first started operating in Iraq (as al-Qaeda in Iraq) it targeted civilians as well as military personnel. Most ISIS fighters are members of the Sunni Muslim sect, and at first ISIS primarily went after Shi'ite targets. (Shi'ites are a majority in Iraq as a whole but a minority in ISIS-dominated northern Iraq). In 2014, however, ISIS began targeting other ethnic minorities including Christians, Yazidis, Shabak, Shi'ite Turkmen, and those Sunni Muslims who disagreed with ISIS's religious philosophy and actions.

While ISIS's actions against the minority populations are heinous, there has long existed a question as to whether they meet the strict interpretation of genocide that international tribunals typically require.[9] On his 2015 trip to Latin America, Pope Francis said he was dismayed "to see how in the Middle East and elsewhere in the world many of our brothers and sisters are persecuted, tortured and killed for their faith in Jesus." He went on: "In this third world war, waged piecemeal, which we are now experiencing, a form of genocide is taking place, and it must end."[10] In 2016, much of the world community (including the U.S. Department of State and the European Union) also applied the label of genocide to these activities.[11] Unfortunately, ISIS remains (and will remain for the foreseeable future) beyond the reach of the ICC.

---

8. Report on the Protection of Civilians in Armed Conflict in Iraq: 11 September–10 December 2014, http://www.ohchr.org/Documents/Countries/IQ/UNAMI_OHCHR_Sep_Dec_2014.pdf.

9. See generally Beth Van Schaack & Ronald C. Slye, *International Criminal Law and Its Enforcement* (2d ed. 2010), 451.

10. Monica Cantilero, "Pope Francis sees Christian 'genocide' as persecution affects 200 million Christians," *Christian Today*, July 29, 2015, http://www.christiantoday.com/article/pope.francis.sees.christian.genocide.as.persecution.affects.200.million.christians/60393.htm.

11. Tom Gjelton, "State Department Declares ISIS Attacks on Christians Constitute Genocide," *National Public Radio*, March 17, 2016, http://www.npr.org/2016/03/17/470861310/state-department-declares-isis-attacks-on-christians-constitute-genocide. Following the announcement from the U.S. State Department, a senior official said that this declaration placed "no new obligations" on the United States in its

The Failed Promise of the International Criminal Court

The Lack of Police Power

As an initial matter, before the ICC can have any impact on ISIS leaders, those leaders must be brought before the court. Before any criminal can be tried, he or she must be arrested. This requires some kind of police action. Unfortunately, the ICC does not have its own police force; it relies on State cooperation. According to the Rome Statute, States Parties are required to cooperate fully with the Court in its investigation and prosecution of crimes within the jurisdiction of the Court.

When it comes to a group like ISIS, the arrest is the most difficult part. If those who commit these crimes are captured, trial in a national court, a special tribunal (like those that were established for Rwanda and the former Yugoslavia), or the ICC would likely be equally effective. The arrest, however, is the problem.

As the Court was planned, assistance of member states was axiomatic. In practice, however, this has not been the case. In several cases, the tyrants have simply been able to avoid capture by State forces. For instance, State Parties have failed to capture Joseph Kony or other Lord's Resistance Army (LRA) leaders in Uganda. Assistance in capture would be far more helpful than the promise of an eventual trial.

In other cases, State Parties have had the opportunity to cooperate but have failed to act. For instance, Sudanese president Omar al-Bashir has made more than seventy-five international trips since the ICC issued arrest warrants for alleged war crimes, crimes against humanity, and genocide in Darfur, Sudan. He has traveled to Chad, Nigeria, and South Africa, all State Parties to the ICC. None of those nations, however, agreed to arrest him. In fact, many African nations that are obligated to capture him under the ICC appear also to be obligated not to detain him under certain African Union treaties.[12]

Moreover, even when arrests are made, the terror may not end.

---

ongoing campaign against ISIS, but the designation would seem to provide a basis for the ICC to assert jurisdiction. Adam Chandler, "How Meaningful Is the ISIS 'Genocide' Designation?" *The Atlantic*, March 19, 2016, http://www.theatlantic.com/international/archive/2016/03/isis-genocide-designation/474414/.

12. Max du Plessis, Tiyanjana Maluwa, and Annie O'Reilly, "Africa and the International Criminal Court" (Chatham House, July 2013), https://www.chathamhouse.org/sites/files/chathamhouse/public/Research/International%20Law/0713pp_iccafrica.pdf.

There are times when a new bad actor simply steps into fill the gap. Thomas Lubanga Dyilo ("Lubanga"), former commander of the Patriotic Forces for the Liberation of the Congo militia and president of the Union of Congolese Patriots, was arrested in 2006 and charged with several crimes for which he stood trial at the ICC. Eventually he was convicted. Some observers were disappointed with his relatively light sentence, but at one point along the way the Court had decided to stop the case and release him due to prosecutorial unfairness. Fortunately, the Appeals Chamber reversed that ruling and the trial proceeded.

It took six years to complete, but eventually the ICC convicted him of the war crimes of enlisting and conscripting children and using them to participate in hostilities. Unfortunately, as soon as Lubanga was arrested, General Bosco Ntaganda, chief of military operations under Lubanga, stepped up and filled the leadership role.[13] In 2008, his forces were accused of massacring sixty-seven civilians in the town of Kiwandja in North Kivu. The head of the U.N. Human Rights Commission, Navi Pillay, called it a war crime. Even though Lubanga was convicted, it did not bring peace.

Even when the defendants are made available, that does not assure that the legal process will play out appropriately. Kenya's President Uhuru Kenyatta was indicted by the ICC in connection with post-election ethnic violence in 2007–08, in which 1,200 people died. The case against him collapsed, according to the prosecutor's office, when the Kenyan government refused to hand over evidence vital to the case. President Kenyatta said he was "excited" and "relieved," adding that his "conscience is absolutely clear." Many others, however, saw this as a reflection of the inability of the ICC to assure the delivery of evidence and as a potentially fatal flaw in the structure of the Court.[14]

---

13. Ntaganda stepped down and turned himself in to authorities in 2013. He is now facing trial at the ICC, but terror groups still torment the Democratic Republic of the Congo.

14. Anna Holligan, "Uhuru Kenyatta case: Most high-profile collapse at ICC," *BBC News*, December 5, 2014, http://www.bbc.com/news/world-africa-30353311 (The withdrawal of the charges has also called into question the credibility of the already controversial court and raises questions about the ability of the prosecution to actually secure the evidence against those it accuses of being responsible for the gravest

The Failed Promise of the International Criminal Court

The Jurisdictional Issue

Assuming that ISIS leaders could be captured, it is not clear that the ICC would have jurisdiction. Article Five of the Rome Statute gives the ICC jurisdiction to try individuals charged with committing genocide, crimes against humanity, war crimes, or the crime of aggression. The ICC may exercise jurisdiction over these crimes in three situations: (1) if a State Party refers a situation to the Prosecutor in accordance with Article Fourteen of the Rome Statute, (2) the United Nations Security Council refers a situation to the Prosecutor (in accordance with Chapter VII of the Charter of the United Nations), or (3) the Prosecutor initiates an investigation in accordance with Article Fifteen of the Rome Statute. In addition, a private party may petition the Court to open an investigation.[15] If the Prosecutor investigates the allegations and determines that one or more individuals should be charged and prosecuted, then proceedings before the ICC can begin.

Perhaps most importantly though, the Rome Statute asserts jurisdiction over defendants only if either the "State on the territory of which" a crime was committed or "the State of which the person accused of the crime is a national" has ratified the statute. On August 4, 2015, ICC Prosecutor Fatou Bensouda issued a statement on the difficulty of prosecuting the alleged crimes committed by ISIS. According to Bensouda, her office had been receiving "disturbing allegations of widespread atrocities" committed by ISIS in Syria and Iraq since the summer of 2014. This included "mass executions, sexual slavery, rape and other forms of sexual and gender-based violence, torture, mutilation, enlistment and forced recruitment of children and the persecution of ethnic and religious minorities, not to mention the wanton destruction of cultural property." Impor-

---

crimes.); see also Eric Posner, "Assad and the Death of the International Criminal Court: The failure to prosecute him will be the end for the ICC's brand of global justice," *Slate* (Sept. 19, 2013), http://www.slate.com/articles/news_and_politics/view_from_chicago/2013/09/failing_to_prosecute_assad_will_be_the_death_of_the_international_criminal.html

15. Each year since it was founded, the ICC has received about 1,000 private-party petitions, but fourteen years into its existence, it has never opened an investigation on that basis.

tantly for ICC jurisdictional purposes, she noted that "genocide has also been alleged."

Bensouda agreed that these crimes "undoubtedly constitute serious crimes of concern to the international community and threaten the peace, security and well-being of the region, and the world," but she noted that Syria and Iraq are not parties to the Rome Statute. "Therefore, the Court has no territorial jurisdiction over crimes committed on their soil." She went on to note that the ICC may "exercise *personal jurisdiction* over alleged perpetrators who are nationals of a State Party, even where territorial jurisdiction is absent." Information gathered by the prosecutor's office "indicates that several thousand foreign fighters have joined the ranks of ISIS..., including significant numbers of State Party nationals." However, because "ISIS is a military and political organisation primarily led by nationals of Iraq and Syria," the prospects of the ICC prosecutor's office prosecuting the leadership of ISIS "appear limited." In fact, Bensouda has concluded "that the jurisdictional basis for opening a preliminary examination into this situation is too narrow at this stage."

Bensouda went on to emphasize that "the primary responsibility for the investigation and prosecution of perpetrators of mass crimes rests, in the first instance, with the national authorities." She pledged to "consult with relevant States to coordinate, and possibly exchange information on crimes allegedly committed by their nationals to support domestic investigations and prosecutions, as appropriate."

It is, of course always possible that the U.N. Security Council could make a referral for prosecution. In fact, such a referral was seriously contemplated in 2014. Unfortunately, both Russia and China exercised their veto power to prevent such an action.[16] Because of that, and due to the threat of repeated vetoes, there has been no further serious contemplation of another Security Council referral. So, for the time being, it appears that the ICC will not be prosecuting ISIS leaders.[17]

---

16. U.N. News Centre, Russia, China block Security Council referral of Syria to International Criminal Court (May 22, 2014), http://www.un.org/apps/news/story.asp?NewsID=47860#.V2gNtLgrKUk.

17. Statement of the Prosecutor of the International Criminal Court, Fatou Bensouda, on the alleged crimes committed by ISIS (August 4, 2015), https://www.icc-cpi.int/Pages/item.aspx?name=otp-stat-08-04-2015-1.

The Failed Promise of the International Criminal Court

How the ICC Could Make Things Worse

Due to the issues set forth by Fatou Bensouda, the ICC has a very limited role to play in countering ISIS. Unfortunately, that does not end the inquiry. There is a serious possibility that the ICC could exacerbate the problems associated with terrorist groups.

Catholic social teaching distinguishes three dimensions of basic justice: legal justice, distributive justice, and commutative justice. Others may also speak of eternal justice or global justice. St. Augustine wrote of friendship or communal harmony as a form of justice. The ICC, however, is premised upon the idea that wrongdoers must be tried and, if convicted, punished so that others will be deterred.[18] It is thus built upon the ideas of retributive justice and deterrence. In the normal course of events, by punishing the guilty and not punishing the innocent, a system of criminal law affirms shared values and supports social cohesion. It might even be said that in most cases society owes an obligation to the citizens to punish those who have committed bad acts.[19]

It is hard to believe, however, that ISIS leaders are actually fearful of being put on trial before the ICC. With or without the ICC, terror leaders commit gross violations of human rights because they assume that they will not be taken into custody. The court is an irrelevancy.

Observers of popular social sciences argue that certainty of punishment (and to a much lesser extent, severity of punishment) is the key to effective deterrence. Certainty of punishment, especially when it comes to leaders of ISIS from a court that lacks an effective enforcement mechanism, is not attainable. Accordingly, if deterrence is dependent on both factors, increasing the penalty is the more efficient way to deter crime. The ICC, however, does not have authority to impose the death penalty. One might wonder whether a court that offers due process, legal advice, and no death penalty might actually

---

18. According to the Rome Statue's preamble, its primary goal is "to put an end to impunity for the perpetrators...of the most serious crimes of concern to the international community as a whole."

19. See Ronald J. Rychlak, "Society's Moral Right to Punish: A Further Exploration of the Denunciation Theory of Punishment," 65 *Tulane L. Rev.* 299 (1990).

decrease the fear (and hence deterrence) of a terrorist who is willing to plot and plan (if not personally carry out) suicide bombings.[20]

There are times when a society needs reconciliation rather than punishment. For instance, consider the case of striking police or firefighters. That is frequently an illegal act, but after the strike is settled, do we really want prosecutions? More dramatically, consider the United States shortly after the Civil War. Abraham Lincoln legitimately could have ordered the hanging of anyone guilty of treason, which would have resulted in uncountable executions. Fortunately, Lincoln recognized that reunification was more important than retribution.

Alexander Hamilton wrote in Federalist Paper 74: "In seasons of insurrection or rebellion, there are often critical moments, when a well-timed offer of pardon to the insurgents or rebels may restore the tranquility of the commonwealth; and which, if suffered to pass unimproved, it may never be possible afterwards to recall." In other words, in some circumstances, plea-bargaining, prosecutorial discretion, executive clemency, amnesty, and jury nullification can do more to serve the common good than would punishment. Even statutes of limitation are based on the idea of putting other considerations above retributive justice. Unfortunately, the structure of the ICC calls for prosecution in all cases. In fact, the ICC is not required to recognize amnesties granted by national jurisdictions, since that could mean that a wrongdoer would escape retributive justice. The ICC is designed to make certain that *all* tyrants who commit crimes that fall under its jurisdiction are prosecuted.

This concept removing politics from the equation is derived from the Nuremberg trials after World War II.[21] Those trials provided a legalistic solution to the problem of how to administer justice to Nazi war criminals. This approach was successful in that circumstance because Nazi Germany was a conquered nation and most of the principle defendants were already in custody. In fact, this approach was

---

20. It is worth noting that existing tribunals have not contributed to regional reconciliation or deterred violence. Both Srebrenica and Kosovo happened during the era of international tribunals. Moreover, since international trials are slow and expensive, they draw resources from other initiatives that might do more good.

21. London Charter, Agreement for the Prosecution and Punishment of the Major War Criminals of the European Axis, Aug. 8, 1945, 82 U.N.T.S. 280.

The Failed Promise of the International Criminal Court

largely foreordained when the Allies, during the war, made the demand for an unconditional surrender.[22] The dynamics are very different in a society that is in the midst of (or just emerging from) a civil war.

The Truth and Reconciliation Commission process must receive credit for South Africa's bloodless transition, even though it permitted notorious wrongdoers to escape criminal punishment. South African Archbishop Desmond Tutu has explained:

> [R]etributive justice—in which an impersonal state hands down punishment with little consideration for victims and hardly any for the perpetrator—is not the only form of justice. I contend that there is another kind of justice, restorative justice, which was characteristic of traditional African jurisprudence. Here the central concern is not retribution or punishment but, in the spirit of *ubuntu*, the healing of breaches, the redressing of imbalances, the restoration of broken relationships. This kind of justice seeks to rehabilitate both the victim and the perpetrator, who should be given the opportunity to be reintegrated into the community he or she has injured.[23]

Unfortunately, the ICC structure elevates retributive justice over other concerns, such as restorative justice.

If a nation decides not to prosecute perpetrators of human rights abuses, opting instead to grant amnesties in exchange for peace, the ICC (assuming it has jurisdiction) would have the power to prosecute them under the doctrine of complementarity. Serious conflicts between national decision-makers and the ICC have already developed in Uganda, the Democratic Republic of the Congo, South Africa, and Kenya. Even if the prosecutors and judges of the ICC later decide not to prosecute, the mere threat of such a prosecution might be sufficient to foreclose the kind of bloodless, negotiated settlements that took place in South Africa and Chile.

The effort to remove politics from the equation and create an international system based purely on law may have originated with the best of intentions. Politics cannot, however, be fully removed

---

22. Pope Pius XII opposed this demand, fearing that it would prolong the war. The Nazis did indeed use this demand to encourage Germans to fight until the bitter end, and General (later President) Eisenhower believed that it had prolonged the war.

23. Desmond Tutu, *No Future Without Forgiveness* (1999), 52.

from any system of justice created by humans.[24] In fact, political issues rose to the surface before the Rome Conference was even over, and they have continued, with the ICC process frequently being misused, to do nothing more than make political statements. Moreover, it turns out that political solutions sometimes are necessary to achieve peace. Recently, both political misuse of the Court and the Court's jurisdictional inability to use political solutions have threatened its continued viability.

No caring person wants a tyrant to escape justice; nor do they oppose the efforts of those associated with the ICC to discourage tyrants of the future. Unfortunately, those efforts and the structure of the ICC tend to elevate justice over peace and create many difficulties for the pursuit of true justice.

Consider the example of Chile under Augusto Pinochet. The Pinochet regime regularly violated human rights as a means of consolidating power and imposing its will on the nation. When a free vote revealed the high level of hostility toward that regime, Pinochet agreed to leave office, but only after securing a lifetime senatorial appointment and the promise of immunity from prosecution.[25] As it turned out, he was later stripped of much of his immunity, but while it was in place, could it be said that Chile was unwilling or unable to prosecute Pinochet? If the ICC had been in existence, its judges may well have so determined. Of course, if that threat were known to Pinochet, he might never have left office. Would that have been better for the people of Chile?

In his 1945 encyclical *Communium Interpretes Doloraum* (An Appeal for Prayers for Peace), Pope Pius XII said: "Do you want peace? Do justice, and you will have peace." That is good advice, but it evolved into the slogan: "No Peace without justice." Improperly understood, that becomes not analysis, but a threat. Pope John Paul II helped clarify the misunderstanding by adding a provision: "No jus-

---

24. John M. Czarnetzky and Ronald J. Rychlak, "An Empire of Law?: Legalism and the International Criminal Court," 79 *Notre Dame Law Review* 55 (2003).

25. "Had South African apartheid leaders not been granted amnesty, they would not have left power, at least non-violently. When Chilean general Augusto Pinochet consented to a referendum on his presidency in 1988, he did so sheltered by an amnesty. In both cases, amnesty facilitated a transition to a healthy democracy following a long period of dictatorship." Daniel Philpott, "Peace After Genocide," *First Things*, June/July 2012.

The Failed Promise of the International Criminal Court

tice without forgiveness."[26] Unfortunately, the unclarified slogan became very popular with supporters of the ICC. Professor Cherif Bassiouni, often called "the Godfather of International Criminal Law" and widely recognized for his contributions to the creation of the ICC,[27] wrote: "My experience chairing U.N. commissions of inquiry has led me to conclude that there is no peace without justice."[28]

Not only *can* peace and justice exist independently, sometimes they are in conflict. For justice to prevail, the society needs stability, which punishment (even deserved punishment) can undermine. In a stable society, peace is within the reach of a flexible response to crime, even an "unjust" response. It happens all the time! Without stability, discontent can grow into conflict that should have been avoided. That does not serve the common good.

Consider the situation in Uganda. Jan Egeland, former U.N. Under-Secretary-General for Humanitarian Affairs, described Northern Uganda as "the world's terrorism epicenter." One of the main terror groups, the LRA, has killed thousands of people. In July, 2006, however, the prospects for peace brightened dramatically. President Yoweri Museveni offered an amnesty for crimes committed in northern Uganda and LRA leader, Joseph Kony, accepted. The offer required the LRA to commit to peace talks and renounce violence.[29] Leader of the Opposition in Parliament Ogenga Latigo said: "I think for us in the opposition and particularly the [sub-region most affected by the war], this is something we shall embrace. The

---

26. "No Peace Without Justice, No Justice Without Forgiveness," Message Of His Holiness Pope John Paul II for the Celebration of the World Day of Peace, January 1, 2002.

27. Philippe Kirsch, "Cherif Bassiouni and the International Criminal Court," 75 *International Review of Penal Law* 695 (2004).

28. Cherif Bassiouni, "Israel and Palestine Need a Joint Truth Commission," *Haaretz*, June 14, 2015.

29. As explained in an article written in 2012:

> Eventually Ugandans themselves shared the judgment that prosecutions were perpetuating the war. Whereas a 2005 survey conducted by the Human Rights Center at the University of California, Berkeley showed 53 percent of the public preferring peace with trials, by 2007, 80 percent had come to prefer peace with amnesty. In March 2008, even Uganda's President Yoweri Museveni reversed his position, announcing that traditional tribal reintegration rituals and national tribunals could together replace trials at The Hague. Ugandans had become weary of the ICC.

Daniel Philpott, "Peace After Genocide," *First Things*, June/July 2012.

amnesty will pave way for reconciliation. In our hearts we are prepared to forgive and start a new chapter." Unfortunately the peace process failed.

The ICC had issued an arrest warrant for Kony. While Uganda was willing—even eager—to dismiss its warrants in exchange for amnesty, the ICC was not. As one account reported at the time: "Already, the government and the ICC are knocking heads over the amnesty matter. The ICC, which has indicted and issued arrest warrants for the LRA leadership, says Kony and his men should be arrested, not granted amnesty. The Ugandan government thinks otherwise, for the sake of peace."[30] Christian Palme, the acting ICC spokesperson, said: "The governments of Uganda, Sudan and Democratic Republic of Congo are obligated to give effect to the arrest warrants, and we are confident that they will honour their joint commitment to do so."[31]

Catholic Archbishop John Baptist Odama advocated reconciliation in Uganda. As Daniel Philpott explained in the journal *First Things*:

> Brandishing the credibility that he has gained by venturing through the bush several times to meet with Kony in his hideout, Odama is a leading voice among Ugandans who oppose the ICC's indictments. Instead he exhorts Ugandans to forgive perpetrators and to reintegrate soldiers into their villages through rituals that involve repentance, restitution, and forgiveness.[32]

Unfortunately, the time for amnesty and peace talks passed, and the LRA continued with its horrifically violent ways. One can never know whether peace talks would have been successful and the amnesty would have held, but the ICC took one of the tools for peace off of the table, and the violence continued. In 2012 it was written: "Today, the four indicted LRA leaders thought to be still alive are on the lam; Kony is probably in the eastern Congo. President Barack Obama recently sent special forces to apprehend them, but it is unclear whether the United States would turn Kony over to the ICC."[33]

---

30. Emma Mutaizibwa, "Govt Happy Kony is for Amnesty," *The Monitor* (Kampala), July 9, 2006.
31. "LRA Leader Must Be Arrested, ICC Insists," Global Policy Forum: Integrated Regional Information Networks, July 5. 2006, https://www.globalpolicy.org/component/content/article/165/29603.html.
32. Daniel Philpott, "Peace After Genocide," *First Things*, June/July 2012.
33. Ibid.

The Failed Promise of the International Criminal Court

It is worth noting that, contrary to the idea behind the ICC, honest trials are not very good places to convey messages to the people. Courts do not write histories; prosecutors should try for conviction, not a historical record. One problem with the prosecution's case in the Slobodan Milosevic trial was that it tried to tell the whole story of the war and eventually drowned in its own narrative. Milosevic died as an unconvicted prisoner. Moreover, the idea of a message can cut two ways. As the *New York Times* wrote: Saddam Hussein turned his trial into a "theater of defiance." Hitler did the same thing when put on trial in Germany for his failed Beer Hall Putsch.[34]

These problems with the ICC were apparent from very early in the process. When former President Bill Clinton signed the Rome Statute on December 31, 2000, he expressed concerns about its "significant flaws" and added: "I will not, and do not recommend that my successor submit the treaty to the Senate for advice and consent until fundamental concerns are satisfied."[35] President George W. Bush later took the unprecedented step of declaring that the United States was "unsigning" the Rome Statute.[36] (The world's four largest nations, the United States, Russia, China, and India, are not parties to the Rome Statute.)

Americans are used to checks and balances, but the ICC is an independent entity. There is no legislative or executive branch to hold this judiciary in check. An unchecked prosecutor should concern people from all political backgrounds. Perhaps more importantly from the American perspective, the ICC does not provide defendants with the full array of Constitutional safeguards that Americans are accustomed to having, including the right to a jury trial and the prohibition against double jeopardy.

---

34. Ronald J. Rychlak, *Hitler, the War, and the Pope* (rev. ed. 2010), 45.
35. Statement by United States President Bill Clinton, authorizing the U.S. signing of the Rome Statute of the International Criminal Court, December 31, 2000, http://www.iccnow.org/documents/USClintonSigning31Dec00.pdf.
36. Brett D. Schaefer, "The Bush Administration's Policy on the International Criminal Court Is Correct," The Heritage Foundation, Backgrounder #1830 on International Criminal Court, March 8, 2005, http://www.heritage.org/research/reports/2005/03/the-bush-administrations-policy-on-the-international-criminal-court-is-correct.

Rights of Defendants

If the U.S. were to ratify the Rome Statute, it would be necessary to amend many state and federal statutes, and probably the federal Constitution and many state constitutions as well. A manual on the ratification and implementation of the Rome Statutes explains that "the ICC is no ordinary international regulatory or institutional body." This manual asserts that modifications must be made to a state's "code of criminal law...and human rights legislation" because "should there be a conflict between the ICC legislation and existing [state] legislation," international law established under the ICC "takes precedence." Accordingly, "[i]t would be prudent" for states "to incorporate all acts defined as crimes" into their own "national laws."[37] The Lawyers Committee for Human Rights has said that "it will be legally and politically difficult to justify a two-tiered system of rights, one for ICC and another for purely domestic purposes."[38] In other words, all nations will have to reduce their domestic rights down until they are the same as the international standard.[39]

Considering the Constitution of the United States, it might be worth noting that American judges have used that document to cre-

---

37. *Manual for the Ratification and Implementation of the Rome Statute*, published by the International Centre for Human Rights and Democratic Development (Montreal, Quebec, Canada) and The International Centre for Criminal Law Reform and Criminal Justice Policy (Vancouver, British Columbia, Canada).

38. Lawyers' Committee for Human Rights, "Pre-Trial Rights in the Rules of Procedure and Evidence," vol. 2, No. 3, *International Criminal Court Briefing Series* (Feb. 1999) (expressing concern that the ICC Statute does not protect persons suspected but not yet charged, and calling for additional procedural protections, particularly during interrogation and arrest).

39. A booklet issued by The Women's Caucus for Gender Justice asserts that "ratification of the treaty creating the Court will necessitate in many cases that national laws be in conformity with the ICC Statute." Women's Caucus for Gender Justice, *The International Criminal Court: The Beijing Platform in Action (Putting the ICC on the Beijing +5 Agenda)*, 8. The caucus states that implementation of the ICC Statute will provide an opportunity for groups "all over the world to initiate and consolidate law reforms." Indeed, the gender caucus asserts that "[i]t is this aspect of the Court—the possibility of national law reform—which may present the most far-reaching potential" for change "in the long run." According to the Caucus, "States parties will be required to review their domestic criminal laws and fill in the gaps to ensure that the crimes enumerated in the ICC Statute are also prohibited domestically."

The Failed Promise of the International Criminal Court

ate new rights, such as the rights to contraception and abortion, which do not appear in the text of that document. What is to stop ICC judges from inventing new crimes, new rights, or otherwise trampling on national sovereignty?[40] Why should we not expect its jurisdiction to expand in the same way that the jurisdiction of the federal courts has expanded?

There have already been calls to expand the ICC's jurisdiction. Representatives from the nation of Turkey have proposed adding the crime of terrorism to the ICC's jurisdiction. There have also been proposals to add international drug transactions to the list of ICC crimes. With eighteen judges (balanced in terms of gender, geography, and legal systems) and a potentially slow docket (there have been less than a handful of tribunals to handle cases like this in the past sixty years), there is every reason to think that ICC judges will start looking for something to do. Suppose they conclude that denial of the right to euthanasia constitutes a violation of human rights? Or what if they find that a society must offer socialized medicine, same-sex marriage, or offer all women the right to an abortion? In such a case, the ICC would be trampling on the sovereignty of many nations. Without co-equal branches of government, how would those nations voice their objections?

Considering the lack of flexibility in the ICC structure, the lack of effective political checks and balances, the difficulty that the Court could pose to negotiating resolutions of conflicts, the impact that it may have on national sovereignty, and way it can be and has been misused for political purposes, the ICC as currently structured poses a significant threat to the common good.

While the Holy See participated in the negotiations that led to the creation of the ICC, its negotiators foresaw these problems. Unlike the United States and Israel, both of which signed then "unsigned" the Rome Statue, the Holy See never signed on to start with. Others are now beginning to see the problem created by the elimination of

---

40. Sharon Dijksma, deputy chair of the Dutch Labor Party, said "A highly-educated woman who chooses to stay at home and not to work—that is destruction of capital.... If you receive the benefit of an expensive education at society's expense, you should not be allowed to throw away that knowledge unpunished." "Dutch Labor MP wants stay-at-home moms punished," religionandspirituality.com, April 5, 2006 (in the Netherlands, the state pays for college tuition).

political considerations. A comprehensive strategy to combat serious violations of international criminal law must incorporate amnesties, immunities, truth commissions, exile for entrenched leaders, lustration for mid-level officials, and civil compensation. It should prioritize domestic processes—and have the courage not to insist on trials in countries that are not ready for them. It must also recognize that, sometimes, the energy expended on tribunals might be better invested in building consensus on robust, timely intervention when crimes are being committed rather than seeking punishment afterward.[41]

Even the godfather of international law and a principal architect of the ICC, Cherif Bassiouni, has started to come to this realization. In 2006, he wrote about the "objective difficulties" that the ICC had to face in its "initial stage," but he hoped that the Lubanga trial would "help to ease many doubts about the direction of the Court."[42] By 2010, the doubts seemed not to have been eased. In a keynote speech associated with the Phillip C. Jessup International Law Moot Court Competition, Bassiouni implied that the expense of the ICC and its bureaucratic framework was leading to the Court's irrelevancy. He was "quite doubtful" that the ICC would be able to meet the expectations of the international community. He predicted a shift from supranational criminal courts (like the ICC) to national courts, which he said would be more successful in prosecuting the guilty.[43] In 2015, Bassiouni called for a truth and reconciliation commission to deal with the conflict between Israel and Palestine.[44] That, of course, would entail some form of amnesty or immunity, running counter to the theory that underlies the ICC.

The *ad hoc* tribunal system that has been used in Rwanda and the former Yugoslavia is not ideal, but it does have the advantage of being flexible enough to adjust to specific local concerns. Over time, the

41. Timothy Waters, "What now for war trials after Milosevic?" *Christian Science Monitor*, March 16, 2006.
42. Cherif Bassiouni, "The ICC—Quo Vadis?" *Journal of International Criminal Justice*, vol. 4, Issue 3 (2006), 421–27.
43. Renee Dopplick, "Bassiouni 'Quite Doubtful' International Criminal Court Will Succeed—The Failures, Challenges, and Future of International Criminal Law," *Inside Justice*, March 31, 2010, http://www.insidejustice.com/intl/2010/03/31/cherif_bassiouni_international_criminal/.
44. Bassiouni, "The ICC—Quo Vadis?"

The Failed Promise of the International Criminal Court

cost of these tribunals can be reduced and procedural concerns minimized. Most importantly, such a system does not foreclose negotiated settlements in those situations where they may be helpful.[45]

Defining the crimes of genocide, aggression, war crimes, and crimes against humanity will certainly help overcome future objections based on the claim of "victor's justice" or *ex post facto*. It is also wise to develop basic standard procedures that will help assure that future trials run smoothly. The idea, however, of a standing court with incentive to grow, a "one size fits all" approach to diverse international problems, and vulnerability to people who would misuse it for their own political purposes, is extraordinarily unwise and may do great damage to the common good. It is, unfortunately, not an effective tool for countering ISIS and its terrorist acts.

---

45. With the horrors in Syria being beyond the jurisdiction of the ICC, a growing number of governments—including Germany, Sweden, and France—have started prosecuting suspected war criminals in their own courts. The U.S. House of Representatives has voted for the creation of a temporary U.N. criminal tribunal for Syria. Coalition for the ICC, "Preparing for justice for Syria," April 15, 2016.

Nineveh Plain, Iraq. Damaged Christian church (November, 2016).

12

The Zhejiang Cross Problem: An Argument for an International Convention Prohibiting (Religious) Cultural Genocide

Richard V. Meyer

IN A *New York Times* article of May 21, 2016, Pulitzer Prize winning author Ian Johnson drew the world's attention to the Chinese government's campaign to remove crosses from atop Christian steeples in the Zhejiang Province.[1] Johnson cited sources claiming that "1200 to 1700" churches had had their crosses removed in that province in the last two years alone.[2] This is not the first time this story had broken into the international news or even been covered by the *New York Times*. Just over a year earlier, Michael Forsythe had introduced the world to a draft regulation that Zhejiang Province planned to use to implement the cross removal program.[3] Forsythe's article mentioned violent attacks on peaceful protests, imprisonment, and that the recent regulation was just a continuation of the "storm of toppling

---

1. Ian Johnson, "Decapitated Churches in China's Christian Heartland," *New York Times*, May 21, 2016 (Asia Pacific Edition), http://www.nytimes.com/2016/05/22/world/asia/china-christians-zhejiang.html?_r=0. Johnson won the Pulitzer Prize in 2001 for his revealing stories about China's brutal suppression of the Falun Gong movement and the implications of that campaign.

2. Ibid.

3. Michael Forsythe, "Chinese Province Issues Draft Regulation on Church Crosses," *New York Times*, May 8, 2015 (Asia Pacific Edition), http://www.nytimes.com/2015/05/09/world/asia/china-church-crosses.html.

crosses" and links all of these acts to a national campaign focused on reining in the power of religious groups with foreign links. The Central Government has called for Christianity to adapt and become more in alignment with traditional Chinese values; values that emphasize one's role as part of a collective and the acceptance of one's lot in life.[4] Christian values that prioritize individual responsibility, morality that supersedes positive law, and a mandate to seek justice are seen as infected with democracy and therefore in opposition to the Communist Party values.

That the regulation justifying the removal of crosses was still in draft form years after the policy of cross removal began gives credence to allegations that the destruction was an attack on the faith itself, and not merely enforcement of a building code. Johnson's article, if anything, shows that there has been no reprieve in the Government's actions against organized Christianity despite a wave of international attention and condemnation. Pastors were still being imprisoned using vague political charges, churches were coerced into promoting socialist values, a legal representative was arrested, and Christians generally were trying to "keep their heads low" to avoid the attention of the Government.[5]

These two articles, published a year apart, do not contain any new facts. That Maoist Communism views Christianity as a threat is no surprise; the actions of the North Korean government to stamp out Christianity evince that axiom.[6] What these two articles do show, however, is the general powerlessness of the international community to prevent this type of government oppression of a religious culture. Despite a wave of condemnation in the media and blogosphere, the People's Republic of China (PRC) has not even blinked.[7] Unlike the violent suppression of the Falun Gong, the PRC has limited its actions against Christianity to attacks on the culture and the use of soft power, exploiting a gap in international law.

---

4. Ibid.
5. Johnson.
6. 2016 Annual Report of the United States Commission on International Religious Freedom, April, 2016, 51–54.
7. A Google search on June 30, 2016 returned over 120 articles and blogs commenting on or criticizing the Chinese government for the removal of the crosses in Zhejiang province.

The Zhejiang Cross Problem

This gap was identified over seventy-two years ago by the father of the Genocide Convention, Raphael Lemkin.[8] Lemkin saw that attacks on culture should be prohibited even when those attacks would not result in the physical destruction of a group.[9] However, the international community of post World War II was not ready for this much of a restriction on sovereign power, so that was left out of the Genocide Convention of 1948.[10] As a result, non-lethal governmental action against Christians and other minorities has continued across the globe. Allegations of officially sanctioned Christian church destructions in the Sudan,[11] Vietnam,[12] and Syria,[13] and dozens of other countries in a swath across the globe from East Africa to the Far East show how exploitation of this gap has become commonplace.

It is time to revisit Lemkin's original proposal and develop an international prohibition of cultural genocide. This chapter addresses this thesis in three parts. The first section applies the current international laws to the problems of Zhejiang Province and shows that they either do not apply or do not contain a sufficient enforcement mechanism to be effective. Part two looks at Lemkin's original analysis of Genocide and the inclusion of Cultural Genocide, and part three explores the difficulties in identifying specific elements of a crime of cultural genocide.

The Gap in International Law

There are four different international legal regimes/paradigms that might be considered to force the prevention of or punishment for the

---

8. Raphael Lemkin, "Genocide—A Modern Crime," http://www.preventgenocide.org/lemkin/freeworld1945.htm.

9. Ibid.

10. Convention on the Prevention and Punishment of the Crime of Genocide, adopted 1948, entry into force 1951 [hereinafter Genocide Convention], https://treaties.un.org/doc/Publication/UNTS/Volume%2078/volume-78-I-1021-English.pdf.

11. "Sudanese police destroy churches, beat Christians," *The Baptist Press*, http://bpnews.net/43857/sudanese-police-destroy-churches-beat-christians.

12. Statement by the Montagnard Foundation, May 28, 2009, http://www.unpo.org/content/view/9642/236/.

13. Yasmine Hafiz, "Syria Conflict Destroys Churches & Mosques, Desecrates Icons," *The Huffington Post*, August 6, 2013, http://www.huffingtonpost.com/2013/08/06/syria-conflict-destroys-mosques-churches_n_3709262.html.

systemic removal of crosses from Christian churches in the Zhejiang Province of China: A) The 1948 Convention on the Prevention and Punishment of the Crime of Genocide; B) The Crime Against Humanity of Persecution within the jurisdiction of the ad hoc United Nations (U.N.) tribunals and the International Criminal Court (ICC); C) The 1954 Convention for the Protection of Cultural Property & International Humanitarian Law; and D) Human Rights Law and the United Nations.

Any discussion of international law dealing with the protection of religious groups normally starts, or at least includes a discussion of the "crime of crimes."[14] The 1948 Genocide Convention was revolutionary in that it was the first ever international convention that traveled so quickly from genesis to enactment, and it was largely the product of the mind and effort of a single man.[15]

Raphael Lemkin observed the actions and policy of the Nazi Germany regime regarding Jews, Catholics, Roma, "inferior Slav peoples," and the Germanic relatives of "the Dutch, the Norwegian, the Alsatians."[16] He then realized that international law did not have a label for a crime whose goal was the elimination of a people. Lemkin coined the term "genocide" based on a combination of the "Greek word *genes* meaning tribe or race and the Latin *cide* meaning killing."[17] Lemkin had listened to the words of Adolf Hitler who had discussed the victor's "prerogative to destroy tribes, entire peoples." Lemkin defined his new term to refer to a "coordinated plan aimed at destruction of the essential foundations of the life of national groups so that these groups wither and die like plants that have suffered a blight." Lemkin identified eight different aspects that could be subjected to genocidal attack: the political, social, cultural, moral, and economic identities of the targeted groups, as well as their biological and physical existence. Lemkin desired a law that would serve to pro-

---

14. For an excellent book on the law of genocide, see William Schabas, *Genocide in International Law: The Crime of Crimes* (Cambridge University Press, 2nd ed., 2009).

15. Lemkin coined the term "genocide" in 1943 and was able to get the Convention adopted within five years.

16. Lemkin, "Genocide."

17. Ibid.

The Zhejiang Cross Problem

tect all of these "essential foundations" of a group from attack, but the political realities of the time forced him to accept a Convention that outlawed only the final two.[18]

The Genocide Convention defines the crime of genocide as the intentional commission of any of five *actus rei*:

(a) Killing members of the group;

(b) Causing serious bodily or mental harm to members of the group;

(c) Deliberately inflicting on the group conditions of life calculated to bring about its physical destruction in whole or in part;

(d) Imposing measures intended to prevent births within the group; or

(e) Forcibly transferring children of the group to another group.[19]

This must be done with the specific intent to destroy, in whole or in substantial part, "a national, ethnical, racial, or religious group, as such."[20] The jurisprudence from the International Court of Justice (ICJ) and the *ad hoc* tribunals have limited the crime to acts intended to bring about the biological/physical destruction of the group.[21] In other words, even if one or more of the *actus rei* were committed with the intent of forcing the remaining group to abandon its identity, this would not be Genocide because the intent was not the actual

---

18. Genocide Convention, Article II.
19. Ibid. There are actually two *mens rea* for the crime of genocide. The five *actus rei* must be done intentionally and with the special intent to bring about the physical destruction of a protected group. If, for example, a genocidaire who intended to kill all Wiccans accidently hit and killed a Wiccan while driving to a meeting of accomplices would not satisfy the *actus reus* requirement because that killing was not the result of an intentional act.
20. The "as such" requirement is that the destruction must be motivated by the victim's membership within the protected group. The word "substantial" was originally part of the U.S. reservations to the Convention. It has since been adopted as part of the Convention by the International Court of Justice (ICJ). See Application of the Convention on the Prevention and Punishment of the Crime of Genocide (Bosn. & Herz. v. Serb. & Mont), Judgment, 2007 I.C.J. 91, at para. 198, http://www.icj-cij.org/docket/files/91/13685.pdf, [hereinafter Bosnia v. Serbia].
21. Bosnia v. Serbia, para. 190.

elimination of the physical existence of the group's individual members.[22]

In addition to identifying the crime of genocide, the 1948 Convention spawned the international law concept of the Responsibility to Protect (RtP) by the wording in its first article: "The Contracting Parties confirm that genocide, whether committed in time of peace or in time of war, is a crime under international law which they undertake to prevent and to punish."[23] This single sentence article was paradigm shifting in the field of International Criminal Law. First, unlike the application of the laws of war, this *lex specialis* would not require an armed conflict in order to apply. Second, this responsibility to "prevent and to punish" was not limited to areas and persons within the control of a given signatory to the Convention. The International Court of Justice has interpreted this Article to require all signatories to "employ all means reasonably available to them" to prevent genocide wherever it could occur.[24] This duty persists even after the issue has been referred to the competent branch of the United Nations. According to that Court, a State could be found liable under the Convention if the State "manifestly failed to take all measures to prevent genocide which were within its power and might have contributed to preventing the genocide."[25] However, the Court was careful to limit its decision to the crime of genocide. Thus, if the removal of the crosses in China does not constitute the crime of genocide, the terms of Article 1 do not apply.

The forced removal of the crosses, and even the imprisonment of those who oppose the removal, do not qualify as one of the five *actus rei* of the Genocide Convention. More importantly, even in a light least favorable to the Central Government, the goal appears to be the elimination of Christianity in China rather than the physical destruction of Chinese Christians. The Genocide Convention in its current form does not serve to prevent or punish the removal of the crosses.

The Crime against Humanity of Persecution seems to be a much

---

22. See Prosecutor v. Radislav Krstić, IT-98-33-T, Trial Chamber Judgment, 2 August 2001, para. 562; and Prosecutor v. Milomir Stakić, IT-97-24-T, Trial Chamber Judgment, 31 July 2003, para. 519.
23. Genocide Convention, Article I.
24. Bosnia v. Serbia, para. 430.
25. Ibid.

stronger lead in the effort to find international law that will protect persecuted Christians, but it too ultimately falls short. The crime of persecution was included in the Charter of the International Military Tribunal at Nuremberg, but as the Trial Chamber of the International Criminal Tribunal for the Former Yugoslavia (ICTY) noted, the crime lacked both definition and any record of domestic application.[26] Fausto Pocar notes that the jurisprudence of both the ICTY and the ICTR (Rwanda) have worked together to define the crime of persecution as:

> The *actus reus* of the crime consists of an underlying act which discriminates in fact and must deny a fundamental human right laid down in international law. The *mens rea* of persecution is discrimination on one of the listed grounds (at the ICTY, these are political, racial and religious grounds).[27]

The Rome Statute prohibits persecution against "any identifiable group or collectivity on political, racial, national, ethnic, cultural, religious, gender ... grounds ... in connection with any act referred to in this paragraph or any crime within the jurisdiction of the Court."[28] While the ICC would limit the prosecution of persecution to acts of genocide, war crimes, or one of the other listed crimes against human-

---

26. Prosecutor v. Tadic, Case No. IT-94-I-T, Opinion and Judgment (May 7, 1997), para. 694, http://www.icty.org/x/cases/tadic/tjug/en/tad-tsj70507JT2-e.pdf.

27. Fausto Pocar, "Persecution as a Crime Under International Criminal Law," 2 J. *Nat'l Security L. & Pol'y* 355 (2008), 358 [hereinafter Pocar].

28. The Rome Statute, Article 7(1)(h). The Elements of Crimes for the International Criminal Court (ICC) further identifies six elements for the crime of Persecution:

1. The perpetrator severely deprived, contrary to international law, one or more persons of fundamental rights.

2. The perpetrator targeted such person or persons by reason of the identity of a group or collectivity or targeted the group or collectivity as such.

3. Such targeting was based on political, racial, national, ethnic, cultural, religious, gender as defined in article 7, paragraph 3, of the Statute, or other grounds that are universally recognized as impermissible under international law.

4. The conduct was committed in connection with any act referred to in article 7, paragraph 1, of the Statute or any crime within the jurisdiction of the Court.

5. The conduct was committed as part of a widespread or systematic attack directed against a civilian population.

6. The perpetrator knew that the conduct was part of or intended the conduct to be part of a widespread or systematic attack directed against a civilian population.

ity, Pocar argues that the *ad hoc* tribunals would also include any other acts that violate a fundamental right as long as those acts rise to "the same level of gravity as a crime against humanity."[29]

Persecution seems much closer to our situation since it covers acts to intentionally deprive a religious group of a fundamental right (religion). The destruction of Christian artifacts may be both widespread and systemic. However, even under Pocar's more relaxed standard, cutting down crosses would not rise to the same level of gravity as the Holocaust (the world's first identified crime against humanity) or the equivalent acts contemplated by the ICTs and the ICC. Perhaps even more problematic is that these acts do not fall under the jurisdiction of the International Criminal Court and would probably never fall under the jurisdiction of an *ad hoc* tribunal due to China's veto power as a permanent member of the U.N. Security Council.[30]

When the target of attacks is property rather than people, the 1954 Hague Convention for the Protection of Cultural Property would be the next avenue to explore.[31] The first problem is that this is not the complete name of the Convention; we must include the narrowing language of "in the event of an armed conflict." This places the convention within the realm of International Humanitarian Law (IHL). IHL is sometimes called the law of war or the law of armed conflict. IHL is an area of specialized law developed by custom and primarily encapsulated within treaties such as the Hague and Geneva Conventions.[32] As a specialized area of law, or *lex specialis*, when it applies it takes priority over more general laws, such as human rights law.[33] The condition precedent for IHL is the existence of an armed conflict.

---

29. Pocar, 359.

30. The jurisdiction of *ad hoc* tribunals is determined by their Statute as approved by Security Council Resolution. See chapter eleven of this book.

31. Convention for the Protection of Cultural Property in the Event of Armed Conflict, May 14, 1954, 249 U.N.T.S. 215 [hereinafter 1954 Hague Convention], http://portal.unesco.org/en/ev.php-URL_ID=13637&URL_DO=DO_TOPIC&URL_SECTION=201.html.

32. The Hague Conventions of 1907 and the Geneva Conventions of 1948 plus the Additional Protocols contain much of the substance of IHL.

33. The legal maxim is *lex specialis derogate legi generali*, or a law governing a specific matter overrides a law that concerns general matters. Human Rights law covers all situations, so it is a general law.

The Zhejiang Cross Problem

If an armed conflict exists, the 1954 Hague Convention and its 1999 Second Protocol would require a government to "respect cultural property situated within their territory."[34] Specifically, it could not conduct military activities near cultural property that would place it at risk of being collaterally damaged within the armed conflict.[35] The 1954 Convention did not revolutionize IHL regarding cultural property; it was already prohibited to intentionally target civilian property.[36] The Convention clarified that cultural property is and should remain civilian property and should not be employed militarily.[37] The Convention also requires states to take actions during peacetime to ensure the protection of cultural property during future armed conflicts.[38] The requirement to safeguard cultural property applies to both international and non-international armed conflicts.

If the resistance to destruction of artifacts is violent and widespread enough to constitute armed conflict, then the Central Government would be prohibited from doing any damage to the churches unless they were being used militarily. This protection would come from traditional IHL and would not require the 1954 Convention. However, this protection would end once the armed conflict ended. As an added problem, even if armed conflict existed, the crosses would probably not constitute cultural property under the Convention. Cultural property, according to the Convention, is "property of great importance to the cultural heritage of every people."[39] Only buildings of significant historic or artistic importance would be considered cultural property. The Chinese crosses were relatively modern and there is no evidence that they had any artistic significance. Some of them were even made of neon.

Given that no armed conflict existed and there is no evidence that the churches were of historic or artistic importance, the *lex specialis* of IHL and the 1954 Convention do not apply to the destruction of church crosses in Zhejiang Province.

---

34. 1954 Hague Convention, Article 4(1).
35. Ibid.
36. This prohibition can be traced back at least as far as the *Lieber Code* (General Orders 100) of 1863.
37. 1954 Hague Convention, Articles 3, 4 & 7.
38. Ibid., Art. 3.
39. Ibid., Art. 1

The final international legal regime to explore is the seemingly omnipresent and all-powerful field of human rights law and its enforcer, the United Nations. The foundational document in this regime that protects religious rights is the 1966 International Covenant on Civil and Political Rights (ICCPR).[40] This Covenant, when combined with the Universal Declaration of Human Rights and the International Covenant on Economic, Social and Cultural Rights constitutes the International Bill of Human Rights. Article 18 of the Covenant states:

1. Everyone shall have the right to freedom of thought, conscience and religion. This right shall include freedom to have or to adopt a religion or belief of his choice, and freedom, either individually or in community with others and in public or private, to manifest his religion or belief in worship, observance, practice and teaching.

2. No one shall be subject to coercion which would impair his freedom to have or to adopt a religion or belief of his choice.

3. Freedom to manifest one's religion or beliefs may be subject only to such limitations as are prescribed by law and are necessary to protect public safety, order, health, or morals or the fundamental rights and freedoms of others.

4. The States Parties to the present Covenant undertake to have respect for the liberty of parents and, when applicable, legal guardians to ensure the religious and moral education of their children in conformity with their own convictions.[41]

Paragraph three seems to directly address the destruction of the crosses in Zhejiang. The cross atop a church building would appear to qualify as a manifestation of religious belief and practice. The Central government would be free to remove the cross for public safety as detailed above. The sheer number of cross removals (1200–1700) in a single year in a single province without evidence of other rooftop sign removals belies a more religiously targeted motive that would violate the Covenant. However, even if the Central Government's conduct were considered to be a violation of Article 18 of the ICCPR, there is no international authority capable of enforcing the Covenant.

---

40. International Covenant on Civil and Political Rights, adopted Dec. 19, 1966, 999 U.N.T.S. 171 (entered into force Mar. 23, 1976), [hereinafter ICCPR].

41. ICCPR at article 18.

The Zhejiang Cross Problem

For enforcement, the ICCPR established the Human Rights Committee (HRC) that would receive and evaluate reports from the State Parties. These reports would document the "measure they have adopted which give effect to the rights recognized herein and on the progress made in the enjoyment of those rights."[42] A State Party may also, by separate action, authorize the HRC to receive complaints from other Parties about their failures to comply with the Covenant.[43] The HRC then has the power to mediate a solution, or appoint an *ad hoc* Conciliation Commission (with the consent of both Parties) to further study the matter.[44] Linked to the ICCPR is the first Optional Protocol (ICCPR-OP1), by which States grant the HRC the authority to receive and consider complaints from individuals that claim violations of their rights identified within the Covenant.[45]

The first problem is that although China signed the ICCPR on October 5, 1998, it has never ratified the Covenant, so it is not subject to the jurisdiction of the HRC. Nor has China signed or ratified the ICCPR-OP1.[46] Thus, the HRC does not have the authority to request a report on an ICCPR violation in China or even to receive such a report from another State Party or an individual victim. The second problem is that even if China were subject to the jurisdiction of the HRC, its powers are limited to reporting deficiencies, more of a public shaming than actual enforcement. Only the Security Council has the powers to force compliance with the Covenant and only in the event the conduct rises to the level where it would constitute a threat to international peace and security.[47] Further, as men-

---

42. Ibid., Art. 40(1).
43. Ibid., Art. 41(1).
44. Ibid., Art. 41–42.
45. The Office of the United Nations High Commissioner on Human Rights, "Optional Protocol to the International Covenant on Civil and Political Rights," http://www.ohchr.org/EN/ProfessionalInterest/Pages/OPCCPR1.aspx [hereinafter I CCPR-OP1].
46. The Office of the High Commissioner tracks singings and ratifications by China to the Human Rights Treaties at http://tbinternet.ohchr.org/_layouts/TreatyBodyExternal/Countries.aspx?CountryCode=CHN&Lang=EN. As of June 30, 2016, the page reflected that China had signed but not ratified the IPPRC but had not signed IPPRC-OP1.
47. Charter to the United Nations, chapter VII.

tioned earlier, China has veto power over any Security Council action.

In the absence of an armed conflict, International Human Rights enforcement depends almost exclusively on a public shaming power and even that is prevented if the violating Party does not elect to be subject to the shaming mechanism. It will not help solve the Zhejiang cross problem.

Despite the existence of four different regimes of international law (Genocide Convention, Persecution as a Crime before International Tribunal, Protection of Cultural Property & IHL, and Human Rights Law) that exist to protect religious minorities from government oppression, as evidenced by the Zhejiang Cross problem, there remains a huge gap that continues to be exploited.

Raphael Lemkin's Solution

The gap in International Law identified earlier in this paper is neither new nor was it unpredictable. Over 70 years ago, the Father of the Genocide Convention foresaw this gap and attempted to seal it closed. Lemkin's solution A) identified many more genocidal acts and a broader genocidal intent than those that would come under the current Convention; B) emphasized the importance of genocidal intent; and C) the world has already suffered because of failure to implement his entire plan.

Although Lemkin's legal offspring is the Genocide Convention, his aim was much more ambitious. As mentioned above, Lemkin identified eight different methods of attack against a protected group that could result in genocide, but the Convention prohibited only two. In addition to the attacks directed against the biological person and their continued physical existence that are prohibited by the Convention, Lemkin wanted to prohibit the use of political, social, cultural, religious, moral, and economic attacks against a group's identity.

To Lemkin, the goal was to protect not just the people in a group but also the unified identity of the group. Lemkin understood that a group could be destroyed by the elimination of its religious identity even if it survived physically.[48] Lemkin provided examples of how the

---

48. Daphne Anayiotos, "The Cultural Genocide Debate: Should the U.N. Genocide Convention Include a Provision on Cultural Genocide, or Should the Phenom-

The Zhejiang Cross Problem

Germans used the other six forms of attack to destroy the unifying identity of a group. The Germans employed cultural attacks in the Alsace-Lorraine area of France by renaming streets and locations, replacing signs and inscriptions in French with signs and inscriptions in German and banning the speaking of French. In Poland they denied any artistic training and censored all artistic expression of Polish culture to prevent "independent [Polish] national thinking."[49]

Lemkin claimed that the Germans employed a moral attack against the primarily conservative Roman Catholic Polish population by "foisting" pornographic publications and movies upon them, changing the local laws to allow and encourage gambling, and manipulating the market to keep the cost of alcohol low. Poles, Luxembourgers, and Alsatians were also attacked economically by confiscation of assets and the denial of trade licenses; only accepting a "germanization" of their identity would allow them to reclaim their economic life.

Lemkin alleged religious attacks in Croatia when the entire Orthodox hierarchy was discarded and a new government that sanctioned patriarchy was established and when the Germans banned the criticism of any child who chose to discard their religious identity in order to join a German Youth group. The imprisonment/targeted killings of Roman Catholic clergy in Slovenia as well as intelligentsia in Slovenia, Poland, and Holland are examples of social attacks to a group's identity. Finally, the creation of new puppet governments in Norway, Greece, and France led by national Nazi parties were examples of political attacks against national identity according to Lemkin.

He was not alone in his condemnation of acts that destroyed identity but stopped short of destroying physical existence. As part of a trial that occurred contemporaneous with the debate on the Genocide Convention, the prosecution charged a group of German defendants with a series of "acts, conduct, plans, and enterprises . . . [that] . . . were carried out as part of a systematic program of genocide, aimed at the destruction of foreign nations and ethnic groups, in

---

enon be Encompassed in a Separate International Treaty?" 22 *N.Y. Int'l L. Rev.* 99, 102 (2009) citing Raphael Lemkin, "Genocide as a Crime Under International Law," 41:1 *Am. J. Int'l L.* 145–51 (1947), http:// www.preventgenocide.org/lemkin/ASIL1947.htm [hereinafter Anayiotos].

49. See Lemkin, note 48.

part by murderous extermination, and in part by elimination and suppression of national characteristics."[50] Thus, even though that tribunal was not empowered to adjudicate charges of genocide,[51] the prosecutors used Lemkin's new term to describe acts committed with the intent of destroying a group's identity and not just their physical bodies.

What makes genocide unique is not the *actus rei*. For example, when an independent fact-finding committee found that the "*actus reus* of genocide" had occurred in the conflict in Gaza, it bore no legal significance because any time two members of the same protected group are intentionally killed, that element is satisfied.[52] Said another way, the *actus reus* of genocide has occurred in every single armed conflict in the history of mankind, so that is hardly what makes the situation special. No, what makes genocide the "crime of crimes" is genocidal intent; when the *actus reus* is committed with the intent to eliminate a protected group in whole or in part. Over seventy years ago, Lemkin recognized that attempts to eliminate any cultural, religious, ethnical, or national group was a huge loss for the entire world even if their physical bodies survived.

If the allegations in the Johnson article are correct, then the Chinese Central Government's destruction of the church crosses is part of a systemic plan to eliminate Christianity in Zhejiang Province and eventually all of China. What is frustrating is that even if the Central Government admitted that it removed the crosses with that specific intent, there is no existing international law paradigm to prevent or punish those acts.

This is not the first time China has decided to eliminate a spiritual group. Johnson has also written extensively of the systemic elimination of the Falun Gong by the Chinese government. When one looks at the alleged actions against the Falun Gong, the Government's attacks on Chinese Christians seem trivial by comparison.

---

50. Anayiotos, 109 (citing U.S. v. Greifelt, in *Trials Of War Criminals Before The Nuremberg Military Tribunals Under Control Council Law No. 10* (1950), 88–89).

51. The decision predates the enactment of the Genocide Convention.

52. Executive Summary, "No Safe Place: Report of the Independent Fact Finding Committee on Gaza," June 3, 2009, para. 29. http://palestinefreevoice.blogspot.com / 2009/10/gaza-no-safe-place-independent-fact.html.

The Zhejiang Cross Problem

Li Hongzhi founded the Falun Gong practice in 1992.[53] Based on meditation and principles of truth-benevolence-compassion, the Falun Gong practice gathered tens of millions of followers within its first decade. This rapid growth attracted the attention of the Central Government who feared that the organization could morph into a rebellious group.[54] The PRC decided to ban the group in an effort to combat "superstition and unscientific ideas."[55] They formed a special office, called the "610 Office" that employed more than 3,000 agents tasked with investigating the Falun Gong and developing a unified approach to the "Falun Gong problem."[56] Starting in 1999, Falun Gong members began being arrested, over 1.5 million books and other publications were collected and destroyed, and all websites were shut down.[57]

Despite never being involved in any violence, threat of violence, or even any political activity besides a single comparatively small peaceful political protest against a government publication that denigrated the movement, the Falun Gong was officially banned on July 22, 1999.[58] An unknown number of Falun Gong are still incarcerated, and horrifying allegations that they are being harvested for their organs have arisen.[59] Just like with the Zhejiang Cross problem, even though the Chinese Central Government, by banning the practice, has thereby publicly admitted an intent to eliminate the Falun Gong, except for perhaps the horrific final allegation, none of the acts above could be prevented or punished by current international law regimes. The time has come to implement Lemkin's original proposal of an

---

53. Jennifer L. Zegel, "Bloody Persecution: Plight of the Falun Gong," 9 *Rutgers J. L. & Religion* 8 (2007) citing Li Hongzhi, *Zhuan Falun ii* (Eng. ed., 1999) ("Falun Gong is a method of mind and body cultivation. It seeks to develop practitioners' heart and character in accordance with the principles of Truthfulness-Compassion-Forbearance") [hereinafter Zegel].

54. Michael J. Greenlee, "A King Who Devours His People: Jiang Zemin and the Falun Gong Crackdown: A Bibliography," 34 *Int'l J. Legal Info.* 556 (2006), 559 [hereinafter Greenlee].

55. Ibid.
56. Zegel, 10; Greenlee, 561.
57. Greenlee, 562.
58. Ibid., 561.
59. Zegel, 10.

international convention against cultural genocide; however, the devil is in the details.

A Modest Proposal for the Elements of the International Crime of Cultural Genocide[60]

Like the current crime of genocide under the Convention, the crime of cultural genocide must identify A) the specific intent required; B) the applicable *actus rei* and the theories of liability; and C) it should also include the recognized mandate that all signatories will take reasonable acts to prevent and punish acts of cultural genocide.

The specific intent of genocide seems a good place to build upon to create Cultural genocide intent: "acts committed with the intent to destroy, in whole or in part, a national, ethnical, racial or religious group, as such."[61] From multiple cases before both ICTs as well as the ICJ we have learned that genocidal intent: is not the equivalent of motive;[62] it can be inferred from comments or a pattern of actions;[63] that the destruction must be in whole or in substantial part; that a substantial part could be determined by sheer numbers, proportion, or importance within the group;[64] and that it must be for the physical destruction of the group.[65] Other than the final aspect, the rest could apply equally to cultural genocidal intent. We also know that four types of protected groups (racial, national, ethnical, and religious) are descriptive rather than an actual exhaustive list. We know that a protected group is based on a stable, somewhat permanent aspect that is normally determined involuntarily. It would include race, ethnicity, nation, and religion, but exclude political affiliation.

Since cultural genocide would prohibit acts that are not intended

---

60. Daphne Anayiotos has a more thorough proposal, but there are some important differences discussed below.
61. Genocide Convention, Art. 2.
62. Prosecutor v. Goran Jelisić, Case No. IT-95-10, Trial Judgment (July 5, 2001), http://www.icty.org/x/cases/jelisic/tjug/en/jel-tj991214e.pdf (para. 111).
63. Prosecutor v. Nahimana, Case No. ICTR 99-52-T, Judgment & Sentence (Dec. 3, 2003).
64. Prosecutor v. Radislav Krstić, Case No. IT-98-33 (April 19, 2004).
65. See notes 26 & 27.

to result in actual deaths, it needs a different term than "destroy."[66] Alternate terminology is necessary to create clear demarcation between genocide and cultural genocide. A Google search for images of the word "destroy" produces pages of pictures of physical destruction. This is misleading since the target of cultural genocide is the group's identity, which is intangible. A Google search of the word "eliminate," however, contains pictures of a delete key and an eraser clearing words from a chalkboard.[67] This seems to be a better verb to reflect the actions to be prevented.

While the current crime of genocide protects members of a group from destruction based upon their membership in the group, a prohibition against cultural genocide would seek to protect the group's identity as a group. Thus, a cultural genocidaire targets that which unifies the group and gives it identity. For religious groups that is easy to identify as the religion itself. This issue is more problematic for other groups such as nations or ethnicities; however, since the Zhejiang Cross problem involves a religious group, I will leave those problems for others to solve. Thus, limiting the proposal to the cultural genocide of religious groups, it would punish "acts committed with the intent to eliminate a religion."

Moving on to the *actus reus*, I would be tempted to start the list with the five *actus rei* contained within genocide and then start adding to the list with acts such as the intentional seizure or destruction of private property.[68] However, in keeping with my "don't reinvent the wheel" philosophy in deciding the *mens rea*, I believe this list has already been created for us.

Part III of the ICCPR contains twenty separate articles that contain prohibitions against: murder, torture, slavery, arbitrary arrest, violations of dignity, separations of youths and adults, restrictions on movement, wrongful prosecution, denial of religious practice or expression, denial of free expression, speech or association, denial of

---

66. Daphne Anayiotos does not share this view and includes the word "destroy" and "Destruction" in her proposal for a new Convention against cultural genocide. See Anayiotos, 145–146.

67. Search conducted on June 20, 2016.

68. If all the Roman Catholic priests in an area were killed with the intent to eliminate Catholicism, it would not be genocide if the physical existence of their respective parishes was not threatened, but it would be cultural genocide if the intent was to eliminate the religion.

suffrage and denial of language.[69] So the *actus rei* are any acts that would violate Articles 6 through 27 of the ICCPR, provided that the act was committed in a State subject to that Covenant.

Article 1 of the Genocide Convention requires all State Parties to "undertake to prevent and punish" the crime of genocide. As noted above, the ICJ has interpreted this to mean that States must take reasonable acts to prevent genocide even if it is occurring outside their borders. This language should also be included in any prohibition of cultural genocide, but the document should also add more information about which undertakings are "reasonable." For example, the new Convention should authorize the HRC to investigate cultural genocide anywhere on the globe (and not just within the borders of a State Party).[70] A "reasonable" undertaking would be to refer an allegation of cultural genocide to the HRC. It is possible that this referral to the HRC may satisfy a State's duties under the Covenant.[71] Compared to the crime of genocide, acts of cultural genocide are normally less permanent. Therefore, there is less of a need for immediate (and possibly unilateral) action by a State Party for acts occurring outside its borders. While I need to research this idea further, I am intrigued by the idea that the Convention would modify the WTO regulations and allow individual members the power (and possibly the responsibility) to enact unilateral trade restrictions against countries after the HRC has made findings that said country's government is engaging in genocide or cultural genocide.

One final, but very important part of the genocide Convention that should be included in a new Convention is the compulsory jurisdiction of the International Court of Justice. Article IX of the Convention gives the ICJ power to decide issues of "interpretation, application or fulfillment of" the Convention.[72] The United States has been a persistent objector to this provision since, like China, it

---

69. ICCPR, Articles 6–27.

70. This right of investigation would not contain any powers over a non-signatory, so HRC investigators could request, but not demand, the cooperation of a non-party government.

71. This would also include the duty of a State Party to cooperate fully with any resultant HRC investigation.

72. Genocide Convention, Art. IX.

never likes to cede sovereign power to an international body.[73] Unlike other organs of the United Nations, the ICJ is less susceptible to the veto, economic, and political power of a permanent member. To combat the protectionism of these permanent members, the new convention would contain a requirement that State parties cannot object/abstain from the compulsory jurisdiction of the ICJ.

Conclusion

Raphael Lemkin was a prophetic genius who identified the need for a prohibition on not just genocide but also cultural genocide. The minorities of the world have suffered and will continue to suffer because we failed to adopt his full proposal.

My modest proposal is an incomplete solution at best. It still does not answer the problem of enforcement against a permanent member, nor is China any more likely to ratify this Convention than the ICCPR. However, the creation and implementation of the proposed Convention Prohibiting Cultural Genocide will make a powerful statement about the seriousness of attempting to eliminate a religious group's identity. Shame is not the best enforcement method, but it is currently the only method available against superpowers like the United States and China.

Genocide is a very powerful term in modern international discourse and even allegations draw the ear of the entire world. The time has long since come for it to apply to more than just a physical destruction.

---

73. All reservations to the Genocide Convention can be found at http://www.preventgenocide.org/law/convention/reservations/.

Bartella, Iraq. Syriac Catholic Archbishop Petros Moshe of Mosul holds a broken image of Our Lady (December, 2016).

13

Under Caesar's Sword: A Report on the Conference

Al Kresta

AS GLOBALIZATION continues and cultures interpenetrate one another, we can expect varying degrees of conflict over the core values and ideas that form these differing cultures. Disagreements over concepts like religious liberty, religious toleration, the right to worship, liberty of conscience, the free exercise of religion, and establishment of religion are not new and will continue. In the modern age, every social order must balance the religious and civil obligations of its adherent's citizens. In the West this debate is commonly described as the conflict between "altar and throne," "church and state," "Christ and Caesar." How do Christians render to Caesar what is Caesar's and to God what is God's?

The practical and painful significance of these ideas was on display in Rome on December 10–12, 2015, at the international conference, "Under Caesar's Sword: Christians in Response to Persecution," hosted by the University of Notre Dame's Center for Civil and Human Rights and Georgetown University's Religious Freedom Project. The conference convened nearly 250 prominent Christian leaders, policy makers, religious freedom advocates, scholars, human rights activists, and interested observers at the Pontifical Urban Institute in Rome.[1] "The uniqueness of this conference is its focus on

---

1. The project "Under Caesar's Sword: A Christian Response to Persecution" is the result of a partnership of the Notre Dame Center for Ethics and Culture, the Religious Freedom Institute, and Georgetown University's Religious Freedom Project, with the support of the Templeton Religion Trust. It has involved three years

what Christians are doing to respond, how they are responding, and how Christians in the West can respond with them," said Dr. Timothy Shah, assistant director of Georgetown's Religious Freedom Project.

Dr. Daniel Philpot, director of Notre Dame's Center for Civil and Human Rights added that the conference was designed to increase solidarity with suffering, persecuted Christians throughout the world. To that end, he set forth four objectives:

1. To roll out the results of the world's first systematic global investigation into responses of Christian communities to violation of their religious freedom;

2. To commemorate the fiftieth anniversary of *Dignitatis Humanae*, the Second Vatican Council's declaration on religious freedom and compare the threats to religious freedom at the time of the declaration (Dec. 7, 1965) and those that Christians face today;

3. To engender discussion of the global persecution of Christians among journalists, government officials, human rights activists, church leaders, representatives of world religions, scholars, students, and the interested public; and

4. To draw public attention to the plight of persecuted Christian communities, promote cooperation among Christian churches in assisting these communities, and encourage global solidarity with them.

Three core questions drove the fifty plus presentations, formed the agenda of the scholarly research findings, and served as touchstones for conversation among all the attendees over the three days:

How do Christian communities respond to repression?

Why do they choose the responses that they do?

What results follow from their choices?

---

of collaborative global research that investigated how Christian communities have responded to violations of their freedom of religion. The key questions explored are as follows: How do Christian communities respond to repression? Why do they choose the responses that they do? What are the results of these responses? The conclusions were rolled out in the international conference held in Rome (December 2015), which corresponded with the 50th anniversary of the Second Vatican Council's Declaration on Religious Freedom, *Dignitatis Humanae*. More information is available at http://ucs.nd.edu/rome-conference/.

Under Caesar's Sword: A Report on the Conference

Along with the academic research findings, these three questions were illustrated and corroborated through personal stories of harassment and direct persecution under many regimes.

The conference also provided opportunity for shared prayer and worship including a beautiful and haunting ecumenical prayer service at the Church of San Bartolomeo, which was established by Pope John Paul II as a shrine to contemporary martyrs and is now run by the Community of Sant'Egidio. Cardinal John Onaiyekan's homily traced the reality of martyrdom in the Christian life. On December 12, the Feast of Our Lady of Guadalupe, many participants celebrated Mass with Pope Francis in Saint Peter's Basilica. The Pope's homily focused on mercy—a theme especially relevant to those living "under Caesar's sword."

Western media have paid scant attention to the plight of persecuted Christians and other religious minorities around the world. This is especially vexing given the scope and extent of persecution through the last and current centuries. Pope John Paul II, other Christian leaders, and human rights monitoring organizations claim that today's persecution of Christians far exceeds previous centuries. But in spite of being rich in suspense, sacrificial love, bloodshed, and heroic courage, these stories of modern martyrdom and persecution have not captured the imagination of our political and media elite.

Occasionally a repentant voice is heard. A.M. Rosenthal, former executive editor of the *New York Times*, admitted: "I realized that in decades of reporting, writing, assigning stories on human rights, I rarely touched on one of the most important. Political human rights, legal, civil, and press rights, emphatically and often, BUT the right to worship where and how God or conscience leads, almost never." His admission is the exception that proves the rule. "Under Caesar's Sword," however, did generate some media interest with, at least, the *Wall Street Journal*, Reuters, National Public Radio, *L'Osservatore Romano*, the *Boston Globe*, *Commonweal*, *Christianity Today*, Ave Maria Radio, and EWTN all present.

The indifference of the media has often reflected the nonchalance and incomprehension of political leaders. Religious freedom activist Michael Horowitz tells of challenging a high-level Clinton State Department official to do something to lift the oppression of suffering believers. The frustrated official asked: "Why are you people working so hard on this issue of religious persecution? Don't you understand how divisive this is? You know we are working to promote democracy... for the right to vote. Don't you understand that when we have the right to vote, people will be able to go to church?" For this official, religious liberty needed to wait in line behind more significant political problems. People wanting to go to church could take their place with those pushing for hunting licenses or a public safety clearance to import avocadoes.

This lack of urgency has afflicted both sides of the political aisle. When human rights activist Nina Shea urged George W. Bush's Secretary of State Condoleezza Rice to highlight the persecution of Christians in the Middle East, the Secretary dismissed her plea by claiming: "We can't be sectarian," as though Shea wished to exclude other persecuted groups like the Yazidis or minority Muslims.

This relative indifference is a far cry from esteeming religious liberty as our "first, most cherished liberty," as described by the U.S. Conference of Catholic Bishops. For many policy makers and opinion shapers, religious liberty shrinks under the demands of trade treaties and other geopolitical considerations. For them, "religion" cannot be permitted to interfere with McDonald's (Mae Dang Lao's) golden arches appearing on the streets of Beijing or air pollution standards to be established in New Delhi. Apparently, to challenge the internal religious policies of China, Malaysia, Egypt, or Saudi Arabia is a breach of diplomatic etiquette, a faux pas caused by Eurocentric conceit. After all, they ask reproachfully, "Who are we to insist that our values are universal or that human rights are inalienable and inviolable?"

Many conference participants admitted that the West may not always know how best to serve the cause of persecuted indigenous Christians or how best to pressure offending nations. The primacy of religious liberty, however, should not be dismissed because of practical difficulties confronted when supporting fellow Christians or other religious believers suffering "under Caesar's sword."

Apart from the fog of political self-interest and media indifference, the enormity of global persecution is also obscured by dismissing the social importance of religion. Leaders of Western societies generally assume that religious ideas, influences, institutions, and individuals are losing their cultural relevance and public moral authority even as there is a growing number of competing religious voices in our society. Sociologists use words like "secularization," "pluralization," and

Under Caesar's Sword: A Report on the Conference

"privatization" to get at this phenomenon. Popularly put, it means that each time a journalist or lawmaker looks out his window, he sees less and less religion operating in the public square. Religion, for many complex reasons, they say, is being pushed to the margins of our shared social space. Religious faith does not disappear; it just goes inward and becomes "privatized" or outward to the margins and becomes "secularized." In either case, religious faith loses major social influence.

For many educated, socially concerned citizens, especially those in the "chattering" or "knowledge class" (i.e., those whose lives are immersed in the world of ideas, politics, media, and academia), faith is a purely personal matter. It possesses the status of a hobby like collecting Star Wars figurines or learning to play the sackbut. Faith is something to be done in one's free time. In that sense, religious faith can be privately engaging but remains socially irrelevant. For such analysts, faith is like spit; it's probably good to have some but you had better keep it to yourself.

Worse, other analysts regard public expressions of faith as socially divisive. In their minds, religion separates people into communities whose chief allegiance is to private truths that cannot be verified in any public way. Competing religious truth-claims cannot be reconciled through logic or science or even popular vote. This produces bitter conflict and endless squabbling with the inevitable attempt to use government to favor one group over others. Even worse, according to these analysts, these communities of faith compete with the state for the final allegiance of its members. Leaders of the state generally assume that they, as the publicly recognized authority over the nation, deserve to be regarded as the "supreme court" of appeal. After all, they say, the state serves all; these religious clans serve only their members.

Both these attitudes contrast with the holdings of Christian anthropology, which teaches that freedom of religion is necessary for moral choice. The liberty to make and act upon moral choices is foundational to human nature. Without opportunity to exercise freedom, virtue cannot be formed. Protecting religious liberty serves the common, social good. In short, God made man for himself, to love and serve other humans, and to cultivate and steward the created order. Generally, people flourish best when left free to live out their experiments in faith. This Christian understanding, however, no longer animates public discussion over the social utility of religious faith. Consequently, religious faith, state leaders claim, is dangerously subjective and subversive of public order.

The prophets of secularization seem unaware of a looming irony. The irony is that in spite of Western assumptions about secularization and the privatizing of religion, nearly every continent has seen the resurgence of publicly and culturally formative religion and associated value systems over the last generation. Serious researchers have noted this reversal of secularization.[2]

The evidence is not hidden. It has either been ignored or the dots have not been connected between major world events and the growing global social influence of religious faith. The reassertion of religious faith has been propping up headlines since the late 1970s. For instance, Shia Islam was the dominant force in the 1979 revolution against the secular Shah of Iran that created the Islamic Republic of Iran under the leadership of the Ayatollah Khomeini. Similarly, Sunni Islam has seen a revival of "fundamentalist" or Salafist groups, including violent extremists like ISIS, launching a new jihad—a new struggle to establish authentic Islamic governance in North Africa, Central Asia, the Middle East, and other lands. Hindu nationalism has reasserted itself on the Indian subcontinent through the BJP party. From Myanmar to Tibet, saffron-robed Buddhist monks have been taking to the streets in protest against political repression, and in Sri Lanka, "engaged" Buddhists urge the spiritual and moral use of public power.

In the United States, a resurgence of conservative Christian political influence formed the now-defunct Moral Majority, the Religious Roundtable, and elevated Ronald Reagan to the presidency in 1980. Religious broadcaster Pat Robertson established the Christian Coalition and sought the Republican nomination for president in 1988. Today groups like United In Purpose, American Family Association, The Family Research Council, The Catholic Vote, and My Faith Votes

---

2. See Peter L. Berger, ed. *The Desecularization of the World: Resurgent Religion and World Politics* (Grand Rapids, MI: William B. Eerdmans, 1999); Monica Duffy Toft, Daniel Philpott, and Timothy Samuel Shah, *God's Century: Resurgent Religion and Global Politics* (New York: W.W. Norton, 2011); and Scott M. Thomas, *The Global Resurgence of Religion and the Transformation of International Relations: The Struggle for the Soul of the Twenty-First Century* (New York: Palgrave McMullan, 2005).

are operating across the nation. Communist China is recovering Confucian wisdom to lend transcendent order and moral structure to relationships between ruler and subject, father and son, husband and wife, etc. Even Judaism with its Abrahamic covenant, prophetic ethics, and respect for tradition wields significant social influence in the secular state of Israel. Regardless of whether one welcomes these developments, they counter the lazy claim that publicly significant religion is waning.

Besides political indifference and secularization, there is another reason why religious persecution has not arrested the attention of the press or the politicians—the fragmentation of the Christian community. When Baptist missionaries are kidnapped in Peru, major newspapers offer few headlines. The story only resonates within their denominational circles, and Christians outside those circles may never hear of it. Even if they do hear of it, they may be preoccupied with problems within their own tradition. The global forces of Christianity are not mobilized.

This was addressed during the conference by Dr. Elisabeth Prodromou from Tufts University's Fletcher School of Law and Diplomacy where she teaches conflict resolution: "We need to recognize that the current state of fracture in the Church is having a terrible impact" on the ability to mobilize support for at-risk Christians. Disunity undermines the urgency of Christian claims of persecution. If some unknown Pentecostal preacher is jailed in Pakistan, the world finds it easy to shrug it off as just another discrete act of repression. After all, it says, the Christians themselves are not shouting about it. Catholics aren't raising their voices, Baptists aren't raising their voice. Why should we?

This fracturing has led to the near elimination of Christians in the Middle East. In the Gaza Strip, for instance, Christians now number 100–150. In Iraq, a population of 2.5 million may have been reduced to 250,000 since the American military initiative of 2003. For all his manifest evils, Saddam Hussein at least kept the lid on the boiling pot of sectarian violence and protected Christians from religious cleansing. Patriarch Ignatius Youseff III, the Patriarch of Antioch and All the East for the Syriac Catholic Church, lamented that "Middle Eastern Christians have been forgotten, abandoned, even betrayed by the Western countries.... The whole Middle East without exception is presently engulfed by a nightmare that seems to have no end and that undermines the very existence of minorities, particularly of Christians, in lands known to be the cradle of our faith and early Christian communities."

To trumpet the plight of the persecuted, even among Christians, an intentional ecumenism was the *sine qua non* of the conference. To that end, "Under Caesar's Sword" was an interdenominational cornucopia. Christians of all stripes came expecting to be heard and expecting to learn from fellow believers regardless of their denominational affiliation and theological tradition.

Accordingly, the conference was attended by a startling array of Christians and other believers. Roman Catholic, evangelical Protestant, Coptic, Orthodox, Jewish, Disciples of Christ, Muslim, Chaldean Catholic, Eastern Orthodox, Reformed, Baptist, Syriac Catholic, Episcopalian, Ukrainian Greek Catholic, Presbyterian, Anglican, and Methodist. Multiple ethnicities were also striking, with Assyrian, Hin-du, Pakistani, Egyptian, Anglo, American, Eritrean, Dutch, Burmese, Czech, Central African, Nigerian, Spanish, Italian, Chaldean, Iraqi, Syriac, Ukrainian, and more participating.

Since at least the New Testament, it has been known that those suffering for their faith easily discern kindred souls from other Christian traditions. This ecumenism of the trenches has been growing whenever fellow Christians hear of each other's exploits and labors. Near the end of World War II, German Lutheran pastor/theologian Dietrich Bonhoeffer found himself reading the Catholic teachers Cyprian and Tertullian while incarcerated in Tegel prison. Writing to a friend, he was amazed that these ancient Catholic fathers better addressed the persecuted Church than even the magisterial Protestant Reformers. Persecution sensitizes and opens one to the suffering of Christians from very different traditions.

Time and again, participants and presenters returned to what was often called "the scandal of disunity." These divisions discredit the gospel in the eyes of nonbelievers even as they leave members of Christ's body without the universal support they should be able to count on.

Prior to the conference, I had interviewed one of evangelical Protestantism's leading missiologists in Southeast Asia. When asked what was the greatest impediment to the spread of the Gospel in his area, he responded without a moment's hesitation: "Disunity among Christians." From different theological traditions, he and Pope St.

Under Caesar's Sword: A Report on the Conference

John Paul II shared a common analysis: "When nonbelievers meet missionaries who do not agree among themselves, even though they all appeal to Christ, will they be in a position to receive the true message?" Division among Christians undermines the claim that God was in Christ reconciling the world to himself. The world has a right to judge Christians. If Christ's disciples cannot reconcile their differences, why should the watching world credit the Christian claim that they who are baptized into Christ Jesus are ministers of reconciliation? Our disunity speaks louder than our gospel presentations. And this disunity also leaves all Christians vulnerable to persecution.

Prior to the conference, Dr. Thomas Farr, director of the Religious Freedom Project at Georgetown and one of the conference organizers wrote: "By now, the scale of Christian persecution has been amply documented. But nobody has examined systematically and globally what these communities do when they are under massive repression. Do they flee? Resist? Work with outsiders to build safe havens? Accommodate? Forgive? Or what?"

The "Under Caesar's Sword" project was conceived in order to find out. With a $1.1 million grant from the Templeton Religious Trust, a team of 14 leading scholars, was selected and commissioned to travel around the world studying 100 beleaguered Christian communities in over 30 countries including China, Indonesia, Nigeria, Syria, Egypt, Iraq, Pakistan, and India.

Dan Philpott explained: "Central to the conference was the presentation of the findings of *Under Caesar's Sword's* 14 scholars, who had been researching some 30 countries where Christians have suffered persecution." Findings were clustered into five regions:

1. The Middle East and North Africa

2. Europe and the Americas

3. Southern Asia

4. Sub-Saharan Africa

5. China and Post-Soviet Countries

The report found that persecution is happening in far more places and at the hands of far more perpetrators than most people imagine. Timothy Shah expressed alarm: "We are seeing a global catastrophe for Christians. Sometimes it takes the form of horrible, violent attacks, beheadings, but in many cases, it takes the form of lower level aggression. Whatever form it takes, millions of Christians face systematic attack. It has been growing in recent years, and yet there is a gap, an incredible lack of awareness and concern, first of all, among our fellow Christians."[3]

While persecution in Muslim countries is most common, Communist regimes in Vietnam, China, and North Korea are also active persecutors. In democratic and pluralist India, the resurgence of Hindu nationalism over the last generation has resulted in martyrdom for Christians. The Western democracies do not escape severe criticism.

Dr. Paul Marshall, senior fellow of the Hudson Institute's Center for Religious Freedom, reported on religious persecution, harassment, and repression in Western Europe and North America. While the West avoids direct persecution, there has been an attempt to shrink the scope of religious liberty. He pointed to a 2015 Pew Research Center report, "Latest Trends in Religious Restrictions and Hostilities." As of December 2013, Europe's religion-related social hostilities were the second highest of any of Pew's five world regions. Marshall cited Swedish historian Eli Gondor who describes a "great animosity" toward religion in Sweden: "I don't think that an openly religious person has the same chance to have a political career, or any other career, as a secular person." In the United States there has been executive action that, wittingly or unwittingly, sought to reduce the liberty of Christians and Christian institutions. The Obama administration's HHS mandate tried to force religious organizations opposed to contraception to provide contraceptive health care coverage. The Obama administration also attempted to tell a Lutheran church school who could be counted as a "minister" and who could not.

Recently, the American Civil Liberties Union (ACLU) reversed its long-standing support for the Religious Freedom Restoration Act (RFRA) for fear it will be used to deny wedding cakes, floral arrangements, chapels, etc., to same sex couples planning weddings. Many observers have noted a tendency to reduce the exercise of religious liberty to merely a right to worship or right to believe.

The report also identified three strategies used by Christians in responding to persecution: Coping, Constructing, and Confronting.

---

3. Under Caesar's Sword: Christians in Response to Persecution, December 10–12, 2015, Pontifical Urban University, Rome, Italy (Final Report).

Under Caesar's Sword: A Report on the Conference

Coping strategies take at least three forms: fleeing, conforming, and hiding. In what has been labeled as the worst refugee crisis on the Old Continent since the Second World War, Bishop Anba Angaelos, leader of the Egyptian Coptic Orthodox Church in the UK, described thousands of Christians from the Middle East and Africa fleeing their counties in rubber boats across the Mediterranean Sea to reach Europe. The slow death of displacement and dislocation seems the only alternative to a quick death by bullets and bombs. As this chapter was being written in the last week of May, 2016, 700 refugees were reported drowned in three separate incidents just south of Italy in the Mediterranean. Fleeing, "getting out of Dodge" for survival's sake, is one response to persecution.

Christians are leaving the Holy Land of Israel/Palestine. Christianity has not fared well in the land of its origin. HAMAS (an acronym in Arabic for Islamic Resistance Movement) developed in 1987 as an offshoot of the Egyptian Muslim Brotherhood, successfully challenged the secular PLO (Palestinian Liberation Organization, and now the less secular Palestinian Authority) for the allegiance of Palestinians. Since 2007, HAMAS has governed the Gaza Strip in Palestine. Christians are now virtually extinct in the Gaza Strip. Largely ignored by Western media, a systematic campaign of religious cleansing is being practiced by Muslims against the Christians in Palestinian areas. In 1950, Christians comprised roughly 15 percent of the Palestinian population. Today it is 2 percent. During the "Under Caesar's Sword" conference, it was announced that the number of individual Christians in Gaza has been reduced to between 100 and 150.

Will Christians even survive in the land of Christianity's origin? "There are tensions between day-to-day immediate coping strategies and ideas of long-term survival," reported Mariz Tadros, a fellow at the Institute of Development Studies at Sussex University. Can Christian families be expected to think in terms of centuries when the life and future of their children are at stake? "In Gaza, this cognitive fear [of ISIS] has meant that they see their survival as being contingent on their immigration. This is at odds with the church leadership who see that up-rootedness is not a survival option. To the contrary, perseverance is the only way to preserve the Christian heritage on those lands."[4]

4. Ibid.

Persecution & Genocide of Christians in the Middle East

His Beatitude Mar Louis Raphael I Sako, the Chaldean Catholic Patriarch of Babylon and head of the Chaldean Catholic Church, has earned a reputation as a champion of religious toleration and inter-religious cooperation, but even he is forced to urge parishioners to resist the understandable impulse to flee. He especially rejects incentives to emigrate to the West. "The West should not encourage Christians to leave the region. Instead, Western governments and churches in the West could help with the financing of particular projects that will enable Christians to stay, not least in the countryside." He urges priests and families to stand firm but understands the risk. Can families think in terms of centuries when violence is in the air their children breathe and the water they drink?

Another way of coping is to conform in areas that do not violate the Christian conscience. For instance, when Christian women come under tremendous pressure to cover their hair and change their mode of attire, they may choose to don various head covers or long robes. It restricts their mobility and their presence in public spaces but it also reduces their vulnerability to more oppressive measures. Similarly, Christian men grow their beards to fit in with their Muslim counterparts. Why emphasize one's otherness needlessly. One has to choose his battles.

A third way of coping is to hide one's light under a bushel-basket, at least temporarily. A U.S. ally, Saudi Arabia is an Islamic theocratic monarchy. Non-Muslims cannot be citizens or even enter the holy city of Mecca. Conversion from Islam to another religion can be punished by death. Blasphemy can also be punished by death or life imprisonment. Saudi customs officials regularly open mail and cargo to search for non-Muslim materials, such as Bibles and recordings of sermons.

Saudi Arabia engages roughly nine million migrant workers, one to three million of whom are Christians from the Philippines or India. So many of them are Catholic that the Catholic Church claims Saudi Arabia as the second largest Catholic country in the Middle East. Their families back home depend upon them for financial support. But in Saudi Arabia, these Christian workers are forbidden to have Bibles, wear religious symbols identifying themselves as Christians, never mind boldly proclaiming the core Christian message that "Jesus is Lord, God in human flesh." Baylor Associate Professor of Religious Studies Christian van Gorder noted that in 2011, a visiting soccer player from Columbia was expelled from Saudi Arabia for

Under Caesar's Sword: A Report on the Conference

wearing a tattoo of the face of Jesus. Another example of misplaced state zeal for Islamic law concerns an expatriate who cursed his Saudi taxi driver using Christ's name. The charge? Not blasphemy but unauthorized prayer in public.

Muslims who convert to Christ are maximally vulnerable. *Voices of the Martyrs* reported that in August, 2008, a Muslim cleric and member of Saudi Arabia's Commission for the Promotion of Virtue and Prevention of Vice killed his 26-year-old sister Fatima Al-Mutairi after she proclaimed her faith in Christ to her family. While this was not a state action, it was a matter of family honor carried out by someone with state authority. How do Christian migrant workers cope in such a repressive environment? Hide their Bibles and tattoos. Hidden away, in fact, are a few underground churches for expatriates.

Construction is the second broad way of response. Using works of mercy and service to other faith communities, some Christian groups build bridges to fellow citizens. This is the "good neighbor" strategy that hopefully overcomes suspicions and avoids confrontation with the oppressive regimes. By using the freedoms they do have to serve non-Christians, they hope to overcome being seen as a threat, an alien, or an "other."

This is important. Even in lands once considered part of Christendom, Christians are being defined as "other," outside the mainstream. Often, this outsider status does not result in benign indifference but active animosity. Dr. Paul Marshall, senior fellow of the Hudson Institute's Center for Religious Freedom describes the work of Norway's Eilif Haland who deliberately established the FHR (Association for the Right to Conscientious Objection for Health Care Workers) without any overt religious affiliation or concern. By doing so, he felt, it was easier to invite all people of good will who wanted to join him in actively working for legislation that respected the fundamental rights of conscientious objection. In this way he is building bridges between different faith communities but also between humanist secularity and the Christian community.

Sara Singha of Georgetown's Berkley Center points to Pakistan where Christian leaders and the laity are active in promoting peace and good will among their Muslim neighbors. How do they do this? By cooperating with Muslim organizations in both rural areas and urban slums to protect young women, promote education, and resolve shared challenges such as lack of clean water and sanitation.

Another way of bridge building is described by Robert Dowd, political science professor at Notre Dame. Nigerian Christians, who have chosen not to take up arms against Boko Haram, an Islamist terror group, petition the state to defend the Christian community against these non-state terrorists. Since Boko Haram is not an agent of the state, and in fact is perceived by the state as an enemy, the government is moved to recognize the Christians as faithful Nigerian citizens. According to Dowd, preliminary evidence suggests that appealing to Muslim leaders for protection has been effective in certain areas of Kenya and Nigeria when the persecution stems from non-state actors. In these cases, cooperation with the civil authorities leads to increased protection and fortifies the state's awareness of Christians as legitimate citizens interested in cooperating with and dependent upon the civil authorities.

Robert Hefner, director of the Institute on Culture, Religion, and World Affairs at Boston University notes minority Christian leaders in Indonesia, the world's largest Muslim country, reaching out to majority Muslim leaders for state protection. Indonesia is a non-Arab Muslim land with less Salafist or "fundamentalist" influence and because Indonesian officials profess citizen equality, they heed the concerns of Christians.

Fenggang Yang, director of the Center on Religion and Chinese Society at Purdue University describes a number of Chinese Christians in the social gospel movement who originally believed that the Chinese Communists were carrying out God-given social and political reforms. Why not cooperate for the sake of the common good? Because cooperation can sometimes lead to compromise, accommodationism, and a chameleon Christianity that becomes indistinguishable from the surrounding culture dictated by oppressive regimes.

This problem is illustrated in the life and career of Wu Yaozong, founder of the *Three-Self Patriotic Movement*. In September 1950, Wu Yaozong published "Channels Through Which China's Christianity Makes an Effort in the Construction of a New China." He believed that Christ's love was necessary for the flourishing of his homeland. Was not Jesus's identification with the poor and oppressed compatible with Communist teaching on class struggle? The Communist party called him a "role model for patriotic religious people."

In time, it became clear that Wu's bridge only served traffic traveling in one direction. According to Robert Fu of China Aid, Wu's son

Under Caesar's Sword: A Report on the Conference

now admits that the Chinese government co-opted his father's intentions and used him to legitimize atheistic rule. "There was an evil backstage manipulator behind everything my father did, and this manipulator was the Chinese Communist Party."

When Mao's Cultural Revolution broke out in 1966, Yaozong belatedly struggled against the revolution that had no use for Christianity, closed churches, and forbade public expression of Christian faith. He was sent to a labor camp and died tragically, rejected by the party and regarded as a compromiser by the underground church movement. The lesson? Cooperation does not always lead to spiritual health. Confrontation with the authorities can sharpen the Church's sense of mission. Indeed, China's persecuted church grew by three times during Mao's Cultural Revolution (1966–76), when no churches were open and church leaders were imprisoned.

Confrontation is the third response to persecution and includes protests, underground organized opposition, legal challenges, etc. In Pakistan, Christian leaders in major cities such as Karachi and Lahore have organized rallies and marches to protest various forms of persecution and violence against them. The most unorthodox protest was the public suicide of the first native Pakistani Catholic bishop, John Joseph of Faisalabad, who shot himself on May 6, 1998, to protest the execution of a Christian man on blasphemy charges.

Pakistan's blasphemy law also motivated Shahbaz Bhatti, at that time, the only Christian in the Pakistani cabinet. He criticized Pakistan's policy not as an offense against Catholics but as an offense against human dignity and human rights. His brother, Paul Bhatti, told how Shahbaz had lived with death threats for two years. Finally, on March 2, 2011, the Pakistani Taliban assassinated him for opposition to the blasphemy laws. Presciently, Bhatti left behind a recording to be viewed upon his death. He wanted his motives to be absolutely clear. "I believe in Jesus Christ who has given his own life for us, and I am ready to die for a cause. I'm living for my community . . . and I will die to defend their rights." At the time, Pakistani bishops asked Pope Benedict XVI to recognize Bhatti as a martyr. His brother, Paul continues Shahbaz's reform initiatives as advisor to the Prime Minister of Pakistan for Minority Affairs.

Some Pakistani Muslims see the deaths of Bishop Joseph and Shahbaz Bhatti as acts of heroic civic virtue. According to an October 26, 2007, *Catholic News Asia* report, the Bishop John Joseph Memorial Hall in Darul uloom Jamia Rehmania Madrassa in Faisalabad was dedicated on March 31, 2007. No other Islamic seminary in the country has a building named after a Catholic priest. Here the strategy of confrontation led to cooperation, just as cooperation with the regime can generate enough goodwill to tolerate confrontation against aspects of the regime.

The Copts of Egypt recently employed a strategy of confrontation. During the "Arab Spring," they opposed the regime of democratically elected Mohammed Morsi because of his association with the Muslim Brotherhood. In retaliation, Morsi and Muslim Brotherhood forces targeted the Copts for persecution. At the end of June 2013, Egyptians rose up and defied Morsi and the Muslim Brotherhood. The Copts joined the revolt in large numbers and documented the systematic torching of churches, commercial property, school, homes, and associations. They deliberately avoided seeking international intervention for their protection. They expected a new regime would bring new citizenship rights for all and trusted they would be protected and rewarded for their confrontation with the Brotherhood. While conditions improved, some sectarian violence and discriminatory policies continued, and the model for new citizenship failed to materialize. Their coping strategy has shifted from open confrontation to one of maximizing citizenship entitlements and, finally, minimizing vulnerability to persecution. Compared to their open challenging of Morsi and the Muslim Brotherhood, their current resistance is low key.

The sessions at the conference were seasoned with testimonies of personal and collective grace under fire. The Eritrean Christian vocalist, Helen Berhane refused to be silenced about her love of Jesus. Shortly after she released an album of Christian music, she was arrested on May 13, 2004. Refusing to sign a document renouncing her singing and preaching, she was detained at a military camp, separated from her family, forced to live in a shipping container, and denied legal representation and medical care for over two years.

In late October, 2006, Amnesty International pressured the president of Eritrea, and she was released. With her daughter Eva, Helen fled to the Sudanese capital of Khartoum for refuge until granted asylum in Denmark. She continues singing the Gospel.

Bishop Borys Gudziak, Eparch of the Ukrainian Greek Catholic Eparchy of Paris, recounted the remarkable resurrection of faith in his church after a long period of devastating destruction. "In 1918, there were 100 bishops in the country; by 1989, there were four. We had had 3,000 priests; by 1989, we had 300, average age 70, who lived in the catacombs."

During the 1920s and '30s, the Soviet Union destroyed the Church in eastern Ukraine. After World War II, the Soviets made the Ukrainian Greek Catholic Church illegal throughout all of Ukraine. "From 1945–89, we were the biggest illegal Church in the world and the largest body of social opposition to the Soviet Union."

Because the Ukrainian Greek Catholic Church operated underground and never collaborated with the regime, her members were hounded and always at risk of losing their jobs or being thrown into prison. Since the collapse of the oppressive Soviet Union, however, the priesthood has grown from 300 priests with an average age of 70 to 3,000 with an average age of 40. The episcopacy has grown from four to forty-seven. Even though the Ukrainian Greek Catholic Church was a minority church, she has retained great moral authority for her refusal to collaborate during the years of Soviet persecution. She has played an indispensable role in helping the entire Ukrainian people move from fear to dignity after the collapse of the Soviet Union.

Perhaps most inspirational are the examples of persecuted Christians imitating their Master despite the open violence poured out upon them. No one claims perfection, but Dan Philpott observed that there were "remarkably few examples of Christians resorting to violence and no known examples of a terrorist dynamic." The example of Jesus turning the other cheek, refusing the option of the sword, and urging love of enemies leads to similar practices on the part of his disciples. Bishop Anba Angaelos, leader of the Egyptian Coptic Orthodox Church in the UK, said Christians are trained not to retaliate. "In 2013, dozens of Christian churches were burned down, and the response was to paint in their crumbling walls: 'Love your enemy.'"

The lessons of the conference were many. The greatest problem, however, facing the global Christian mission is widespread ignorance among Christians that their fellow Christians are, in fact, living "under Caesar's sword." When this ignorance begins to yield to awareness and knowledge, another problem presents itself. There is a widespread notion that somehow more Christian-friendly governments, like the United States or Great Britain, are routinely engaged in protecting religious minorities as an affront to our deepest civil beliefs and values. Unfortunately, that is not the case.

Even if friendly states rose to defend Christians, Timothy Shah stressed, that "we cannot subcontract our sense of solidarity with fellow Christians to the government. If we Christians are not on our knees, if we Christians are not mobilizing our parishes, it is a gross hypocrisy to expect our government to do something. If we were to mobilize our churches, if we were to raise awareness, if we were to do teachings in our churches, if we were to insist that our priests preach about this issue, if we were to insist that our 'prayers of the faithful' contain not just a phrase but a few sentences invoking God's protection of fellow Christians, we would see these governments acting." In other words, if fellow Christians do not behave as though persecution is a primary concern, why should we expect the world's Caesars to appropriately value it?

Since the conference, there are signs that change may be coming. In early February 2016, the European Parliament, for the first time, called ISIS's persecution of Christian and other religious minorities "genocide." The following month, the U.S. House unanimously passed a resolution declaring that the Islamic State is committing "genocide" against Christians, Yazidis, Kurds, and other ethnic and religious minorities in Iraq and Syria. Then U.S. Secretary of State John Kerry officially condemned ISIS's "genocidal action" against Christians and other religious minorities. On April 17, 2016, "Stand with the Persecuted Sunday," nearly 40,000 churches in the United States were asked pray for the persecuted, participate in practical ministry, and promote public policy to protect the persecuted. The event was coordinated by largely evangelical Protestant organizations including the Family Research Council, Open Doors, The Voice of the Martyrs, Institute of Religion and Democracy, In Defense of Christians, Christian Solidarity Worldwide-USA, The 21st Century Wilberforce Initiative, and International Christian Concern.

Aid to the Church in Need, a Catholic charity directly under the influence of Pope Francis, has also made the persecution of Christians its chief priority. The Knights of Columbus "have raised seven million dollars to help Christian in the Middle East in the last few months and have spent five million of it to help Christians on the ground," explained Timothy Shah. Before the conference, Supreme

Under Caesar's Sword: A Report on the Conference

Knight Carl Anderson testified in front of Congress calling for a recognition of genocide. Vice President of the Knights of Columbus, Patrick Kelly, gave the concluding address at the conference.

Even if we are not ignorant, we often feel impotent. When we see twenty-one Coptic Christians beheaded in Libya or 90 percent of Christians driven from their homes and churches in Mosul, Iraq, we may be moved but left paralyzed by the horror that the problem is too large, too distant, too complicated. It is not. "Under Caesar's Sword" called for Christians to be in practical and effective solidarity with the persecuted. "The uniqueness of this conference is its focus is on what Christians are doing to respond, how they are responding, and how Christians in the West can respond with them. There are things we can do. We can make a difference." Time will eventually render the judgment.

Al-Qaryatayn, Syria. Burnt chalice found in the monastery of St. Elian (April, 2016).

Glossary

Allahu Akbar: Allah is the greatest.

Al-Qaeda (or Al-Qa'ida) al-Jihad: Literally, "the base of holy war." A terrorist group that emerged as a network in the Soviet-Afghan conflict.

Al-Qaeda in Iraq (AQI): The organization that became ISIS. Formal affiliation was disavowed by Al-Qaeda in 2014.

AQ: see Al-Qaeda.

Bay'at: Pledging spiritual allegiance; surrendering one's self to a Spiritual Master (Murshid) to be guided to Allah.

Boko Haram: An Islamic jihadist and terrorist organization based in northeast Nigeria.

Caliph: The chief Muslim civil and religious ruler, regarded as the successor of Muhammad.

Caliphate: The area ruled by a caliph; also considered an area of Islamic supremacy.

Chapeau: The element of a statute that identifies its character (particularly with regard to an international crime).

Crimes against Humanity: International criminal offenses that aggrieve not only the victims and their own communities, but that violate core human values.

Crime of Aggression: Waging (especially commencing) an unjust war.

Customary International Law: Those elements of international law that are widely recognized and binding.

Dabiq: ISIS propaganda magazine.

Da'esh: The Arabic acronym for "*al-Dawla al-Islamiya al-Iraq wa-ash-Shaam*," the Islamic State of Iraq and Syria or ISIS.

Daftar: Slang term for ransom or jizya.

Dhimma contract: An agreement for protection between an Islamic government and a non-Muslim.

Dhimmis: Non-Muslims who are supposed to be protected by an Islamic government, but it may involve heavy taxation, segregation, and humiliation.

Geneva Conventions: International limitations (by agreement) on waging war.

Genocide: Violent acts committed with intent to destroy, in whole or in part, a national, ethnical, racial or religious group.

HAMAS: An acronym in Arabic for Islamic Resistance Movement, developed in 1987 as an offshoot of the Egyptian Muslim Brotherhood.

Holy See: The ecclesiastical jurisdiction of the Roman Catholic Church, an independent sovereign entity.

Human Rights Watch: An American-based international non-governmental organization that conducts research and advocacy on human rights.

Ijtihad: Referring to independent reasoning or the thorough exertion of a jurist's mental faculty in finding a solution to a legal question.

Ijma: The agreement on a particular issue by the Muslim community.

International Humanitarian Law (IHL): Those conventions from the law of war that protect the victims, along with Customary International Law. Also known as the Law of War or the Law of Armed Conflict.

Irhabi: those who practice "the Lesser Jihad" or "violent struggle on behalf of Islam."

Glossary

ISIL: See ISIS.

ISIS (or ISIL): the Islamic State of Iraq and Syria or the Islamic State of Iraq and the Levant. See DAESH and the Islamic State.

Islamic State: the Islamic State of Iraq and Syria. Also ISIS or ISIL. See DAESH.

Jihad: A struggle or fight against the enemies of Islam or the spiritual struggle within oneself against sin. See lesser jihad.

Jihadis: Those who struggle under juhad. The term is used by members of groups such as al-Qaeda to describe themselves. See "mujahedeen."

Jizya: a traditional Islamic tax, paid as an alternative to death, deportation, or forcible conversion.

Kafir: A "rejector" or "one who covers." When used theologically in Arabic-Islamic literature, it refers to one who "rejects the truth of Islam."

Knights of Columbus: An association of Catholic men, founded in the United States but with branches around the world.

Kurds: Islamic people living in parts of eastern Turkey, northern Iraq, western Iran, and eastern Syria.

Lesser Jihad: Fighting against an outer enemy of Islam. Struggling within one's self is the greater jihad.

Mens rea: The mental element required to prove a crime.

Montevideo Convention: A treaty signed in 1933 that codifies the declarative theory of statehood as accepted as part of customary international law.

Mujahedeen: Holy warriors, commonly used to refer to Muslims engaged in the Lesser Jihad. See "Jihadis."

Muslim Brotherhood: Founded in Egypt in 1928, it spawned many of the more violent Islamic groups that came later. Its stated goal is to instill the Quran and the Sunnah as the sole reference point for ordering the life of the Muslim family, individual, community and state.

Murshid: Spiritual Master.

Non-Governmental Organization (NGO): A not-for-profit organization, independent from states and international organizations, usually involved in trying to shape international agreements.

Qiyas: The deduction and articulation of a juridical solution through legal analogy.

Open Doors USA: A watchdog group supporting Christians in about 60 countries where they are persecuted.

Organization of Islamic Cooperation (OIC): Composed of fifty-seven nations and describing itself as "the collective voice of the Muslim world."

Palestinian Authority (or Palestinian National Authority): The semi-official, self-governing Palestinian body established in 1994 in accordance with the Israel-PLO Declaration of Principles on behalf of the Palestine Liberation Organization.

Palestinian Liberation Organization (PLO): Founded in 1964 with the purpose of the "liberation of Palestine" through armed struggle, with much of its violence aimed at Israeli civilians. Precursor of the less secular Palestinian Authority.

People of the Book: An Islamic term for Christians and Jews.

Qu'ran (or Koran): Holy book of Islam.

Rome Statute: The foundational document for the International Criminal Court.

Salafism: An ideology and reform movement calling for a return to Islam as it was practiced in the days of Muhammad.

Sharia: Strict Islamic canonical law based on the teachings of the Qu'ran and the traditions of the Prophet Muhammad.

Glossary

Shia: A branch of Islam which holds that Muhammad designated Ali ibn Abi Talib as his successor. This is in conflict with Sunni Islam, whose adherents believe that Muhammad did not appoint a successor and consider Abu Bakr (who was appointed Caliph through a Shura, i.e. consensus) to be the correct Caliph.

Shlomo: A lawyers' group comprised of Christian survivors now displaced in Kurdistan.

Sunni: A branch of Islam. See Shia.

Syriac Catholic Church: A Christian church in the Levant which uses the Syrian Ritea and has many practices in common with the Syriac Orthodox Church but is in full communion with the Holy See.

Takfir: Proclaiming a Muslim as an apostate and thus sanctioning violence against him.

The Taliban: A Sunni Islamic fundamentalist political movement in Afghanistan which recently changed its name and identity to Islamic Emirate of Afghanistan.

Torture Act: An American federal law (18 U.S.C. § 2340) that prohibits torture.

Turkmens: A Turkic people located primarily in Turkmenistan, but also in Iran, Afghanistan, North Caucasus (Stavropol Krai), and northern Pakistan.

Universal Declaration on Human Rights: A declaration adopted by the United Nations General Assembly in December 1948.

Wahhabi: A radicalized Islamic fundamentalism associated with the theologian Muhammad bin 'Abdil-Wahhab.

Yazidis: An ethnically Kurdish religious community indigenous to northern Mesopotamia.

Contributor Biographies

Jane F. Adolphe is an Associate Professor of Law at Ave Maria School of Law, in Naples, Florida (2001–present) and an expert with the Holy See, Secretariat of State, Relations with States, residing in Rome (2011–present). She is also an Adjunct Professor at the Law School of the University of Notre Dame Australia, Sydney Campus (2016–present). She has served as Visiting Fellow in Canon Law, Faculty of Law, University of Calgary (2016) and as a member of the Editorial Board of the canon law *Collection Gratianus Series*. She has a Licentiate and Doctorate in Canon law (JCL/JCD) from the Pontifical University of the Holy Cross, Rome; Common Law and Civil Law degrees (LLB/BCL) from the University of McGill, Montreal; and a Bachelor of Arts (BA) from the University of Calgary. She began her legal career clerking for the Alberta Court of Appeal and Court of Queen's Bench, after practicing with the Law Firm of Bennett Jones Verchere, she served as a prosecutor with the Alberta Crown Prosecutor's Office, then later as a legal consultant for a law firm in Rome and as a legal advisor to the Holy See (2003–2011), which included her participation on various delegations of the Holy See at Conferences and meetings within the United Nations system. Her courses have included Canon Law, International Law and the Holy See, International Law, and International Human Rights. She writes in the field of International Human Rights as they relate to the Holy See and the rights of children, women, parents, and the family.

Mark Healy Bonner graduated from the Portsmouth Abbey School, received an AB in History from Georgetown University, and a JD from the Washington College of Law of American University. He also studied in Tours, France, and Fribourg, Switzerland. He met his wife Beth in Fribourg; they have been married for forty years. After clerking for a U.S. Senator in Washington, DC, and for a Federal Judge in Manhattan, he began a twenty-nine-year career in the U.S. Department of Justice, which included work in the Legislation and Special

Contributor Biographies

Projects Section of the Criminal Division, followed by appointment as Assistant U.S. Attorney for the Central District of California (Los Angeles). He later served in the Terrorism and Violent Crime Section of the Criminal Division in Washington, DC, and served for two years as Resident Legal Advisor at the U.S. Embassy in Moscow. He was an Adjunct Professor at Georgetown University Law Center for thirteen years. In 2000 he was appointed as Senior Advisor and Chief of Staff to the Undersecretary of the Treasury for Enforcement. He was a delegate to the U.S.-China Joint Economic Committee in Beijing with Treasury Secretary Paul O'Neill on September 11, 2000. When the Department of Homeland Security was created (incorporating most of Treasury Enforcement, including U.S. Customs, the U.S. Secret Service, and the U.S. Coast Guard) Bonner became a Senior Advisor in the Policy Directorate of DHS and was in charge of DHS's work in the G8, principally through the Lyon-Roma Group, Ministerial meetings, and the annual G8 Summit. In 2008 he left public service to become a Professor of Law at Ave Maria School of Law. Bonner teaches Evidence, Criminal Law, Criminal Procedure, Complex Criminal Litigation, and runs the school's Moot Court program.

Kevin Cieply, President and Dean, Ave Maria School of Law. Prior to his appointment at Ave Maria School of Law, Cieply served as the Associate Dean for Academic Affairs and Associate Professor at Atlanta's John Marshall Law School. Cieply also served for more than twenty-two years in the Army and Wyoming Army National Guard as a helicopter pilot, Company Commander, and a Judge Advocate General Corps (JAG) Officer. As a JAG Officer, his practice included prosecuting courts-martial cases, prosecuting major criminal procurement fraud cases in federal courts as a full-time Special Assistant U.S. Attorney, and serving as the Senior Legal Advisor on all military matters for the Wyoming Army National Guard. Dean Cieply's last military assignment was as the Chief, Legal Operations (Land), North American Aerospace Defense Command (NORAD) and U.S. Northern Command (NORTHCOM), concentrating on counterterrorism and Defense Support of Civilian Authorities. Cieply retired from the military with the rank of Colonel. He is admitted to practice in Arizona, Colorado, Florida, Georgia, and Wyoming, the Ninth and Tenth Circuit Courts of Appeal, and the U.S. Supreme Court.

Persecution & Genocide of Christians in the Middle East

John M. Czarnetzky is Professor and Mitchell McNutt and Jessie Puckett Lecturer in Law at the University of Mississippi School of Law. He earned his BS at the Massachusetts Institute of Technology and his JD at the University of Virginia School of Law. Prof. Czarnetzky is an advisor to the Holy See's delegation to the United Nations and a former member of the Mississippi Advisory Committee to the U.S. Civil Rights Commission. He teaches and writes on bankruptcy, corporate, and commercial law. Prof. Czarnetzky also has taught a freshman seminar on Catholic Social Doctrine, and has applied its tenets in his scholarship. His chapter is dedicated to the late Robert J. Araujo, SJ, who was a scholar, diplomat, lawyer mentor and friend, and who is sorely missed.

Robert A. Destro is Professor of Law and founding Director of the Interdisciplinary Program in Law & Religion at The Catholic University of America's Columbus School of Law. He has been a member of the faculty since 1982 and served as Interim Dean from 1999 to 2001. From 1983 to 1989, Destro served as a Commissioner on the United States Commission on Civil Rights, and led the Commission's discussions in the areas of discrimination on the basis of disability, national origin, and religion. He has served as Special Counsel to the Ohio Attorney General and the Ohio Secretary of State on election law matters from 2004 to 2006; as General Counsel to the Catholic League for Religious and Civil Rights from 1977 to 1982, and as an Adjunct Associate Professor of Law at Marquette University from 1978 to 1982.

Robert Fastiggi holds a BA from Dartmouth College and a MA and a PhD in theology from Fordham University. From 1985 to 1999, he taught at St. Edward's University in Austin, Texas, and since 1999 he has been on the faculty of Sacred Heart Major Seminary, Detroit, Michigan, where he's Professor of Systematic Theology. In addition to his own publications, he served as co-editor of the English translation of the 43rd edition of the Denzinger-Hünermann *Compendium of Creeds, Definitions, and Declarations on Matters of Faith and Morals* (Ignatius Press, 2012) and as executive editor of the 2009–2013 supplements to the *New Catholic Encyclopedia* (Gale Cengage Learning in cooperation with the Catholic University of America). Dr. Fastiggi is a member of the Society for Catholic Liturgy, the Academy of

Contributor Biographies

Catholic Theology, and the Mariological Society of America (for which he served as president from 2014 to 2016).

Kevin H. Govern is Professor at the Ave Maria School of Law. He began his legal career as an Army Judge Advocate, serving twenty years at every echelon during peacetime and war in worldwide assignments involving every legal discipline. He has also served as an Assistant Professor of Law at the United States Military Academy and has taught at John Jay College and at California University of Pennsylvania. He has published widely and spoken frequently on international and comparative law, national security and homeland security law, military operations, and professional ethics.

Al Kresta is President and CEO of Ave Maria Communications and host of Kresta in the Afternoon, a two-hour daily national talk program distributed by EWTN and heard on 350 stations nationally and Sirius XM. His program monitors global persecution of Christians and was broadcast from the "Under Caesar's Sword" Conference in Rome. Besides regular commentaries, he has authored four books including *Dangers to the Faith: Catholicism's 21st Century Opponents*.

Fr. Piotr Mazurkiewicz is a Professor of political science at the Institute of Political Science of Cardinal Stefan Wyszynski University. From 2002 to 2014, he served as a member of the Scientific Council of the Institute of Political Studies, from 2001 to 2008 he was a member of the board of the European Society for Research in Ethics "Societas Ethica," and from 2008 to 2012 was Secretary-General of the Commission of the Bishops' Conferences of the European Community. His areas of research include political philosophy, political ethics, Catholic social teaching, European integration, and religion in public life. He is the author of *The Church and Democracy* (2001), *The Europeanization of Europe. Europe's cultural identity in the context of integration processes* (2001), *Violence in Politics* (2006), and *In the Land of Celibacy* (2014).

Richard V. Meyer is the Director of the LLM. Program at Mississippi College School of Law. He writes and teaches in the areas of Humanitarian Law, Military Justice, International Criminal Law, Comparative Criminal Law, Contracts, and Torts. Professor Meyer's recent publications concern targeted killing, The Military Commissions Act of 2006, and humanitarian interventions. He has presented on these topics at law schools and cities around the country and the globe, including: Brasilia, Yale, Columbia, Pennsylvania, West Point, Amsterdam, Beijing, Chongqing, Monrovia, Munich, Wuerzburg, Nuremberg, ChengDu, and Washington DC. Prior to joining the faculty of Mississippi College, Professor Meyer served as an Associate Professor of Law at the United States Military Academy at West Point and also taught at Columbia Law School. He holds an LLM. from Columbia, and LLM. from the Judge Advocate General's School, a JD from Northern Illinois, and a BA from Illinois State. He is completing his JSD at Columbia studying the future of the military jurisdiction. Professor Meyer is a retired Army Judge Advocate who practiced in the United States, Europe, and Asia in the fields of: military justice, international law, administrative law, intelligence law, humanitarian law, and environmental law, among others. He is married to his wife of twenty-four years, Melissa, and they have five children ages five to eighteen.

Ronald J. Rychlak is the Jamie L. Whitten Chair of Law and Government and Professor of Law at the University of Mississippi. He also serves as the university's Faculty Athletic Representative, and he is the former Associate Dean for Academic Affairs. He is a graduate of Wabash College (BA) and Vanderbilt University (JD). Prior to joining the faculty, he practiced law with Jenner & Block in Chicago, and he served as a clerk to Hon. Harry W. Wellford of the U.S. Sixth Circuit Court of Appeals. Prof. Rychlak is an advisor to the Holy See's delegation to the United Nations and a member of the Mississippi Advisory Committee to the U.S. Civil Rights Commission. He is on the committee appointed by the Mississippi Supreme Court to revise the state's criminal code and serves on Advisory Boards for the Catholic League for Religious and Civil Rights, Ave Maria School of Law, and the Society of Catholic Social Scientists. He has authored or edited a dozen books, including *Hitler, the War, and the Pope* and *Disinformation* (with Ion M. Pacepa).

Nina Shea is a Hudson Institute senior fellow, where she directs the Center for Religious Freedom; a former commissioner on the U.S. Commission on International Religious Freedom; and an international human rights lawyer. She helped organize and lead a coalition of churches and religious groups that worked to end a religious war against non-Muslims and dissident Muslims in southern Sudan; in 2004 and 2005 she advised in the drafting of the religious freedom provisions in Iraq's constitution. Her publications include: *Persecuted: The Global Assault on Christians* (2013, with Paul Marshall and Lela Gilbert), *Silenced: How Apostasy and Blasphemy Codes are Choking Freedom Worldwide* (2011, with Paul Marshall), *In the Lion's Den: A Shocking Account of Persecution and Martyrdom of Christians Today and How We Should Respond* (1996), *Saudi Arabia's Curriculum of Intolerance* (2006), and *Saudi Publications on Hate Ideology Invade American Mosques* (2005). Shea is a graduate of Smith College and American University's Washington College of Law. Her chapter in this book is derived from her new report for the Hudson Institute, "The ISIS Genocide of Middle Eastern Christian Minorities and Its Jizya Propaganda Ploy," August 2016.

Geoffrey Bedford Strickland, JD, JCL, serves as Rome Office Director for Priests for Life/Gospel of Life Ministries and as Director of the Middle East and North Africa Region for the International Center for Law, Life, Faith and Family. In his role as Rome Office Director and International Associate, he provides research and analysis of canonical and international legal themes pertaining to life and family issues. As a Regional Director for the International Center on Law, Life, Faith and Family he provides analysis upon themes related to the rights of life and religious freedom, particularly with regard to the Persecution of Christians in the region. He formerly served as an internal legal analyst for the Pontifical Council for the Family, where his work focused upon areas pertaining to the family, dignity of human life, demographics, and gender ideologies. He continues to serve as an external collaborator to the Roman Curia for translation and interpretation of Spanish, Portuguese, French, Italian, and Arabic.

Made in the USA
Monee, IL
24 July 2025